T0334606

Applied Time Series Analysis

Applied Time Series Analysis

A Practical Guide to Modeling and Forecasting

Terence C. Mills
Loughborough University, Loughborough, United Kingdom

ACADEMIC PRESS

An imprint of Elsevier

Academic Press is an imprint of Elsevier
125 London Wall, London EC2Y 5AS, United Kingdom
525 B Street, Suite 1650, San Diego, CA 92101, United States
50 Hampshire Street, 5th Floor, Cambridge, MA 02139, United States
The Boulevard, Langford Lane, Kidlington, Oxford OX5 1GB, United Kingdom

Notices
Knowledge and best practice in this field are constantly changing. As new research and experience broaden
our understanding, changes in research methods, professional practices, or medical treatment may become
necessary.

Practitioners and researchers must always rely on their own experience and knowledge in evaluating and
using any information, methods, compounds, or experiments described herein. In using such information or
methods they should be mindful of their own safety and the safety of others, including parties for whom
they have a professional responsibility.

To the fullest extent of the law, neither the Publisher nor the authors, contributors, or editors, assume any
liability for any injury and/or damage to persons or property as a matter of products liability, negligence or
otherwise, or from any use or operation of any methods, products, instructions, or ideas contained in the
material herein.

British Library Cataloguing-in-Publication Data
A catalogue record for this book is available from the British Library

Library of Congress Cataloging-in-Publication Data
A catalog record for this book is available from the Library of Congress

ISBN: 978-0-12-813117-6

For Information on all Academic Press publications
visit our website at https://www.elsevier.com/books-and-journals

  Working together
to grow libraries in
Book Aid International developing countries

www.elsevier.com • www.bookaid.org

Publisher: Candice Janco
Acquisition Editor: J. Scott Bentley
Editorial Project Manager: Susan Ikeda
Production Project Manager: Vijayaraj Purushothaman
Cover Designer: Christian J. Bilbow

Typeset by MPS Limited, Chennai, India

Contents

Introduction

0.1 Data taking the form of time series, where observations appear sequentially, usually with a fixed time interval between their appearance (every day, week, month, etc.,), are ubiquitous. Many such series are followed avidly: for example, the Dow Jones Industrial stock market index opened 2017 with a value of 20,504, closing the year on 24,719; a rise of 20.6%, one of the largest annual percentage increases on record. By January 26, 2018, the index had reached an intraday high of 26,617 before declining quickly to close on February 8 at 23,860; a value approximately equal to that of the index at the end of November 2017 and representing a fall of 10.4% from its peak. Five days later, it closed on February 13 at 24,640; 3.3% above this "local minimum." By the end of May 2018, the index stood at 24,415; little changed over the ensuing 3 months.

This "volatility," which was the subject of great media and, of course, stock market attention, was surpassed by the behavior of the price of the crypto-currency bitcoin during a similar period. Bitcoin was priced at $995 at the start of 2017 and $13,850 at the end of the year; an astonishing almost 1300% increase. Yet, during December 17, just a fortnight before, it had reached an even higher price of $19,871; an almost 1900% increase from the start of the year. The decline from this high point continued into the new year, the price falling to $5968 on February 6 (a 70% decline from the peak price less than 2 months prior), before rebounding again to close at $8545 on February 13. Since then the price has increased to $11,504 on March 4 before falling back to $6635 on April 6. At the end of May 2018, the price stood at $7393.

0.2 While financial time series observed at high frequency often display such wildly fluctuating behavior, there are many other time series, often from the physical world, which display interesting movements over longer periods. Fig. I.1 shows the decadal averages of global temperatures from the 1850s onward. The behavior of temperature time series, whether global or regional, have become the subject of great interest and, in some quarters, great concern, over the past few decades. Fig. I.1 shows why. Global temperatures were relatively constant from the 1850s to the 1910s before increasing over the next three decades. There was then a second "hiatus" between the 1940s and 1970s before temperatures began to increase rapidly

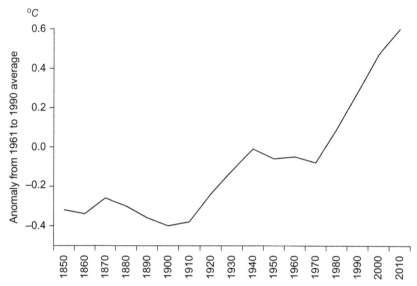

FIGURE I.1 Average decadal global temperatures, 1850–2010.

from the 1980s onward. Such behavior, in which trends are interspersed with periods of relative stability, is a feature of many time series.

0.3 How to model time series statistically is the concern of this book, in which, as its title suggests, I emphasize the practical, applied, aspects of statistical time series modeling. While a formal theoretical framework is, as we shall see, an unavoidable necessity, I do not overburden the reader with "technical niceties" that have little practical impact—my aim is always to provide methods that may be used to analyze and understand time series that occur in the "real world" that researchers face.[1] Examples are, therefore, drawn from a variety of fields that I am familiar with and have indeed researched in.

0.4 Chapter 1, Time Series and Their Features, initiates our analysis by considering some of the features that may be exhibited by an individual time series or a group of time series, and this leads naturally to Chapter 2, Transforming Time Series, where a variety of transformations are introduced that enable observed time series to become more amenable to statistical analysis. Chapter 3, ARMA Models for Stationary Time Series, introduces the basic formal concepts of stochastic processes and stationarity that underpin all statistical time series models. It then develops the basic class of univariate time series models, the autoregressive-moving average (ARMA) process, which is the core model used throughout the book. Not every time series is stationary, however: indeed, many require transforming to stationarity. Integrated processes, which may be made stationary by differencing, are an important class of nonstationary processes and Chapter 4, ARIMA Models for Nonstationary Time Series, thus extends ARMA models to the AR-integrated-MA (or ARIMA) class of processes.[2]

An important aspect of applied modeling is that of determining whether a time series is stationary or nonstationary and, if found to be the latter, of determining what form of nonstationarity it takes. Chapter 5, Unit Roots, Difference and Trend Stationarity, and Fractional Differencing, considers this problem within the context of testing for unit roots, discriminating between difference and trend stationarity, and investigating whether fractional differencing is required. The analysis is extended in Chapter 6, Breaking and Nonlinear Trends, to consider models having breaking and nonlinear trends.

An important use of time series models is in forecasting future, and hence unobserved, values of a series. Chapter 7, An Introduction to Forecasting With Univariate Models, thus introduces the theory of univariate time series forecasting based on the range of models introduced so far. Chapter 8, Unobserved Component Models, Signal Extraction, and Filters and Chapter 9, Seasonality and Exponential Smoothing, both focus on other types of univariate models, the former on unobserved component models, the latter on exponential smoothing techniques, which are particularly useful when seasonality, which is also discussed in this chapter, is a feature of the time series.

Chapter 10, Volatility and Generalized Autoregressive Conditional Heteroskedastic Processes, considers volatility, characterized by a time-varying variance, and consequently introduces the generalized autoregressive conditional heteroskedastic (GARCH) process to model such volatility. A time-varying variance may be regarded as a form of nonlinearity, but there are many other types of nonlinear processes and these are reviewed in Chapter 11, Nonlinear Stochastic Processes.

The remainder of the book deals with multivariate models, beginning in Chapter 12, Transfer Functions and Autoregressive Distributed Lag Modeling, with an introduction to transfer functions and autoregressive-distributed lag (ARDL) models, in which an "endogenous" time series is influenced by one or more "exogenous" series. The endogenous/exogenous distinction may be relaxed to allow a group of time series to all be considered endogenous. This leads to the vector autoregressive (VAR) model and the related concept of (Granger) causality which is the topic of Chapter 13, Vector Autoregressions and Granger Causality.

These two chapters are restricted to analyzing groups of stationary time series, but when integrated series are allowed, some important new concepts need to be introduced. The inclusion of integrated series in an ARDL model requires consideration of the related concepts of error correction and cointegration, as outlined in Chapter 14, Error Correction, Spurious Regressions, and Cointegration. Chapter 15, VARs With Integrated Variables, Vector Error Correction Models, and Common Trends, extends these concepts to a VAR setting, which leads to the vector error correction model (VECM) and the concept of common trends.

Chapter 16, Compositional and Count Time Series, focuses on both the modeling of time series that come as "counts," that is, small integer values for which the usual assumption of a continuous measurement scale is untenable, and the implications of modeling a set of time series that form a "composition." These are series that are shares of a whole and must, therefore, satisfy the twin constraints of taking only values between zero and unity and of summing to unity for every observation, constraints which must, for example, be satisfied by forecasts of future shares. Chapter 17, State Space Models, introduces a general setup known as the state space form, which enables many of the models introduced in the book to be cast in a single framework, which may be analyzed using a powerful technique known as the Kalman filter. Chapter 18, Some Concluding Remarks, provides some concluding remarks about the nature of applied time series modeling.

0.5 Each chapter contains applied examples, some of which are "developed" over several chapters. All computations use the *Econometric Views, Version 10 (EViews 10)* software package and full details on how the computations were performed are provided in the computing exercises that accompany each chapter. *EViews 10* was used as it is an excellent and popular package developed specifically for the time series techniques discussed in the book. However, I am aware that many researchers outside the economics and finance area use the statistical programming language R, and *EViews 10* contains links between *EViews* routines and R routines, which those researchers may wish to consult.

0.6 It is assumed that the reader has a background in introductory statistics (at the level of Mills, 2014, say) and some basic knowledge of matrix algebra (Mills, 2013a, Chapter 2, provides a convenient presentation of the material required).

0.7 A brief word on notation. As can be seen, chapter sections are denoted **x.y**, where **x** is the chapter and **y** is the section (this chapter is numbered **0**). This enables the latter to be cross-referenced as §**x.y**. Matrices and vectors are always written in bold font, upper case for matrices, lower case for vectors wherever possible. The latter are regarded as column vectors unless otherwise stated: thus, **A** denotes a matrix while **a** is a vector.

ENDNOTES

1. There are several highly technical treatments of time series analysis, most notably Brockwell and Davis (1991) and Hamilton (1994), which the interested reader may wish to consult.
2. Acronyms abound in time series analysis and have even prompted a journal article on them (Granger, 1982), although in the almost four decades since its publication many, many more have been suggested!

Chapter 1

Time Series and Their Features

Chapter Outline

1.1 As stated in the Introduction, time series are indeed ubiquitous, appearing in almost every research field where data are analyzed. However, their formal study requires special statistical concepts and techniques without which erroneous inferences and conclusions may all too readily be drawn, a problem that statisticians have found necessary to confront since at least Udny Yule's Presidential Address to the Royal Statistical Society in 1925, provocatively titled "Why do we sometimes get nonsense-correlations between time series? A study in sampling and the nature of time series."[1]

1.2 In general, a time series on some variable x will be denoted as x_t, where the subscript t represents time, with $t = 1$ being the first observation available on x and $t = T$ being the last. The complete set of times $t = 1, 2, \ldots, T$ will often be referred to as the *observation period*. The observations are typically measured at equally spaced intervals, say every minute, hour, or day, etc., so the order in which observations arrive is paramount. This is unlike, say, data on a cross section of a population taken at a *given* point in time, where the ordering of the data is usually irrelevant unless some form of spatial dependence exists between observations.[2]

1.3 Time series display a wide variety of features and an appreciation of these is essential for understanding both their properties and their evolution, including calculating future forecasts and, therefore, unknown values of x_t at, say, times $T + 1$, $T + 2$, $\ldots$, $T + h$, where h is referred to as the *forecast horizon*.

Fig. 1.1 shows monthly observations of an index of the North Atlantic Oscillation (NAO) between 1950 and 2017. The NAO is a weather phenomenon in the North Atlantic Ocean and measures fluctuations in the difference

Applied Time Series Analysis. DOI: https://doi.org/10.1016/B978-0-12-813117-6.00001-6
1

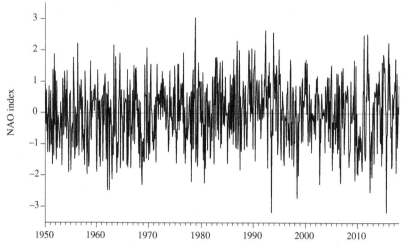

FIGURE 1.1 NAO index: monthly, January 1950–December 2017. *NAO*, North Atlantic Oscillation. *Data from Climate Prediction Center, NOAA Center for Weather and Climate Prediction.*

of atmospheric pressure at sea level between two stable air pressure areas, the Subpolar low and the Subtropical (Azores) high. Strong positive phases of the NAO tend to be associated with above-normal temperatures in eastern United States and across northern Europe and with below-normal temperatures in Greenland and across southern Europe and the Middle East. These positive phases are also associated with above-normal precipitation over northern Europe and Scandinavia and with below-normal precipitation over southern and central Europe. Opposite patterns of temperature and precipitation anomalies are typically observed during strong negative phases of the NAO (see Hurrell et al., 2003).

Clearly, being able to identify recurring patterns in the NAO would be very useful for medium- to long-range weather forecasting, but, as Fig. 1.1 illustrates, no readily discernible patterns seem to exist.

AUTOCORRELATION AND PERIODIC MOVEMENTS

1.4   Such a conclusion may, however, be premature for there might well be internal correlations within the index that could be useful for identifying interesting periodic movements and for forecasting future values of the index. These are typically referred to as the *autocorrelations* between a current value, x_t, and previous, or lagged, values, x_{t-k}, for $k = 1, 2, \ldots$. The *lag-k (sample) autocorrelation* is defined as

$$
r_k = \frac{\sum_{t=k+1}^{T} (x_t - \bar{x})(x_{t-k} - \bar{x})}{Ts^2} \tag{1.1}
$$

where

$$\bar{x} = T^{-1} \sum_{t=1}^{T} x_t \tag{1.2}$$

and

$$s^2 = T^{-1} \sum_{t=1}^{T} (x_t - \bar{x})^2 \tag{1.3}$$

are the sample mean and variance of x_t, respectively. The set of sample auto-correlations for various values of k is known as the *sample autocorrelation function* (SACF) and plays a key role in time series analysis. An examination of the SACF of the NAO index is provided in Example 3.1.

1.5 A second physical time series that has a much more pronounced periodic movement is the annual sunspot number from 1700 to 2017 as shown in Fig. 1.2. As has been well-documented, sunspots display a periodic cycle (the elapsed time from one minimum (maximum) to the next) of approximately 11 years; see, for example, Hathaway (2010). The SACF can be used to calculate an estimate of the length of this cycle, as is done in Example 3.3.

1.6 Fig. 1.3 shows the temperature of a hospital ward taken every hour for several months during 2011 and 2012 (see Iddon et al., 2015, for more details and description of the data). Here there is a long cyclical move-ment—an annual swing through the seasons—superimposed upon which are short-term diurnal movements as well as a considerable amount of random

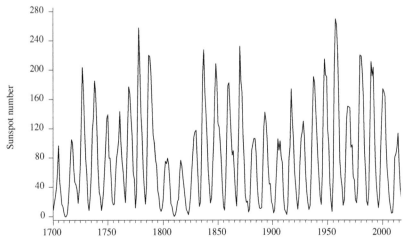

FIGURE 1.2 Annual sunspot numbers: 1700–2017. *Data from WDC-SILSO, Royal Observatory of Belgium, Brussels.*

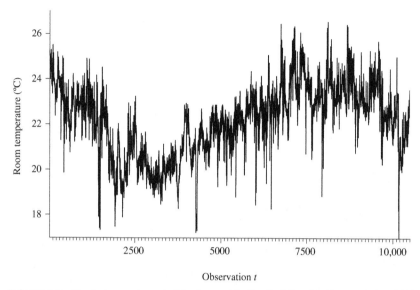

FIGURE 1.3 Hourly temperatures in °C of a ward in Bradford Royal Infirmary during 2011 and 2012. *Data from Iddon, C.R., Mills, T.C., Giridharan, R., Lomas, K.J., 2015. The influence of ward design on resilience to heat waves: an exploration using distributed lag models. Energy Build., 86, 573−588.*

fluctuation (known as *noise*), typically the consequence of windows being left open on the ward for short periods of time and more persistent movements which are related to external temperatures and solar irradiation (sunshine).

SEASONALITY

1.7 When a time series is observed at monthly or quarterly intervals an annual *seasonal pattern* is often an important feature. Fig. 1.4 shows quarterly United Kingdom beer sales between 1997 and 2017 that have a pronounced seasonal pattern that has evolved over the years: first quarter sales are always the lowest, fourth quarter sales are usually, but not always, the highest, while the relative size of second and third quarter sales seems to fluctuate over the observation period.

STATIONARITY AND NONSTATIONARITY

1.8 An important feature of Figs. 1.1−1.3 is the absence of any sustained increase or decline in the level of each series over the observation period; in other words, they fluctuate around a constant mean level which is clearly to be expected from the physical nature of each series. A constant mean level is one, but not the only, condition for a series to be *stationary*. In contrast, beer

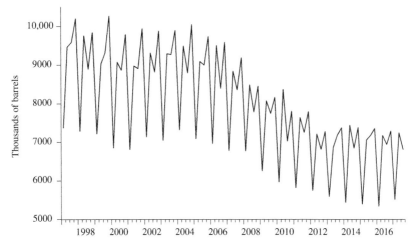

FIGURE 1.4   United Kingdom beer sales (thousands of barrels): quarterly, 1997–2017. *Data from the British Beer & Pub Association.*

FIGURE 1.5 $–£ Exchange rate: daily observations, January 1975–December 2017. *Data from Bank of England.*

sales in Fig. 1.4 show a decline throughout the observation period, most noticeably from 2004 onwards. Clearly beer sales have not fluctuated around a constant mean level; rather, the mean level has fallen in recent years which has been a well-documented concern of UK brewers.

1.9   If the mean level cannot be regarded as constant then a series is said to be *nonstationary*. Nonstationarity, however, can appear in many guises. Fig. 1.5 plots daily observations on the US dollar–UK sterling ($–£)

exchange rate from 1975 to 2017, a period in which this exchange rate fluctuated widely. The rate fell from around $2.50 at the start of the 1980s to almost parity by the middle of that decade, before rebounding to about $2 at the beginning of the 1990s. In the past 25 years it has undergone three further steep declines, known as depreciations, corresponding to the United Kingdom's exit in October 1992 from the European Exchange Rate Mechanism, the onset of the global financial crisis during 2008, and the Brexit referendum of June 2016, interspersed by a major appreciation from around $1.4 to over $2 between 2003 and 2008.

Clearly, the assumption of a constant mean level for the exchange rate would not be appropriate either statistically or, indeed, economically, for this would imply an equilibrium level for the exchange rate which would, consequently, provide a "one-way bet" for dealers whenever the rate got too far from this level, either above or below. The exchange rate thus exhibits a form of nonstationarity that can be termed *random walk* or *unit root* nonstationarity, terms that will be defined and discussed in detail in Chapter 4, ARIMA Models for Nonstationary Time Series, and Chapter 5, Unit Roots, Difference and Trend Stationarity, and Fractional Differencing.

TRENDS

1.10 Just as clearly, the exchange rate does not exhibit an overall *trend* throughout the observation period, this being informally thought of as a generally monotonic upward or downward movement, which would here imply either a perpetual appreciation or depreciation of the currency; a movement that could not happen in practice as it would, again, offer a one-way bet to dealers in what is perhaps the most efficient of financial markets.

1.11 Trends, however, are to be found in many time series.[3] Fig. 1.6 shows per capita wine and spirits consumption for the United Kingdom from 1950 to 2015. Both show positive trends; that for wine being stronger than that for spirits with, to a first approximation, both trends having reasonably constant slopes. The two series, thus, appear to exhibit *linear trends*.

1.12 Many trends, though, do not have constant slopes and hence are *nonlinear*. Monthly observations from 1948 to 2017 on the UK retail price index are shown in Fig. 1.7, and the index clearly has a nonconstant slope. Since the slope measures the change in the index, it is related to, but is not identical with, inflation and the shifting slopes thus reveal the evolution of price increases in the United Kingdom during the postwar period (how measures of inflation might in practice be constructed from a price index is discussed

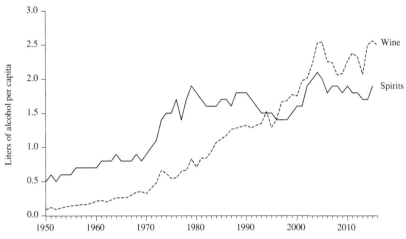

FIGURE 1.6   Annual consumption of wines and spirits in the United Kingdom: liters of alcohol per capita, 1950−2015. *Data from megafile_of_global_wine _data_1835_to_2016 _031117.xlxs. Available from: <www.adelaide.edu.au/wine-econ/databases>.*

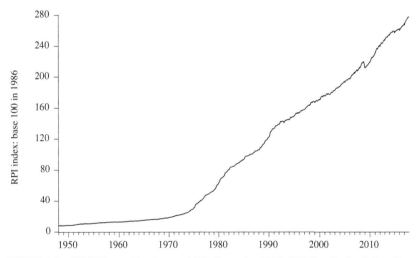

FIGURE 1.7   UK RPI: monthly, January 1948−December 2017. *RPI*, Retail price index. *Data from U.K. Office of National Statistics.*

in Chapter 2: Transforming Time Series). Note the sequence of falling prices in the latter half of 2008 at the height of the global financial crisis which produced a brief period of deflation; a rare event in developed economies in the postwar era.

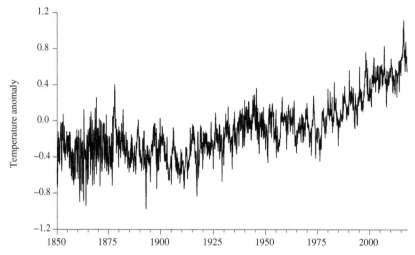

FIGURE 1.8 Global temperature: monthly, January 1850–December 2017. *Data from Met Office Hadley Centre for Climate Science and Services.*

1.13 Ascertaining whether a time series contains a trend may be quite difficult. Consider Fig. 1.8 which shows monthly global temperatures from 1850 to 2017. While there is certainly a general upward movement during the observation period, it is by no means monotonic, with several sustained periods of relative constancy and even decline, thus seeming to rule out a linear trend for the entire observation period. For the anthropogenic global warming hypothesis to hold, this series must exhibit random walk nonstationarity with a *positive drift*. Whether the drift is significantly positive will be considered in Example 4.3.

VOLATILITY

1.14 A second condition of stationarity is that of constant variance. Fig. 1.9 shows the daily percentage change in the $–£ exchange rate plotted in Fig. 1.5. Although the plot of the percentage changes is dominated by the 8% point decline in sterling on June 24, 2016, after the announcement of the Brexit referendum result, the entire sequence of changes is characterized by periods of relative calm interspersed by bursts of volatility, so that the variance of the series changes continuously. Thus, although the daily percentage change in the $–£ rate certainly fluctuates around a mean that is constant and virtually zero (being −0.003) it is nevertheless nonstationary as the variance cannot be regarded as constant. A specific time series process, the GARCH process, is introduced in Chapter 7, An

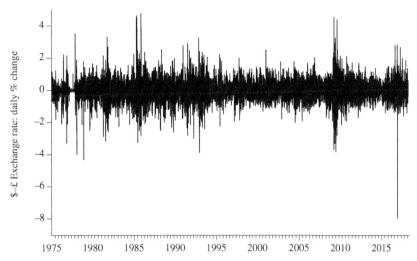

FIGURE 1.9   % Daily change in the $-£ exchange rate: January 1975–December 2017.

Introduction to Forecasting With Univariate Models, to model a variance that changes through time.[4]

COMMON FEATURES

1.15 Two or more time series may contain *common* features. Consider Fig. 1.10 where the top panel shows long (the yield on 20-year gilts, $R20$) and short (the yield on 3-month Treasury bills, RS) UK interest rates monthly from 1952 to 2017. Both exhibit random walk nonstationarity, but appear to have a strong tendency to be "bound together" over time, as will be demonstrated in Example 14.1.

The bottom panel of Fig. 1.10 shows the "spread" between the rates, defined as $S = R20 - RS$, which is stationary, albeit exhibiting persistent (highly positively autocorrelated) deviations from the sample mean of 1.2%. The nonstationarity in the individual series has, thus, been "annihilated" by taking the difference between them. The interest rates thus share a common trend and are said to *cointegrate*; a potential property of nonstationary time series that will be extensively developed in Chapter 14, Error Correction, Spurious Regressions, and Cointegration, and Chapter 15, VARs with Integrated Variables, VECMs, and Common Trends.

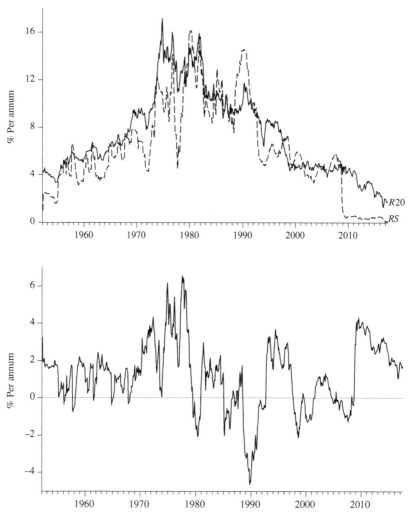

FIGURE 1.10 Long (*R*20) and short (*RS*) interest rates for the United Kingdom and their spread $S = R20 - RS$: monthly, January 1952–June 2017. *Data from Bank of England.*

TIME SERIES HAVING NATURAL CONSTRAINTS

1.16 Some time series have natural constraints placed upon them. Fig. 1.11, for example, shows the consumption (*c*), investment (*i*), government (*g*), and "other" (*x*) shares in the United Kingdom's gross final expenditure for the period 1955q1 to 2017q2. Because these shares must be lie between zero and one and must also add up to one for each observation, these restrictions need to be accounted for, as to ignore them would make

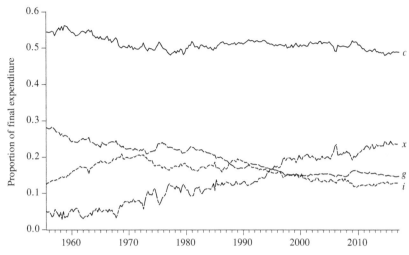

FIGURE 1.11   Shares in the United Kingdom's total final expenditure: c consumption; i investment; g government; x "other." Quarterly, 1955q1–2017q2. *Data from U.K. Office for National Statistics.*

standard analysis of covariances and correlations invalid. Such *compositional time series* require distinctive treatment through special transformations before they can be analyzed, as is done in Chapter 16, Compositional and Count Time Series.

1.17   All the time series introduced so far may be regarded as being measured on a continuous scale, or at least can be assumed to be well-approximated as being continuous. Some series, however, occur naturally as (small) integers and these are often referred to as *counts*. Fig. 1.12 shows the annual number of North Atlantic storms and hurricanes (the latter being a subset of the former) between 1851 and 2017. The annual number of storms ranges from a minimum of one (in 1914) to a maximum of 28 in 2005; that year also saw the maximum number of hurricanes, 15, while there were no hurricanes in either 1907 and 1914. The figure uses spike graphs to emphasize the integer nature of these time series and this feature requires special techniques to analyze count data successfully, and will be discussed in Chapter 16, Compositional and Count Time Series.

1.18   Understanding the features exhibited by time series, both individually and in groups, is a key step in their successful analysis and clearly a great deal can be learnt by an initial plot of the data. Such plots may also suggest possible transformations of the data which may expedite formal analysis and modeling of time series, and it is to this topic that Chapter 2, Transforming Time Series, is devoted.

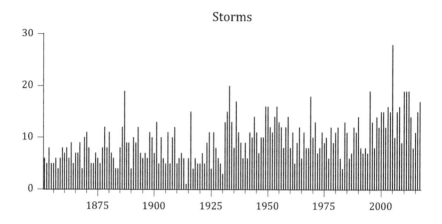

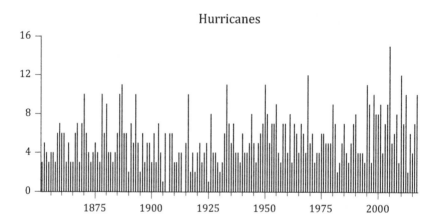

FIGURE 1.12   Number of North Atlantic storms and hurricanes, annually 1851–2017. *Data from Hurricane Research Division, NOAA.*

ENDNOTES

1. This was published as Yule (1926). George Udny Yule was a famous British statistician during the first half of the 20th century, working in many areas and making fundamental contributions in most of them. Mills (2017a) is the first biography of this important figure in the history of statistics.
2. Arbia (2014) is an introductory text on modeling spatial data.
3. As Phillips (2010) remarks, "trends have an elusive quality. No one understands them, but everyone sees them in the data." A history of modeling trends, albeit with an emphasis on economics, is provided by Mills and Patterson (2015), while formal definitions of many varieties of trends may be found in White and Granger (2011).
4. Daily financial data often display volatility of this type. Financial time series are also available at frequencies higher than daily, these often being referred to as *high frequency* or *tick-by-tick* data. Such time series typically have various features that are idiosyncratic to financial markets and a new discipline of high frequency econometrics has, thus, been developed in recent years. This is too specialized an area of time series analysis to be considered in this book. For a review see, for example, Aït-Sahalia and Jacod (2014).

Chapter 2

Transforming Time Series

Chapter Outline

2.1 Prior to analyzing, statistically, an individual or a group of time series, it is often appropriate to transform the data, with an initial plot of the series often providing clues as to what transformation(s) to use. There are three general classes of transformations for time series—distributional, stationarity inducing, and decompositional—and these may often be combined to produce an appropriate variable to analyze.

DISTRIBUTIONAL TRANSFORMATIONS

2.2 Many statistical procedures perform more effectively on data that are normally distributed, or at least are symmetric and not excessively kurtotic (fat-tailed), and where the mean and variance are approximately constant. Observed time series frequently require some form of transformation before they exhibit these distributional properties, for in their "raw" form they are often asymmetric. For example, if a series is only able to take positive (or at least nonnegative) values, then its distribution will usually be skewed to the right, because although there is a natural lower bound to the data, often zero, no upper bound exists and the values are able to "stretch out," possibly to infinity. In this case a simple and popular transformation is to take logarithms, usually to the base e (natural logarithms).

2.3 Fig. 2.1 displays histograms of the levels and logarithms of the monthly UK retail price index (RPI) series plotted in Fig. 1.7. Taking logarithms clearly reduces the extreme right-skewness found in the levels, but it certainly does not induce normality, for the distribution of the logarithms is distinctively bimodal.

The reason for this is clearly seen in Fig. 2.2, which shows a time series plot of the logarithms of the RPI. The central part of the distribution, which

Applied Time Series Analysis. DOI: https://doi.org/10.1016/B978-0-12-813117-6.00002-8
13

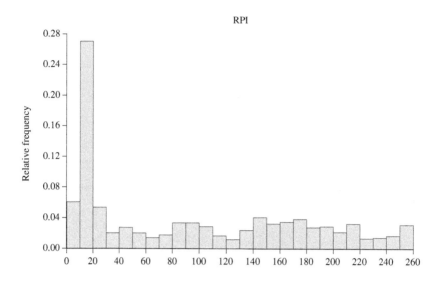

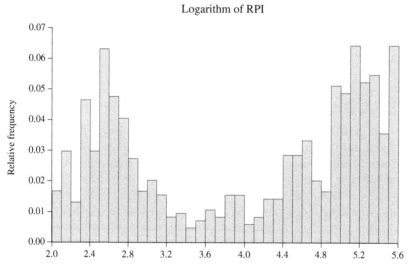

FIGURE 2.1 Histograms of RPI and its logarithm.

has the lower relative frequency, is transited swiftly during the 1970s, as this was a decade of high inflation characterized by the steepness of the slope of the series during this period.

Clearly, transforming to logarithms does not induce stationarity, but on comparing Fig. 2.2 with Fig. 1.7, taking logarithms does "straighten out" the trend, at least to the extent that the periods before 1970 and after 1980 are both approximately linear with roughly the same slope.[1] Taking logarithms

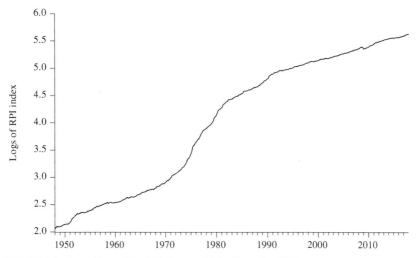

FIGURE 2.2   Logarithms of the RPI: January 1948–December 2017.

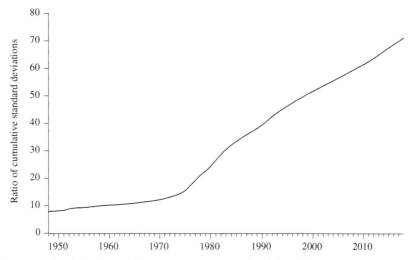

FIGURE 2.3   Ratio of cumulative standard deviations $s_i(\text{RPI})/s_i(\log \text{RPI})$.

also stabilizes the variance. Fig. 2.3 plots the ratio of *cumulative standard deviations*, $s_i(\text{RPI})/s_i(\log \text{RPI})$, defined using (1.2) and (1.3) as:

$$s_i^2(x) = i^{-1} \sum_{t=1}^{i} (x_t - \overline{x}_i)^2 \qquad \overline{x}_i = i^{-1} \sum_{t=1}^{i} x_t$$

Since this ratio increases monotonically throughout the observation period, the logarithmic transformation clearly helps to stabilize the variance and it will, in fact, do so whenever the standard deviation of a series is proportional to its level.[2]

2.4 It is also clear that for attaining approximate normality, the availability of a more general class of transformations would be useful. A class of *power transformations* that contains the logarithmic as a special case is that proposed by Box and Cox (1964) for positive x:[3]

$$f^{BC}(x_t, \lambda) = \begin{cases} (x_t^\lambda - 1)/\lambda & \lambda \neq 0 \\ \log x_t & \lambda = 0 \end{cases} \tag{2.1}$$

Fig. 2.4 shows monthly rainfall for England and Wales between 1875 and 2017. Observed rainfall is plotted in the top panel and the empirical density shown in the left sidebar reveals that the distribution is markedly skewed to the right. The lower panel plots the Box–Cox transformed series for $\lambda = 0.5$, essentially a square root transformation, and this series is now symmetric and, indeed, approximately normally distributed.[4]

2.5 The restriction to positive values that is required by the Box–Cox transformation can be relaxed in several ways. A shift parameter may be introduced in (2.1) to handle situations where x may take negative values but is still bounded below, but this may lead to inferential problems when λ is estimated as in §**2.6**. Possible alternatives are the *signed power* transformation proposed by Bickel and Doksum (1981):

$$f^{SP}(x_t, \lambda) = \left(\text{sgn}(x_t)|x_t^\lambda| - 1\right)/\lambda \quad \lambda > 0 \tag{2.2}$$

or the generalized power (GP) transformation suggested by Yeo and Johnson (2000) shown in (2.3)

$$f^{GP}(x_t, \lambda) = \begin{cases} ((x_t+1)^\lambda - 1)/\lambda & x_t \geq 0, \lambda \neq 0 \\ \log(x_t + 1) & x_t \geq 0, \lambda = 0 \\ -((-x_t+1)^{2-\lambda} - 1)/(2-\lambda) & x_t < 0, \lambda \neq 2 \\ -\log(-x_t + 1) & x_t < 0, \lambda \neq 2 \end{cases} \tag{2.3}$$

A further alternative is the *inverse hyperbolic sine* (IHS) transformation suggested by Burbidge et al. (1988) to deal with extreme values of either sign:

$$f^{IHS}(x_t, \lambda) = \frac{\sinh^{-1}(\lambda x_t)}{\lambda} = \log \frac{\lambda x_t + (\lambda^2 x_t^2 + 1)^{1/2}}{\lambda} \quad \lambda > 0 \tag{2.4}$$

2.6 The transformation parameter λ may be estimated by the method of maximum likelihood (ML). Suppose that for a general transformation $f(x_t, \lambda)$, the model $f(x_t, \lambda) = \mu_t + a_t$ is assumed, where μ_t is a model for the mean of $f(x_t, \lambda)$ and a_t is assumed to be independent and normally distributed with

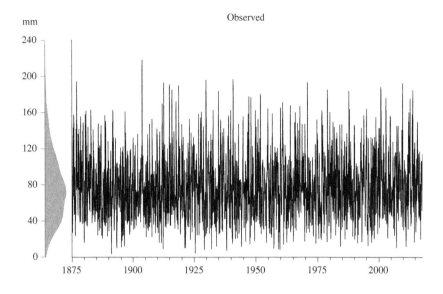

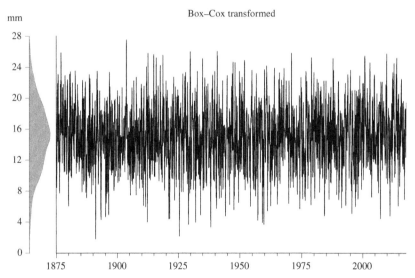

FIGURE 2.4 England and Wales rainfall (in mm): monthly, January 1875–December 2017. Top panel: observed rainfall; bottom panel: Box–Cox transformed with $\lambda = 0.5$. *Data from Met Office Hadley Centre for Climate Science and Services.*

zero mean and constant variance. The ML estimator $\hat{\lambda}$ is then obtained by maximizing over λ the concentrated log-likelihood function:

$$\ell(\lambda) = C_f - \left(\frac{T}{2}\right) \sum_{t=1}^{T} \log \hat{a}_t^2 + D_f(x_t, \lambda) \tag{2.5}$$

where $\hat{a}_t = f(x_t, \lambda) - \hat{\mu}_t$ are the residuals from ML estimation of the model, C_f is a constant and $D_f(x_t, \lambda)$ depends on which of the transformations (2.1)−(2.4) is being used:

$$D_f(x_t, \lambda) = (\lambda - 1)\sum_{t=1}^{T}\log|x_t| \qquad \text{for (2.1) and (2.2)}$$

$$= (\lambda - 1)\sum_{t=1}^{T}\mathrm{sgn}(x_t)\log(|x_t| + 1) \quad \text{for (2.3)}$$

$$= -\frac{1}{2}\sum_{t=1}^{T}\log\left(1 + \lambda^2 x_t^2\right) \qquad \text{for (2.4)}$$

If $\hat{\lambda}$ is the ML estimator and $\ell\left(\hat{\lambda}\right)$ is the accompanying maximized likelihood from (2.5), then a confidence interval for λ can be constructed using the standard result that $2\left(\ell\left(\hat{\lambda}\right) - \ell(\lambda)\right)$ is asymptotically distributed as $\chi^2(1)$, so that a 95% confidence interval, for example, is given by those values of λ for which $\ell\left(\hat{\lambda}\right) - \ell(\lambda) < 1.92$.

2.7 For the rainfall series in Fig. 2.4, μ_t was chosen to be a linear function of seasonal means and trends, that is, $\mu_t = \sum_{i=1}^{12}(\alpha_i + \beta_i t)s_{i,t}$, where the "seasonal dummy" $s_{i,t}$ takes a value of unity for month i and is zero otherwise ($i = 1$ for January, etc.): see Mills (2017b) for a justification for this choice of model. Since all the values of x_t are positive (there has never been a completely dry month in England and Wales, as residents of these countries will surely attest!), the Box−Cox transformation (2.1) is appropriate. The ML estimate is $\hat{\lambda} = 0.55$ with an accompanying 95% confidence interval of (0.48, 0.62), hence the choice of $\lambda = 0.5$ with which to transform the series. Note that both $\lambda = 0$, the logarithmic transformation, and $\lambda = 1$, effectively no transformation, lie well outside this interval.

2.8 The top panel of Fig. 2.5 shows another monthly rainfall series for the Greek island of Kefalonia between 2003 and 2017. As is typical for an island in the Ionian chain, there is little rain in the summer months but often considerable winter rainfall. Consequently, the series contains zero values and is highly skewed to the right, making it a candidate for either a GP or an IHS transformation.

The middle panel shows the series after a GP transformation with $\hat{\lambda} = 0.16$ [95% confidence interval (0.08, 0.24)], while the bottom panel shows the IHS transformation of the series (in both cases the seasonal mean model $\mu_t = \sum_{i=1}^{12}\alpha_i s_{i,t}$ was used). In the IHS transformation the parameter $\lambda = 1$ is used, because although the ML estimate is $\hat{\lambda} = 0.65$, it is accompanied by a wide 95% confidence interval running from 0.29 to 1.82; this is a consequence of an extremely flat likelihood function, thus implying that

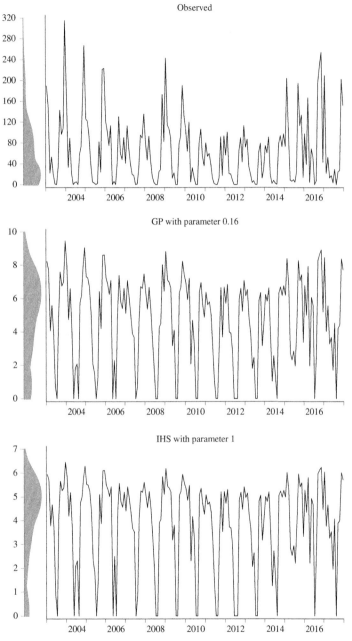

FIGURE 2.5 Kefalonia rainfall (in mm): monthly, January 2003−December 2017. *Data from Personal communication.*

many values of the IHS parameter could be chosen to transform the series. Clearly both transformed series are now left-skewed but look to be more stable in terms of variation.

STATIONARITY INDUCING TRANSFORMATIONS

2.9 A simple stationarity transformation is to take successive differences of a series, on defining the *first-difference* of x_t as $\nabla x_t = x_t - x_{t-1}$. Fig. 2.6

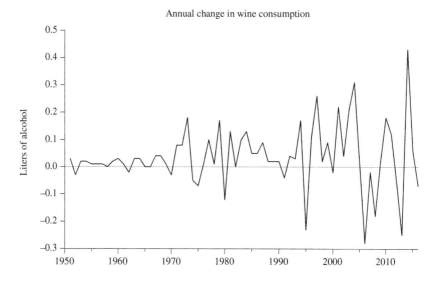

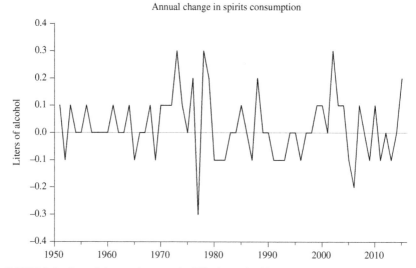

FIGURE 2.6 Annual changes in per capita UK wine and spirits consumption; 1951–2015.

shows the first-differences of the wine and spirits consumption series plotted in Fig. 1.6, that is, the annual changes in consumption. The trends in both series have been eradicated by this transformation and, as will be shown in Chapter 4, ARIMA Models for Nonstationary Time Series, differencing has a lot to recommend it both practically and theoretically for transforming a nonstationary series to stationarity.

First-differencing may, on some occasions, be insufficient to induce stationarity and further differencing may be required. Fig. 2.7 shows successive temperature readings on a chemical process, this being Series C of Box and Jenkins (1970). The top panel shows observed temperatures. These display a distinctive form of nonstationarity, in which there are almost random switches in trend and changes in level. Although first differencing (shown as the middle panel) mitigates these switches and changes, it by no means eliminates them; second-differences are required to achieve this, as shown in the bottom panel.

2.10   Some caution is required when taking higher-order differences. The second-differences shown in Fig. 2.7 are defined as the first-difference of the first-difference, that is, $\nabla\nabla x_t = \nabla^2 x_t$. To provide an explicit expression for second-differences, it is convenient to introduce the *lag operator B*, defined such that $B^j x_t \equiv x_{t-j}$, so that:

$$\nabla x_t = x_t - x_{t-1} = x_t - B x_t = (1 - B)x_t \tag{2.6}$$

Consequently:

$$\nabla^2 x_t = (1-B)^2 x_t = \left(1 - 2B + B^2\right)x_t = x_t - 2x_{t-1} + x_{t-2} \tag{2.7}$$

which is clearly *not* the same as $x_t - x_{t-2} = \nabla_2 x_t$, the *two-period* difference, where the notation $\nabla_j = 1 - B^j$ for the taking of *j*-period differences has been introduced. The distinction between the two is clearly demonstrated in Fig. 2.8, where second- and two-period differences of Series C are displayed.

2.11   For some time series, interpretation can be made easier by taking *proportional* or *percentage* changes rather than simple differences, that is, transforming by $\nabla x_t / x_{t-1}$ or $100 \nabla x_t / x_{t-1}$. For financial time series these are typically referred to as the *return*. Fig. 2.9 plots the monthly price of gold and its percentage return from 1980 to 2017. The price is clearly nonstationary, the series being dominated by the upward swing from around $270 per ounce in the summer of 2001 to almost $1750 in the autumn of 2012, but the monthly returns are trend-free, albeit with considerable variation, ranging from −15% to 20%.

2.12   When attention is focused on the percentage change in a price index, then these changes are typically referred to as the *rate of inflation*. There may be several different rates of inflation depending on the frequency of observation, say monthly, quarterly, or annually, and the *span* over which the inflation rate is calculated. For example, the annual rate of inflation of a

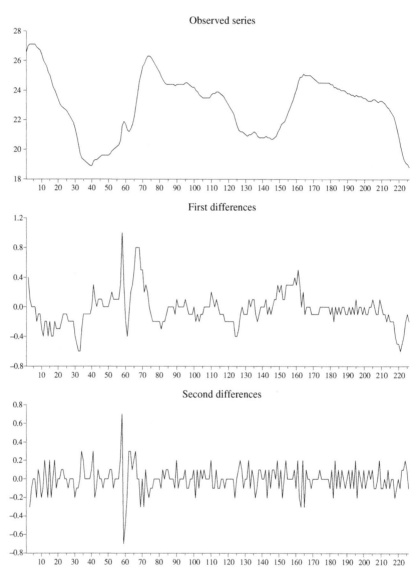

FIGURE 2.7 Chemical process temperature readings: levels, first- and second-differences. *From Box, G.E.P., Jenkins, G.M., 1970. Time Series Analysis: Forecasting and Control. San Francisco: Holden-Day, Series C.*

monthly price index is defined as $100\nabla_{12}x_t/x_{t-12}$, so that it is the percentage change in the index from a given month of one year to that month of the next year: see Fig. 2.10 for the annual rate of inflation of the monthly RPI.[5]

2.13   While transforming to an annual rate of inflation certainly eradicates the trend in the monthly RPI series, it is important to realize that such a

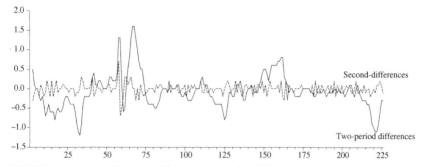

FIGURE 2.8   Second-differences $\nabla^2 x_t$ and two-period differences $\nabla_2 x_t$ of chemical process temperature readings.

transformation does *not* necessarily induce stationarity and it certainly does not in Fig. 2.10, which can be compared with the monthly rate of inflation shown in Fig. 2.11, which is more obviously stationary. Why then, are annual rather than monthly rates of inflation typically discussed by economic commentators? Stationarity is clearly not much of a concern to them, whereas the relative smoothness of annual inflation compared to the much higher volatility of monthly inflation allows the former to be more readily interpretable in terms of evolving patterns of price behavior.

2.14   There is a useful relationship between the rate of change of a variable and its logarithm that is often worth bearing in mind, namely:

$$\frac{x_t - x_{t-1}}{x_{t-1}} = \frac{x_t}{x_{t-1}} - 1 \approx \log\frac{x_t}{x_{t-1}} = \log x_t - \log x_{t-1} = \nabla\log x_t \qquad (2.8)$$

where the approximation follows from the fact that $\log(1 + y) \approx y$ for small y. Thus, if $y_t = (x_t - x_{t-1})/x_{t-1}$ is small, rates of inflation can be closely approximated by the change in the logarithms, which is often a more convenient transformation to work with.

DECOMPOSING A TIME SERIES AND SMOOTHING TRANSFORMATIONS

2.15   It is often the case that the long-run behavior of a time series is of particular interest and attention is then focused on isolating these "permanent" movements from shorter-run, more "transitory," fluctuations, that is, by separating the observations through a *decomposition*, generally of the form "data = fit + residual." Because such a decomposition is more than likely going to lead to a *smooth* series, this might be better thought of as "data = smooth + rough," terminology borrowed from Tukey (1977). Tukey himself favored *running* or *moving medians* to do this, but *moving averages* (MAs) have become by far the most popular approach to smoothing a time series.

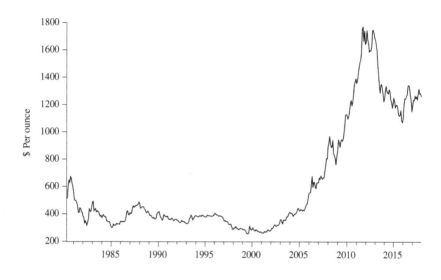

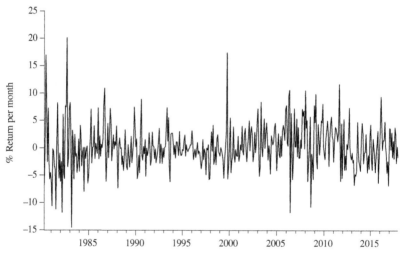

FIGURE 2.9 Monthly gold price and return: January 1980–December 2017. *Readily available online.*

2.16 The simplest MA replaces x_t with the average of itself, its predecessor, and its successor, that is, by the MA(3) $\frac{1}{3}(x_{t-1} + x_t + x_{t+1})$. More complicated formulations are obviously possible: the $(2n + 1)$-term *weighted* and *centered* MA [WMA$(2n + 1)$] replaces x_t with

$$\text{WMA}_t(2n + 1) = \sum_{i=-n}^{n} \omega_i x_{t-i} \qquad (2.9)$$

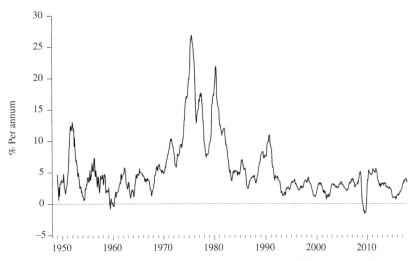

FIGURE 2.10   Annual % rate of inflation of monthly RPI: January 1949–December 2017.

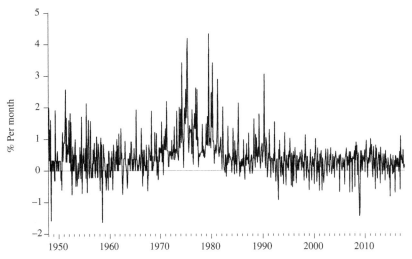

FIGURE 2.11   Monthly % rate of RPI inflation: February 1948–December 2017.

where the *weights* ω_i are restricted to sum to unity: $\sum_{i=-n}^{n} \omega_i = 1$. The weights are often symmetrically valued about the central weight ω_0 and because there is an odd number of weights in (2.9), $\text{WMA}_t(2n+1)$ "matches up" with x_t, hence the use of the term "centered".

As more terms are included in the MA, the smoother it becomes, albeit with the trade-off that since n observations are "lost" at the beginning and at the end of the sample, more observations will be lost the larger n is. If observations at the end of the sample, the most "recent", are more important than those at the start of the sample, then an *uncentered* MA may be considered, such as $\sum_{i=0}^{n} w_i x_{t-i}$, where only current and past observations appear in the MA, which is then said to be "backward looking" or "one-sided," in contrast to the two-sided WMA of (2.9).

2.17 WMAs may also arise when a simple MA with an even number of terms is used but centering is required. For example, a four-term MA may be defined as:

$$\text{MA}_{t-1/2}(4) = \frac{1}{4}(x_{t-2} + x_{t-1} + x_t + x_{t+1})$$

where the notation makes clear that the "central" date to which the MA relates to is a noninteger, being halfway between $t-1$ and t, that is, $t - (1/2)$, but of course $x_{t-(1/2)}$ does not exist and the centering property is lost. At $t + 1$, however, the MA is:

$$\text{MA}_{t+(1/2)}(4) = \frac{1}{4}(x_{t-1} + x_t + x_{t+1} + x_{t+2})$$

which has a central date of $t + (1/2)$. Taking the average of these two simple MAs produces a weighted MA centered on the average of $t - (1/2)$ and $t + (1/2)$, which is, of course, t:

$$\text{WMA}_t(5) = \frac{1}{8}x_{t-2} + \frac{1}{4}x_{t-1} + \frac{1}{4}x_t + \frac{1}{4}x_{t+1} + \frac{1}{8}x_{t+2} \qquad (2.10)$$

This is an example of (2.9) with $n = 2$ and where there are "half-weights" on the two extreme observations of the MA.

2.18 Fig. 2.12 plots two simple MAs for the daily observations on the \$–£ exchange rate shown in Fig. 1.5. The centered MA(251) has a span of approximately one year, while the backward looking one-sided MA(60) has a span stretching back over the last three months (5-day working weeks and 20-day working months being assumed here). Naturally, the former MA is much smoother, missing out on the sharper peaks and troughs captured by the latter, but reproducing the longer-term undulations of the exchange rate, known as "long swings." It also loses the last 125 days (approximately 6 months), which might be regarded as a drawback if recent movements are thought to be of special importance.

2.19 Weighted MAs lie behind many of the *trend filters* that have been proposed over the years and which will be introduced in Chapter 8, Unobserved Component Models, Signal Extraction, and Filters: see Mills (2011, chapter 10) for a historical discussion. Fig. 2.13 shows the global temperature series originally plotted in Fig. 1.8 with a popular trend filter, known as the *Hodrick–Prescott* (H–P) filter, superimposed. Details of this filter are provided in §§**8.13–8.18**, it being a symmetric weighted MA with end-point corrections that allow the filter to be computed right up to the end of the sample,

FIGURE 2.12   Daily $–£ exchange rate: centered MA(251) (———); backward looking MA(60) (----). *MA*, Moving average.

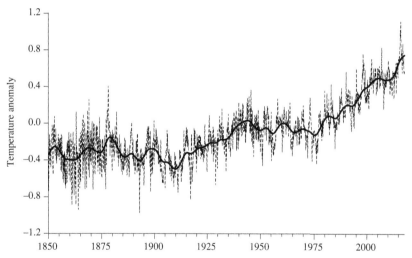

FIGURE   2.13   Monthly   global   temperatures   with   HP   trend   superimposed.   *HP*, Hodrick–Prescott.

thus avoiding any loss of observations. This is important here, because global temperatures are quite volatile and extracting the recent trend is essential for providing an indication of the current extent of any global warming. The weights of the MA depend on choosing a value for the *smoothing parameter*: here a large value has been chosen to produce a relatively "smooth trend" that focuses on the longer run movements in temperature.

2.20   The MAs fitted in the previous examples have been interpreted as trends; the long-run, smoothly evolving component of a time series, that is, the "smooth" of a two-component decomposition (recall §**2.15**). When a time series is observed at a frequency greater than annual, say monthly or quarterly, a three-component decomposition is often warranted, with the observed series, now denoted X_t, being decomposed into trend, T_t, seasonal, S_t, and irregular, I_t, components. The decomposition can either be *additive:*

$$X_t = T_t + S_t + I_t \qquad (2.11)$$

or *multiplicative*

$$X_t = T_t \times S_t \times I_t \qquad (2.12)$$

although the distinction is to some extent artificial, as taking logarithms of (2.12) will produce an additive decomposition for $\log X_t$. The seasonal component is a regular, short-term, annual cycle, while the irregular component is what is left over after the trend and seasonal components have been removed; it should with thus be random and hence unpredictable.

The *seasonally adjusted* series is then defined as either:

$$X_t^{SA,A} = X_t - S_t = T_t + I_t \qquad (2.13)$$

or

$$X_t^{SA,M} = \frac{X_t}{S_t} = T_t \times I_t \qquad (2.14)$$

depending on which form of decomposition is used.

2.21   The dominant features of the beer sales series shown in Fig. 1.4 were the downward trend in the second half of the observation period and the prominent seasonal pattern of sales. A simple method of seasonal adjustment is to first estimate the trend component using a MA. Since beer sales are observed quarterly, (2.10) may be used as the centered MA, and assuming an additive decomposition (2.11), the "trend-free" series may then be obtained by subtracting this MA from the observed series:

$$X_t - T_t = X_t - \text{WMA}_t(5) = S_t + I_t$$

This trend-free series is the sum of the seasonal and irregular components, which somehow need to be disentangled. To do this the "identifying" assumption that I_t should, on average, be zero may be made (if it was not then a portion of I_t would be predictable and should be part of either the trend or the seasonal). This allows S_t to be calculated by taking the average of each quarter across years; for example, the seasonal *factor* for the first quarter is given by:

$$S_t(Q1) = \frac{X_{1997Q1} + X_{1998Q1} + \cdots + X_{2017Q1}}{21}$$

with the factors for the other three quarters being given analogously. For beer sales, these factors are calculated to be[6]:

$$S_t(Q1) = -1523.2 \quad S_t(Q2) = 485.1 \quad S_t(Q3) = 151.2 \quad S_t(Q4) = 886.9$$

The large negative first quarter factor is compensated by offsetting positive factors for the other three quarters, by far the largest being the fourth. Hence, beer sales tend to be highest in the fourth quarter of the year, in the run up to Christmas and the New Year, with sales being lowest during the subsequent quarter in the aftermath of these festivities.

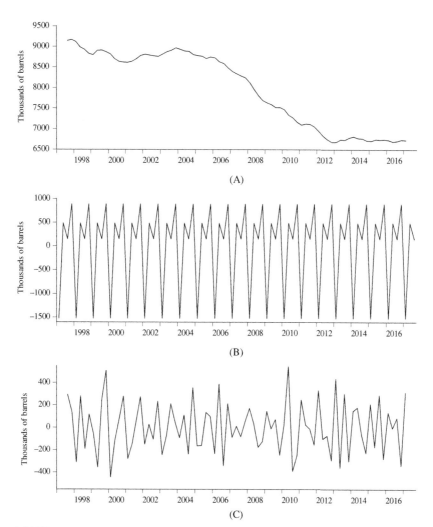

FIGURE 2.14 Additive decomposition of quarterly U K beer sales. (A) Trend; (B) Seasonal; (C) Irregular.

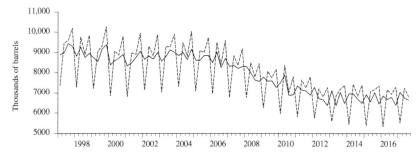

FIGURE 2.15 Observed and seasonally adjusted quarterly UK beer sales.

The trend and seasonal components are shown in Fig. 2.14, panels A and B, respectively. The declining trend in beer sales from 2003 to 2012 is clearly seen, although the trend has flattened off since then. The seasonal pattern is forced by this method to be "constant" over time, which is probably adequate for the relatively brief period for which observations are available here, but more sophisticated seasonal adjustment procedures allow seasonal patterns to evolve.[7]

2.22 The irregular is now calculated "by residual" as:

$$I_t = X_t - T_t - S_t$$

and is plotted as shown in Fig. 2.14C. It is clearly random, and since it ranges from -440 to 540 thousand barrels, is relatively large, reflecting the many factors that influence beer sales in any quarter. Seasonally adjusted beer sales are computed from (2.13) and are shown, with unadjusted sales, in Fig. 2.15. Being the sum of the trend and irregular, the seasonally adjusted series reflects both the underlying trend and the random, and sometimes large, shocks that impact on beer sales.

ENDNOTES

1. If x_t is generated by the exponential trend $x_t = Ae^{\beta t}$ then on taking logarithms, $\log x_t = \log A + \beta t$ is a linear trend function. Thus, the slope $\beta = d\log x_t/dt = (dx_t/dt)/x_t$ is the rate of change of x, i.e., the (instantaneous) rate of inflation if x is a price level.
2. See, for example, Mills (1990, chapter 6.2) for a formal derivation of this result.
3. The "simple" power transformation x_t^λ is modified because the limiting value of $(x_t^\lambda - 1)/\lambda$ as $\lambda \to 0$ is $\log x_t$ and so continuity is preserved in the region of $\lambda = 0$.
4. The moment measures of skewness for observed and transformed rainfall are 0.60 and -0.05 respectively. The square root transformation is recommended when the variance is proportional to the level of the series.
5. Occasionally an "annualized" one-period rate of inflation is used. This is defined for monthly data as $100\left(\left(1 + \nabla x_t/x_{t-1}\right)^{12} - 1\right)$.
6. These factors are required to sum to zero, and so would need adjusting if the raw calculations lead to a nonzero sum: if this sum is $a \neq 0$, say, then $a/4$ should be subtracted from each factor.
7. *EViews 10* provides several specialist seasonal adjustment procedures that are extremely sophisticated but too advanced and detailed to be discussed in this book.

Chapter 3

ARMA Models for Stationary Time Series

Chapter Outline

STOCHASTIC PROCESSES AND STATIONARITY

3.1 The concept of a stationary time series was introduced informally in Chapter 1, Time Series and Their Features, but to proceed further it is necessary to consider the concept rather more rigorously. To this end, it is often useful to regard the observations $x_1, x_2, \ldots, x_T$ on the series x_t as a *realization* of a stochastic process. In general, such a stochastic process may be described by a T-dimensional probability distribution, so that the relationship between a realization and a stochastic process is analogous, in classical statistics, to that between a sample and the population from which it has been drawn from.

Specifying the complete form of the probability distribution, however, will typically be too ambitious a task, so attention is usually concentrated on the first and second moments; the T means:

$$E(x_1), E(x_2), \ldots, E(x_T)$$

T variances:

$$V(x_1), V(x_2), \ldots, V(x_T)$$

and $T(T-1)/2$ covariances:

$$Cov(x_i, x_j), \quad i < j$$

If the distribution could be assumed to be (multivariate) normal, then this set of expectations would completely characterize the properties of the stochastic process. As has been seen from the examples in Chapter 2, Transforming

Applied Time Series Analysis. DOI: https://doi.org/10.1016/B978-0-12-813117-6.00003-X

Time Series, however, such an assumption will not always be appropriate, but if the process is taken to be *linear*, in the sense that the current value x_t is generated by a linear combination of previous values $x_{t-1}, x_{t-2}, \ldots$ of the process itself plus current and past values of any other related processes, then again this set of expectations would capture its major properties.

In either case, however, it will be impossible to infer all the values of the first and second moments from just a single realization of the process, since there are only T observations but $T + T(T + 1)/2$ unknown parameters. Consequently, further simplifying assumptions must be made to reduce the number of unknown parameters to more manageable proportions.

3.2 It should be emphasized that the procedure of using a single realization to infer the unknown parameters of a joint probability distribution is only valid if the process is *ergodic*, which roughly means that the sample moments for finite stretches of the realization approach their population counterparts as the length of the realization becomes infinite. Since it is difficult to test for ergodicity using just (part of) a single realization, it will be assumed that this property holds for every time series.[1]

3.3 Perhaps the most important simplifying assumption has already been introduced in Chapter 1, Time Series and Their Features, that of *stationarity*, which, as we have seen, requires the process to be in a state of "statistical equilibrium." A stochastic process is said to be *strictly stationary* if its properties are unaffected by a change of time origin, that is, the joint probability distribution at *any* set of times $t_1, t_2, \ldots, t_m$ must be the same as the joint probability distribution at $t_{1+k}, t_{2+k}, \ldots, t_{m+k}$, where k is an arbitrary shift in time. For $m = 1$, strict stationarity implies that the marginal probability distributions at $t_1, t_2, \ldots$ do not depend on time, which in turn implies that as long as $E|x_t^2| < \infty$ (which is part of a finite second moment assumption) both the mean and variance of x_t must be constant, so that:

$$E(x_1) = E(x_2) = \cdots = E(x_T) = \mu$$

and

$$V(x_1) = V(x_2) = \cdots = V(x_T) = \sigma_x^2$$

If $m = 2$, strict stationarity implies that all bivariate distributions do not depend on time, so that covariances are functions of the time-shift (or lag) k only, hence implying that for all k,

$$Cov(x_1, x_{1+k}) = Cov(x_2, x_{2+k}) = \cdots = Cov(x_{T-k}, x_T) = Cov(x_t, x_{t-k})$$

This leads to the definition of the lag-k *autocovariance* as:

$$\gamma_k = Cov(x_t, x_{t-k}) = E((x_t - \mu)(x_{t-k} - \mu))$$

so that

$$\gamma_0 = E(x_t - \mu)^2 = V(x_t) = \sigma_x^2$$

and the lag-k *autocorrelation* may then be defined as

$$\rho_k = \frac{Cov(x_t, x_{t-k})}{(V(x_t)V(x_{t-k}))^{1/2}} = \frac{\gamma_k}{\gamma_0} = \frac{\gamma_k}{\sigma_x^2} \qquad (3.1)$$

The set of assumptions that the mean and variance of x_t are both constant and the autocovariances and autocorrelations depend only on the lag k is known as *weak* or *covariance stationarity*.

3.4 While strict stationarity (with finite second moments) thus implies weak stationarity, the converse does not hold, for it is possible for a process to be weakly stationary but *not* strictly stationary. This would be the case if higher moments, such as $E(x_t^3)$, were functions of time and an important example of this is considered in Chapter 10, Volatility and GARCH Processes. If, however, joint normality could be assumed so that the distribution was entirely characterized by the first two moments, weak stationarity would indeed imply strict stationarity.

3.5 The set of autocorrelations (3.1), when considered as a function of k, is referred to as the (*population*) *autocorrelation function* (ACF). Since:

$$\gamma_k = Cov(x_t, x_{t-k}) = Cov(x_{t-k}, x_t) = Cov(x_t, x_{t+k}) = \gamma_{-k}$$

it follows that $\rho_{-k} = \rho_k$ and so only the positive half of the ACF is usually given. The ACF plays a major role in modeling dependencies between the values of x_t since it characterizes, along with the process mean $\mu = E(x_t)$ and variance $\sigma_x^2 = \gamma_0 = V(x_t)$, the stationary stochastic process describing the evolution of x_t. It therefore indicates, by measuring the extent to which one value of the process is correlated with previous values, the length and strength of the "memory" of the process.

WOLD'S DECOMPOSITION AND AUTOCORRELATION

3.6 A fundamental theorem in time series analysis, known as *Wold's decomposition*, states that every weakly stationary, purely nondeterministic, stochastic process $x_t - \mu$ can be written as a linear combination (or linear *filter*) of a sequence of uncorrelated random variables.[2] "Purely nondeterministic" means that any deterministic components have been subtracted from $x_t - \mu$. Such components are those that can be perfectly predicted from past values of themselves and examples commonly found are a (constant) mean, as is implied by writing the process as $x_t - \mu$, periodic sequences (e.g., sine and cosine functions), and polynomial or exponential sequences in t.

This linear filter representation is given by:

$$x_t - \mu = a_t + \psi_1 a_{t-1} + \psi_2 a_{t-2} + \cdots = \sum_{j=0}^{\infty} \psi_j a_{t-j} \quad \psi_0 = 1 \qquad (3.2)$$

The a_t, $t = 0, \pm 1, \pm 2, \ldots$ are a sequence of uncorrelated random variables, often known as *innovations*, drawn from a fixed distribution with:

$$E(a_t) = 0 \quad V(a_t) = E\left(a_t^2\right) = \sigma^2 < \infty$$

and

$$Cov(a_t, a_{t-k}) = E(a_t a_{t-k}) = 0, \quad \text{for all } k \neq 0$$

Such a sequence is known as a *white noise* process, and occasionally the innovations will be denoted as $a_t \sim \text{WN}(0, \sigma^2)$.[3] The coefficients (possibly infinite in number) in the linear filter (3.2) are known as ψ-*weights*.

3.7 It is easy to show that the model (3.2) leads to autocorrelation in x_t. From this equation it follows that:

$$E(x_t) = \mu$$

and

$$
\begin{aligned}
\gamma_0 &= V(x_t) = E(x_t - \mu)^2 \\
&= E\left(a_t + \psi_1 a_{t-1} + \psi_2 a_{t-2} + \cdots\right)^2 \\
&= E\left(a_t^2\right) + \psi_1^2 E\left(a_{t-1}^2\right) + \psi_2^2 E\left(a_{t-2}^2\right) + \cdots \\
&= \sigma^2 + \psi_1^2 \sigma^2 + \psi_2^2 \sigma^2 + \cdots \\
&= \sigma^2 \sum_{j=0}^{\infty} \psi_j^2
\end{aligned}
$$

by using the white noise result that $E\left(a_{t-i} a_{t-j}\right) = 0$ for $i \neq j$. Now:

$$
\begin{aligned}
\gamma_k &= E(x_t - \mu)(x_{t-k} - \mu) \\
&= E\left(a_t + \psi_1 a_{t-1} + \cdots + \psi_k a_{t-k} + \cdots\right)\left(a_{t-k} + \psi_1 a_{t-k-1} + \cdots\right) \\
&= \sigma^2\left(1 \cdot \psi_k + \psi_1 \psi_{k+1} + \psi_2 \psi_{k+2} + \cdots\right) \\
&= \sigma^2 \sum_{j=0}^{\infty} \psi_j \psi_{j+k}
\end{aligned}
$$

and this implies

$$\rho_k = \frac{\displaystyle\sum_{j=0}^{\infty} \psi_j \psi_{j+k}}{\displaystyle\sum_{j=0}^{\infty} \psi_j^2}$$

If the number of ψ-weights in (3.2) is infinite, the weights must be assumed to be absolutely summable, so that $\sum_{j=0}^{\infty} |\psi_j| < \infty$, in which case the linear filter representation is said to *converge*. This condition can be shown to be equivalent to assuming that x_t is stationary, and guarantees that all moments exist and are independent of time, in particular that the variance of x_t, γ_0, is finite.

FIRST-ORDER AUTOREGRESSIVE PROCESSES

3.8 Although Eq. (3.2) may appear complicated, many realistic models result from specific choices for the ψ-weights. Taking $\mu = 0$ without loss of generality, choosing $\psi_j = \phi^j$ allows (3.2) to be written as:

$$\begin{aligned} x_t &= a_t + \phi a_{t-1} + \phi^2 a_{t-2} + \cdots \\ &= a_t + \phi(a_{t-1} + \phi a_{t-2} + \cdots) \\ &= \phi x_{t-1} + a_t \end{aligned}$$

or

$$x_t - \phi x_{t-1} = a_t \tag{3.3}$$

This is known as a *first-order autoregressive* process, often given the acronym AR(1).[4]

3.9 The lag operator B introduced in §**2.10** allows (possibly infinite) lag expressions to be written in a concise way. For example, by using this operator the AR(1) process can be written as:

$$(1 - \phi B)x_t = a_t$$

so that

$$\begin{aligned} x_t &= (1 - \phi B)^{-1} a_t = \left(1 + \phi B + \phi^2 B^2 + \cdots\right) a_t \\ &= a_t + \phi a_{t-1} + \phi^2 a_{t-2} + \cdots \end{aligned} \tag{3.4}$$

This linear filter representation will converge if $|\phi| < 1$, which is, therefore, the *stationarity condition*.

3.10 The ACF of an AR(1) process may now be deduced. Multiplying both sides of (3.3) by x_{t-k}, $k > 0$, and taking expectations yields:

$$\gamma_k - \phi \gamma_{k-1} = E(a_t x_{t-k}). \tag{3.5}$$

From (3.4), $a_t x_{t-k} = \sum_{i=0}^{\infty} \phi^i a_t a_{t-k-i}$. As a_t is white noise, any term in $a_t a_{t-k-i}$ has zero expectation if $k + i > 0$. Thus (3.5) simplifies to:

$$\gamma_k = \phi \gamma_{k-1} \quad \text{for all } k > 0$$

and, consequently, $\gamma_k = \phi^k \gamma_0$. An AR(1) process, therefore, has an ACF given by $\rho_k = \phi^k$. Thus, if $\phi > 0$ the ACF decays exponentially to zero, while if $\phi < 0$ the ACF decays in an oscillatory pattern, both decays being slow if ϕ is close to the nonstationary boundaries of $+1$ and -1.

3.11 The ACFs for two AR(1) processes with (A) $\phi = 0.5$ and (B) $\phi = -0.5$ are shown in Fig. 3.1, along with generated data from the two processes with a_t assumed to be normally and independently distributed with $\sigma^2 = 25$, denoted $a_t \sim \text{NID}(0, 25)$, and with starting value $x_0 = 0$ (essentially a_t is normally distributed white noise since under normality independence implies uncorrelatedness). With $\phi > 0$ adjacent values of x_t are positively correlated and the

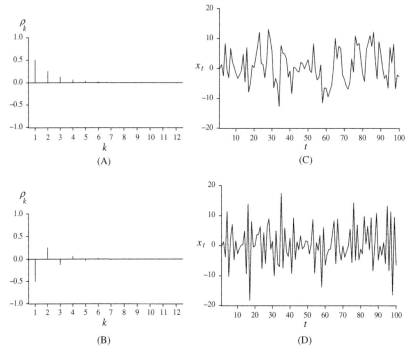

FIGURE 3.1 ACFs and simulations of AR(1) processes. (A) $\phi = 0.5$ (B) $\phi = -0.5$ (C) $\phi = 0.5$, $x_0 = 0$ (D) $\phi = -0.5$, $x_0 = 0$. *ACFs*, Autocorrelation functions.

generated series tends to be smooth, exhibiting runs of observations having the same sign. With $\phi < 0$, however, adjacent values are negatively correlated and the generated series displays violent, rapid oscillations.

FIRST-ORDER MOVING AVERAGE PROCESSES

3.12   Now consider the model obtained by choosing $\psi_1 = -\theta$ and $\psi_j = 0$, $j \geq 2$, in (3.2):

$$x_t = a_t - \theta a_{t-1} \tag{3.6}$$

or

$$x_t = (1 - \theta B)a_t$$

This is known as the *first-order moving average* (MA(1)) process and it follows immediately that:[5]

$$\gamma_0 = \sigma^2 \left(1 + \theta^2\right) \quad \gamma_1 = -\sigma^2 \theta \quad \gamma_k = 0 \text{ for } k > 1$$

and, hence, its ACF is described by

$$\rho_1 = -\frac{\theta}{1+\theta^2} \quad \rho_k = 0 \text{ for } k > 1$$

Thus, although observations one period apart are correlated, observations more than one period apart are not, so that the memory of the process is just one period: this "jump" to zero autocorrelation at $k = 2$ may be contrasted with the smooth, exponential decay of the ACF of an AR(1) process.

3.13 The expression for ρ_1 can be written as the quadratic equation $\rho_1\theta^2 + \theta + \rho_1 = 0$. Since θ must be real, it follows that $|\rho_1| < 0.5$.[6] However, both θ and $1/\theta$ will satisfy this equation, and thus, two MA(1) processes can always be found that correspond to the same ACF.

3.14 Since any MA model consists of a finite number of ψ-weights, all MA models are stationary. To obtain a converging autoregressive representation, however, the restriction $\theta < 1$ must be imposed. This restriction is known as the *invertibility* condition and implies that the process can be written in terms of an infinite autoregressive representation:

$$x_t = \pi_1 x_{t-1} + \pi_2 x_{t-2} + \cdots + a_t$$

where the π-*weights* converge: $\sum_{j=1}^{\infty} |\pi_j| < \infty$. In fact, the MA(1) model can be written as:

$$(1 - \theta B)^{-1} x_t = a_t$$

and expanding $(1 - \theta B)^{-1}$ yields

$$\left(1 + \theta B + \theta^2 B^2 + \cdots\right) x_t = a_t.$$

The weights $\pi_j = \theta^j$ will converge if $|\theta| < 1$; in other words, if the model is invertible. This implies the reasonable assumption that the effect of past observations decreases with age.

3.15 Fig. 3.2 presents plots of generated data from two MA(1) processes with (A) $\theta = 0.8$ and (B) $\theta = -0.8$, in each case, again, with $a_t \sim \text{NID}(0, 25)$. On comparison of these plots with those of the AR(1) processes in Fig. 3.1, it is seen that realizations from the two processes are often quite similar (the ρ_1 values are 0.488 and 0.5, respectively, for example), thus suggesting that it may, on occasion, be difficult to distinguish between the two.

GENERAL AR AND MA PROCESSES

3.16 Extensions to the AR(1) and MA(1) models are immediate. The general autoregressive model of order p (AR(p)) can be written as:

$$x_t - \phi_1 x_{t-1} - \phi_2 x_{t-2} - \cdots - \phi_p x_{t-p} = a_t$$

or

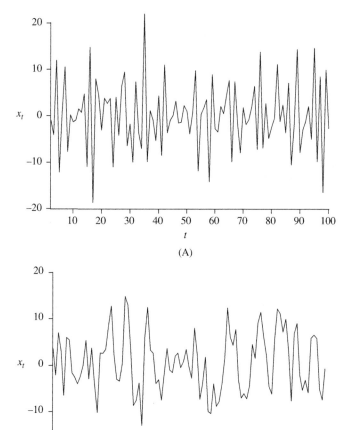

FIGURE 3.2 Simulations of MA(1) processes. (A) $\theta = 0.8$ (B) $\theta = -0.8$. *MA*, Moving average.

$$\left(1 - \phi_1 B - \phi_2 B^2 - \cdots - \phi_p B^p\right) x_t = \phi(B) x_t = a_t$$

The linear filter representation $x_t = \phi^{-1}(B) a_t = \psi(B) a_t$ can be obtained by equating coefficients in $\phi(B)\psi(B) = 1$.[7]

3.17 The stationarity conditions required for convergence of the ψ-weights are that the roots of the characteristic equation:

$$\phi(B) = (1 - g_1 B)(1 - g_2 B) \cdots \left(1 - g_p B\right) = 0$$

are such that $|g_i| < 1$ for $i = 1, 2, \ldots, p$. The behavior of the ACF is determined by the difference equation:

$$\phi(B)\rho_k = 0 \quad k > 0 \tag{3.7}$$

which has the solution

$$\rho_k = A_1 g_1^k + A_2 g_2^k + \cdots + A_p g_p^k$$

Since $|g_i| < 1$, the ACF is thus described by a mixture of damped exponentials (for real roots) and damped sine waves (for complex roots). As an example, consider the AR(2) process:

$$\left(1 - \phi_1 B - \phi_2 B^2\right) x_t = a_t$$

with characteristic equation

$$\phi(B) = (1 - g_1 B)(1 - g_2 B) = 0$$

The roots g_1 and g_2 are given by:

$$g_1, g_2 = \tfrac{1}{2}\left(\phi_1 \pm \left(\phi_1^2 + 4\phi_2\right)^{1/2}\right)$$

and can both be real, or they can be a pair of complex numbers. For stationarity, it is required that the roots be such that $|g_1| < 1$ and $|g_2| < 1$, and it can be shown that these conditions imply this set of restrictions on ϕ_1 and ϕ_2:[8]

$$\phi_1 + \phi_2 < 1 \quad -\phi_1 + \phi_2 < 1 \quad -1 < \phi_2 < 1$$

The roots will be complex if $\phi_1^2 + 4\phi_2 < 0$, although a necessary condition for complex roots is simply that $\phi_2 < 0$.

3.18 The ACF of an AR(2) process is given by:

$$\rho_k = \phi_1 \rho_{k-1} + \phi_2 \rho_{k-2}$$

for $k \geq 2$ with starting values $\rho_0 = 1$ and $\rho_1 = \phi_1 / (1 - \phi_2)$. The behavior of this ACF for four combinations of (ϕ_1, ϕ_2) is shown in Fig. 3.3. If g_1 and g_2 are real (cases (A) and (C)), the ACF is a mixture of two damped exponentials. Depending on their sign, the autocorrelations can also damp out in an oscillatory manner. If the roots are complex (cases (B) and (D)), then the ACF follows a damped sine wave. Fig. 3.4 shows plots of generated time series from these four AR(2) processes, in each case with $a_t \sim \text{NID}(0, 25)$. Depending on the signs of the real roots, the series may be either smooth or jagged, while complex roots tend to induce "periodic-type" behavior.

3.19 Since all AR processes have ACFs that "damp out", it is sometimes difficult to distinguish between processes of different orders. To aid with such discrimination, the *partial ACF* (PACF) may be used. In general, the correlation between two random variables is often due to both variables being correlated with a third. In the present context, a sizeable portion of the correlation between x_t and x_{t-k} may be due to the correlation that this pair

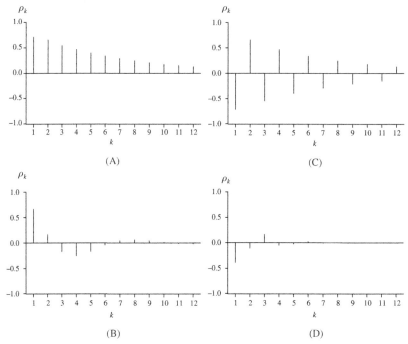

FIGURE 3.3   ACFs of various AR(2) processes. (A) $\phi_1 = 0.5$, $\phi_2 = 0.3$ (B) $\phi_1 = 1$, $\phi_2 = -0.5$ (C) $\phi_1 = -0.5$, $\phi_2 = 0.3$ (D) $\phi_1 = -0.5$, $\phi_2 = -0.3$. ACF, Autocorrelation function.

have with the intervening lags $x_{t-1}, x_{t-2}, \ldots, x_{t-k+1}$. To adjust for this "internal" correlation, the *partial autocorrelations* may be calculated.

3.20   The kth partial autocorrelation is the coefficient ϕ_{kk} in the AR(k) process:

$$x_t = \phi_{k1}x_{t-1} + \phi_{k2}x_{t-2} + \cdots + \phi_{kk}x_{t-k} + a_t \tag{3.8}$$

and measures the additional correlation between x_t and x_{t-k} after adjustments have been made for the intervening lags.

In general, the ϕ_{kk} can be obtained from the *Yule–Walker* equations that correspond to (3.8). These are given by the set shown in Eq. (3.7) with $p = k$ and $\phi_i = \phi_{ii}$, and solving for the last coefficient ϕ_{kk} using Cramer's Rule leads to:

$$\phi_{kk} = \frac{\begin{vmatrix} 1 & \rho_1 & \cdots & \rho_{k-2} & \rho_1 \\ \rho_1 & 1 & \cdots & \rho_{k-3} & \rho_2 \\ \vdots & \vdots & \cdots & \vdots & \vdots \\ \rho_{k-1} & \rho_{k-2} & \cdots & \rho_1 & \rho_k \end{vmatrix}}{\begin{vmatrix} 1 & \rho_1 & \cdots & \rho_{k-2} & \rho_{k-1} \\ \rho_1 & 1 & \cdots & \rho_{k-3} & \rho_{k-2} \\ \vdots & \vdots & \cdots & \vdots & \vdots \\ \rho_{k-1} & \rho_{k-2} & \cdots & \rho_1 & 1 \end{vmatrix}}$$

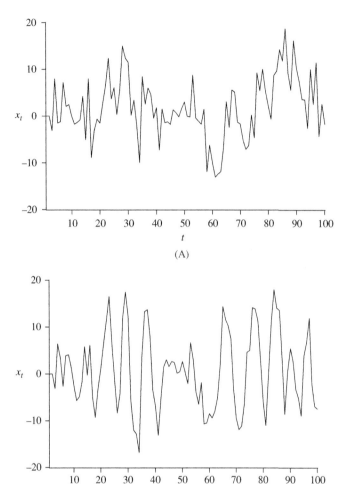

FIGURE 3.4 Simulations of various AR(2) processes. (A) $\phi_1 = 0.5$, $\phi_2 = 0.3$, $x_0 = x_1 = 0$ (B) $\phi_1 = 1$, $\phi_2 = -0.5$, $x_0 = x_1 = 0$. *AR*, Autoregressive.

Thus, for $k = 1$, $\phi_{11} = \rho_1 = \phi$, while for $k = 2$,

$$\phi_{22} = \frac{\begin{vmatrix} 1 & \rho_1 \\ \rho_1 & \rho_2 \end{vmatrix}}{\begin{vmatrix} 1 & \rho_1 \\ \rho_1 & 1 \end{vmatrix}} = \frac{\rho_2 - \rho_1^2}{1 - \rho_1^2}$$

It then follows from the definition of ϕ_{kk} that the PACFs of AR processes follow the pattern:

$$\text{AR(1):} \quad \phi_{11} = \rho_1 = \phi \qquad\qquad\qquad \phi_{kk} = 0 \text{ for } k > 1$$

$$\text{AR(2):} \quad \phi_{11} = \rho_1 \quad \phi_{22} = \frac{\rho_2 - \rho_1^2}{1 - \rho_1^2} \qquad \phi_{kk} = 0 \text{ for } k > 2$$

$$\vdots$$

$$\text{AR(p):} \quad \phi_{11} \neq 0, \; \phi_{22} \neq 0, \dots, \; \phi_{pp} \neq 0 \quad \phi_{kk} = 0 \text{ for } k > p$$

Hence, the partial autocorrelations for lags larger than the order of the process are zero. Consequently, an AR(p) process is described by:

1. an ACF that is infinite in extent and is a combination of damped exponentials and damped sine waves, and
2. a PACF that is zero for lags larger than p.

3.21 The general MA of order q (MA(q)) can be written as:

$$x_t = a_t - \theta_1 a_{t-1} - \cdots - \theta_q a_{t-q}$$

or

$$x_t = \left(1 - \theta_1 B - \cdots - \theta_q B^q\right) a_t = \theta(B) a_t$$

The ACF can be shown to be:

$$\rho_k = \frac{-\theta_k + \theta_1 \theta_{k+1} + \cdots + \theta_{q-k} \theta_q}{1 + \theta_1^2 + \cdots + \theta_q^2} \quad k = 1, 2, \dots, q$$

$$\rho_k = 0 \quad k > q$$

The ACF of an MA(q) process therefore cuts off after lag q; the memory of the process extends q periods, observations more than q periods apart being uncorrelated.

3.22 The weights in the AR(∞) representation $\pi(B)x_t = a_t$ are given by $\pi(B) = \theta^{-1}(B)$ and can be obtained by equating coefficients of B^j in $\pi(B)\theta(B) = 1$. For invertibility, the roots of

$$\left(1 - \theta_1 B - \cdots - \theta_q B^q\right) = \left(1 - h_1 B\right) \cdots \left(1 - h_q B\right) = 0$$

must satisfy $|h_i| < 1$ for $i = 1, 2, \dots, q$.

3.23 Fig. 3.5 presents generated series from two MA(2) processes, again using $a_t \sim \text{NID}(0, 25)$. The series tend to be fairly jagged, similar to AR(2) processes with real roots of opposite signs, and, of course, such MA processes are unable to capture periodic-type behavior.

3.24 The PACF of an MA(q) process can be shown to be infinite in extent, so that it tails off. Explicit expressions for the PACFs of MA processes are complicated but, in general, are dominated by combinations of exponential decays (for the real roots in $\theta(B)$) and/or damped sine waves (for the complex roots). Their patterns are, thus, similar to the ACFs of AR processes.

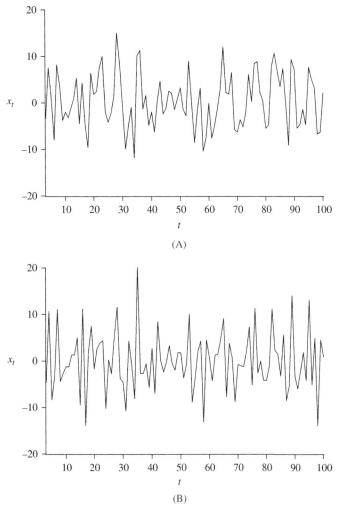

FIGURE 3.5 Simulations of MA(2) processes. (A) $\theta_1 = -0.5$, $\theta_2 = 0.3$ (B) $\theta_1 = 0.5$, $\theta_2 = 0.3$. *MA*, Moving average.

Indeed, an important duality between AR and MA processes exists: while the ACF of an AR(p) process is infinite in extent, the PACF cuts off after lag p. The ACF of an MA(q) process, on the other hand, cuts off after lag q, while the PACF is infinite in extent.

AUTOREGRESSIVE-MOVING AVERAGE MODELS

3.25 We may also entertain combinations of autoregressive and moving average models. For example, consider the natural combination of the AR(1) and MA(1) models, known as the *first-order autoregressive-moving average,* or ARMA(1,1), process:

$$x_t - \phi x_{t-1} = a_t - \theta a_{t-1} \tag{3.9}$$

or

$$(1 - \phi B)x_t = (1 - \theta B)a_t$$

The ψ-weights in the MA(∞) representation are given by:

$$\psi(B) = \frac{(1 - \theta B)}{(1 - \phi B)}$$

so that

$$x_t = \psi(B)a_t = \left(\sum_{i=0}^{\infty} \phi^i B^i \right)(1 - \theta B)a_t = a_t + (\phi - \theta) \sum_{i=1}^{\infty} \phi^{i-1} a_{t-i} \tag{3.10}$$

Likewise, the π-weights in the AR(∞) representation are given by:

$$\pi(B) = \frac{(1 - \phi B)}{(1 - \theta B)}$$

so that

$$\pi(B)x_t = \left(\sum_{i=0}^{\infty} \theta^i B^i \right)(1 - \phi B)x_t = a_t$$

or

$$x_t = (\phi - \theta) \sum_{i=1}^{\infty} \theta^{i-1} x_{t-i} + a_t$$

The ARMA(1,1) process, thus, leads to both MA and autoregressive representations having an infinite number of weights. The ψ-weights converge for $|\phi| < 1$ (the stationarity condition) and the π-weights converge for $|\theta| < 1$ (the invertibility condition). The stationarity condition for the ARMA(1,1) process is, thus, the same as that for an AR(1).

3.26 It follows from Eq. (3.10) that any product $x_{t-k}a_{t-j}$ has zero expectation if $k > j$. Thus, multiplying both sides of (3.9) by x_{t-k} and taking expectations yields:

$$\gamma_k = \phi\gamma_{k-1} \quad \text{for } k > 1$$

whilst for $k = 0$ and $k = 1$ we obtain, respectively

$$\gamma_0 - \phi\gamma_1 = \sigma^2 - \theta(\phi - \theta)\sigma^2$$

and

$$\gamma_1 - \phi\gamma_0 = -\theta\sigma^2$$

Eliminating σ^2 from these two equations allows the ACF of the ARMA(1,1) process to be given, after some algebraic manipulation, by:

$$\rho_1 = \frac{(1 - \phi\theta)(\phi - \theta)}{1 + \theta^2 - 2\phi\theta}$$

and

$$\rho_k = \phi\rho_{k-1} \quad \text{for } k > 1$$

The ACF of an ARMA(1,1) process is, therefore, similar to that of an AR(1) process, in that the autocorrelations decay exponentially at a rate ϕ. Unlike the AR(1), however, this decay starts from ρ_1 rather than from $\rho_0 = 1$. Moreover, $\rho_1 \neq \phi$ and if both ϕ and θ are positive with $\phi > \theta$, ρ_1 can be much less than ϕ if $\phi - \theta$ is small.

3.27 More general ARMA models are obtained by combining AR(p) and MA(q) processes:

$$x_t - \phi_1 x_{t-1} - \cdots - \phi_p x_{t-p} = a_t - \theta_1 a_{t-1} - \cdots - \theta_q a_{t-q}$$

or

$$\left(1 - \phi_1 B - \cdots - \phi_p B^p\right)x_t = \left(1 - \theta_1 - \cdots - \theta_q B^q\right)a_t \qquad (3.11)$$

which may be written more concisely as

$$\phi(B)x_t = \theta(B)a_t$$

The resultant ARMA(p,q) process has the stationarity and invertibility conditions associated with the constituent AR(p) and MA(q) processes respectively. Its ACF will eventually follow the same pattern as that of an AR(p) process after $q - p$ initial values $\rho_1, \ldots, \rho_{q-p}$, while its PACF eventually (for $k > q - p$) behaves like that of an MA(q) process.

3.28 Throughout this development, it has been assumed that the mean of the process, μ, is zero. Nonzero means are easily accommodated by replacing x_t with $x_t - \mu$ in (3.11), so that in the general case of an ARMA (p,q) process, we have:

$$\phi(B)(x_t - \mu) = \theta(B)a_t$$

Noting that $\phi(B)\mu = \left(1 - \phi_1 - \cdots - \phi_p\right)\mu = \phi(1)\mu$, the model can equivalently be written as:

$$\phi(B)x_t = \theta_0 + \theta(B)a_t$$

where $\theta_0 = \phi(1)\mu$ is a constant or intercept.

ARMA MODEL BUILDING AND ESTIMATION

3.29 An essential first step in fitting ARMA models to observed time series is to obtain estimates of the generally unknown parameters μ, σ_x^2, and the ρ_k. With the stationarity and (implicit) ergodicity assumptions, μ and σ_x^2 can be estimated by the sample mean and sample variance, respectively, of the realization $x_1, x_2, \ldots, x_T$, that is, by Eqs. (1.2) and (1.3). An estimate of ρ_k is then provided by the lag k sample autocorrelation given by Eq. (1.1), which, because of its importance, is reproduced here:

$$r_k = \frac{\sum\limits_{t=k+1}^{T} (x_t - \bar{x})(x_{t-k} - \bar{x})}{Ts^2} \quad k = 1, 2, \ldots$$

Recall from §**1.2** that the set of r_ks defines the sample ACF (SACF), which is sometimes referred to as the *correlogram*.

3.30 Consider a time series generated as independent observations drawn from a fixed distribution with finite variance (i.e., $\rho_k = 0$ for all $k \neq 0$). Such a series is said to be *independent and identically distributed* or i.i.d. For such a series the variance of r_k is approximately given by T^{-1}. If T is large as well, $\sqrt{T}r_k$ will be approximately standard normal, so that $r_k \overset{a}{\sim} N(0, T^{-1})$, implying that an absolute value of r_k in excess of $2/\sqrt{T}$ may be regarded as "significantly" different from zero at the 5% significance level. More generally, if $\rho_k = 0$ for $k > q$, the variance of r_k, for $k > q$, is:

$$V(r_k) = T^{-1}\left(1 + 2\rho_1^2 + \cdots + 2\rho_q^2\right). \tag{3.12}$$

Thus, by successively increasing the value of q and replacing the ρ_ks by their sample estimates, the variances of the sequence $r_1, r_2, \ldots, r_k$ can be estimated as T^{-1}, $T^{-1}(1 + 2r_1^2), \ldots, T^{-1}(1 + 2r_1^2 + \cdots + 2r_{k-1}^2)$, and, of course, these will be larger for $k > 1$ than those calculated using the simple formula T^{-1}. Taking the square root of $V(r_k)$ gives the standard error to be attached to r_k and these are often referred to as *Bartlett standard errors*, as (3.12) was derived in Bartlett (1946).

3.31 The *sample partial ACF* (SPACF) is usually calculated by fitting autoregressive models of increasing order; the estimate of the last coefficient in each model is the sample partial autocorrelation, $\hat{\phi}_{kk}$.[9] If the data follow an AR(p) process then for lags greater than p the variance of $\hat{\phi}_{kk}$ is approximately T^{-1}, so that $\hat{\phi}_{kk} \overset{a}{\sim} N(0, T^{-1})$.

3.32 Given the r_k and $\hat{\phi}_{kk}$, the approach to ARMA model building proposed by George Box and Gwilym Jenkins—the Box and Jenkins (1970) approach—may be followed. This is a three-stage procedure, the first of which, known as the *identification* stage, is essentially to match the behavior of the SACF and SPACF of a time series with that of various theoretical

ACFs and PACFs. This may be done by assessing individual sample autocorrelations and partial autocorrelations for significance by comparing them to their accompanying standard errors computed according to the formulae of §§**3.30**–**3.31**. Additionally, a "portmanteau" statistic based on the complete set of r_ks may be constructed. On the hypothesis that $x_t \sim \text{WN}(\mu, \sigma^2)$, then Ljung and Box (1978) show that:

$$Q(k) = T(T+2) \sum_{i=1}^{k} (T-i)^{-1} r_i^2 \overset{a}{\sim} \chi^2(k) \qquad (3.13)$$

and this statistic may be used to assess whether an observed series departs significantly from white noise (but see §**11.5** for more specific assumptions concerning x_t).

3.33 Having picked the best match (or set of matches), the second stage is to estimate the unknown model parameters (the ϕ_is, θ_is, μ, and σ^2). If the model is a pure autoregression, then ordinary least squares (OLS) is an efficient and perfectly acceptable estimation method as it produces the *conditional ML* estimates of the parameters; here "conditional" means that the likelihood function is maximized conditional on regarding $x_1, x_2, \ldots, x_p$ as deterministic and, hence, given by their observed values rather than as being taken as random variables drawn from the underlying distribution. If the sample size T is large, then these first p observations make a negligible contribution to the total likelihood and conditional ML will have the same large-sample distribution for the estimates $\hat{\phi}_1, \hat{\phi}_2, \ldots, \hat{\phi}_p, \mu, \hat{\sigma}^2$ as *exact* ML.

If there is an MA component, then a simple approach is to condition on the assumption that $a_{p-q+1}, a_{p-q+2}, \ldots, a_p$ all take their expected value of zero. This is known as conditional least squares (CLS) and, again, is equivalent to exact ML in large samples; the estimates of the additional MA parameters being denoted $\hat{\theta}_1, \hat{\theta}_2, \ldots, \hat{\theta}_q$. Other approaches to computing exact ML estimates in small samples are available if necessary.

3.34 Finally, the third stage, *diagnostic checking*, is to examine the residuals:

$$\hat{a}_t = x_t - \hat{\phi}_1 x_{t-1} - \cdots - \hat{\phi}_p x_{t-p} - \hat{\theta}_1 \hat{a}_{t-1} - \cdots - \hat{\theta}_q \hat{a}_{t-q}$$

from the fitted model(s) for any possible misspecifications. Misspecifications typically take the form of autocorrelated residuals, so that the SACF of the $\hat{a}_t$ will contain one or more significant values. Significance can be assessed by comparing individual residual autocorrelations, say $\hat{r}_k$, with their standard error, which will be $T^{-1/2}$ under the null that the residuals are not misspecified and, hence, are white noise. Alternatively, the portmanteau statistic (3.13) may be computed, although the degrees of freedom for Q must now be decreased to $k - p - q$ if an ARMA(p,q) has been fitted.

A further check on the adequacy of the fitted model is to *overfit*, say by estimating an ARMA($p + 1,q$) or an ARMA($p,q + 1$) process and checking whether the additional fitted parameter is significant or not. If any deficiencies in the model(s) are encountered, then further rounds of model building must be undertaken until a well-specified model with no obvious deficiencies is obtained.[10]

3.35 This three-stage approach, developed in the 1960s when computing power was extremely limited and software unavailable (indeed, Box and Jenkins had to write all their programs from scratch), may strike modern readers as unnecessarily labor intensive, although it will become apparent that it does have some important advantages in that it enables analysts to obtain a detailed "feel" of the data. Consequently, an alternative approach that harnesses modern computer power and software availability is to select a set of models based on prior considerations of maximum settings of p and q, estimate each possible model, and select that which minimizes a chosen selection criterion based on goodness of fit considerations.

3.36 There are a variety of selection criteria that may be used to choose an appropriate model, of which perhaps the most popular is Akaike's (1974) Information Criteria (AIC), defined as:

$$AIC(p, q) = \log \hat{\sigma}^2 + 2(p + q)T^{-1}$$

although a criterion that has better theoretical properties is the BIC of Schwarz (1978)

$$BIC(p, q) = \log \hat{\sigma}^2 + (p + q)T^{-1} \log T.$$

The criteria are used in the following way. Upper bounds, say p_{max} and q_{max}, are set for the orders of $\phi(B)$ and $\theta(B)$, with $\bar{p} = \{0, 1, \ldots, p_{max}\}$ and $\bar{q} = \{0, 1, \ldots, q_{max}\}$, orders p_1 and q_1 are selected such that, for example;

$$AIC(p_1, q_1) = \min AIC(p, q) \quad p \in \bar{p}, \quad q \in \bar{q}$$

with parallel strategies obviously being employed in conjunction with BIC. One possible difficulty with the application of this strategy is that no specific guidelines on how to determine $\bar{p}$ and $\bar{q}$ seem to be available, although they are tacitly assumed to be sufficiently large for the range of models to contain the "true" model, which may be denoted as having orders (p_0, q_0): these, of course, will not necessarily be the same as (p_1, q_1), the orders chosen by the criterion under consideration.

Given these alternative criteria, are there reasons for preferring one to the other? If the true orders (p_0, q_0) are contained in the set (p, q), $p \in \bar{p}$, $q \in \bar{q}$, then for all criteria, $p_1 \geq p_0$ and $q_1 \geq q_0$, almost surely, as $T \to \infty$. However, BIC is *strongly consistent* in the sense that it will determine the true model asymptotically, whereas for AIC an over-parameterized model will emerge no matter how long the available realization. Of course, such properties are not necessarily guaranteed in finite samples, so that both criteria are often used together.[11]

These model building procedures will not be discussed in any further detail; rather, they will be illustrated by way of a sequence of examples designed to bring out many of the features encountered in practice when using these procedures.

EXAMPLE 3.1 An ARMA Process for the NAO

The monthly observations of the North Atlantic Oscillation (NAO) index from 1950 to 2017 plotted in Fig. 1.1 are clearly stationary around a mean estimated to be $\bar{x} = -0.015$ with standard deviation 1.012. They are also approximately normally distributed, with moment measures of skewness and kurtosis being -0.10 and 2.67, respectively. These moment measures, which should be zero and 3 under normality, may be jointly tested for departures from this distribution by computing the Jarque and Bera (1980) test. This yields a test statistic of 5.13, which is asymptotically distributed as $\chi^2(2)$ (note that $T = 816$ here) and, hence, has a marginal probability (or p-value) of 0.08.[12]

Fig. 3.6 reproduces the NAO series in its bottom panel along with a simulation of a NID(0, 1), that is, standard normal, white noise of the same length (given that the mean and standard deviation of the NAO series are so close to zero and one respectively). A visual comparison of the two suggests that the NAO may not be completely random but may exhibit low order, albeit weak, autocorrelation.

Is this perceived autocorrelation merely in the "eye of the beholder" or does it, in fact, really exist? Table 3.1 reports the SACF and SPACF up to $k = 12$, along with accompanying standard errors. The lag-one sample autocorrelation r_1, and hence $\hat{\phi}_{11}$, are estimated to be 0.19 and are significant as their accompanying standard error is 0.035. All other r_k and $\hat{\phi}_{kk}$ are insignificant so that both the SACF and SPACF may be regarded as "cutting-off" at lag one, thus identifying either an AR(1) or MA(1) process as likely to be generating the series.

This lag-one cut-off in both the SACF and SPACF is a common occurrence in time series that display weak, albeit significant, autocorrelation. From §**3.10**, an AR(1) process with $\phi = 0.2$ would have autocorrelations exponentially declining as $\rho_k = 0.2^k$, which, even for a sample size in excess of 800 would lead to sample autocorrelations that would be insignificantly different from zero for $k = 2$ onwards. $Q(k)$ statistics are also reported in Table 3.1 for $k = 1, 2, \ldots, 12$, and they confirm that there is evidence of autocorrelation concentrated at lag-one.

Estimating by OLS an AR(1) model obtains:

$$x_t = \underset{(0.034)}{0.186} x_{t-1} + \hat{a}_t \quad \hat{\sigma} = 0.994$$

while the CLS estimated MA(1) process is[13]

$$x_t = \hat{a}_t + \underset{(0.035)}{0.175} \hat{a}_{t-1} \quad \hat{\sigma} = 0.995$$

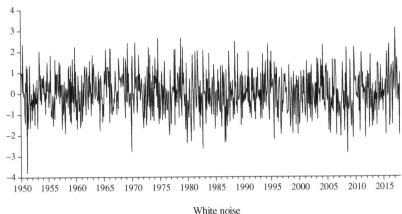

White noise

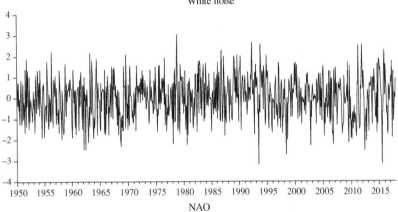

NAO

FIGURE 3.6 Normal white noise and monthly NAO.

where in both regressions standard errors are shown in parentheses. The models are essentially identical in terms of fit.

The residual SACFs from the two models contain no individually significant autocorrelations, while the portmanteau statistics computed from (3.13) for the first 12 residual autocorrelations are $Q(12) = 8.4$ and $Q(12) = 10.4$, respectively, noting that in both models one degree of freedom is lost when comparing these statistics to χ^2 critical values, that is, they are asymptotically distributed as $\chi^2(11)$ variates.

It would, thus, appear that either an AR(1) or MA(1) process adequately fits the monthly NAO series. However, although the fitted parameter is highly significant in both models, with the "t-ratios" being over 5 in both cases, little (less than 4%) of the variation in the NAO can be explained by its past behavior; the traditional R^2 measures of regression goodness of fit being just 0.035 and 0.032, respectively.

TABLE 3.1 SACF and SPACF of the NAO

k	r_k	$se(r_k)$	$\hat{\phi}_{kk}$	$se\left(\hat{\phi}_{kk}\right)$	$Q(k)$
1	0.186	0.035	0.186	0.035	28.34
2	0.054	0.036	0.020	0.035	30.76
3	0.007	0.036	− 0.007	0.035	30.80
4	− 0.048	0.036	− 0.051	0.035	32.67
5	0.024	0.036	0.044	0.035	33.16
6	− 0.016	0.036	− 0.025	0.035	33.37
7	− 0.020	0.036	− 0.016	0.035	33.71
8	− 0.009	0.036	0.015	0.035	33.78
9	0.044	0.036	0.047	0.035	35.39
10	0.040	0.036	0.020	0.035	36.72
11	0.031	0.037	0.018	0.035	37.51
12	0.059	0.037	0.052	0.035	40.37

SACF, sample autocorrelation function; SPACF, sample partial autocorrelation function.

EXAMPLE 3.2 Modeling the United Kingdom Interest Rate Spread

The "spread," the difference between long and short interest rates, is an important variable in testing the expectations hypothesis of the term structure of interest rates. Fig. 1.10 showed the spread between 20-year United Kingdom gilts and three-month Treasury bills using monthly observations from January 1952 to June 2017 ($T = 786$), and Table 3.2 now reports the SACF and SPACF up to $k = 12$, again with accompanying standard errors.

The evolution of the spread is considerably smoother than one might expect if it was a realization from a white noise process, and is certainly much smoother than that of the NAO in Example 3.1. This is confirmed by the SACF, whose values are all positive and significant, with the accompanying portmanteau statistic being $Q(12) = 5872$! The SPACF has both $\hat{\phi}_{11}$ and $\hat{\phi}_{22}$ significant, after which there is a cut-off, thus identifying an AR(2) process. Fitting such a model to the series by OLS regression yields:

$$x_t = \underset{(0.017)}{0.036} + \underset{(0.035)}{1.193}\, x_{t-1} - \underset{(0.035)}{0.224}\, x_{t-2} + \hat{a}_t \quad \hat{\sigma} = 0.394$$

Figures in parentheses are, again, standard errors and the intercept implies a fitted mean of $\hat{\mu} = \hat{\theta}_0 / \left(1 - \hat{\phi}_1 - \hat{\phi}_2\right) = 1.140$, with standard error 0.448. The model can, therefore, be written in "mean deviation" form as:

TABLE 3.2 SACF and SPACF of the United Kingdom Interest Rate Spread

k	r_k	$se(r_k)$	$\hat{\phi}_{kk}$	$se\left(\hat{\phi}_{kk}\right)$
1	0.974	0.036	0.974	0.036
2	0.938	0.061	-0.221	0.036
3	0.901	0.077	0.017	0.036
4	0.865	0.089	-0.005	0.036
5	0.828	0.099	-0.044	0.036
6	0.790	0.108	-0.046	0.036
7	0.751	0.115	-0.008	0.036
8	0.714	0.121	-0.006	0.036
9	0.680	0.126	0.043	0.036
10	0.651	0.131	0.039	0.036
11	0.623	0.135	-0.006	0.036
12	0.595	0.139	-0.016	0.036

SACF, sample autocorrelation function; SPACF, sample partial autocorrelation function.

$$x_t = 1.140 + 1.193(x_{t-1} - 1.140) - 0.224(x_{t-2} - 1.140) + \hat{a}_t$$

Since $\hat{\phi}_1 + \hat{\phi}_2 = 0.969$, $-\hat{\phi}_1 + \hat{\phi}_2 = -1.417$, and $\hat{\phi}_2 = -0.224$, the stationarity conditions associated with an AR(2) process are satisfied, but although $\hat{\phi}_2$ is negative, $\hat{\phi}_1^2 + 4\hat{\phi}_2 = 0.526$, so that the roots are real, being $g_1 = 0.96$ and $g_2 = 0.23$. The spread is therefore stationary around an "equilibrium" level of 1.14% per annum: equivalently, in equilibrium long rates are 1.14% higher than short rates. The closeness of g_1 to unity will be discussed further in Example 4.1, but its size means that shocks that force the spread away from its equilibrium will take a long time to dissipate and, hence, the spread will exhibit extended departures away from this level, although as the roots are real these departures will not follow any periodic or cyclical pattern.

Having fitted an AR(2) process, it is now necessary to establish whether this model is adequate. With $k = 12$, the residuals yield the value $Q(12) = 7.57$, which is asymptotically distributed as $\chi^2(10)$ and, hence, gives no evidence of model inadequacy.

Overfitting may also be undertaken. For example, an AR(3) process or, perhaps, an ARMA(2,1) may be fitted to the series. These yield the pair of models:

$$x_t = \underset{(0.017)}{0.036} + \underset{(0.036)}{1.194} x_{t-1} - \underset{(0.055)}{0.224} x_{t-2} - \underset{(0.036)}{0.001} x_{t-3} + \hat{a}_t$$

$$x_t = \underset{(0.018)}{0.037} + \underset{(0.156)}{1.144} x_{t-1} - \underset{(0.152)}{0.177} x_{t-2} + \hat{a}_t + \underset{(0.158)}{0.051} \hat{a}_{t-1}$$

The additional parameter is insignificant in both models, thus confirming the adequacy of the original choice of an AR(2) process.

EXAMPLE 3.3 Modeling the Sunspot Number

The annual sunspot numbers from 1700 to 2017 shown in Fig. 1.2 reveals a stationary series having an approximately periodic cycle of around 11 years. Fig. 3.7 portrays the SACF and SPACF of the numbers in graphical form for k up to 50, reflecting the fact that the periodicity in the series imparts a cyclical pattern onto the autocorrelations, which decays only slowly. The SPACF, although dominated by large values for $\hat{\phi}_{11}$ and $\hat{\phi}_{22}$, also has several other higher-order partial autocorrelations that are significantly different from zero, thus making the identification of an ARMA process rather difficult using the Box–Jenkins approach.

Restricting attention to pure autoregressions, Table 3.3 reports AIC and BIC values for AR processes up to order 20, with both criteria selecting an AR(9) as the best fit.[14] OLS estimates of the AR(9) model are shown in Table 3.4. The portmanteau statistic for residual autocorrelation indicates no model misspecification and, indeed, none of the first 20 residual autocorrelations approach significance. On examining the individual estimated ϕs, $\hat{\phi}_3$ to $\hat{\phi}_8$ are all insignificant, with several of them taking on very small values. A restricted AR(9) process was thus considered, where the restriction $\phi_3 = \phi_4 = \cdots = \phi_8 = 0$ is imposed. A standard F-test of this restriction yields a statistic of 0.74 with a p-value of just .62, so that the restricted model is perfectly acceptable, and the estimates of this model are also reported in Table 3.4.

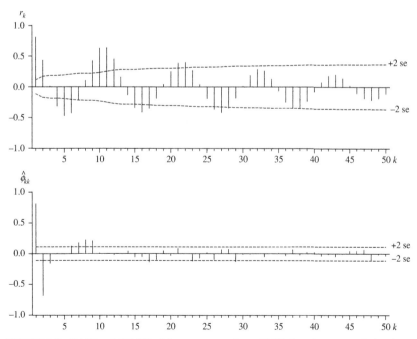

FIGURE 3.7   SACF and SPACF of the sunspot numbers. *SACF*, Sample autocorrelation function; *SPACF*, sample partial autocorrelation function.

TABLE 3.3 AIC and BIC Values for AR Models of the Sunspot Number

k	AIC	BIC	k	AIC	BIC
1	10.001	10.024	11	9.231	9.377
2	9.355	9.391	12	9.240	9.398
3	9.342	9.389	13	9.248	9.419
4	9.350	9.410	14	9.254	9.437
5	9.360	9.432	15	9.259	9.455
6	9.349	9.433	16	9.264	9.473
7	9.294	9.390	17	9.248	9.337
8	9.254	9.363	18	9.243	9.478
9	**9.213**	**9.334**	19	9.251	9.498
10	9.223	9.377	20	9.258	9.519

Bold values signify minimum AIC and BIC values.

TABLE 3.4 AR(9) Estimates for the Sunspot Number

	AR(9)	Restricted AR(9)	AR(2)
$\hat{\theta}_0$	81.044 (8.696)	81.144 (12.339)	79.415 (4.691)
$\hat{\phi}_1$	1.169 (0.056)	1.222 (0.044)	1.382 (0.041)
$\hat{\phi}_2$	−0.419 (0.088)	−0.524 (0.044)	−0.693 (0.041)
$\hat{\phi}_3$	−0.134 (0.091)	−	−
$\hat{\phi}_4$	0.105 (0.091)	−	−
$\hat{\phi}_5$	−0.072 (0.091)	−	−
$\hat{\phi}_6$	0.005 (0.091)	−	−
$\hat{\phi}_7$	0.022 (0.091)	−	−
$\hat{\phi}_8$	−0.053 (0.088)	−	−
$\hat{\phi}_9$	0.222 (0.056)	0.192 (0.026)	−
$\hat{\sigma}$	23.848	23.786	25.888
R^2	0.858	0.856	0.825
$Q(20)$	16.27 [0.132]	17.43 [0.426]	45.67 [0.000]

Standard errors shown in (...); p-values shown in [...].

Autoregressions, particularly when, as here, they are of high order, can be difficult to interpret in terms of just the ϕ coefficients. Recalling §**3.17**, interpretation may be facilitated by considering the roots of the characteristic equation $\phi(B) = 0$. The behavior of the ACF of an AR process can be described by a mixture of damped exponentials (for the real roots) and damped sine waves (for the complex roots). The AR(9) process fitted to the sunspot number has nine roots. From the restricted model, these turn out to be a single real root of 0.95 and four complex conjugates, $0.80 \pm 0.55i$, $0.29 \pm 0.79i$, $-0.29 \pm 0.70i$, and $-0.67 \pm 0.28i$ (the roots from the unrestricted fit are almost identical to these).

For a pair of complex roots $\alpha \pm \beta i$ the period of the related cycle, f, is obtained by solving:

$$\cos\frac{2\pi}{f} = \frac{|\alpha|}{\sqrt{\alpha^2 + \beta^2}}$$

The periods of the four implied cycles are therefore calculated to be 10.43, 5.15, 5.33, and 15.87 years, respectively. The cycle damping factor is given by the denominator of this expression, and so the factors are 0.97, 0.84, 0.76, and 0.73, respectively, so that the cycle with a period closest to 11 years quickly dominates ($0.97^{10} = 0.74$ while $0.73^{10} = 0.04$, for example).

It is interesting to compare this model with the simpler "single cycle" AR(2) model originally fitted by Yule (1927), the estimates of which are shown in the right-hand column of Table 3.4. This model has a pair of complex roots $0.69 \pm 0.46i$, which imply a cyclical period of 10.63 years with a damping factor of 0.83. Unfortunately, the fit of the AR(2) is inferior to that of the AR(9) and, perhaps more importantly, it is a seriously inadequate model in that the Q-statistic signals significant residual autocorrelation, a consequence of omitting the statistically important lag-nine term.

ENDNOTES

1. Technical details on ergodicity may be found in Granger and Newbold (1986, chapter 1) and Hamilton (1994, chapter 3.2), with Domowitz and El-Gamal (2001) providing a method of testing for the property.
2. Wold's decomposition takes its name from Theorem 7 of Wold (1938, pages 84–89), although he does not refer to this theorem as a decomposition. Peter Whittle, in "Some recent contributions to the theory of stationary processes", which is Appendix 2 of the second edition of Wold's book, seems to be the first to refer to it as such. See also Mills (2011, chapter 7) for a detailed discussion of the theorem.
3. The term "white noise" was coined by physicists and engineers because of its resemblance, when examined in the frequency domain, to the optical spectrum of white light, which consists of very narrow lines close together: see Jenkins (1961). The term "innovation" reflects the fact that the current error a_t is, by definition, independent of all previous values of both the error and x, and hence represents unforecastable "news" that becomes available at time t.
4. Autoregressions were first introduced by Yule (1927). For details on the historical development of these models, see Mills (2013).
5. Moving average processes were introduced and analyzed in detail by Wold (1938).

6. The solution to the quadratic $\rho_1 \theta^2 + \theta + \rho_1 = 0$ is:

$$\theta = \frac{-1 \pm \sqrt{1 - 4\rho_1^2}}{2\rho_1}$$

The restriction that θ be real requires that $1 - 4\rho_1^2 > 0$, which implies that $\rho_1^2 < 0.25$ and hence $-0.5 < \rho_1 < 0.5$.

7. As an example of this technique, consider the AR(2) process for which $\phi(B) = 1 - \phi_1 B - \phi_2 B^2$. The ψ-weights are then obtained by equating coefficients in

$$\left(1 - \phi_1 B - \phi_2 B^2\right)\left(1 + \psi_1 B + \psi_2 B^2 + \cdots\right) = 1$$

or

$$1 + \left(\psi_1 - \phi_1\right)B + \left(\psi_2 - \phi_1\psi_1 - \phi_2\right)B^2 + \left(\psi_3 - \phi_1\psi_2 - \phi_2\psi_1\right)B^3 + \cdots = 1$$

For this equality to hold, the coefficients of B^j, $j \geq 0$, on each side of the equation must be the same. Thus:

$$B^1: \psi_1 - \phi_1 = 0 \qquad \therefore \psi_1 = \phi_1$$
$$B^2: \psi_2 - \phi_1\psi_1 - \phi_2 = 0 \qquad \therefore \psi_1^2 = \phi_1^2 + \phi_2$$
$$B^3: \psi_3 - \phi_1\psi_2 - \phi_2\psi_1 = 0 \qquad \therefore \psi_1^3 = \phi_1^3 + 2\phi_1\phi_2$$

Noting that $\psi_3 = \phi_1\psi_2 + \phi_2\psi_1$, the ψ-weights can then be derived recursively for $j \geq 2$ from $\psi_j = \phi_1\psi_{j-1} + \phi_2\psi_{j-2}$.

8. See Hamilton (1994, pages 17−18) for a derivation of this set of restrictions.

9. The successive sample partial autocorrelations may be estimated recursively using the updating equations proposed by Durbin (1960), which are known as the *Durbin−Levinson algorithm*.

10. This is the classic reference to time series analysis: the latest edition is the fourth: Box et al. (2008).

11. See Tremayne (2006) for more discussion of information criteria, for which several others have been proposed, and for a survey of many current issues in ARMA modeling.

12. If m_3 and m_4 are the estimated moment measures of skewness and kurtosis respectively, then the Jarque−Bera statistic is:

$$JB = \left(\frac{T}{6}\right)m_3^2 + \left(\frac{T}{24}\right)(m_4 - 3)^2$$

13. When intercepts are included in the models they are found to be insignificant.

14. It is interesting to note that when Yule (1927) introduced autoregressive processes his example was indeed the sunspot numbers for the truncated period 1749−1924, where he fitted an AR(2) to the series.

Chapter 4

ARIMA Models for Nonstationary Time Series

Chapter Outline

NONSTATIONARITY

4.1 The autoregressive-moving average (ARMA) class of models relies on the assumption that the underlying process is weakly stationary, which restricts the mean and variance to be constant and requires the autocovariances to depend only on the time lag. As we have seen, however, many time series are certainly not stationary, for they tend to exhibit time-changing means and/or variances.

4.2 To deal with such *nonstationarity*, we begin by characterizing a time series as the sum of a nonconstant mean level plus a random error component:

$$x_t = \mu_t + \varepsilon_t \tag{4.1}$$

The nonconstant mean level μ_t in (4.1) can be modeled in a variety of ways. One potentially realistic possibility is that the mean evolves as a (nonstochastic) polynomial of order d in time, with the error ε_t assumed to be a stochastic, stationary, but possibly autocorrelated, zero mean process. This, in fact, is always possible given Cramer's (1961) extension of Wold's decomposition theorem to nonstationary processes. Thus, we may have:

$$x_t = \mu_t + \varepsilon_t = \sum_{j=0}^{d} \beta_j t^j + \psi(B)a_t \tag{4.2}$$

Since:

$$E(\varepsilon_t) = \psi(B)E(a_t) = 0,$$

Applied Time Series Analysis. DOI: https://doi.org/10.1016/B978-0-12-813117-6.00004-1

we have

$$E(x_t) = E(\mu_t) = \sum_{j=0}^{d} \beta_j t^j$$

and, as the β_j coefficients remain constant through time, such a trend in the mean is said to be *deterministic*.

4.3 Trends of this type can be removed by a simple transformation. Consider the linear trend obtained by setting $d = 1$, where, for simplicity, the error component is assumed to be a white noise sequence:

$$x_t = \beta_0 + \beta_1 t + a_t \tag{4.3}$$

Lagging (4.3) one period yields:

$$x_{t-1} = \beta_0 + \beta_1(t - 1) + a_{t-1} = \beta_0 - \beta_1 + \beta_1 t + a_{t-1}$$

and subtracting this from (4.3) itself yields

$$x_t - x_{t-1} = \beta_1 + a_t - a_{t-1} \tag{4.4}$$

The result is a difference equation following an ARMA(1,1) process in which, since $\phi = \theta = 1$, both autoregressive and moving average roots are unity and the model is neither stationary nor invertible. If, however, we consider the first-differences $w_t = \nabla x_t$ then (4.4) can be written as:

$$w_t = \beta_1 + \nabla a_t$$

and w_t is therefore generated by a stationary, since $E(w_t) = \beta_1$ is constant, but not invertible MA(1) process.

4.4 In general, if the trend polynomial is of order d and ε_t is characterized by the ARMA process $\phi(B)\varepsilon_t = \theta(B)a_t$, then $\nabla^d x_t = (1-B)^d x_t$, obtained by first-differencing x_t d times, will follow the process:

$$\nabla^d x_t = \theta_0 + \frac{\nabla^d \theta(B)}{\phi(B)} a_t$$

where $\theta_0 = d!\beta_d$. Thus, the moving average (MA) part of the process generating $\nabla^d x_t$ will also contain the factor ∇^d and will, therefore, have d roots of unity. Note also that the variance of x_t will be the same as the variance of ε_t and so will be constant for all t. Fig. 4.1 shows plots of generated data for both linear and quadratic ($d = 2$) trend models. Because the variance of the error component, here assumed to be white noise and distributed as NID(0, 9), is constant and independent of the level, the variability of each of the series is bounded about the expected value, and the trend components are clearly observed in the plots.

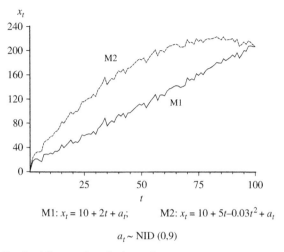

M1: $x_t = 10 + 2t + a_t$;   M2: $x_t = 10 + 5t - 0.03t^2 + a_t$

$a_t \sim$ NID $(0,9)$

FIGURE 4.1   Simulated linear and quadratic trends.

4.5   An alternative way of generating a nonstationary mean level is to employ ARMA models whose autoregressive parameters do not satisfy stationarity conditions. For example, consider the AR(1) process:

$$x_t = \phi x_{t-1} + a_t \tag{4.5}$$

where $\phi > 1$. If the process is assumed to have started at time $t = 0$, the difference equation Eq. (4.5) has the solution:

$$x_t = x_0 \phi^t + \sum_{i=0}^{t} \phi^i a_{t-i} \tag{4.6}$$

The "complementary function" $x_0 \phi^t$ can be regarded as the *conditional expectation* of x_t at time $t = 0$ and is clearly an increasing function of t. The conditional expectation of x_t at subsequent times $t = 1, 2, \ldots$ will depend on the sequence of random shocks $a_1, a_2, \ldots$ and, hence, since this conditional expectation may be regarded as the trend of x_t, the trend changes *stochastically*.

The variance of x_t is given by:

$$V(x_t) = \sigma^2 \frac{\phi^{2t} - 1}{\phi^2 - 1}$$

which is also an increasing function of time and becomes infinite as $t \to \infty$.[1]In general, x_t will have a trend in both mean and variance, and such processes are said to be *explosive*. A plot of generated data from the process (4.5) with $\phi = 1.05$ and $a_t \sim$ NID$(0, 9)$, and having starting value $x_0 = 10$, is shown in Fig. 4.2. We see that, after a short "induction period," the series

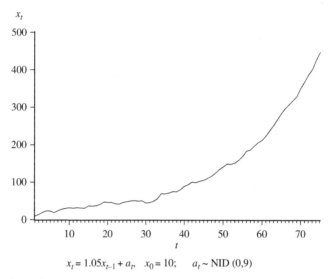

$$x_t = 1.05x_{t-1} + a_t, \quad x_0 = 10; \quad a_t \sim \text{NID}\,(0,9)$$

FIGURE 4.2 A simulated explosive AR(1) model.

essentially follows an exponential curve with the generating a_ts playing almost no further part. The same behavior would be observed if additional autoregressive and moving average terms were added to the model, as long as the stationarity conditions are violated.

ARIMA PROCESSES

4.6 As we can see from (4.6), the solution to (4.5) is explosive if $\phi > 1$ but stationary if $\phi < 1$. The case $\phi = 1$ produces a process that is neatly balanced between the two. If x_t is generated by the model:

$$x_t = x_{t-1} + a_t \tag{4.7}$$

then x_t is said to follow a *random walk*.[2] If we allow a constant, θ_0, to be included, so that:

$$x_t = x_{t-1} + \theta_0 + a_t \tag{4.8}$$

then x_t will follow a *random walk with drift*. If the process starts at $t = 0$, then:

$$x_t = x_0 + t\theta_0 + \sum_{i=0}^{t} a_{t-i},$$

so that

$$\mu_t = E(x_t) = x_0 + t\theta_0$$

$$\gamma_{0,t} = V(x_t) = t\sigma^2$$

and

$$\gamma_{k,t} = Cov(x_t, x_{t-k}) = (t-k)\sigma^2 \quad k \geq 0$$

are all functions of t and, hence, are time-varying.

4.7 The autocorrelation between x_t and x_{t-k} is then given by:

$$\rho_{k,t} = \frac{\gamma_{k,t}}{\sqrt{\gamma_{0,t}\gamma_{0,t-k}}} = \frac{t-k}{\sqrt{t(t-k)}} = \sqrt{\frac{t-k}{t}}$$

If t is large compared to k, then all the $\rho_{k,t}$ will be approximately unity. The sequence of x_t values will, therefore, be very smooth, but will also be nonstationary since both the mean and variance of x_t will change with t. Fig. 4.3 shows generated plots of the random walks (4.7) and (4.8) with

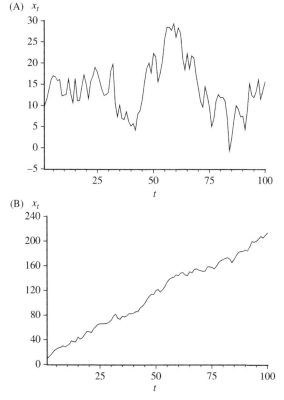

FIGURE 4.3 Simulated random walks. (A) $x_t = x_{t-1} + a_t$, $x_0 = 10$; $a_t \sim \text{NID}(0,9)$ and (B) $x_t = 2 + x_{t-1} + a_t$, $x_0 = 10$; $a_t \sim \text{NID}(0,9)$.

$x_0 = 10$ and $a_t \sim \text{NID}(0,9)$. In part (A) of the figure the drift parameter, θ_0, is set to zero while in part (B) we have set $\theta_0 = 2$. The two plots differ considerably, but neither show any affinity with the initial value x_0: indeed, the expected length of time for a random walk to pass again through an arbitrary value is infinite.

4.8 The random walk is an example of a class of nonstationary models known as *integrated processes*. Eq. (4.8) can be written as:

$$\nabla x_t = \theta_0 + a_t$$

and so first-differencing x_t leads to a stationary model, in this case the white noise process a_t. Generally, a series may need first-differencing d times to attain stationarity, and the series so obtained may itself be autocorrelated.

If this autocorrelation is modeled by an ARMA(p,q) process, then the model for the original series is of the form:

$$\phi(B)\nabla^d x_t = \theta_0 + \theta(B)a_t \tag{4.9}$$

which is said to be an *autoregressive-integrated-moving average* (ARIMA) process of orders p, d and q, or ARIMA(p,d,q), and x_t is said to be integrated of order d, denoted $I(d)$.[3]

4.9 It will usually be the case that the order of integration d or, equivalently, the degree of differencing, will be 0, 1 or, occasionally, 2 (recall the examples in §§**2.9–2.10**). It will continue to be the case that the autocorrelations of an ARIMA process will be close to 1 for all nonlarge k. For example, consider the (stationary) ARMA(1,1) process:

$$x_t - \phi x_{t-1} = a_t - \theta a_{t-1}$$

whose ACF has been shown to be (§**3.26**)

$$\rho_1 = \frac{(1 - \phi\theta)(\phi - \theta)}{1 + \theta^2 - 2\phi\theta} \qquad \rho_k = \phi\rho_{k-1} \text{ for } k > 1$$

As $\phi \to 1$, the ARIMA(0,1,1) process:

$$\nabla x_t = a_t - \theta a_{t-1}$$

results, and all the ρ_k tend to unity.

4.10 Several points concerning the ARIMA class of models are of importance. Consider again (4.9), with $\theta_0 = 0$ for simplicity:

$$\phi(B)\nabla^d x_t = \theta(B)a_t$$

This process can equivalently be defined by the two equations:

$$\phi(B)w_t = \theta(B)a_t$$

and

$$w_t = \nabla^d x_t \tag{4.10}$$

so that, as previously noted, the model corresponds to assuming that $\nabla^d x_t$ can be represented by a stationary and invertible ARMA process. Alternatively, for $d \geq 1$, (4.10) can be inverted to give:

$$x_t = S^d w_t \tag{4.11}$$

where S is the infinite summation, or *integral*, operator defined by

$$S = \left(1 + B + B^2 + \cdots\right) = (1 - B)^{-1} = \nabla^{-1}$$

Eq. (4.11) implies that x_t can be obtained by summing, or "integrating," the stationary series w_t d times; hence, the term integrated process.

4.11   This type of nonstationary behavior is often referred to as *homogenous nonstationarity*, and it is important to discuss why this form of nonstationarity is felt to be useful when describing the behavior of time series from many fields. Consider again the first-order autoregressive process (4.2). A basic characteristic of the AR(1) model is that, for both $|\phi| < 1$ and $\phi > 1$, the "local" behavior of a series generated from the model is heavily dependent on the level of x_t. In the former case local behavior will always be dominated by an affinity to the mean, while in the latter the series will eventually increase rapidly with t. For many time series, however, local behavior appears to be roughly independent of level, and this is what we mean by homogenous nonstationarity.

4.12   If we want to use ARMA models for which the behavior of the process is indeed independent of its level, then the autoregressive polynomial $\phi(B)$ must be chosen so that:

$$\phi(B)(x_t + c) = \phi(B)x_t$$

where c is any constant. Thus:

$$\phi(B)c = 0$$

implying that $\phi(1) = 0$, so that $\phi(B)$ must be able to be factorized as

$$\phi(B) = \phi_1(B)(1 - B) = \phi_1(B)\nabla,$$

in which case the class of processes that need to be considered will be of the form

$$\phi_1(B)w_t = \theta(B)a_t$$

where $w_t = \nabla x_t$. Since the requirement of homogenous nonstationarity precludes w_t increasing explosively, either $\phi_1(B)$ is a stationary operator or $\phi_1(B) = \phi_2(B)(1 - B)$, so that $\phi_2(B)w_t^* = \theta(B)a_t$, where $w_t^* = \nabla^2 x_t$. Since this argument can be used recursively, it follows that for time series that are homogenously nonstationary, the autoregressive lag polynomial must be of the form $\phi(B)\nabla^d$, where $\phi(B)$ is a stationary polynomial. Fig. 4.4 plots generated data from the model $\nabla^2 x_t = a_t$, where $a_t \sim \text{NID}(0, 9)$ and $x_0 = x_1 = 10$,

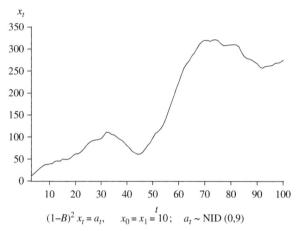

$$(1-B)^2 x_t = a_t, \qquad x_0 = x_1 = 10; \quad a_t \sim \text{NID}(0,9)$$

FIGURE 4.4 A simulated "second-difference" model.

and such a series is seen to display random movements in both level and slope.

4.13 In general, if a constant is included in the model for dth differences, then a deterministic polynomial trend of degree d is automatically allowed for. Equivalently, if θ_0 is taken to be nonzero, then:

$$E(w_t) = E\left(\nabla^d x_t\right) = \mu_w = \frac{\theta_0}{\left(1 - \phi_1 - \phi_2 - \cdots - \phi_p\right)}$$

is nonzero, so that an alternative way of expressing (4.9) is as

$$\phi(B)\tilde{w}_t = \theta(B)a_t$$

where $\tilde{w}_t = w_t - \mu_w$.

Fig. 4.5 plots generated data for $\nabla^2 x_t = 2 + a_t$, where, again, $a_t \sim \text{NID}(0,9)$ and $x_0 = x_1 = 10$. The inclusion of the deterministic quadratic trend has a dramatic effect on the evolution of the series, with the nonstationary "noise" being completely swamped after a few periods.

Model (4.9) therefore allows both stochastic and deterministic trends to be modeled. When $\theta_0 = 0$ only a stochastic trend is incorporated, while if $\theta_0 \neq 0$ the model may be interpreted as representing a deterministic trend (a polynomial of order d) buried in nonstationary and autocorrelated noise, the latter containing a stochastic trend. The models presented in §§**4.2**–**4.4** could be described as deterministic trends buried in *stationary* noise, since they can be written as:

$$\phi(B)\nabla^d x_t = \phi(1)\beta_d d! + \nabla^d \theta(B)a_t$$

the stationary nature of the noise in the level of x_t being manifested in d roots of the moving average lag polynomial being unity.

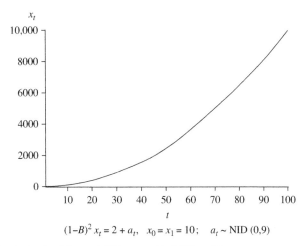

$$(1-B)^2 x_t = 2 + a_t, \quad x_0 = x_1 = 10; \quad a_t \sim \text{NID}(0,9)$$

FIGURE 4.5   A simulated "second-difference with drift" model.

ARIMA MODELING

4.14   Once the order of differencing d has been established, then since $w_t = \nabla^d x_t$ is, by definition, stationary, the ARMA model building techniques discussed in §§**3.29−3.35** may be applied to the suitably differenced series. Establishing the correct order of differencing is by no means straightforward however, and is discussed in detail in §§**5.4−5.7**. We content ourselves here with a sequence of examples illustrating the modeling of ARIMA processes when d has already been chosen; the suitability of these choices will be examined through examples in Chapter 5, ARIMA Models for Nonstationary Time Series.

EXAMPLE 4.1 Modeling the United Kingdom Spread as an Integrated Process

In Example 3.2, we modeled the spread of UK interest rates as a stationary, AR(2), process. There we noted that the roots of this process were 0.96 and 0.23, so that the model could be written as:

$$(1 - 0.23B)(1 - 0.96B)(x_t - 1.14) = a_t$$

or as

$$(1 - 0.96B)(x_t - 1.14) = 0.23(1 - 0.96B)(x_{t-1} - 1.14) + a_t$$

i.e., as being close to an ARIMA(1,1,0) process. Consequently, here we consider modeling the spread assuming that it is an $I(1)$ process, so that we examine the behavior of the SACF and SPACF of $w_t = \nabla x_t$. Table 4.1 provides these estimates up to $k = 12$ and suggests that as both functions cut-off at $k = 1$, either an AR(1) (as suggested previously) or an MA(1) process could be identified. Estimation of the former obtains:

$$w_t = -\underset{(0.0142)}{0.0017} + \underset{(0.035)}{0.209}\, w_{t-1} + \hat{a}_t, \qquad \hat{\sigma} = 0.398$$

The residuals are effectively white noise, as they yield a portmanteau statistic of $Q(12) = 8.81$, and the mean of w_t is seen to be insignificantly different from zero. The spread can therefore be modeled as an ARIMA(1,1,0) process but without drift. In fact, fitting an ARIMA(0,1,1) process obtains almost identical estimates, with θ estimated to be -0.204 and $\hat{\sigma} = 0.398$.

The implication of this model is that the spread evolves as a driftless random walk with AR(1) innovations. Being nonstationary, the spread therefore has no equilibrium level to return to and thus "wanders widely" but without any drift up or, indeed, down. All innovations consequently have *permanent* effects, in direct contrast to the AR(2) model of Example 3.2, in which the spread is stationary about an equilibrium level, so that since the series always reverts back to this level, all innovations can have only *temporary* effects. A method of distinguishing between these alternative models is introduced in Chapter 5, ARIMA Models for Nonstationary Time Series.

TABLE 4.1 SACF and SPACF of the First Difference of the UK Spread

k	r_k	$s.e.(r_k)$	$\hat{\phi}_{kk}$	$s.e.\left(\hat{\phi}_{kk}\right)$
1	0.209	0.036	0.209	0.036
2	-0.027	0.038	-0.018	0.036
3	-0.020	0.038	-0.023	0.036
4	0.015	0.038	0.026	0.036
5	0.033	0.038	0.026	0.036
6	0.003	0.038	-0.011	0.036
7	-0.016	0.038	-0.014	0.036
8	-0.071	0.039	-0.066	0.036
9	-0.082	0.039	-0.057	0.036
10	-0.037	0.039	-0.009	0.036
11	-0.009	0.039	-0.001	0.036
12	-0.021	0.039	0.024	0.036

EXAMPLE 4.2 Modeling the \$–£ Exchange Rate

As was noted in §**1.6**, the daily observations of the \$–£ exchange rate plotted in Fig. 1.5 exhibit the wandering movement of a driftless random walk: the SACF in fact has $r_1 = 0.999$, $r_2 = 0.997$, $r_{10} = 0.986$, $r_{50} = 0.919$, and $r_{100} = 0.829$, thus displaying the slow, almost linear, decline typical of an $I(1)$ process (this is discussed further in §**5.2**).

The differences are almost identical to the percent daily change in the rate shown in Fig. 1.9 and are stationary about zero and appear to show no discernible autocorrelation pattern. Indeed, they are close to being white noise, the only significant sample autocorrelation being $r_1 = 0.06$, on noting that here the standard error of r_1 is $10818^{-1/2} \approx 0.010$. Although the parameter estimates are significant on fitting either an AR(1) or MA(1) process, the R^2 statistic associated with each model is around 0.0036, which, of course, is equal to r_1^2. Thus, although changes in the exchange rate bear some correlation with past changes, this correlation is small and, although seemingly statistically significant, it is unlikely that it will be economically significant in the sense that it could be used to develop trading rules, say. A resolution to this apparent departure from the efficient markets hypothesis will be provided in Example 10.1.

EXAMPLE 4.3 Modeling Global Temperatures

The anthropogenic global warming (AGW) hypothesis may be taken to imply that the global monthly temperature series shown in Fig. 1.8 must be nonstationary, for if it was not then temperatures would fluctuate around a constant mean and all discussion of global warming would be moot. On the assumption, therefore, that $d = 1$, Fig. 4.6 shows the SACF and SPACF of the first-differences of temperatures. Whilst only r_1 and r_3 are significant, the SPACF exhibits a decline toward zero, with all the first 12 sample autocorrelations being negative, most being significantly so. An ARIMA(0,1,3) process may therefore be identified, which was estimated by CLS to be:

$$\nabla x_t = \underset{(0.00078)}{0.00052} + \hat{a}_t - \underset{(0.022)}{0.506}\,\hat{a}_{t-1} - \underset{(0.025)}{0.090}\,\hat{a}_{t-2} - \underset{(0.022)}{0.119}\,\hat{a}_{t-3}$$

$$\hat{\sigma} = 0.1236 \quad Q(12) = 11.75$$

This model shows no misspecification, but it does have an interesting implication. The intercept, which measures the drift of the series and, hence, in this case, the slope of a deterministic linear trend in temperatures, implies a trend increase of $0.00052 \times 1200 = 0.62°C$ per century, but is, in fact, insignificantly different from zero, having a t-ratio of just 0.66. The model therefore implies that although temperatures are nonstationary, they can be interpreted as evolving as an autocorrelated but driftless random walk, so that there is no long-run tendency for temperatures to drift inexorably upward over time, which must put the model at odds with the AGW hypothesis.

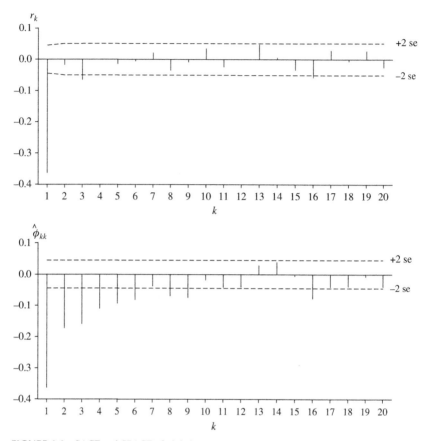

FIGURE 4.6 SACF and SPACF of global temperatures.

ENDNOTES

1. This expression for the variance of x_t is obtained by noting that:

$$\begin{aligned} V(x_t) &= E(x_t^2) = E\left(a_t + \phi a_{t-1} + \phi^2 a_{t-2} + \cdots + \phi^{2t-1}a_1\right)^2 \\ &= \sigma^2\left(1 + \phi^2 + \phi^4 + \cdots + \phi^{2t-1}\right) \\ &= \sigma^2\frac{1 - \phi^{2t}}{1 - \phi^2} = \sigma^2\frac{\phi^{2t} - 1}{\phi^2 - 1} \end{aligned}$$

on using the white noise assumptions and the standard result that

$$1 + z + z^2 + \cdots + z^{t-1} = \frac{(1 - z^t)}{(1 - z)}$$

with $z = \phi^2$.

2. The term random (or drunkard's) walk was coined by Karl Pearson in correspondence with Lord Rayleigh in the journal *Nature* in 1905. Although first employed by Pearson to describe

a mosquito infestation in a forest, the model was subsequently, and memorably, used to describe the optimal "search strategy" for finding a drunk who had been left in the middle of a field in the dead of night! The solution is to start exactly where the drunk had been placed, as that point is an unbiased estimate of the drunk's future position, and then walk in a randomly selected straight line, since he will presumably stagger along in an unpredictable and random fashion.

Pearson's metaphor was, of course, in terms of *spatial* displacement, but the time series analogy should be clear. Random walks were, in fact, first formally introduced in continuous time by Louis Bachelier in his 1900 doctoral dissertation *Theorie de Speculation* to describe the unpredictable evolution of stock prices. They were independently discovered by Albert Einstein in 1905 and have since played a fundamental role in mathematics and physics as models of, for example, waiting times, limiting diffusion processes, and first-passage problems.

3. This terminology was introduced in Box and Jenkins (1970).

Chapter 5

Unit Roots, Difference and Trend Stationarity, and Fractional Differencing

Chapter Outline

DETERMINING THE ORDER OF INTEGRATION OF A TIME SERIES

5.1 As we have shown in §§**4.5**−**4.13**, the order of integration, d, is a crucial determinant of the properties exhibited by a time series. If we restrict ourselves to the most common values of zero and one for d, so that x_t is either $I(0)$ or $I(1)$, then it is useful to bring together the properties of these two processes.

If x_t is $I(0)$, which we will sometimes denote $x_t \sim I(0)$ even though such a notation has been used previously to denote the distributional characteristics of a series, then, if we assume for convenience that x_t has zero mean;

1. the variance of x_t is finite and does not depend on t;
2. the innovation a_t has only a temporary effect on the value of x_t;
3. the expected length of time between crossings of $x = 0$ is finite, so that x_t fluctuates around its mean of zero;
4. the autocorrelations, ρ_k, decrease steadily in magnitude for large enough k, so that their sum is finite.

Applied Time Series Analysis. DOI: https://doi.org/10.1016/B978-0-12-813117-6.00005-3

If, on the other hand, $x_t \sim I(1)$ with $x_0 = 0$, then;

1. the variance of x_t goes to infinity as t goes to infinity;
2. an innovation a_t has a permanent effect on the value of x_t because x_t is the sum of all previous innovations: recall from §**4.10** that $x_t = \nabla^{-1} a_t = Sa_t = \sum_{i=0}^{t-1} a_{t-i}$;
3. the expected time between crossings of $x = 0$ is infinite;
4. the autocorrelations $\rho_k \to 1$ for all k as t goes to infinity.

5.2 As was shown in Chapter 2, Transforming Time Series, the fact that a time series is nonstationary is often self-evident from a plot of the series. Determining the actual *form* of nonstationarity, however, is not so easy from just a visual inspection and, consequently, an examination of the SACFs for alternative differences of the series may be required.

To see why this may be so, recall from §**3.17** that a stationary AR(p) process requires that all roots g_i in

$$\phi(B) = (1 - g_1 B)(1 - g_2 B)\ldots\left(1 - g_p B\right)$$

must be such that $|g_i| < 1$. Now suppose one of them, say g_1, approaches 1, so that $g_1 = 1 - \delta$, where δ is a small positive number. The autocorrelations

$$\rho_k = A_1 g_1^k + A_2 g_2^k + \cdots + A_p g_p^k$$

will then become dominated by the lead term $A_1 g_1^k$, since all others will go to zero more rapidly, i.e., $\rho_k \cong A_1 g_1^k$. Moreover, because g_1 is close to 1, the exponential decay $A_1 g_1^k$ will be slow and almost linear, since

$$A_1 g_1^k = A_1 (1 - \delta)^k = A\left(1 - \delta k + \delta^2 k^2 - \ldots\right) \cong A_1(1 - \delta k)$$

Hence, the failure of the SACF to die down quickly is an indication of nonstationarity, its behavior tending to be rather that of a slow, linear decline. If the original series x_t is found to be nonstationary, the first-difference ∇x_t is then analyzed. If ∇x_t is still nonstationary, the second-difference $\nabla^2 x_t$ is analyzed, the procedure being repeated until a stationary difference is found, although in practice d will not exceed 2.

5.3 Sole reliance on the SACF can sometimes lead to problems of *overdifferencing*. Although further differences of a stationary series will themselves be stationary, overdifferencing can lead to serious difficulties. Consider the stationary MA(1) process $x_t = (1 - \theta B)a_t$. The first-difference of this is

$$\begin{aligned}
\nabla x_t &= (1 - B)(1 - \theta B)a_t \\
&= \left(1 - (1 + \theta)B + \theta B^2\right)a_t \\
&= \left(1 - \theta_1 B - \theta_2 B^2\right)a_t.
\end{aligned}$$

We now have a more complicated model containing two parameters rather than one and, moreover, one of the roots of the $\theta(B)$ polynomial will be unity since $\theta_1 + \theta_2 = 1$. The model is, therefore, not invertible, so that the AR(∞)

representation of ∇x_t does not exist and attempts to estimate this model will almost surely run into difficulties.

TESTING FOR A UNIT ROOT

5.4   Given the importance of choosing the correct order of differencing, we should have available a formal testing procedure to determine d. To introduce the issues involved in developing such a procedure, we begin by considering the simplest case, that of the zero mean AR(1) process:

$$x_t = \phi x_{t-1} + a_t \quad t = 1, 2, \dots, T \tag{5.1}$$

where $a_t \sim \text{WN}(0, \sigma^2)$ and $x_0 = 0$. The OLS estimator of ϕ is given by

$$\hat{\phi}_T = \frac{\sum_{t=1}^{T} x_{t-1} x_t}{\sum_{t=1}^{T} x_t^2}$$

As we have seen, x_t will be $I(0)$ if $|\phi| < 1$, but will be $I(1)$ if $\phi = 1$, so that testing this null hypothesis, that of a "unit root," becomes a method of determining the correct order of differencing/integration. Given the estimate $\hat{\phi}_T$, a conventional way of testing the null hypothesis would be to construct the t-statistic

$$t_\phi = \frac{\hat{\phi}_T - 1}{\hat{\sigma}_{\hat{\phi}_T}} = \frac{\hat{\phi}_T - 1}{\left(s_T^2 / \sum_{t=1}^{T} x_{t-1}^2 \right)^{1/2}} \tag{5.2}$$

where

$$\hat{\sigma}_{\hat{\phi}_T} = \left(\frac{s_T^2}{\sum_{t=1}^{T} x_{t-1}^2} \right)^{1/2}$$

is the usual OLS standard error for $\hat{\phi}_T$ and s_T^2 is the OLS estimator of σ^2:

$$s_T^2 = \frac{\sum_{t=1}^{T} \left(x_t - \hat{\phi}_T x_{t-1} \right)^2}{T - 1}$$

5.5   Unfortunately, the distribution of t_ϕ does not have the usual limiting standard normal distribution when $\phi = 1$. Rather, its distribution is as shown in Fig. 5.1, where it is called the τ-distribution in recognition of its nonnormality. The test statistic (5.2) is renamed τ, rather than t_ϕ, and is often known as the *Dickey–Fuller* test, as indeed is the distribution.[1]

Fig. 5.1 shows that the limiting distribution of τ is approximately standard normal, but shifted to the left by roughly 0.3: the large T 5%, 2.5%, and 1% critical values for τ are -1.95, -2.23, and -2.58, rather than the standard normal critical values of -1.65, -1.96, and -2.33.

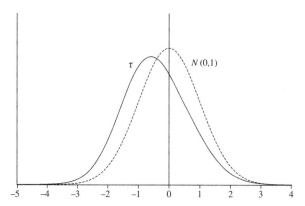

FIGURE 5.1 Limiting distribution of τ.

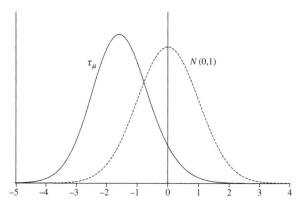

FIGURE 5.2 Limiting distribution of τ_μ.

5.6 This case has the merit of being simple, but is not particularly realistic, for it implies that the alternative to a driftless random walk is a stationary AR(1) process about a *zero* mean, which would rule out series that can take only positive values, of which there are many (most economic and financial time series, for example). A more sensible alternative would be for the AR(1) process to fluctuate about a nonzero mean, so that we have the model:

$$x_t = \theta_0 + \phi x_{t-1} + a_t \quad t = 1, 2, \ldots, T \tag{5.3}$$

in which the unit root null is parameterized as $\theta_0 = 0$, $\phi = 1$. The presence of an intercept alters the distribution of the test statistic, which is now denoted τ_μ to emphasize that a nonzero mean is allowed for in the regression (5.3).[2] Fig. 5.2 presents the distribution of τ_μ. With a nonzero mean, the distribution under the unit root null deviates further from the standard normal than when the mean is zero (compare with Fig. 5.1), with the large T 5%, 2.5%, and 1% critical values now being -2.86, -3.12, and -3.43.

5.7 A further generalization is to allow the innovations to be autocorrelated. Suppose that x_t is generated by the AR(p) process:

$$\left(1 - \phi_1 B - \phi_2 B^2 - \cdots - \phi_p B^p\right)x_t = \theta_0 + a_t$$

or

$$x_t = \theta_0 + \sum_{i=1}^{p} \phi_i x_{t-i} + a_t \tag{5.4}$$

A more convenient representation is obtained by defining

$$\phi = \sum_{i=1}^{p} \phi_i$$

$$\delta_i = - \sum_{j=i+1}^{p-1} \phi_j \quad i = 1, 2, \ldots, p-1$$

so that (5.4) can be written, with $k = p - 1$,

$$x_t = \theta_0 + \phi x_{t-1} + \sum_{i=1}^{k} \delta_i \nabla x_{t-i} + a_t \tag{5.5}$$

The unit root null is, thus, $\phi = \sum_{i=1}^{p} \phi_i = 1.$[3] OLS provides consistent estimators of the coefficients of (5.5) and a test of $\phi = 1$ can be constructed as

$$\tau_\mu = \frac{\hat{\phi}_T - 1}{se\left(\hat{\phi}_T\right)}$$

where $se\left(\hat{\phi}_T\right)$ is the OLS standard error attached to the estimate $\hat{\phi}_T$ (recall §5.4). This statistic is also denoted τ_μ because it has the *same* limiting distribution as the statistic obtained from the AR(1) model (5.3), although it is often referred to as the *augmented Dickey–Fuller* (ADF) test. In a similar vein, Eq. (5.5) is known as the ADF *regression*.

5.8 The analysis of §§5.4–5.7 has implicitly assumed that the AR order p is known, so that we are certain that x_t is generated by a pth order autoregression. If the generating process is an ARMA(p,q), then the τ_μ statistic obtained from estimating the model:

$$x_t = \theta_0 + \phi x_{t-1} + \sum_{i=1}^{p} \delta_i \nabla x_{t-i} + a_t - \sum_{j=1}^{q} \theta_j a_{t-j}$$

has the same limiting distribution as that calculated from (5.5). The problem here, of course, is that p and q are assumed known, and this is unlikely to be the case in practice. When p and q are unknown, the test statistic obtained from (5.5) can still be used if k, the number of lags of ∇x_t

introduced as regressors, increases with the sample size T. Typically, setting k at $\left[T^{0.25}\right]$ should work reasonably well in practice, where $[\cdot]$ denotes the operation of taking the integer part of the argument: for example, for $T = 50$, $T^{0.25} = 2.659$, so that k is set at 2; for $T = 500$, $T^{0.25} = 4.729$ and, hence, $k = 4$. This adjustment is necessary because, as the sample size increases, the effects of the correlation structure of the residuals on the shape of the distribution of τ_μ become more precise. A more accurate setting of k may be determined by using, for example, information criteria or by implementing a sequence of t-tests on the lags, once a suitable maximum value for k has been chosen, perhaps by the rule of thumb discussed.

EXAMPLE 5.1 Unit Root Tests on the Spread and the $–£ Exchange Rate

Examples 3.2 and 4.1 examined two models for the United Kingdom interest rate spread: a stationary AR(2) process and an $I(1)$ process without drift. We are now able to discriminate between the two through the application of a unit root test. The fitted AR(2) model:

$$x_t = \underset{(0.017)}{0.036} + \underset{(0.035)}{1.193}\, x_{t-1} - \underset{(0.035)}{0.224}\, x_{t-2} + \hat{a}_t$$

can equivalently be written as

$$x_t = \underset{(0.017)}{0.036} + \underset{(0.008)}{0.969}\, x_{t-1} + \underset{(0.035)}{0.224}\, \nabla x_{t-1} + \hat{a}_t$$

so that $\tau_\mu = -0.0314/0.0078 = -4.03$, which is significant at the 1% level, this critical value being -3.44. Note that the τ_μ statistic can be obtained directly as the t-ratio on x_{t-1} from rewriting the model again as

$$\nabla x_t = \underset{(0.017)}{0.036} - \underset{(0.008)}{0.031}\, x_{t-1} + \underset{(0.035)}{0.224}\, \nabla x_{t-1} + \hat{a}_t$$

We may, therefore, conclude that the spread does not contain a unit root and that the appropriate specification is the stationary AR(2) model in which there are temporary, albeit highly persistent, deviations away from an equilibrium level of 1.14%.

A similar approach to testing for a unit root in the $–£ exchange rate, the presence of which was assumed in Example 4.2, leads to the estimated equation:

$$\nabla x_t = \underset{(0.0007)}{0.0019} - \underset{(0.0004)}{0.0012}\, x_{t-1} + \underset{(0.0096)}{0.0607}\, \nabla x_{t-1} + \hat{a}_t$$

Here we have $\tau_\mu = -2.96$, and since the 1% critical value is -3.43, this is insignificant at this level, although it is certainly significant at the 5% level (the P-value is .039). Thus, even though the largest autoregressive root is estimated to be 0.9988, there is still some doubt as to whether the appropriate model for the $–£ exchange rate is indeed a (possibly autocorrelated) random walk or whether it is stationary around an "equilibrium" level, estimated here to be 1.712.[4] This latter model would have the implication that any deviation from this level would only be temporary and foreign exchange traders would then have a "one-way" bet in that such deviations must eventually be reversed, which seems highly unlikely in such a competitive and efficient market. A resolution of this apparent "paradox" will be provided in Example 10.1.

EXAMPLE 5.2 Is There a Unit Root in Global Temperatures?

It was assumed in Example 4.3 that global temperatures were $I(1)$. A proponent of the absence of global warming would require this series to be $I(0)$, and should, thus, demand that a unit root test be carried out to determine the appropriate level of differencing. Since the AR order in the ADF regression is unknown, k may be selected using the rule of thumb suggested in §**5.8**, which here gives $k = \left[2016^{0.25}\right] = 6$. Using the BIC to select the lag augmentation also gives this value for k, so leading to the ADF regression

$$\nabla x_t = -\underset{(0.003)}{0.002} - \underset{(0.009)}{0.032}\, x_{t-1} + \sum_{i=1}^{6} \hat{\delta}_i \nabla x_{t-i} + \hat{a}_t$$

Here $\tau_\mu = -0.0319/0.0092 = -3.48$, which is significant at the 1% level, this critical value being -3.43 (the p-value is .009). There is, thus, considerable doubt as to whether this global temperature series is actually $I(1)$, as is necessary for the AGW hypothesis, although it is not sufficient because, as we have seen in Example 4.3, even on the $I(1)$ assumption the drift is insignificantly different from zero.

TREND VERSUS DIFFERENCE STATIONARITY

5.9   In the unit root testing strategy outlined previously, the implicit null hypothesis is that the series is generated as a driftless random walk with, possibly, autocorrelated innovations. In popular terminology introduced by Nelson and Plosser (1982), x_t is said to be *difference stationary* (DS),

$$\nabla x_t = \varepsilon_t \tag{5.6}$$

where $\varepsilon_t = \theta(B)a_t$, while the alternative is that x_t is *stationary* in levels. While the null of a driftless random walk is appropriate for many time series, others often do contain a drift, so that the relevant null becomes

$$\nabla x_t = \theta + \varepsilon_t \tag{5.7}$$

In this case, a plausible alternative is that x_t is generated by a linear trend buried in stationary noise (see §**4.13**), now termed *trend stationarity* (TS):

$$x_t = \beta_0 + \beta_1 t + \varepsilon_t \tag{5.8}$$

Unfortunately, the τ_μ statistic obtained from (5.5) is incapable of distinguishing a stationary process around a linear trend [model (5.8)] from a process

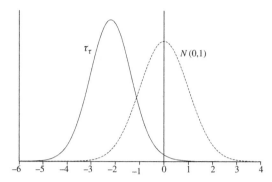

FIGURE 5.3 Limiting distribution of τ_τ.

with a unit root and drift [model (5.7)]. Indeed, rejection of a null hypothesis of a unit root is unlikely using this statistic if the series is stationary around a linear trend and becomes impossible as the sample size increases, i.e., the test is inconsistent, results that were first announced by Perron (1988).[5]

5.10 A test of (5.7) against (5.8) is, however, straightforward to carry out by using an extension of the testing methodology previously discussed: the ADF regression (5.5) is simply extended by the inclusion of the time trend t as an additional regressor,

$$x_t = \beta_0 + \beta_1 t + \phi x_{t-1} + \sum_{i=1}^{k} \delta_i \nabla x_{t-i} + a_t \tag{5.9}$$

and the statistic

$$\tau_\tau = \frac{\hat{\phi}_T - 1}{se\left(\hat{\phi}_T\right)}$$

is calculated. This "t-statistic" is denoted τ_τ to distinguish it from τ_μ because it has a different limiting distribution, which is shown in Fig. 5.3. The large T 5%, 2.5%, and 1% critical values are now -3.41, -3.66, and -3.96, and since these are "more negative" than their τ_μ counterparts, a greater deviation from $\phi = 1$ is required before the DS null can be rejected.

EXAMPLE 5.3 Trends in Wine and Spirit Consumption

Fig. 1.6 showed annual United Kingdom wine and spirits consumption, in which positive linear trends were clearly apparent, thus suggesting that these series may have been generated as TS processes. The first-differences of these series (i.e., the annual changes) were shown in Fig. 2.6, and here the trends have been eradicated, implicitly suggesting that the series could be DS processes. To distinguish between these two possibilities, the trend-included ADF regressions (5.9) were estimated, with lag augmentation being determined using the BIC ($k = 0$ for both wine and spirits):

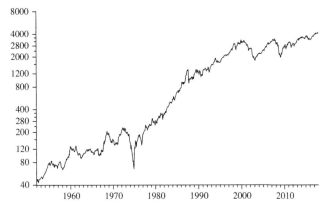

FIGURE 5.4   FTSE *All Share* index: monthly, January 1952–December 2017; logarithmic scale.

Wine

$$\nabla x_t = -\underset{(0.035)}{0.048} + \underset{(0.0030)}{0.0093}\, t - \underset{(0.072)}{0.213}\, x_{t-1} + \hat{a}_t$$

Spirits

$$\nabla x_t = \underset{(0.047)}{0.112} + \underset{(0.0016)}{0.0022}\, t - \underset{(0.061)}{0.121}\, x_{t-1} + \hat{a}_t$$

The τ_τ statistics are -2.97 and -1.89 respectively, so both are clearly insignificant as the 10% critical value is -3.17. Each series is, thus, confirmed as a DS, rather than TS, process.

EXAMPLE 5.4 Are United Kingdom Equity Prices Trend or Difference Stationary?

Fig. 5.4 plots, on a logarithmic scale, monthly observations from 1952 to 2017 on the FTSE *All Share* stock market index; the broadest based of the London Stock Exchange's price indices. The index has a pronounced tendency to drift upwards, albeit with some major "wanderings" about trend, most notably over the past decade and a half of the sample period, roughly since the beginning of the 2000s. We may, thus, investigate whether a DS representation of the logarithms of the index is appropriate or whether a TS model would be preferable.

Setting the lag augmentation at $k = 1$, as suggested by the BIC, leads to the trend-included ADF regression:

$$\nabla x_t = \underset{(0.020)}{0.049} + \underset{(0.000033)}{0.000064}\, t - \underset{(0.005)}{0.011}\, x_{t-1} + \underset{(0.035)}{0.118}\, \nabla x_{t-1} + \hat{a}_t$$

This yields the test statistic $\tau_\tau = -2.13$. Since the 10% critical value is -3.13, there is no evidence against the hypothesis that the logarithm of the index is DS. If the logarithms of the index had been TS, this would have implied that they evolved as autocorrelated deviations about a linear trend, again providing traders with a one-way bet whenever the index got too far away from this trend. Even a cursory examination of Fig. 5.4 shows that such a representation is clearly false.

EXAMPLE 5.5 Are Shocks to British GDP Temporary or Permanent?

Fig. 5.5 shows the logarithms of British real GDP per capita annually over the period of 1822–1913, i.e., from just after the end of the Napoleonic wars to the beginning of World War I, a period which covers the whole of the Victorian era. A linear trend line has been superimposed on the plot, calculated from a model of the form of (5.8):

$$x_t = \underset{(0.019)}{0.329} + \underset{(0.0004)}{0.0103}\, t + \varepsilon_t$$

$$\varepsilon_t = \underset{(0.076)}{0.696}\, \varepsilon_{t-1} + \hat{a}_t$$

This TS model implies that, since we are dealing with logarithms, trend growth in real GDP per capita was 1.03% per annum, with there being stationary deviations about the trend line. Consequently, all shocks that push real GDP per capita away from its long-run trend path have only short-run, "transitory" impacts, with the series *always* returning to this trend path. Since the error component is modeled by an AR(1) process with a parameter of around 0.7, such shocks die away geometrically and rather quickly; being reduced by over 90% in size after 7 years ($0.7^7 = 0.082$).

Note that the error component displays no evidence of a "business cycle," for this would require ε_t to follow (at least) an AR(2) process with complex roots, for which there is no evidence, since the inclusion of a second autoregressive term produces an insignificant coefficient.

This TS representation may be contrasted with the DS representation

$$\nabla x_t = \underset{(0.0003)}{0.0104} + \hat{a}_t$$

obtained by replacing the autoregressive coefficient of 0.7 with one of unity. This model is a drifting random walk with the drift parameter estimated as 1.04% per annum. The interpretation of this model, however, is one in which all shocks are *permanent*; remaining in the series for all time with no dissipation.

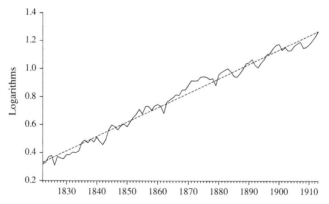

FIGURE 5.5 Logarithm of British real GDP per capita, 1822–1913, with linear trend line superimposed.

The series, therefore, never returns to a *unique* trend growth path: each year the projected trend growth path is reset after the latest shock.

The distinction between the two processes is important for macroeconomists when determining the impact of economic shocks, perhaps induced by a policy shift. Are shocks transitory so that real GDP eventually returns to its underlying trend growth path, in which case policy-induced shocks have only short-run effects? On the other hand, are shocks permanent and so live on forever, never dying out and remaining in the series for all time? To determine which of the two models is appropriate here, a trend-included ADF regression was estimated:

$$\nabla x_t = \underset{(0.025)}{0.108} + \underset{(0.00080)}{0.00313}\, t - \underset{(0.076)}{0.304}\, x_{t-1} + \hat{a}_t$$

from which $\tau_\tau = -0.304/0.076 = -3.98$ is obtained. Since this statistic has a p-value of just 0.013 a TS representation is clearly appropriate. Note that the DF statistic may be interpreted as a t-test of the hypothesis that the autoregressive coefficient of the AR(1) error component in the TS representation is unity, against the alternative that it is less than unity using the appropriate τ_τ critical values. Shocks to real GDP per capita during the period 1822–1913 were, therefore, transitory and the series grew at a trend growth rate of 1% per annum with shocks dissipating at a rate of 70% per annum.

TESTING FOR MORE THAN ONE UNIT ROOT

5.11   This development of unit root tests has been predicated on the assumption that x_t contains *at most* one unit root, so that it is either $I(0)$ or $I(1)$. If the null hypothesis of a unit root is not rejected, then it may be necessary to test whether the series contains a second unit root—in other words whether x_t is $I(2)$ and, thus, needs differencing twice to induce stationarity.

EXAMPLE 5.6 Is Box and Jenkins' Series C $I(2)$?

Fig. 2.7 showed the levels, first- and second-differences of Box and Jenkins' (1970) Series C, these being successive temperature readings on a chemical process. The SACFs for each of these series are now given in Fig. 5.6 and suggest that some order of differencing is required. Box and Jenkins (1970, page 185), in their discussion of these SACFs, thought that the SACF for ∇x_t showed an exponential decline from an r_1 of around 0.8, thus suggesting an ARIMA(1,1,0) process, although they did not rule out the possibility that second-differencing might be required, in which case, given that the SACF for $\nabla^2 x_t$ is that of white noise, an ARIMA(0,2,0) process would be identified.

The choice between the two models can be decided using a unit root test on ∇x_t, the appropriate ADF regression being

$$\nabla^2 x_t = -\underset{(0.038)}{0.187}\, \nabla x_{t-1} + \hat{a}_t$$

This produces a τ statistic of -4.87, noting that neither a constant or trend is included in the regression as their presence would imply that there was at least a

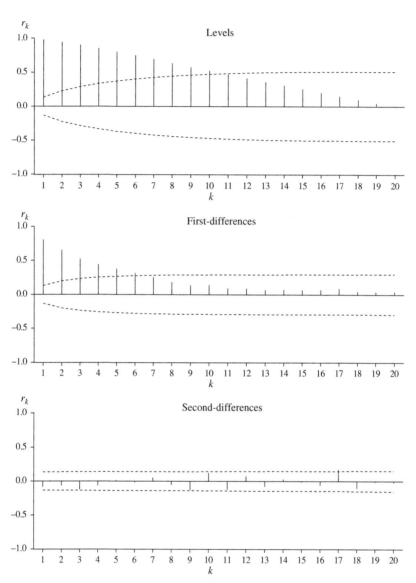

FIGURE 5.6   SACFs for alternative differences of Box and Jenkins Series C.

quadratic trend in x_t itself, which is clearly not the case. The hypothesis of two unit roots is, thus, clearly rejected in favor of there being just one, i.e., the test supports the ARIMA(1,1,0) model for Series C.

However, are we really certain that Series C even contains one unit root? Could it be stationary, having highly persistent cyclical fluctuations produced by complex roots with a modulus that is less than, albeit close to, unity? This would certainly seem plausible, since the series is made up of temperature readings from a presumably regulated chemical process. To investigate this possibility, one not considered by Box and Jenkins, we report an ADF regression for a single unit root:

$$\nabla x_t = \underset{(0.101)}{0.277} - \underset{(0.0044)}{0.0124} x_{t-1} + \underset{(0.038)}{0.815} \nabla x_{t-1} + \hat{a}_t$$

From this we obtain $\tau_\mu = -2.85$, which is close to the 5% critical value of -2.87, the p-value being .053. Thus, the unit root null can be rejected at almost the 5% level and, if we were to do so, the stationary AR(2) model implied by the ADF regression can be written as

$$x_t = \underset{(0.071)}{22.86} + \underset{(0.038)}{1.807} (x_{t-1} - 22.86) - \underset{(0.038)}{0.820} (x_{t-2} - 22.86) + \hat{a}_t$$

This provides a pair of complex roots $0.90 \pm 0.06i$. From the expression given in Example 3.3, the implied cycle is then 113, which is exactly half the available sample of observations and suggests that the cycle is far too long to be anything other than a statistical artefact of imposing a stationary autoregressive structure rather than that of a unit root. On balance, we would agree with Box and Jenkins that their series C is best modeled by the ARIMA(1,1,0) process

$$\nabla x_t = \underset{(0.038)}{0.813} \nabla x_{t-1} + \hat{a}_t$$

OTHER APPROACHES TO TESTING FOR A UNIT ROOT

5.12 An alternative unit root test to the ADF for dealing with autocorrelation in a_t, which also allows for heterogeneity of variance, has been proposed by Phillips and Perron (1988). Rather than including extra lags of ∇x_t to ensure that the errors of (5.4) are indeed white noise, the idea here is to estimate an "unaugmented" model—(5.3), say—and to modify the test statistics so that the effects of any autocorrelation are accounted for. This will enable the same DF limiting distributions and, hence, critical values to be used.

Under a specific set of conditions placed upon a_t, known as *weak dependency*, which are described in detail by Phillips (1987), the τ_μ statistic obtained from the estimation of (5.3) is modified to

$$Z(\tau_\mu) = \tau_\mu (\hat{\sigma}_0 / \hat{\sigma}_\ell) - \frac{1}{2} (\hat{\sigma}_\ell^2 - \hat{\sigma}_0^2) / \Sigma_\ell \tag{5.10}$$

in which

$$\hat{\sigma}_0^2 = T^{-1} \sum_{t=1}^{T} \hat{a}_t^2$$

$$\hat{\sigma}_\ell^2 = \hat{\sigma}_0^2 + 2T^{-1} \sum_{j=1}^{\ell} w_j(\ell) \left(\sum_{t=j+1}^{T} \hat{a}_t \hat{a}_{t-j} \right) \tag{5.11}$$

$$\Sigma_\ell^2 = T^{-2} \hat{\sigma}_\ell^2 \sum_{t=2}^{T} (x_{t-1} - \bar{x}_{-1})^2 \quad \bar{x}_{-1} = (T-1)^{-1} \sum_{t=1}^{T-1} x_t$$

$\hat{\sigma}_{\ell}^2$ is a consistent estimator of the *long-run variance* and employs a window or kernel function $w_j(\ell)$ to weight the sample autocovariances appearing in the formula. This ensures that the estimator remains positive, with ℓ acting as a truncation lag, much like k in the ADF regression. A range of kernel functions are available, such as the "triangular" set of lag weights $w_j(\ell) = \ell - j/(\ell + 1)$. $Z(\tau_\mu)$ is often referred to as the Phillips–Perron (PP) non-parametric unit root test.

$Z(\tau_\mu)$ has the same limiting distribution as τ_μ, so that the latter's critical values may again be used. If x_t has zero mean, the adjusted statistic, $Z(\tau)$, is as in (5.10) with $\bar{x}_{-1}$ removed and has the same limiting distribution as τ. If a time trend is included then a further adjustment is required to enable the statistic, now denoted $Z(\tau_\tau)$, to have the limiting τ_τ distribution (Mills and Markellos, 2008, page 87, for example, provide details).

5.13 Many alternative unit root tests have been developed since the initial ADF and PP tests were introduced. A recurring theme of unit root testing is the low power and severe size distortion inherent in many tests: see, especially, the review by Haldrup and Jansson (2006). For example, the PP tests suffer severe size distortions when there are moving average errors with a large negative root and, although their ADF counterparts are better behaved in this respect, the problem is not negligible even here. Moreover, many tests have low power when the largest autoregressive root is close to, but nevertheless less than, unity.

A related issue is that unlike many hypothesis testing situations, the power of tests of the unit root hypothesis against stationary alternatives depends less on the number of observations per se and more on the *span* of the data (i.e., the length of the observation period). For a given number of observations, power has been found to be highest when the span is longest; conversely, for a given span, additional observations obtained using data sampled more frequently lead to only a marginal increase in power, the increase becoming negligible as the sampling interval is decreased. Hence, a series containing fewer annual observations over an extended time period will often lead to unit root tests having higher power than those computed from a series containing more observations over a shorter period.

5.14 Several subsequent tests have explicitly concentrated on improving power and reducing size distortion. Many of these are based on generalized least squares (GLS) "detrending" prior to calculating a test statistic. The DF-GLS and point optimal unit root tests of Elliott, Rothenberg, and Stock (ERS, 1996) were the initial pair of tests based on this approach, both employing the *quasi-differences*

$$d(x_t|\alpha) = \begin{cases} x_t & \text{if } t = 1 \\ x_t - \alpha x_{t-1} & \text{if } t > 1 \end{cases}$$

The quasi-differences of any intercept and trend regressors may similarly be defined as $d(1|\alpha)$ and $d(t|\alpha)$, respectively. The DF-GLS test then proceeds by first regressing $d(x_t|\alpha)$ on $d(1|\alpha)$ and $d(t|\alpha)$ to obtain the intercept and trend estimates $\hat{\beta}_0(\alpha)$ and $\hat{\beta}_1(\alpha)$ and, hence, the detrended series $x_t^d = x_t - \hat{\beta}_0(\alpha) - \hat{\beta}_1(\alpha)t$. The test statistic is then τ_τ from the ADF-style regression

$$x_t^d = \phi x_{t-1}^d + \sum_{i=1}^{k} \nabla x_{t-i}^d + a_t$$

where, because the data has been detrended, neither an intercept nor a trend need be included as regressors. Critical values for the DF-GLS test are provided by ERS, although if no trend is included in the first-stage detrending regression then τ_μ critical values may continue to be used.

To make the DF-GLS test operational a value of α must be chosen to perform the initial quasi-differencing. ERS suggest using $\overline{\alpha} = 1 - 13.5/T$ when both an intercept and trend are included in the first-stage regression and $\overline{\alpha} = 1 - 7/T$ when just an intercept is included.

The *point optimal* test is the most powerful test of a unit root against a simple point alternative. If we define the residual sum of squares from the first-stage regression as $S(\overline{\alpha})$, then the point optimal test of the null $\phi = 1$ against the alternative $\phi = \overline{\phi} < 1$ is then defined as

$$P_\tau = \frac{S(\overline{\phi}) - \overline{\phi}S(1)}{\hat{\sigma}_\ell^2}$$

where $\hat{\sigma}_\ell^2$ is the estimate of the long-run variance given in (5.10). Critical values of P_τ are provided by ERS, with the null of a unit root being rejected if the test statistic is too small.

5.15 Ng and Perron (2001) construct four further tests that are based on the GLS-detrended data x_t^d. It is useful to define the term

$$\kappa = T^{-2} \sum_{t=1}^{T-1} \left(x_t^d\right)^2$$

whereupon the test statistics are defined as

$$MZ^d(\phi) = \frac{T^{-1}\left(x_T^d\right) - \hat{\sigma}_\ell^2}{2\kappa}$$

$$MSB^d = \left(\frac{\kappa}{\hat{\sigma}_\ell^2}\right)^{1/2}$$

$$MZ_t^d = MZ^d(\phi) \times MSB^d$$

and

$$\text{MP}_T^d(k) = \frac{\bar{c}_k^2 \kappa - (\bar{c}_k - k)T^{-1}\left(x_T^d\right)^2}{\hat{\sigma}_\ell^2}$$

In this last statistic, $k = 0$ if just an intercept is included in the first-stage GLS regression, and $k = 1$ if both an intercept and trend are included; $\bar{c}_0 = -7$ and $\bar{c}_1 = -13.5$.

$\text{MZ}^d(\phi)$ and MZ_t^d are modified versions of non-parametric tests and incorporate the feature that a series converges in distribution with different rates of normalization under the unit root null and stationary alternative hypotheses. The $\text{MP}_T^d(k)$ statistics are similarly modified versions of the point optimal P_τ test, while MSB^d is a modified version of Bhargava's (1986) earlier R_1 statistic. On the stationary alternative, MSB^d tends to zero, so the unit root null is rejected when the statistic is below the critical value.

5.16 Throughout the development of unit root testing procedures, the null hypothesis has been that of a unit root, with a stationary hypothesis (either trend or level stationarity) as the alternative. How might a null of stationarity be tested against a unit root alternative? Consider the ARIMA(0,1,1) process:

$$\nabla x_t = \theta_0 + a_t - \theta a_{t-1}$$

Reversing the argument in §**4.3**, a TS process is obtained if $\theta = 1$, so that this restriction parameterizes the trend stationary null, with the unit root alternative being $\theta < 1$. The statistic proposed to test this null is the KPSS test (after Kwiatkowski et al., 1992), which is defined as

$$\eta_\tau = T^{-2} \sum\nolimits_{t=1}^T \hat{S}_t^2 / \hat{\sigma}_{e\ell}^2$$

Here

$$\hat{S}_t = \sum_{i=1}^t e_i \quad e_t = x_t - \hat{\beta}_0 - \hat{\beta}_1 t$$

and $\hat{\sigma}_{e\ell}^2$ is defined analogously to $\hat{\sigma}_\ell^2$ in (5.10). If there is no trend in x_t under the null, then the residuals are defined as $e_t = x_t - \bar{x}$ and the resulting "level stationarity" test statistic is denoted η_μ. On the null of $\theta = 1$, $\eta_\tau = 0$, while under the alternative, $\eta_\tau > 0$. Critical values of the test statistics are reported in KPSS: the 5% critical value of η_τ is 0.146, the 1% critical value is 0.216. For η_μ these critical values are 0.463 and 0.739, respectively.

EXAMPLE 5.7 More Unit Roots Tests on the *All Share* Index

In Example 5.4 an ADF test could not reject the null hypothesis that the logarithms of the *All Share* index were DS and, hence, contained a unit root. Is this conclusion confirmed by the other available tests? The PP test yields $Z(\tau_\tau) = -1.98$, which has a p-value of just .61. The ERS test statistics are DF-GLS $= -2.17$ and $P_\tau = 9.50$, while the modified tests of Ng and Perron (2001) produce $MZ^d(\phi) = -9.82$, $MZ_t^d = -2.17$, $MSB^d = 0.220$, and $MP_T^d(1) = 9.51$. None of these statistics come close to being significant at the 10% level. The KPSS statistic, on the other hand, is $\eta_\tau = 0.372$, which comfortably exceeds the 1% critical value of 0.216 and so rejects the TS null in favor of the DS alternative, so that the entire battery of tests consistently points to the index having a unit root.

ESTIMATING TRENDS ROBUSTLY

5.17   Consider again the linear trend model (5.8): $x_t = \beta_0 + \beta_1 t + \varepsilon_t$. As we have seen, correct specification of the trend is crucially important for unit root and stationarity testing. As was pointed out in §**5.9**, incorrectly excluding a linear trend renders the τ_μ statistic inconsistent, while it is also the case that unnecessarily including a trend vastly reduces the power of the τ_τ test, with similar problems affecting the KPSS stationarity statistics η_μ and η_τ.

Often, however, the trend parameter β_1 is of direct interest, especially when ascertaining whether a trend is present ($\beta_1 \neq 0$) or not ($\beta_1 = 0$). This may be assessed by either constructing a direct test of the no trend hypothesis $\beta_1 = 0$ or by forming a confidence interval for β_1. Such tests rely on whether ε_t, and hence, x_t, is either $I(0)$ or $I(1)$, but this can only be established after a unit root or stationarity test has been performed—yet the properties of these latter tests rely, in turn, on whether a trend has been correctly included or not! This circularity of reasoning has prompted the development of trend function testing procedures that are *robust*, in the sense that, at least asymptotically, inference on the trend function is unaffected as to whether ε_t is $I(0)$ or $I(1)$.

5.18   To develop robust tests of trend, we start with the simplest case in which $\varepsilon_t = \rho \varepsilon_{t-1} + a_t$, where ε_t is $I(0)$ if $|\rho| < 1$ and $I(1)$ if $\rho = 1$. We then wish to test $H_0: \beta_1 = \beta_1^0$ against the alternative $H_1: \beta_1 \neq \beta_1^0$. If ε_t is *known* to be $I(0)$ then an optimal test of H_0 against H_1 is given by the "slope" t-ratio

$$z_0 = \frac{\hat{\beta}_1 - \beta_1^0}{s_0} \qquad s_0 = \sqrt{\frac{\hat{\sigma}_\varepsilon^2}{\sum_{t=1}^{T}(t-\bar{t})^2}} \tag{5.12}$$

where $\hat{\sigma}_\varepsilon^2 = (T-2)^{-1}\sum_{t=1}^{T}\left(x_t - \hat{\beta}_0 - \hat{\beta}_1 t\right)^2$ is the error variance from OLS estimation of (5.8). Under H_0, z_0 will be asymptotically standard normal.

On the other hand, if ε_t is *known* to be $I(1)$ then the optimal test of H_0 against H_1 is based on the t-ratio associated with the OLS estimator of β_1 in the first-differenced form of (5.8),

$$\nabla x_t = \beta_1 + \nu_t \quad t = 2, \ldots, T \tag{5.13}$$

where $\nu_t = \nabla \varepsilon_t$:

$$z_1 = \frac{\tilde{\beta}_1 - \beta_1^0}{s_1} \quad s_1 = \sqrt{\frac{\tilde{\sigma}_\nu^2}{T-1}}$$

Here

$$\tilde{\beta}_1 = (T-1) \sum_{t=2}^{T} \nabla x_t = (T-1)(x_T - x_1)$$

is the OLS estimator of β_1 in (5.13) and $\tilde{\sigma}_\nu^2 = (T-2)^{-1} \sum_{t=2}^{T} \left(\nabla x_t - \tilde{\beta}_1\right)^2$. Again, under H_0, z_1 will be asymptotically standard normal.

5.19 What if it is *not known* whether ε_t is $I(0)$ or $I(1)$? Harvey, Leybourne, and Taylor (HLT, 2007) show that a weighted average of z_0 and z_1, say

$$z_\lambda = (1 - \lambda(U,S))z_0 + \lambda(U,S)z_1 \tag{5.14}$$

where U is a standard unit root test statistic, S is a standard trend-stationarity test statistic and

$$\lambda = \exp\left(-\kappa \left(\frac{U}{S}\right)^2\right) \tag{5.15}$$

will be asymptotically standard normal under H_0, so providing a convenient test of the trend hypothesis without having to assume a model for the error generating process.

The asymptotic standard normality of z_λ enables approximate confidence bounds for β_1 to be constructed, which hold regardless of whether the errors are $I(0)$ or $I(1)$. If $c_{\alpha/2}$ is the $\alpha/2$ percentage point of the standard normal distribution, e.g., $c_{0.025} = 1.96$, then an approximate $(1 - \alpha)\%$ two-sided confidence interval for β_1 is given by

$$\hat{\beta}_{1,\lambda} \pm c_{\alpha/2} \frac{s_0 s_1}{(1 - \lambda(U,S))s_1 + \lambda(U,S)s_0} \tag{5.16}$$

where

$$\hat{\beta}_{1,\lambda} = \frac{(1 - \lambda(U,S))\hat{\beta}_1 s_1 + \lambda(U,S)\tilde{\beta}_1 s_0}{(1 - \lambda(U,S))s_1 + \lambda(U,S)s_0}$$

with $\hat{\beta}_{1,\lambda}$ being a consistent and asymptotically efficient estimator of β_1, again regardless of whether ε_t is $I(0)$ or $I(1)$.

5.20 In typical applications, the error specification $\varepsilon_t = \rho \varepsilon_{t-1} + a_t$ needs to be extended to incorporate additional autocorrelation, whereupon $\hat{\sigma}_\varepsilon^2$ and $\tilde{\sigma}_\nu^2$ may be replaced by their long-run variance counterparts by using (5.11) to compute s_0 and s_1 and, hence, z_λ and $\hat{\beta}_{1,\lambda}$.

5.21 HLT suggest using the DF-GLS statistic for U and the KPSS η_τ statistic for S, along with setting the constant in (5.15) to $\kappa = 0.00025$. In a typical case in which there is autocorrelation, the augmented versions of these tests should be employed.

5.22 The HLT approach has the advantage that it may be computed using only statistics that are readily available, but no claims can be made for its optimality and other tests may have better size and power properties. Two alternative approaches have been proposed by Bunzel and Vogelsang (2005) and Perron and Yabu (2009), but while the latter approach appears to have some good statistical properties, its resulting trend estimate is rather more complicated to obtain.

EXAMPLE 5.8 Estimating the Trend in Central England Temperatures Robustly

Fig. 5.7 shows the annual Central England temperature (CET) series. This is the longest available recorded instrumental temperature series in existence, beginning in 1659, and establishing its trend is clearly of great interest for debates concerning global warming. If it is assumed that deviations from a linear trend are $I(0)$, then estimating (5.8) with an autocorrelation correction obtains $\hat{\beta}_1 = 0.002749$ with $s_0 = 0.000745$, thus yielding $z_0 = 3.689$, which, when compared to a standard normal distribution, implies that the trend β_1 is significantly positive at $0.27°C$ per century.

On the other hand, assuming that the deviations are $I(1)$ obtains, from estimating (5.13) with an autocorrelation correction, $\tilde{\beta}_1 = 0.004777$, $s_1 = 0.007769$, and $z_1 = 0.615$, thus implying that although the estimate of the trend is nearly 50% higher than the $I(0)$ deviations estimate, it is nevertheless insignificantly different

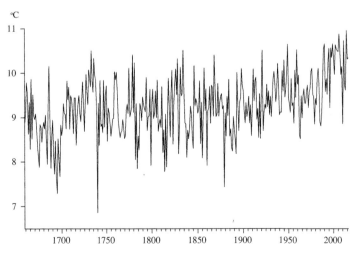

FIGURE 5.7   Central England temperatures, annual, 1659–2016.

from zero, a consequence of s_1 being over ten times as large as s_0. Determining which of the two estimates to use is not resolved by computing unit root and stationarity tests, for $DF - GLS = -9.212$ and $\eta_\tau = 0.189$, the former rejecting the unit root null at the 1% level, the latter rejecting the TS null at the 5% level!

This is clearly a situation when estimating the trend robustly is called for. With the information presented, we obtain $\lambda = 0.554$, $z_{0.554} = 1.987$, $\hat{\beta}_{1,0.554} = 0.002965$, and a 95% confidence interval for β_1 of 0.002965 ± 0.002925, i.e., approximately $0-0.6°C$ per century. The CET, therefore, has a trend that, with a p-value of .023, is a significantly positive $0.3°C$ per century.

FRACTIONAL DIFFERENCING AND LONG MEMORY

5.23 Our analysis has so far only considered cases where the order of differencing, d, is either zero, one, or possibly two. Concentrating on the first two cases, if $x_t \sim I(1)$ then its ACF declines linearly, whereas if $x_t \sim I(0)$ its ACF exhibits an exponential decline, so that observations far apart may be assumed to be independent, or at least nearly so. Many empirically observed time series, however, although appearing to satisfy the assumption of stationarity (perhaps after differencing), nevertheless seem to exhibit some dependence between distant observations that, although small, is by no means negligible. This may be termed *long range persistence* or *dependence*, although the term *long memory* is now popular.[6]

Such series have particularly been found in hydrology, where the long-range persistence of river flows is known as the Hurst effect (see, e.g., Mandelbrot and Wallis, 1969; Hosking, 1984), but many financial time series also exhibit similar characteristics of extremely long persistence. This may be characterized as a tendency for large values to be followed by further large values of the same sign, in such a way that the observations appear to go through a succession of "cycles," including long cycles whose length is comparable to the total sample size.

5.24 The class of ARIMA processes may be extended to model this type of long-range persistence by relaxing the restriction to just integer values of d, so allowing *fractional differencing* within the class of AR-fractionally integrated-MA (ARFIMA) processes. This notion of fractional differencing/integration seems to have been proposed independently by Granger and Joyeux (1980) and Hosking (1981) and is made operational by considering the binomial series expansion of ∇^d for any real $d > -1$:

$$
\begin{aligned}
\nabla^d = (1-B)^d &= \sum_{k=0}^{\infty} \frac{d!}{(d-k)!k!}(-B)^k \\
&= 1 - dB + \frac{d(d-1)}{2!}B^2 - \frac{d(d-1)(d-2)}{3!} + \cdots
\end{aligned}
\tag{5.17}
$$

With this expansion we may define the ARFIMA(0,d,0) process as

$$\nabla^d x_t = \left(1 - \pi_1 B - \pi_2 B^2 - \cdots\right)x_t = a_t \tag{5.18}$$

where, using the gamma function $\Gamma(n) = (n-1)!$, the π-weights are given by

$$\pi_j = \frac{\Gamma(j-d)}{\Gamma(-d)\Gamma(j+1)}$$

This process can, thus, be interpreted as an infinite autoregression and is often referred to as *fractional white noise*. Inverting (5.18) yields the infinite MA representation

$$x_t = \nabla^{-d} a_t = \left(1 - \psi_1 B - \psi_2 B^2 - \cdots\right)a_t$$

with

$$\psi_j = \frac{\Gamma(j+d)}{\Gamma(d)\Gamma(j+1)}$$

For $-1 < d < 0.5$, $d \neq 0$, the autocorrelations are given by

$$\rho_k = \frac{\Gamma(1-d)}{\Gamma(d)} \frac{\Gamma(k+d)}{\Gamma(k+1-d)} \approx \frac{\Gamma(1-d)}{\Gamma(d)} k^{2d-1} = A(d)k^{2d-1} \tag{5.19}$$

where Stirling's approximation for large k, $\Gamma(k+a)/\Gamma(k+b) \approx k^{a-b}$, has been used. The autocorrelations thus exhibit *hyperbolic* decay, the speed of which depends on d, and this property is also found in both the π- and ψ-weights. This decay, being a function of k^{2d-1}, is often referred to as a "power law" decay and will appear for *all* processes exhibiting long range persistence, and is not restricted to just ARFIMA processes (see Lieberman and Phillips, 2008).

Examples of this hyperbolic decay of the autocorrelations are shown in Fig. 5.8 and these may be contrasted with the autocorrelations from an ARMA model, which, for large k, are approximately of the form $A\theta^k$ with $|\theta| < 1$ (recall §**3.10**). These tend to zero at an exponential rate and thus decay quicker than the hyperbolic decline of the autocorrelations given by (5.19).

5.25 As is apparent from (5.19), the process (5.18) will be weakly stationary for $d < 0.5$ and invertible for $d > -0.5$. For $d \geq 0.5$ the variance of x_t is infinite and so the process is nonstationary, but arguably "less nonstationary" than a unit root process (see Robinson, 1994), so smoothly bridging the gulf between $I(0)$ and $I(1)$ processes. Smooth persistent trending behavior and positive dependencies are obtained only when d is positive. Processes having negative d are characterized by a nonsmooth form of persistence, often referred to as *antipersistence*, which is associated with negative short- and long-range dependencies.

These properties are also displayed by the more general ARFIMA(p,d,q) process, although parametric expressions for the π- and ψ-weights are particularly complicated: see Baillie (1996) for these, and Lieberman and Phillips

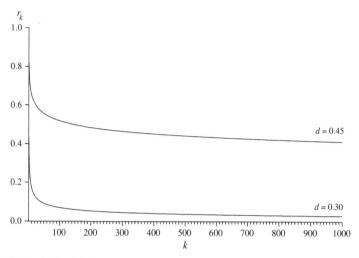

FIGURE 5.8 ACFs of ARIMA(0,d,0) processes with $d = 0.30$ and $d = 0.45$.

(2008) and Phillips (2009) for more general expressions concerning the auto-covariance functions of long memory processes.

5.26 As mentioned in §**5.23**, the long range persistence exhibited by frac-tionally differenced processes is often referred to as *long memory* and the intuition behind this concept and the limitations of the integer-d restriction emerge more clearly in the frequency domain representation of a time series.

While Wold's decomposition (3.2) provides a time domain representation of a stationary series as a linear filter of white noise, an equivalent represen-tation is given by its *spectral density*. Theorem 5 of Wold (1938) states that a necessary and sufficient condition for a stationary process to exist is for the autocorrelations ρ_k to be the coefficients of a nondecreasing function $F(\omega)$, such that $F(0) = 0$, $F(\pi) = \pi$, and

$$\rho_k = \frac{1}{\pi} \int_0^\pi \cos k\omega \cdot dF(\omega)$$

This expression can be inverted to yield the *Fourier transform*

$$F(\omega) = \omega + 2 \sum_{k=1}^\infty \frac{\rho_k}{k} \sin k\omega$$

which is also known as the generating function of the ρ_k. The convergence condition described in §**3.7** then implies that the derivative of $F(\omega)$ exists and is given by

$$f(\omega) = \frac{dF(\omega)}{d\omega} = \sum_{k=-\infty}^\infty \rho_k \cos k\omega = 1 + 2 \sum_{k=1}^\infty \rho_k \cos k\omega \tag{5.20}$$

$F(\omega)$ is known as the *integrated power spectrum* and $f(\omega)$ as the spectral density (or just *spectrum*), with ω being termed the *frequency*. Defining $z = e^{-i\omega}$ enables (5.20) to be written, using the well-known trigonometric Euler equation identity, as

$$f(\omega) = \sum_{k=-\infty}^{\infty} \rho_k z^k$$

5.27 For the AR(1) process $x_t = \phi x_{t-1} + a_t$, the spectrum is given by

$$f(\omega) = 1 + 2 \sum_{k=1}^{\infty} \phi^k \cos k\omega = \frac{\sigma_a^2}{2\pi} \frac{1 - \phi^2}{1 + \phi^2 - 2\phi \cos \omega} \qquad (5.21)$$

where σ^2 is the variance of the white noise innovation a_t. If, as is typically the case, ϕ is positive then the spectrum will be large at low frequencies ω and small at high frequencies, the reverse being true for ϕ negative: these are termed low- and high-frequency spectra respectively. If $\phi = 0$ the spectrum of white noise is obtained, this being simply the constant $\sigma^2/2\pi$ for all ω.

Clearly, if $\phi = 1$ then (5.21) is undefined, so that the spectrum does not exist for an integrated process. However, if $y_t = \nabla^d x_t$, where $x_t \sim I(d)$, then $y_t \sim I(0)$ and will have a well-defined spectrum of the form of (5.20), denoted $f_y(\omega)$, say. Although x_t does not strictly possess a spectrum, it can be thought of as having the "pseudo-spectrum"

$$f_x(\omega) = |1 - z|^{-2d} f_y(\omega) = \left(2 \sin|\omega/2|\right)^{-2d} f_y(\omega) \qquad (5.22)$$

which uses the result $|1 - z|^{-2d} = \left(2\sin\omega/2\right)^{-2d}$. If y_t has the ARMA representation $\phi(B)y_t = \theta(B)a_t$ then, because y_t is stationary, the limiting value of its spectrum $f_y(\omega)$, as ω becomes small, must be a positive constant, say

$$c = \frac{\sigma^2}{2\pi} \left(\frac{\theta(1)}{\phi(1)}\right) > 0$$

It then follows that, for ω small, $2\sin|\omega/2| \approx \omega$ and $f_x(\omega) \propto c\omega^{-2d}$, so that if $d = 1$ the pseudo-spectrum takes the form $f_x(\omega) \approx c\omega^{-2} \to \infty$ as $\omega \to 0$. If, however, d can take on noninteger values then a much richer range of spectral behavior at low frequencies becomes possible, allowing long memory behavior to be captured.

TESTING FOR FRACTIONAL DIFFERENCING

5.28 The "classic" approach to detecting the presence of long memory in a time series is to use the *range over standard deviation* or *rescaled range* (R/S) statistic. This was originally developed by Hurst (1951) when studying river discharges and a revised form was later proposed in an economic context by Mandelbrot (1972). It is defined as the range of partial sums of deviations of a time series from its mean, rescaled by its standard deviation, i.e.,

$$R_0 = \hat{\sigma}_0^{-1} \left[\max_{1 \le i \le T} \sum_{t=1}^{i} (x_t - \bar{x}) - \min_{1 \le i \le T} \sum_{t=1}^{i} (x_t - \bar{x}) \right] \quad \hat{\sigma}_0^2 = T^{-1} \sum_{t=1}^{T} (x_t - \bar{x})^2$$

(5.23)

The first term in brackets is the maximum of the partial sums of the first i deviations of x_t from the sample mean. Since the sum of all T deviations of the x_ts from their mean is zero, this maximum is always nonnegative. The second term is the minimum of the same sequence of partial sums, and hence is always nonpositive. The difference between the two quantities, called the "range" for obvious reasons, is therefore always nonnegative, so that $R_0 \ge 0$.

5.29 Although it has long been established that the R/S statistic is certainly able to detect long-range dependence, it is nevertheless sensitive to short-run influences. Consequently, any incompatibility between the data and the predicted behavior of the R/S statistic under the null of no long run dependence need not come from long memory, but may merely be a symptom of short-run autocorrelation.

The R/S statistic was, thus, modified by Lo (1991), who incorporated short-run dependence into the estimator of the standard deviation, replacing (5.23) with

$$R_q = \hat{\sigma}_q^{-1} \left[\max_{1 \le i \le T} \sum_{t=1}^{i} (x_t - \bar{x}) - \min_{1 \le i \le T} \sum_{t=1}^{i} (x_t - \bar{x}) \right]$$

(5.24)

where

$$\hat{\sigma}_q^2 = \hat{\sigma}_0^2 \left(1 + \frac{2}{T} \sum_{j=1}^{q} w_{qj} r_j \right) \quad w_{qj} = 1 - \frac{j}{q+1}, \quad q < T$$

The r_j, $j = 1, \ldots, q$, are the first q sample autocorrelations of x_t, which are given linearly declining weights in the "correction factor" designed to adjust the estimate of the standard deviation for short-run autocorrelation [cf. (5.10)].

Lo (1991) provides the assumptions and technical details to allow the asymptotic distribution of R_q to be obtained, showing that $T^{-1/2} R_q$ converges in distribution to a well-defined random variable whose significance levels are reported in Table II of his paper. The statistics are consistent against a class of long-range dependent alternatives that include all ARFIMA(p,d,q) models with $-0.5 \le d \le 0.5$.

5.30 Some difficulties have been encountered when applying the R/S statistic. The appropriate choice of q (i.e., how to distinguish between short- and long-range dependencies) remains an unresolved issue. There is also evidence that if the distribution of x_t is fat-tailed then the sampling distribution of R_q is shifted to the left relative to the asymptotic distribution. This would imply that rejection rates in favor of $d < 0$ (antipersistence) are above the nominal sizes given by the asymptotic distribution, whereas rejection rates in favor of $d > 0$ (persistent long memory) are below the nominal size. Lo, consequently, argues that the R/S approach should best be regarded as a kind of exploratory test that may complement, and come prior to, a more comprehensive analysis of long-range dependence.

5.31 An obvious approach to testing for fractional differencing is to construct tests against the null of either $d = 1$ or $d = 0$. ADF and nonparametric tests of $d = 1$ and KPSS tests of $d = 0$ are consistent against fractional d alternatives, but have the drawback that rejection of the respective nulls cannot be taken as evidence of the presence of fractional d.

Extensions of the Dickey–Fuller testing approach have, thus, been proposed, which evaluate the null hypothesis $\delta = 0$ in the model $\nabla^{d+\delta} x_t = a_t$. Breitung and Hassler (2002), building upon the Lagrange Multiplier (LM) approach of Agiakloglou and Newbold (1994), show that a simple test of this null is the t-statistic testing $\phi = 0$ from the regression

$$\nabla^d x_t = \phi x_{t-1}^* + a_t \qquad (5.25)$$

where

$$x_{t-1}^* = \sum_{j=1}^{t-1} j^{-1} \nabla^d x_{t-j}$$

Note that when $d = 1$, $x_{t-1} = \nabla x_1 + \cdots + \nabla x_{t-1}$, so that the only difference between (5.25) and the simple DF regression is the introduction of the weights j^{-1} in the definition of the regressor. The t-statistic has the advantage of being asymptotically standard normal, so that testing is immediate. To incorporate deterministic components and autocorrelation, a first-stage regression may be performed, e.g.,

$$\nabla^d x_t = \hat{\alpha}_0 + \hat{\alpha}_1 t + \sum_{i=1}^{p} \hat{\beta}_i \nabla^d x_{t-i} + \hat{\varepsilon}_t$$

from which the regressor

$$\varepsilon_{t-1}^* = \sum_{j=1}^{t-p-1} j^{-1} \hat{\varepsilon}_{t-j}$$

is defined and the second-stage regression

$$\varepsilon_t = \phi \varepsilon_{t-1}^* + \sum_{i=1}^{p} \gamma_i \nabla^d x_{t-i} + a_t \qquad (5.26)$$

estimated. The LM t-statistic testing $\phi = 0$ is again standard normal.

Dolado et al. (2002) propose a similar DF regression to (5.25) for testing the null that $x_t \sim I(d_0)$ against the alternative that $x_t \sim I(d_1)$, where d_0 and d_1 are real numbers. Their "*FD-F*" regression is

$$\nabla^{d_0} x_t = \phi \nabla^{d_1} x_{t-1} + a_t$$

in which $\nabla^{d_0} x_t$ and $\nabla^{d_1} x_{t-1}$ have been differenced according to their order of integration under the null and alternative hypothesis, respectively. When $d_0 = 1$ and $d_1 = 0$ the conventional Dickey–Fuller testing framework is obtained, so that the t-statistic testing $\phi = 0$ will require DF critical values. More generally, the *FD-F* test statistics will be standard normal if the processes under both hypotheses are stationary ($d_0, d_1 < 0.5$) or when the process is nonstationary under the null ($d_0 \geq 0.5$) and $d_0 - d_1 < 0.5$; otherwise they will have nonstandard distributions, for which critical values are provided by Dolado et al. (2002).

ESTIMATING THE FRACTIONAL DIFFERENCING PARAMETER

5.32 A drawback of the *FD-F* procedure is that, if d_1 is not known a priori, as it is in the standard Dickey–Fuller case, then a consistent estimate must be provided. A variety of estimators have been suggested, many of which involve quite complex calculations. Perhaps the simplest is suggested by R/S analysis and is

$$\tilde{d} = \frac{\log R_0}{\log T} - 0.5$$

A popular and relatively simple estimator is the log-periodogram regression proposed by Geweke and Porter-Hudak (1983, GPH). From (5.22) the spectral density of x_t can be written as

$$f_x(\omega) = \left(4 \sin^2 \left(\frac{\omega}{2} \right) \right)^{-d} f_y(\omega)$$

or, on taking logs,

$$\log f_x(\omega) = \log f_y(\omega) - d \log 4 \sin^2 \left(\frac{\omega}{2} \right)$$

This leads GPH to propose estimating d as (minus) the slope estimator of the regression

$$\log I(\omega_j) = a - d \log 4 \sin^2 \left(\frac{\omega}{2} \right) \tag{5.27}$$

where

$$I(\omega_j) = 2\hat{\sigma}_0^2 \left(1 + 2 \sum_{s=1}^{T-1} r_s \cos s\omega_j \right)$$

is the periodogram estimate of $f_x(\omega)$ at frequencies $\omega_j = 2\pi j/T, j = 1, \ldots, K$, for a suitable choice of K, typically $K = \left[T^{0.5}\right]$. It has been shown that the GPH estimator $\hat{d}$ is consistent for $-0.5 < d < 1$ and asymptotically normal, so that the estimated standard error attached to $\hat{d}$ can be used for inference. Alternatively, the asymptotic result $\sqrt{K}\left(\hat{d} - d\right) \sim N\left(0, \pi^2/24\right)$ may be used.

5.33 With an estimate $\hat{d}$, the "truncated" form of (5.17) may be used to compute the fractionally differenced series

$$y_t = \nabla \hat{d} x_t = \sum_{k=0}^{t-1} \frac{\hat{d}\,!}{\left(\hat{d} - k\right)!k\,!}(-1)^k x_{t-k}$$

where it is explicitly assumed that $y_t = 0$ for $t \leq 0$, and this series can then be modeled as an ARMA process in the usual way.

5.34 Several other estimators of d have been proposed, going under the name of *semiparametric* estimators, but these typically require numerical optimization methods, while it is also possible to estimate d jointly with the ARMA parameters in the ARFIMA process, although specialized software is required for this, which is now available in *EViews 10*.

EXAMPLE 5.9 Persistence in the Nile River Flow

The impetus for H.E. Hurst's initial statistical analysis of persistence in river flow (Hurst, 1951: recall §**5.22**) was provided by his position as Director General of the Physical Department of Egypt, where he was responsible for, amongst other things, studying the hydrology of the Nile basin. For thousands of years the Nile has helped to sustain civilization in an otherwise barren desert, but the economic development of the basin has been severely impeded by the river's regular floods and irregular flows.[7] Hurst and his department were consequently tasked with devising a method of water control for the entire Nile basin, from its sources in the African great lakes, through the Ethiopian plains, to the delta on the Mediterranean, and analyzing the river flow was, thus, central to this.

Fig. 5.9 shows the mean annual flow of the Nile from 1872 to 1970 along with its SACF, which is accompanied by a 2.5% upper bound of $1.96/\sqrt{T} = 0.20$ under the assumption that river flow is i.i.d. (recall §**3.30**). All the first 20 sample autocorrelations are positive, with 11 of the first 13 significantly so, and the overall pattern is one of approximately hyperbolic decline, thus indicating the possibility of long memory in Nile river flow.

The calculation of the LM t-statistic for testing the null that $d = 0$ against the fractional alternative $d > 0$ proceeds with a first-stage regression in which river flow is regressed on a constant and two lags. The residuals are then used in the augmented regression (5.26) to yield $\hat{\phi} = 0.313$ with a standard error of 0.076, thus producing a t-statistic of 4.09, which clearly rejects the null in favor of a positive value of d.

Estimating an ARFIMA(0, d, 0) process yields $\hat{d} = 0.361$, which has an asymptotic standard error of 0.071, so providing evidence in favor of stationary long

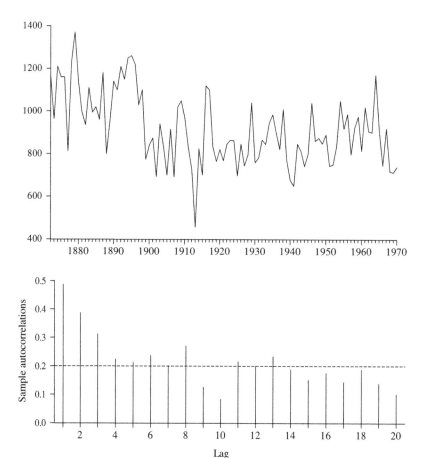

FIGURE 5.9 Mean annual flow of the Nile, 1872–1970, and accompanying SACF with 95% confidence upper bound under the i.i.d. null hypothesis.

memory. Note that the residuals from this model show no evidence of any remaining autocorrelation, so that river flow may indeed be characterized as fractional white noise. The GPH estimate of d is $\hat{d} = 0.471$.

EXAMPLE 5.10 Is There Long Memory in the *S&P 500* Stock Market Index?

Fig. 5.10 shows, on a logarithmic scale, the daily price of the *S&P 500* stock market index from January 1928 to August 1991, a series of $T = 17054$ observations that has been analyzed, in considerable detail, by Granger and his co-workers (see, e.g., Ding et al., 1993). The logarithms of the index are, not surprisingly, nonstationary and are, in fact, DS, with $\tau_\tau = -2.58$ and having a p-value of just .29.

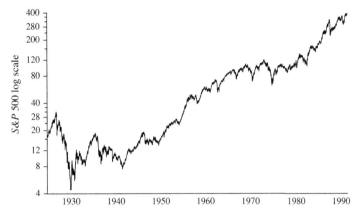

FIGURE 5.10   *S&P 500* stock market index: daily, January 1928−August 1991.

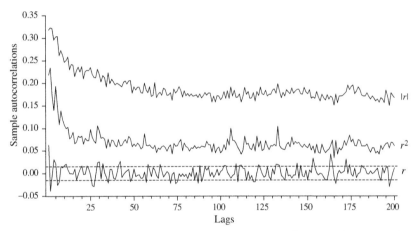

FIGURE 5.11   SACFs of daily returns (r), squared daily returns (r^2), and absolute returns ($|r|$) with 95% confidence bands under the i.i.d. hypothesis.

On denoting the index as p_t, the daily return may be defined as $r_t = \nabla \log p_t$, and Fig. 5.11 shows the first 200 lags of the SACFs for r_t and the squared and absolute returns, r_t^2 and $|r_t|$, along with $\pm 1.96/\sqrt{T} = \pm 0.015$ bounds, which correspond to a 95% confidence interval for the estimated sample autocorrelations if r_t is i.i.d. A considerable number of sample autocorrelations lie outside these bounds, particularly noticeable ones being the first, estimated to be 0.063, and the second, -0.039, so that returns cannot be regarded as a realization from an i.i.d. process.

If r_t really was an i.i.d. process then any transformation, such as r_t^2 or $|r_t|$, would also be i.i.d. These transformations would then also have sample autocorrelations with standard errors $1/\sqrt{T}$ under the i.i.d. null if r_t^2 has finite variance and $|r_t|$ has finite kurtosis. In Fig. 5.11, it is seen that all sample autocorrelations

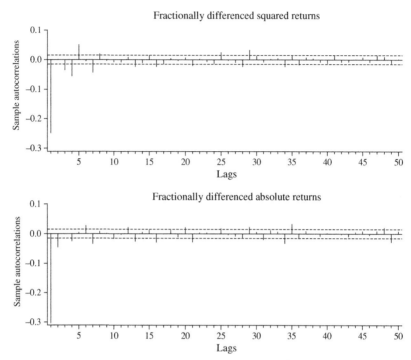

FIGURE 5.12   SACFs of fractionally differenced squared and absolute returns.

for these transformations also fall well outside the i.i.d. 95% confidence bands and, moreover, that they are all positive, with those for absolute returns always being larger than those for squared returns for every one of the first 200 lags. The daily return on the *S&P 500* is clearly not an i.i.d. process, but an interesting question is whether the squared and absolute returns display long memory, for the declines in the SACFs of these transformations shown in Fig. 5.11 are clearly indicative of such a property, being neither linearly nor exponentially declining but somewhere "in between."

R/S statistics with $q = 4$ were calculated to be 1.42, 10.17, and 17.82 for actual, squared and absolute returns, respectively, the latter two being highly significant and, hence, suggestive of long-range persistence. GPH estimates of d, using the common choice of $K = \left[T^{0.5}\right] = 130$ to compute the periodogram in (5.21), were $\hat{d} = 0.04$, $\hat{d} = 0.43$, and $\hat{d} = 0.47$, respectively: since the standard error in each case is 0.06 then again there is evidence that squared and absolute returns exhibit long memory. Fig. 5.12 shows the SACFs of fractionally differenced squared and absolute returns computed using these estimates of d, and these clearly indicate that long memory has been eradicated.

However, the GPH estimates of d produce fitted autocorrelations for squared and absolute returns that are much larger than the sample autocorrelations (see Ding and Granger, 1996, Fig. 4) and this has led to a variety of more sophisticated models being fitted to these series (see Ding et al., 1993; Granger et al., 2000).

ENDNOTES

1. The seminal article on what has become a vast topic, and which gives the distribution and test their eponymous names, is Dickey and Fuller (1979). The statistical theory underlying the distribution is too advanced to be considered here, but see, for example, Patterson (2010) and, at a rather more technical level, Patterson (2011). As will be seen from these texts (and from §§**5.12 to 5.16**), there are now a considerable number of unit root tests, differing in both their size and power properties. Nevertheless, the original Dickey−Fuller tests remain popular and widely used.

2. Strictly, τ_μ tests $\phi = 1$ *conditional* upon $\theta_0 = 0$, so that the model under the null is the drift-less random walk $x_t = x_{t-1} + a_t$. The joint hypothesis $\theta_0 = 0$, $\phi = 1$ may be tested by constructing a standard F-test, although clearly the statistic, typically denoted Φ, will not follow the conventional $F(2, T - 2)$ distribution. For large samples, the 5% and 1% critical values of the appropriate distribution are 4.59 and 6.53, rather than the 2.99 and 4.60 critical values of the $F(2, T - 2)$ distribution: see Dickey and Fuller (1981).

3. This generalization is seen most clearly when $p = 2$, so that

$$x_t = \theta_0 + \phi_1 x_{t-1} + \phi_2 x_{t-2} + a_t$$

This can be written as

$$\begin{aligned} x_t &= \theta_0 + \phi_1 x_{t-1} + \phi_2 x_{t-1} - \phi_2 x_{t-1} + \phi_2 x_{t-2} + a_t \\ &= \theta_0 + (\phi_1 + \phi_2) x_{t-1} - \phi_2 \Delta x_{t-1} + a_t \\ &= \theta_0 + \phi x_{t-1} + \delta_1 \Delta x_{t-1} + a_t \end{aligned}$$

which is (5.5) with $k = 1$.

4. The mean deviation form of the implied stationary AR(2) model for the \$−£ rate is estimated to be

$$x_t = 1.713 + 1.060(x_{t-1} - 1.713) - 0.061(x_{t-2} - 1.713) + a_t$$

which has two real roots of 0.9998 and 0.06.

5. A consistent test is one for which the power of rejecting a false null hypothesis tends to unity asymptotically, i.e., as the sample size becomes infinite.

6. An interesting historical account of "long range dependence," "long range persistence," and "long memory" is provided by Graves et al. (2016), where a much wider perspective of the topic is given than can be provided here.

7. These were later colorfully named the "Joseph Effect" by Mandelbrot and Wallis (1968), a term which alludes to the Old Testament story of Joseph's interpretation of the Pharaoh's dream of seven fat cows and seven gaunt ones to mean that there would be seven prosperous years followed by seven lean ones, this being an example of "long memory" in practice.

Chapter 6

Breaking and Nonlinear Trends

Chapter Outline

BREAKING TREND MODELS

6.1 The trend stationary (TS) versus difference stationary (DS) dichotomy and associated testing procedure outlined in §§**5.9**−**5.10** is both simple and straightforward to implement, but is it necessarily realistic? Could the TS alternative of a "global" linear trend be too simplistic in some situations, thus indicating that a more sophisticated trend function might be warranted? Often a more plausible candidate for a trend is a linear function that "breaks" at one or more points in time.

There are several ways in which a trend may break. Assume, for simplicity, that there is a single break at a *known* point in time T_b^c $(1 < T_b^c < T)$, with the superscript "c" denoting the "correct" break date, a distinction that will become important in due course. The simplest *breaking trend* model is the "level shift" in which the level of x_t shifts from μ_0 to $\mu_1 = \mu_0 + \mu$ at T_b^c. This may be parameterized as

$$x_t = \mu_0 + (\mu_1 - \mu_0)\text{DU}_t^c + \beta_0 t + \varepsilon_t = \mu_0 + \mu\text{DU}_t^c + \beta_0 t + \varepsilon_t \qquad (6.1)$$

where $\text{DU}_t^c = 0$ if $t \leq T_b^c$ and $\text{DU}_t^c = 1$ if $t > T_b^c$. This shift variable may be written more concisely as $\text{DU}_t^c = \mathbf{1}(t > T_b^c)$, where $\mathbf{1}(\cdot)$ is the indicator function, so that it takes the value 1 if the argument is true and 0 otherwise. Another possibility is the "changing growth" model in which the slope of the trend changes from β_0 to $\beta_1 = \beta_0 + \beta$ at T_b^c without a change in level. In this case, the trend function is joined at the time of the break and is often referred to as a *segmented trend*. This model may be parameterized as

$$x_t = \mu_0 + \beta_0 t + (\beta_1 - \beta_0)\text{DT}_t^c + \varepsilon_t = \mu_0 + \beta_0 t + \beta\text{DT}_t^c + \varepsilon_t \qquad (6.2)$$

Applied Time Series Analysis. DOI: https://doi.org/10.1016/B978-0-12-813117-6.00006-5
103

where $\mathrm{DT}_t^c = \mathbf{1}(t > T_t^c)(t - T_t^c)$ models the shift in growth. Both forms of break could, of course, occur simultaneously, so that we would then have the combined model

$$
\begin{aligned}
x_t &= \mu_0 + (\mu_1 - \mu_0)\mathrm{DU}_t^c + \beta_0 t + (\beta_1 - \beta_0)\mathrm{DT}_t^c + \varepsilon_t \\
&= \mu_0 + \mu \mathrm{DU}_t^c + \beta_0 t + \beta \mathrm{DT}_t^c + \varepsilon_t
\end{aligned}
\tag{6.3}
$$

so that x_t undergoes both a shift in level and slope at T_b^c.

6.2   In models (6.1)–(6.3) the error process ε_t has been left unspecified. An obvious choice is that it is an ARMA process, say $\phi(B)\varepsilon_t = \theta(B)a_t$, in which case (6.1)–(6.3) will be *breaking trend-stationary* models. Suppose that the autoregressive polynomial can be factorized as $\phi(B) = (1 - \phi B)\phi_1(B)$. If $\phi(B)$ contains a unit root then $\phi = 1$ and $\phi(B) = \nabla\phi_1(B)$ (cf. §**4.12**), with (6.1) becoming

$$
\nabla x_t = \beta_0 + \mu \nabla \mathrm{DU}_t^c + \varepsilon_t^* = \beta_0 + \mu D(\mathrm{TB}^c)_t + \varepsilon_t^*
\tag{6.4}
$$

where $\phi_1(B)\varepsilon_t^* = \theta(B)a_t$ and where we have defined $D(\mathrm{TB}^c)_t = \nabla\mathrm{DU}_t^c = \mathbf{1}(t = T_b^c + 1)$. This model, therefore, specifies x_t to be an $I(1)$ process with drift plus a dummy variable that takes the value of one at T_b^c and zero elsewhere. Similarly, a unit root in the error process for (6.2) leads to

$$
\nabla x_t = \beta_0 + \beta\nabla\mathrm{DT}_t^c + \varepsilon_t^* = \beta_0 + \beta\mathrm{DU}_t^c + \varepsilon_t^*
\tag{6.5}
$$

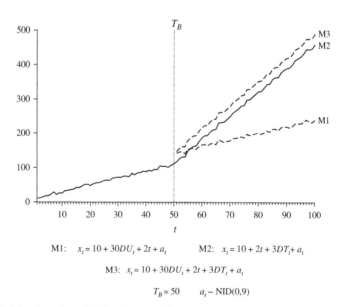

M1: $x_t = 10 + 30DU_t + 2t + a_t$ M2: $x_t = 10 + 2t + 3DT_t + a_t$

M3: $x_t = 10 + 30DU_t + 2t + 3DT_t + a_t$

$T_B = 50$ $a_t \sim NID(0,9)$

FIGURE 6.1   Examples of TS breaking trend functions.

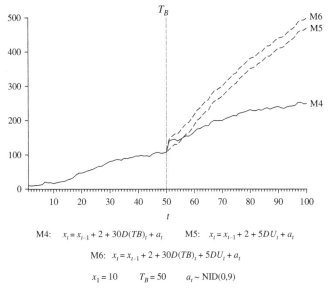

M4: $x_t = x_{t-1} + 2 + 30D(TB)_t + a_t$ M5: $x_t = x_{t-1} + 2 + 5DU_t + a_t$

M6: $x_t = x_{t-1} + 2 + 30D(TB)_t + 5DU_t + a_t$

$x_1 = 10$ $T_B = 50$ $a_t \sim \text{NID}(0,9)$

FIGURE 6.2   Examples of breaking DS processes.

so that the drift changes from β_0 to β_1 at the break point T_b^c. The combined model then becomes

$$\nabla x_t = \beta_0 + \mu \text{D(TB}^c)_t + \beta \text{DU}_t^c + \varepsilon_t^* \qquad (6.6)$$

Examples of these types of breaking trend functions are shown in Fig. 6.1 (for TS breaking trends) and Fig. 6.2 (for breaking DS processes).

BREAKING TRENDS AND UNIT ROOT TESTS

6.3   How can we distinguish between TS breaking trends and breaking DS processes? Clearly unit root tests should be applicable, but what is the influence of breaking trends upon such tests? Perron (1989, 1990: see also Perron and Vogelsang, 1993) was the first to consider the impact of breaking trends and shifting levels on unit root tests, showing that standard tests of the type discussed in Chapter 5, Unit Roots, Difference and Trend Stationarity, and Fractional Differencing, are not consistent against TS alternatives when the trend function contains a shift in slope. Here the estimate of the largest autoregressive root is biased toward unity and, in fact, the unit root null becomes impossible to reject, even asymptotically. Although the tests are consistent against a shift in the intercept of the trend function, their power is nevertheless reduced considerably because the limiting value of the estimated autoregressive root is inflated above its true value.

6.4 Perron (1989) consequently extended the Dickey–Fuller unit root testing strategy to ensure consistency against shifting trend functions by developing two asymptotically equivalent procedures. The first uses initial regressions in which x_t is detrended according to either model (A), the level shift (6.1); model (B), the segmented trend (6.2); or model (C), the combined model (6.3). Thus, let $\tilde{x}_t^i$, $i = A, B, C$, be the residuals from a regression of x_t on (1) $i = A$: a constant, t, and DU_t^c; (2) $i = B$: a constant, t, and DT_t^c; and (3) $i = C$: a constant, t, DU_t^c, and DT_t^c. For models (A) and (C) a modified ADF regression (cf. (5.5)) is then estimated:

$$\tilde{x}_t^i = \tilde{\phi}^i \tilde{x}_{t-1}^i + \sum_{j=0}^{k} \gamma_j D(TB^c)_{t-j} \sum_{j=1}^{k} \delta_j \nabla \tilde{x}_{t-j}^i \quad i = A, C \qquad (6.7)$$

and a t-test of $\tilde{\phi}^i = 1$ is performed (t^i, $i = A, C$). The inclusion of the $k + 1$ dummy variables $D(TB^c)_t, \ldots, D(TB^c)_{t-k}$ is required to ensure that the limiting distributions of t^A and t^C are invariant to the correlation structure of the errors (see Perron and Vogelsang, 1993). For model (B) the "unmodified" ADF regression

$$\tilde{x}_t^B = \tilde{\phi}^i \tilde{x}_{t-1}^B + \sum_{j=1}^{k} \delta_j \nabla \tilde{x}_{t-j}^B + a_t \qquad (6.8)$$

may be estimated to obtain t^B.

6.5 Asymptotic critical values for t^i, $i = A, C$, are provided by Perron (1989, Tables IV.B, VI.B), and for t^B by Perron and Vogelsang (1993, Table 1). These depend on where the break occurs and so are a function of the *break fraction* $\tau^c = T_b^c/T$. For example, for model (A) and $\tau^c = 0.5$ (a break known to occur at the midpoint of the sample), the 5%, 2.5%, and 1% critical values of t^A for testing $\tilde{\phi}^A = 1$ are -3.76, -4.01, and -4.32, respectively, while if the break occurs near the start ($\tau^c = 0.1$) or end ($\tau^c = 0.9$) of the sample, then these critical values are smaller in absolute value, being -3.68, -3.93, -4.30 and -3.69, -3.97, and -4.27, respectively. This is to be expected because the critical values are identical to the standard DF critical values when $\tau^c = 0$ or 1, since in these extreme cases no break can occur. Models (B) and (C) have critical values that are larger in absolute value: for the latter model the midpoint critical values of t^C for testing $\tilde{\phi}^C = 1$ are -4.24, -4.53, and -4.90. All statistics are naturally larger in absolute value, for a given size of test, than the standard DF critical values.

6.6 Perron (1989) pointed out a possible disadvantage of the prior detrending approach, which is that it implies that the change in the trend function occurs instantaneously, so that the shift is akin to what is known as an "additive outlier" (AO) effect in the literature on outliers in time series (see, e.g., Tsay, 1986a). A transition period in which the series reacts gradually to a shock to the trend function may thus be considered. Taking model (A) as an example, this may be specified as:

$$x_t = \mu_0 + \mu\psi(B)\mathrm{DU}_t^c + \beta_0 t + \varepsilon_t$$

where $\psi(B)$ is stationary and invertible with $\psi(0) = 1$. The immediate impact of the shock is μ but the long-run change is $\mu\psi(1)$.

6.7   One way to incorporate such a gradual change into the trend function is to suppose that x_t responds to a trend shock in the same way as it reacts to any other shock. Recalling the ARMA specification for ε_t made in §**6.2**, viz., $\phi(B)\varepsilon_t = \theta(B)a_t$, this would imply that $\psi(B) = \phi(B)^{-1}\theta(B)$, which would be analogous to an "innovation outlier" (IO) model. With this specification, tests for the presence of a unit root can be performed using a direct extension of the ADF regression framework to incorporate dummy variables as appropriate:

$$x_t = \mu^A + \theta^A \mathrm{DU}_t^c + \beta^A t + d^A \mathrm{D(TB}^c)_t + \phi^A x_{t-1} + \sum_{i=1}^{k} \delta_i \nabla x_{t-i} + a_t \qquad (6.9)$$

$$x_t = \mu^B + \theta^B \mathrm{DU}_t^c + \beta^B t + \gamma^B \mathrm{DT}_t^c + \phi^B x_{t-1} + \sum_{i=1}^{k} \delta_i \nabla x_{t-i} + a_t \qquad (6.10)$$

$$x_t = \mu^C + \theta^C \mathrm{DU}_t^c + \beta^C t + \gamma^C \mathrm{DT}_t^c + d^C \mathrm{D(TB}^c)_t + \phi^C x_{t-1} + \sum_{i=1}^{k} \delta_i \nabla x_{t-i} + a_t$$

$$(6.11)$$

The null hypothesis of a unit root imposes the following parameter restrictions on each model: Model (A): $\phi^A = 1$, $\theta^A = \beta^A = 0$; Model (B): $\phi^B = 1$, $\beta^B = \gamma^B = 0$; and Model (C): $\phi^C = 1$, $\beta^C = \gamma^C = 0$. The asymptotic distributions for testing $\phi^A = 1$ and $\phi^C = 1$ are the same as those for $\tilde{\phi}^A = 1$ and $\tilde{\phi}^C = 1$ from (6.7), but the correspondence does not hold for the t-statistic from (6.10). Indeed, Perron argues that testing the segmented trend model should only be done using (6.8).

EXAMPLE 6.1 The Great Crash, the Oil Price Shock, and ADF Tests of Breaking Trend Processes

A key assumption in Perron's testing procedure is that the break date T_b^c is assumed to be known or, equivalently, that the shock producing the break in trend is exogenously determined. Perron's context was that of the United States economy during the 20th century and he postulated that two exogenous shocks to the economy had occurred—the Great (stock market) Crash of 1929 and the oil price shock of 1973. Fig. 6.3 shows the logarithms of the *S&P 500* stock market index annually from 1871 to 2016 with a breaking trend of the form $\tilde{x}_t^C$ with $T_b^c = 59$ (1929) superimposed, which clearly shows the potential for a breaking TS process to adequately model the evolution of the index.

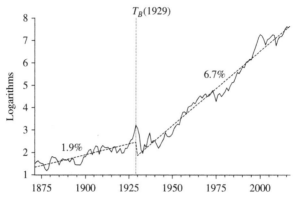

FIGURE 6.3 *S&P 500* index, 1871−2016, with breaking trend at 1929.

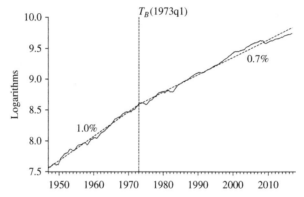

FIGURE 6.4 United States real GNP, quarterly 1947−2016, and segmented trend with break at 1973q1.

Estimating (6.11) with $k = 1$ obtains $\tilde{\phi}^C = 0.757\,(0.045)$ with $t^C = -5.38$, which, with $\tau^c = 58/145 = 0.4$, is significant at the 1% level. Furthermore, β^C and γ^C are both significantly different from zero, so that overall, convincing evidence is provided that the logarithms of the *S&P 500* index can indeed be modeled as a TS process with a one-time break at 1929. As shown in Fig. 6.3, the pre-break trend growth rate of the index is 1.9% per annum, while post-break it is 6.7%, the Crash also producing a 45% fall in the trend level of the index.

Fig. 6.4 shows quarterly observations on the logarithms of the United States real GNP from 1947 to 2016, with a segmented trend $\tilde{x}_t^B$ with a break at 1973q1 ($\lambda^c = 105/284 = 0.37 \approx 0.4$) superimposed. Here the pre-break trend growth rate is 1.0% per quarter while post-break it is reduced to 0.7%. Estimating (6.8) with $k = 2$ obtains $\tilde{\phi}^B = 0.960(0.014)$ and $t^B = -2.86$. As the 5% critical value is -3.91, this statistic is clearly insignificant and, hence, we cannot reject the unit root null hypothesis. This contrasts with Perron's original finding that a unit root could be rejected in favor of a TS segmented break model of the form of Model (B), but this was based on a sample period that ended in 1986q3.[1] Clearly, the accumulation of another 30 years of data has altered the conclusion in favor of breaking difference stationarity, the estimated form of (6.5) being:

$$\nabla x_t = \underset{(0.0011)}{0.0099} - \underset{(0.0017)}{0.0034} \, \mathrm{DU}_t^c + \varepsilon_t$$

$$\varepsilon_t = \underset{(0.048)}{0.350} \, \varepsilon_{t-1} + a_t$$

This implies that the logarithms of real GNP follow a correlated random walk with a one-time shift in the drift from 1.0% per quarter to 0.65% in 1973q1.

6.8 On the face of it, the finding that the *S&P 500* index may be characterized as a breaking TS process looks odd, as it would suggest that (the logarithms) of stock prices evolve as transitory deviations from a linear trend (albeit with a single break at the Great Crash) and, hence, would allow traders to bet successfully on a reversal of price whenever the index moved too far away from the trend line, in sharp contrast to the findings for the UK *All Share Index* in Example 5.4.

Perron (1989) argued, however, that the rejection of the null hypothesis of a unit root, conditional on the possibility of shifts in the underlying trend function at known dates, does *not* imply that the series can necessarily be modeled as stationary fluctuations around a completely deterministic trend function. To do this, Perron invoked the general statistical principle that a rejection of a null hypothesis does not imply the acceptance of any specific alternative hypothesis. What Perron had in mind was the class of maintained hypotheses that could be parameterized as

$$\begin{aligned} x_t &= \eta_t + \varepsilon_t & \eta_t &= \mu_t + \beta_t t \\ \nabla \mu_t &= v(B) v_t & \nabla \beta_t &= \omega(B) w_t \end{aligned} \tag{6.12}$$

where $\phi(B)\varepsilon_t = \theta(B)a_t$. The intercept and slope of the trend function, μ_t and β_t, are taken to be integrated processes with $v(B)$ and $\omega(B)$ being stationary and invertible. However, the timing and occurrence of the shocks v_t and w_t are assumed to be sporadic relative to the sequence of innovations a_t, perhaps being Poisson processes with arrival rates specified such that their occurrences are rare relative to the frequency of the realizations in the a_t sequence.

6.9 The intuitive idea behind the model (6.12) is that the coefficients of the trend function are determined by long-term "fundamentals" which rarely change. The exogeneity assumption about the changes in the trend function is then a device that allows us to take these rare shocks out of the noise and into the trend without having to model specifically the stochastic behavior of μ_t and β_t. Perron's framework is then to test whether the noise ε_t is an integrated process or not by removing those events that occur at dates where nonzero values of v_t and w_t are believed to have occurred and to model these as part of the trend function.

UNIT ROOTS TESTS WHEN THE BREAK DATE IS UNKNOWN

6.10   The procedure set out in §§**6.3**−**6.5** is only valid when the break date is known independently of the data, for if a systematic search for a break is carried out then the limiting distributions of the tests are no longer appropriate. Problems also occur if an incorrect break date is selected exogenously, with the tests then suffering size distortions and loss of power.

Consequently, several approaches have been developed that treat the occurrence of the break date as unknown and needing to be estimated: see, for example, Zivot and Andrews (1992), Perron (1997), and Vogelsang and Perron (1998). Thus, suppose now that the correct break date T_b^c is unknown. Clearly, if this is the case then the models of §§**6.3**−**6.5** are not able to be used until some break date, say $\hat{T}_b$, is selected, since none of the dummy variables that these models require can be defined until this selection has been made.

6.11   Two data-dependent methods for choosing $\hat{T}_b$ have been considered, both of which involve estimating the appropriate detrended AO regression, (6.7) or (6.8), or IO regression (6.9−6.11), for all possible break dates. The first method chooses $\hat{T}_b$ as the break date that is most likely to reject the unit root hypothesis, which is the date for which the t-statistic for testing $\phi = 1$ is minimized (i.e., is most negative).

The second approach involves choosing $\hat{T}_b$ as the break date for which some statistic that tests the significance of the break parameters is maximized. This is equivalent to minimizing the residual sum of squares across all possible regressions, albeit after some preliminary trimming has been performed, that is, if only break fractions $\tau = T_b/T$ between $0 < \tau_{min}, \tau_{max} < 1$ are considered.

6.12   Having selected $\hat{T}_b$ by one of these methods, the procedure set out in §§**6.3**−**6.5** may then be applied conditional upon this choice. Critical values may be found in Vogelsang and Perron (1998) for a variety of cases: typically, they are more negative than the critical values that hold when the break date is known to be at T_b^c.

An important limitation with both these approaches to selecting the break point endogenously is that it must be assumed that no break occurs under the null hypothesis of a unit root, so that $\mu = \beta = 0$ in (6.4)−(6.6), with the break only occurring under the alternative. Vogelsang and Perron (1998) provide some results on what happens to the limiting distributions of unit root tests when μ and β are nonzero under the null, but a full treatment was not developed until Kim and Perron (2009). Unfortunately, the correct testing procedure in this more general framework is rather difficult to implement and is too advanced to be discussed here.[2]

EXAMPLE 6.2 Determining a Break Point for United States Stock Prices

The minimum unit root method of selecting the break point for the *S&P 500* index does indeed select 1929, which yields a DF statistic of −5.11 with a marginal significance level of 0.06. Maximizing the significance of a test on the break parameters also selects 1929.

ROBUST TESTS FOR A BREAKING TREND

6.13   Of course, the broken trend will typically be of interest in itself, and so it is natural for the robust trend analysis of §§**5.17–5.22** to have been extended to cover such specifications, most notably by Harvey, Leybourne, and Taylor (HLT, 2009). If the break date is known to be at T_b^c with break fraction τ_c then, focusing on the segmented trend model (B), the HLT method is extended by focusing on autocorrelation corrected t-tests of $\beta = 0$ in (6.2) and (6.5), which we denote as $t_0(\tau^c)$ and $t_1(\tau^c)$. A weighted average of these two statistics is again considered,

$$t_\lambda = \lambda(S_0(\tau^c), S_1(\tau^c)) \times |t_0(\tau^c)| + (1 - \lambda(S_0(\tau^c), S_1(\tau^c))) \times |t_1(\tau^c)| \quad (6.13)$$

with the weight function now being defined as

$$\lambda(S_0(\tau^c), S_1(\tau^c)) = \exp\left(-(500 S_0(\tau^c) S_1(\tau^c))^2\right)$$

Here $S_0(\tau^c)$ and $S_1(\tau^c)$ are KPSS η_τ statistics (cf. §**5.16**) computed from the residuals of (6.2) and (6.5) respectively. Under $H_0 : \beta = 0$, t_λ will be asymptotically standard normal.

6.14   When τ^c is unknown but is assumed to lie between $0 < \tau_{\min}, \tau_{\max} < 1$ then (6.13) can be replaced by

$$t_\lambda = \lambda(S_0(\hat{\tau}), S_1(\tilde{\tau})) \times |t_0(\hat{\tau})| + m_\xi(1 - \lambda(S_0(\hat{\tau}), S_1(\tilde{\tau}))) \times |t_1(\tilde{\tau})|$$

Here $\hat{\tau}$ and $\tilde{\tau}$ are the break fractions that maximize $|t_0(\tau)|$ and $|t_1(\tau)|$ across all break fractions in the range $\tau_{\min} < \tau < \tau_{\max}$. In these circumstances t_λ is no longer asymptotically standard normal. The constant m_ξ is chosen so that, for a given significance level ξ, the asymptotic null critical value of t_λ is the same irrespective of whether the errors are $I(0)$ or $I(1)$.

6.15   If we have model (C), that is, Eqs. (6.3) and (6.6), then the procedures outlined in §§**6.10–6.11** may again be followed using the t-statistics relating to the null $\beta = 0$. HLT (2009) provide these critical values and m_ξ values for t_λ in the unknown break case:

	Model (A)		Model (C)	
ξ	Critical Value	m_ξ	Critical Value	m_ξ
0.10	2.284	0.835	2.904	1.062
0.05	2.563	0.853	3.162	1.052
0.01	3.135	0.890	3.654	1.037

CONFIDENCE INTERVALS FOR THE BREAK DATE AND MULTIPLE BREAKS

6.16 When the break date is estimated it is often useful to be able to provide a confidence interval for the unknown T_b^c. Perron and Zhu (2005) show that for the segmented trend model (B) and $I(1)$ errors

$$\sqrt{T}(\hat{\tau} - \tau^c) \overset{d}{\sim} N\left(0, 2\sigma^2/15\beta^2\right)$$

while for $I(0)$ errors

$$T^{3/2}(\tilde{\tau} - \tau^c) \overset{d}{\sim} N\left(0, 4\sigma^2/\left(\tau^c(1 - \tau^c)\beta^2\right)\right)$$

so that, for example, a 95% confidence interval for τ^c when the errors are $I(1)$ is given by

$$\hat{\tau} \pm 1.96\sqrt{\frac{2\hat{\sigma}^2}{15T\hat{\beta}^2}}$$

The limiting distributions for the break date do not depend on the autocorrelation structure of the errors, only requiring an estimate of the error variance σ^2. When the errors are $I(1)$ the limiting distribution is invariant to the location of the break, whereas for $I(0)$ errors, the limiting distribution depends on the location of the break in such a way that the variance is smaller the closer the break is to the middle of the sample. In both cases the variance decreases as the shift in slope increases.

For model (C) the limiting distributions for the break date are no longer normal but are complicated functions of nuisance parameters and, thus, can only be simulated, so that no simple results are available.

6.17 In theory, all the procedures available when there is only one break, may be extended to the case of multiple breaks, but, in practice, when there are multiple breaks at unknown times, only the sequential procedure of Kejriwal and Perron (2010), which requires specialized programming, is currently available.

NONLINEAR TRENDS

6.18 A breaking linear trend may be interpreted as a form of *nonlinear* trend and their use begs the question of why not model nonlinear trends explicitly, particularly when the shift in the trend evolves smoothly over a sequence of observations rather than occurring instantaneously with a sharp break. While many types of deterministic nonlinear trends could be specified, the *logistic smooth transition* (LSTR) and *exponential smooth transition* (ESTR) have proved to be popular. The LSTR function may be defined as

$$S_t(\gamma, m) = (1 + \exp(-\gamma(t - mT)))^{-1} \tag{6.14}$$

while the ESTR takes the form

$$S_t(\gamma, m) = 1 - \exp\left(-\gamma(t - mT)^2\right) \tag{6.15}$$

Analogous to (6.1)–(6.3), three alternative smooth transition trend models may then be specified as

$$x_t = \mu_0 + \mu S_t(\gamma, m) + \varepsilon_t \tag{6.16}$$

$$x_t = \mu_0 + \beta_0 t + \mu S_t(\gamma, m) + \varepsilon_t \tag{6.17}$$

$$x_t = \mu_0 + \beta_0 t + \mu S_t(\gamma, m) + \beta t S_t(\gamma, m) + \varepsilon_t \tag{6.18}$$

The parameter m determines the timing of the transition midpoint, since for $\gamma > 0$, $S_{-\infty}(\gamma, m) = 0$, $S_{+\infty}(\gamma, m) = 1$, and $S_{mT}(\gamma, m) = 0.5$. The speed of the transition is determined by the parameter γ. If γ is small then $S_t(\gamma, m)$ takes a long time to traverse the interval $(0, 1)$, and in the limiting case where $\gamma = 0$, $S_t(\gamma, m) = 0.5$ for all t and there is, thus, no transition. For large values of γ, $S_t(\gamma, m)$ traverses the interval $(0, 1)$ rapidly, and as γ approaches $+\infty$, it changes from zero to one instantaneously at time mT, so that a level shift model emerges.

6.19 Thus, in (6.16) x_t is stationary around a mean that changes from an initial value of μ_0 to a final value of $\mu_1 = \mu_0 + \mu$. Model (6.17) is similar with the intercept again changing from μ_0 to $\mu_1 = \mu_0 + \mu$, but it also allows for a fixed slope. In model (6.18) the slope also changes, with the same speed of transition, from β_0 to $\beta_1 = \beta_0 + \beta$. If $\gamma < 0$ then the initial and final model states are reversed but the interpretation of the parameters remains the same. Examples of the smooth transitions of models (6.16)–(6.18) are shown in Fig. 6.5.

6.20 The smooth transition $S_t(\gamma, m)$ does, however, impose the restriction that the transition path is both monotonic and symmetric around the midpoint. More flexible specifications, which allow for nonmonotonic and asymmetric transition paths, could be obtained by including a higher-order time polynomial in the exponential term of $S_t(\gamma, m)$. The constraints that the transitions in intercept and slope occur only once, simultaneously and at the same speed, could also be relaxed, although at some cost to interpretation and ease of estimation.[3]

6.21 Indeed, the ease with which smooth transition models may be estimated may be of some concern because nonlinear least squares (NLS) must be used to estimate models of the form of (6.16)–(6.18), usually with some form of autocorrelation adjustment to deal with an ARMA specification for ε_t (cf. the discussion in §**6.2**). NLS estimation can often be problematic in terms of the convergence of estimates and the computability of the variances and covariances to be attached to these estimates. Consequently, approximating a nonlinear trend by a Fourier series expansion has also become popular.

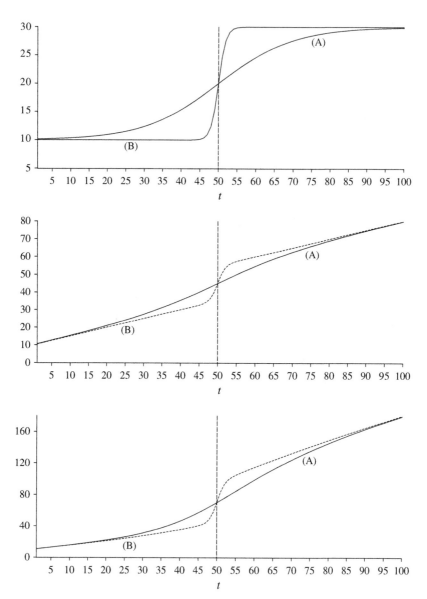

FIGURE 6.5 Smooth transitions (6.16)–(6.18): (A) $\gamma = 0.1$; (B) $\gamma = 1$; $\mu_0 = 10$, $\mu_1 = 20$, $\beta_0 = 0.5$, $\beta_1 = 1$, $m = 0.5$.

Such a model can be written as:

$$x_t = \mu + \beta t + \sum_{f=1}^{n} \gamma_{1f} \sin\left(\frac{2\pi ft}{T}\right) + \sum_{f=1}^{n} \gamma_{2f} \cos\left(\frac{2\pi ft}{T}\right) + \varepsilon_t \qquad (6.19)$$

Here $f = 1, 2, \ldots, n \leq T/2$ are the frequencies contained in the approximation, but it is usual to consider only a limited number of such frequencies, with n typically chosen to be no more than three. This is because a Fourier approximation using a small number of frequency components will often capture the essential characteristics of an unknown nonlinear function. It is also because the evolution of the nonlinear trend is usually assumed to be gradual rather than exhibiting the sharp shifts that will occur when n is chosen to be large.

EXAMPLE 6.3 LSTR and Fourier Models for United States Stock Prices

In Example 6.1 a breaking trend model with both a level and trend shift at 1929 was fitted to the *S&P 500* index. Here an equivalent LSTR model of the form (6.18) is fitted by NLS with AR(2) errors to obtain:

$$x_t = \underset{(0.182)}{1.278} + \underset{(0.0046)}{0.0198\, t} - \underset{(0.414)}{3.891\, S_t(0.685,\ 0.507)} + \underset{(0.0056)}{0.0507\, tS_t(0.685,\ 0.507)} + e_t$$

$$e_t = \underset{(0.085)}{0.913\, e_{t-1}} - \underset{(0.085)}{0.172\, e_{t-1}} + a_t$$

This model can be interpreted as implying that the intercept decreased from 1.28 to -2.61, while trend growth increased from 2.0% per annum to 7.1% per annum across the transition. The midpoint of the smooth transition is estimated to be 1951 and, as $\hat{\gamma} = 0.685$, the speed of the transition is reasonably swift. As can be seen from the smooth transition trend shown in Fig. 6.6, the transition takes about six years to complete and occurs two decades later than the Great Crash of 1929.

Also shown is an $n = 3$ component Fourier approximation obtained by fitting (6.19) by OLS, again with AR(2) errors. This provides a reasonable approximation to the LSTR fit, but tends to produce a sequence of "long swings" rather than a smooth transition from one essentially linear segment to another.

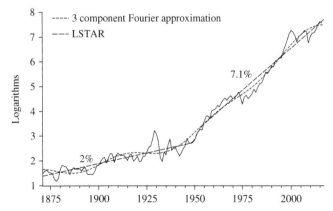

FIGURE 6.6 *S&P 500* index, 1871−2016, with LSTR trend having a midpoint at 1951 and an $n = 3$ component Fourier approximation.

6.22   Of course, the error ε_t in (6.16)−(6.18) may contain a unit root rather than be assumed stationary as in Example 6.3. A simple procedure to test for a unit root when there are smooth transition breaks is to detrend x_t by fitting one of (6.16)−(6.18) and to compute an ADF test using the residuals. Once again standard DF percentiles are invalid but Leybourne et al. (1998) and Kapetanios et al. (2003) provide the necessary critical values, which depend on which smooth transition model is fitted. If the null hypothesis is an $I(1)$ process without drift then all three models are possible alternatives, while if a drift is included under the null then only (6.17) and (6.18) can be considered as realistic alternatives.

A similar procedure may be employed after having fitted a Fourier approximation (6.19), although Enders and Lee (2012) prefer an alternative approach based on the Lagrange Multiplier methodology, which they find to have better size and power properties.

EXAMPLE 6.4 LSTR Versus a Unit Root in United States Stock Prices

A DF unit root test computed using the residuals from the LSTR model fitted in Example 6.3, albeit without an AR(2) error, yielded a value of −4.46. From Table 1 of Leybourne et al. (1998) this is close to being significant at the 10% level and the residuals from the model are well fitted by an AR(4) process with two pairs of complex roots of $0.68 \pm 0.23i$ and $-0.20 \pm 0.57i$. There is, thus, some modest confirmation that stock prices can reasonably be modeled as the sum of a deterministic nonlinear trend and a stationary innovation, although, as we have seen, the transition occurs some 20 years after the Great Crash break in the trend function fitted in Example 6.1.

6.23   As has been repeatedly emphasized, the interaction between specifying a trend component and ascertaining whether a time series has a unit root or not is of considerable importance. Failure to correctly specify the deterministic component of a time series will typically result in inconsistent unit root tests, while the power of such tests to reject the unit root null under a stationary alternative can be markedly reduced when deterministic components are unnecessarily included in the specification.

These issues are magnified when nonlinear trends are being considered. Unless one is committed to a specific parametric trend specification, such as one of the smooth transitions, then a Fourier expansion approximation is required, for which a choice of n in (6.19) is required. If this is to be selected empirically via a statistical test, then knowing whether the errors contain a unit root or not is essential for deriving the correct form of the test, but this knowledge is itself only available after conducting a test whose validity, as we have just pointed out, depends on the very trend specification we are attempting to ascertain.

6.24   This circularity of reasoning must, therefore, be broken by a robust procedure of the type introduced in §§**6.10−6.12**, and this has been provided by Harvey, Leybourne, and Xiao (HLX, 2010). Their focus is on deriving a test of the null of linearity against the alternative of a nonlinear trend in (6.19) that is robust to whether ε_t contains a unit root or not, that is, a test of

$$H_0{:}\gamma_{1f} = \gamma_{2f} = 0, \quad f = 1,\ldots,n$$

against

$$H_1{:} \text{ at least one of } \gamma_{1f}, \gamma_{2f} \neq 0, \quad f = 1,\ldots,n$$

The test is developed using the "partially summed" counterpart to (6.19):

$$z_t = \mu t + \beta y_t + \sum_{f=1}^{n} \gamma_{1f} \sum_{s=1}^{t} \sin\left(\frac{2\pi fs}{T}\right) + \sum_{f=1}^{n} \gamma_{2f} \sum_{s=1}^{t} \cos\left(\frac{2\pi fs}{T}\right) + \eta_t \quad (6.20)$$

where $z_t = \sum_{s=1}^{t} x_s$, $y_t = \sum_{s=1}^{t} s$, and $\eta_t = \sum_{s=1}^{t} \varepsilon_s$. Let RSS_U denote the residual sum of squares from OLS estimation of (6.20) and RSS_R the residual sum of squares from the OLS regression of (6.20) under H_0, that is, the regression of z_t on just t and y_t. A suitable test of H_0 against H_1 (i.e., of the null of zero frequencies against the alternative of $n \geq 1$ frequencies) is then given by the Wald statistic

$$W_0^n = \frac{\text{RSS}_R - \text{RSS}_U}{\text{RSS}_U/T}$$

HLX show that a modified form of this Wald statistic is robust to whether the errors are $I(0)$ or $I(1)$, in the sense that its critical values and significance levels do not depend on this distinction. The modification that they favor is

$$MW_0^n = T^{-1} W_0^n \exp\left(-b_\xi/|DF|\right)$$

where DF is the Dickey–Fuller t-statistic testing $\phi = 0$ from the OLS regression

$$\nabla e_t = \phi e_{t-1} + \sum_{i=1}^{k} \delta_i \nabla e_{t-i} + a_t$$

the e_t being the residuals from OLS estimation of (6.19). Values of b_ξ for significance level ξ and critical values for n up to 3 are given in Table 1 of HLX. For example, for $n = 1$, $\xi = 0.05$ with a trend included, $b_{0.05} = 9.484$ and the critical value is 3.708; if the trend is omitted, $b_{0.05} = 7.096$ and the critical value is 7.439.

6.25 HLX found that the maximum number of frequencies used in the Fourier approximation, n, was a key factor in the performance of the MW_0^n test. Choosing too large a value naturally results in a sacrifice of power, but choosing n too small can also lead to dramatic losses in power. A method of determining n is, therefore, needed and HLX begin by considering robust tests of m versus at most $m - 1$ frequencies, that is, tests of:

$$H_0^*: \gamma_{1m} = \gamma_{2m} = 0; \quad \gamma_{1f}, \gamma_{2f}, \quad f = 1, \ldots, m - 1 \quad \text{unrestricted}$$

against

$$H_1^*: \text{at least one of } \gamma_{1m}, \gamma_{2m} \neq 0$$

The hypothesis H_0^* can be tested by the same approach using the Wald statistic:

$$W_{m-1}^m = \frac{\text{RSS}_R - \text{RSS}_U}{\text{RSS}_U / T}$$

where RSS_R now denotes the residual sum of squares from OLS estimation of (6.20) with n replaced by $m - 1$ and RSS_U is the residual sum of squares from (6.20) with n replaced by m. The modified statistic is then:

$$MW_{m-1}^m = T^{-1} W_{m-1}^m \exp\left(- \frac{b_\varepsilon}{|DF|} \right)$$

The procedure for selecting n is then as follows. In the first step, a maximum value $n_{\max}$ is selected and the sequence of tests MW_0^i, $i = 1, \ldots, n_{\max}$, are conducted. If none of these tests reject, then we conclude that $n = 0$. If any of these tests do reject, we identify the largest value of i for which the null is rejected and set m to this value. If $m = 1$ we conclude that $n = 1$; otherwise, if $m > 1$ we conclude that m is the largest value that n might take. MW_0^{m-1} is then considered and if this fails to reject we set $n = m$. If MW_0^{m-1} does reject, however, MW_{m-1}^m is then considered; if this rejects we again conclude that $n = m$, otherwise m is reduced by one and the loop repeated.

6.26 A natural alternative is to identify n using a model selection criterion. Astill et al. (2015) suggest fitting two sequences of regressions; the first being

$$\nabla x_t = \mu + \beta t + \phi x_{t-1} + \sum_{f=1}^{n} \gamma_{1f} \sin\left(\frac{2\pi f t}{T} \right) + \sum_{f=1}^{n} \gamma_{2f} \cos\left(\frac{2\pi f t}{T} \right)$$

$$+ \sum_{i=1}^{k} \delta_i \nabla x_{t-i} + \varepsilon_t \tag{6.21}$$

the second being (6.21) with the restriction $\phi = 0$ imposed, for $n = \{0, 1, \ldots, n_{\max}\}$ and $k = \{0, 1, \ldots, k_{\max}\}$. From these two sequences the regression that produces the minimum value of, say, BIC then provides the value of n to use in the testing procedure.

Astill et al. also provide an alternative set of test statistics that they claim have superior finite sample size and power properties to the MW-type statistics. These are, however, rather more complicated to construct but may be used if so desired.

EXAMPLE 6.5 Determining a Fourier approximation for United States Stock Prices

In Example 6.3 a Fourier approximation with $n = 3$ was fitted to the *S&P 500* index. The HLX procedure was then applied to ascertain whether this choice was warranted. The sequence of Wald statistics were obtained as $W_0^1 = 6914.76$, $W_0^2 = 7268.96$, and $W_0^3 = 18129.54$. With $DF = -4.551$, and choosing $\xi = 0.05$ as the significance level, so that the b_ξ values are 9.484, 14.193, and 18.349, the modified Wald statistics are $MW_0^1 = 5.893$, $MW_0^2 = 2.101$, and $MW_0^3 = 2.203$ respectively. Since the critical values are 3.708, 6.124, and 8.468, this procedure selects $n = 1$ as the appropriate value to use in the Fourier approximation.

Estimating the two sequences of regressions from (6.21) with $n_{max} = 3$ and $k_{max} = 4$ finds that the joint minimum BIC is provided by $n = 0$ at $k = 0$ i.e., that the most appropriate model is actually a pure random walk with drift, although focusing only on the unrestricted regression yields $n = 1$ at $k = 0$, which is the regression with the second smallest BIC value.

ENDNOTES

1. Repeating the test for the restricted sample ending in 1986q3 yields $\tilde{\phi}^B = 0.885(0.029)$ with $t^B = -3.92$, which is on the border of significance at the 5% level and is similar in value to the statistic obtained by Perron (1989) for an earlier vintage of real GNP data.
2. Tests of stationarity in the presence of structural breaks occurring at unknown times have also been developed: see Busetti and Harvey (2003) and Harvey and Mills (2003, 2004).
3. The LSTR trend model was introduced by Leybourne et al. (1998) and extensions were provided by Sollis et al. (1999) and Harvey and Mills (2002).

Chapter 7

An Introduction to Forecasting With Univariate Models

Chapter Outline

FORECASTING WITH AUTOREGRESSIVE-INTEGRATED-MOVING AVERAGE (ARIMA) MODELS

7.1 An important feature of the univariate models introduced in previous chapters is their ability to provide forecasts of future values of the observed series. There are two aspects to forecasting: the provision of a forecast for a future value of the series and the provision of a forecast error that can be attached to this *point* forecast. This forecast error may then be used to construct *forecast intervals* to provide an indication of the precision these forecasts are likely to possess. The setup is, thus, analogous to the classic statistical problem of estimating an unknown parameter of a model and providing a confidence interval for that parameter.

What is often not realized when forecasting is that the type of model used to construct point and interval forecasts will necessarily determine the properties of these forecasts. Consequently, forecasting from an incorrect or misspecified model may lead to forecasts that are inaccurate and which incorrectly measure the precision that may be attached to them.[1]

7.2 To formalize the forecasting problem, suppose we have a realization $(x_{1-d}, x_{2-d}, \ldots, x_T)$ from a general ARIMA (p,d,q) process

$$\phi(B)\nabla^d x_t = \theta_0 + \theta(B)a_t \qquad (7.1)$$

and that we wish to forecast a future value x_{T+h}, h being known as the *lead time* or *forecast horizon*.[2] If we let

$$\alpha(B) = \phi(B)\nabla^d = \left(1 - \alpha_1 B - \alpha_2 B^2 - \cdots - \alpha_{p+d}B^{p+d}\right)$$

Applied Time Series Analysis. DOI: https://doi.org/10.1016/B978-0-12-813117-6.00007-7

121

then (7.1) becomes, for time $T + h$,

$$\alpha(B)x_{T+h} = \theta_0 + \theta(B)a_{T+h}$$

that is,

$$x_{T+h} = \alpha_1 x_{T+h-1} + \alpha_2 x_{T+h-2} + \cdots + \alpha_{p+d}x_{T+h+p-d} + \theta_0 + a_{T+h}$$
$$- \theta_1 a_{T+h-1} - \cdots - \theta_q a_{T+h-q}$$

Clearly, observations from $T + 1$ onwards are unavailable, but a *minimum mean square error* (MMSE) forecast of x_{T+h} made at time T (known as the *origin*), and denoted $f_{T,h}$, is given by the conditional expectation

$$f_{T,h} = E(\alpha_1 x_{T+h-1} + \alpha_2 x_{T+h-2} + \cdots + \alpha_{p+d}x_{T+h-p-d} + \theta_0 \qquad (7.2)$$
$$+ a_{T+h} - \theta_1 a_{T+h-1} - \cdots - \theta_q a_{T+h-q}|x_T, x_{T-1}, \ldots).$$

This is the forecast that will minimize the variance of the h-step ahead forecast error $e_{T,h} = x_{T+h} - f_{T,h}$, that is, it will minimize $E\left(e_{T,h}^2\right)$. Now it is clear that

$$E\left(x_{T+j}|x_T, x_{T-1}, \ldots\right) = \begin{cases} x_{T+j}, & j \leq 0 \\ f_{T,j}, & j > 0 \end{cases},$$

and

$$E\left(a_{T+j}|x_T, x_{T-1}, \ldots\right) = \begin{cases} a_{T+j}, & j \leq 0 \\ 0, & j > 0 \end{cases},$$

so that, to evaluate $f_{T,h}$, all we need to do is: (1) replace past expectations $(j \leq 0)$ by known values, x_{T+j} and a_{T+j}, and (2) replace future expectations $(j > 0)$ by forecast values, $f_{T,j}$ and 0.

7.3 We will use three processes to illustrate the procedure, with further actual forecasting applications developed as worked examples. Consider first the AR(2) process $\left(1 - \phi_1 B - \phi_2 B^2\right)x_t = \theta_0 + a_t$, so that $\alpha(B) = \left(1 - \phi_1 B - \phi_2 B^2\right)$. Here

$$x_{T+h} = \phi_1 x_{T+h-1} + \phi_2 x_{T+h-2} + \theta_0 + a_{T+h},$$

and, hence, for $h = 1$, we have

$$f_{T,1} = \phi_1 x_T + \phi_2 x_{T-1} + \theta_0$$

For $h = 2$ we have

$$f_{T,2} = \phi_1 f_{T,1} + \phi_2 x_T + \theta_0$$

and, for $h > 2$,

$$f_{T,h} = \phi_1 f_{T,h-1} + \phi_2 f_{T,h-2} + \theta_0$$

An alternative expression for $f_{T,h}$ can be obtained by noting that

$$f_{T,h} = \left(\phi_1 + \phi_2\right)f_{T,h-1} - \phi_2\left(f_{T,h-1} - f_{T,h-2}\right) + \theta_0$$

from which, by repeated substitution, we obtain

$$f_{T,h} = (\phi_1 + \phi_2)^h x_T - \phi_2 \sum_{j=0}^{h-1} (\phi_1 + \phi_2)^j (f_{T,h-1-j} - f_{T,h-2-j}) + \theta_0 \sum_{j=0}^{h-1} (\phi_1 + \phi_2)^j$$

where, by convention, we take $f_{T,0} = x_T$ and $f_{T,-1} = x_{T-1}$. Thus, for stationary processes, that is, those for which $\phi_1 + \phi_2 < 1$, $|\phi_2| < 1$,

$$f_{T,h} \rightarrow \frac{\theta_0}{1 - \phi_1 - \phi_2} = E(x_t) = \mu$$

as $h \rightarrow \infty$, so that for long lead times the best forecast of a future observation will eventually be the mean of the process. This is a general result: for *all* stationary processes, forecasts will eventually converge on the mean of the process, reflecting the *mean reversion* property of such models. Short-term (small h) forecasts may, of course, be different from the mean, as they respond to recent developments in the realization, and the speed with which the forecasts mean revert will depend upon the strength of the autocorrelation in the series (in the AR(2) context, the closer $\phi_1 + \phi_2$ is to unity, the slower the mean reversion).

7.4 Next consider the ARIMA(0,1,1) model $\nabla x_t = (1 - \theta_1 B)a_t$. Here $\alpha(B) = (1 - B)$ so that

$$x_{T+h} = x_{T+h-1} + a_{T+h} - \theta_1 a_{T+h-1}.$$

For $h = 1$, we have

$$f_{T,1} = x_T - \theta_1 a_T$$

for $h = 2$

$$f_{T,2} = f_{T,1} = x_T - \theta_1 a_T$$

and, in general,

$$f_{T,h} = f_{T,h-1} = f_{T,1}, \quad h > 1.$$

Thus, for *all* lead times, forecasts from origin T will follow a straight line parallel to the time axis and passing through $f_{T,1}$. Note that since

$$f_{T,h} = x_T - \theta_1 a_T$$

and

$$a_T = (1 - B)(1 - \theta_1 B)^{-1} x_T$$

the h-step ahead forecast can be written as

$$\begin{aligned} f_{T,h} &= (1 - \theta_1)(1 - \theta_1 B)^{-1} x_T \\ &= (1 - \theta_1)(x_T + \theta_1 x_{T-1} + \theta_1^2 x_{T-2} + \cdots) \end{aligned}$$

so that the forecast for all future values of x is a weighted moving average of current and past values, with the weights geometrically declining (this is also known as an exponentially weighted moving average: see § **9.14**).

The nonstationary nature of the ARIMA(0,1,1) model asserts itself in the absence of mean reversion, with forecasts remaining at $f_{T,1}$ for all lead times. Note that if $\theta_1 = 0$ then the model is a pure random walk and $f_{T,h} = x_T$ for all h, that is, for a random walk without drift the optimal forecast for all lead times is the current value of the series.

If there is a drift, then we have

$$\nabla x_t = \theta_0 + (1 - \theta_1 B)a_t$$

and

$$x_{T+h} = x_{T+h-1} + \theta_0 + a_{T+h} - \theta_1 a_{T+h-1}.$$

For $h = 1$, we now have

$$f_{T,1} = x_T + \theta_0 - \theta_1 a_T,$$

for $h = 2$

$$f_{T,2} = f_{T,1} + \theta_0 = x_T + 2\theta_0 - \theta_1 a_T$$

and, in general,

$$f_{T,h} = f_{T,h-1} + \theta_0 = f_{T,1} + (h - 1)\theta_0 = x_T + h\theta_0 - \theta_1 a_T, \quad h > 1$$

Thus, the inclusion of a drift into the model introduces a linear trend into the forecasts. If again $\theta_1 = 0$ and we have a random walk with drift, the sequence of forecasts is then a linear trend emanating from the last available observation with the slope given by the drift.

7.5 Finally, we consider the ARIMA(0,2,2) process $\nabla^2 x_t = \left(1 - \theta_1 B - \theta_2 B^2\right)a_t$, with $\alpha(B) = (1-B)^2 = \left(1 - 2B + B^2\right)$:

$$x_{T+h} = 2x_{T+h-1} - x_{T+h-2} + a_{T+h} - \theta_1 a_{T+h-1} - \theta_2 a_{T+h-2}$$

For $h = 1$, we have

$$f_{T,1} = 2x_T - x_{T-1} - \theta_1 a_T - \theta_2 a_{T-1}$$

for $h = 2$,

$$f_{T,2} = 2f_{T,1} - x_T - \theta_2 a_T$$

for $h = 3$,

$$f_{T,3} = 2f_{T,2} - f_{T,1}$$

and, thus, for $h \geq 3$,

$$f_{T,h} = 2f_{T,h-1} - f_{T,h-2} = (h - 1)f_{T,2} - (h - 2)f_{T,1}$$

Hence, for all lead times, the forecasts from origin T will follow a straight line passing through the forecasts $f_{T,1}$ and $f_{T,2}$.

7.6 These results may be generalized to ARIMA(p,d,q) processes having d at most 2. After the impact that the autoregressive and moving average components have on short-term forecasts has dissipated, the behavior of long-term forecasts is dependent upon the order of differencing and whether an intercept is included in the process or not. For stationary processes, forecasts will eventually revert to the mean of the process, which will be zero if no intercept is included. For $I(1)$ processes, long-term forecasts will either be horizontal, if there is no intercept, or follow a linear trend when the intercept is nonzero. For $I(2)$ processes a linear trend is automatically inserted if there is no intercept. Including an intercept in an $I(2)$ process will, thus, introduce a quadratic trend into the forecasts, which would in most applications be felt inappropriate; its absence is consistent with the typical finding that estimated intercepts are insignificant in fitted $I(2)$ models.

7.7   The h-step ahead forecast error for origin T, defined in § **7.2**, may be expressed as

$$e_{T,h} = x_{T+h} - f_{T,h} = a_{T+h} + \psi_1 a_{T+h-1} + \cdots + \psi_{h-1} a_{T+1} \qquad (7.3)$$

where $\psi_1, \ldots, \psi_{h-1}$ are the first $h-1$ ψ-weights in $\psi(B) = \alpha^{-1}(B)\theta(B)$. The forecast error is, therefore, a linear combination of the unobservable future shocks entering the system after time T, although the one-step ahead forecast error is simply

$$e_{T,1} = x_{T,1} - f_{T,1} = a_{T+1}.$$

Thus, for a MMSE forecast, the one-step ahead forecast errors must be uncorrelated. However, h-step ahead forecasts made at different origins will not be uncorrelated, and neither will forecasts for different lead times made at the same origin.[3]

7.8   From (7.3), the variance of the forecast error is given by

$$V(e_{T,h}) = \sigma^2 \left(1 + \psi_1^2 + \psi_2^2 + \cdots + \psi_{h-1}^2\right) \qquad (7.4)$$

For the AR(2) model, we have $\psi_1 = \phi_1$, $\psi_2 = \phi_1^2 + \phi_2$ and, for $j > 2$, $\psi_j = \phi_1 \psi_{j-1} + \phi_2 \psi_{j-2}$ (recall §**3.16**). Since we are assuming stationarity, these ψ-weights converge absolutely, which implies that $\sum_{j=1}^{h} \psi_j^2 < \infty$. Consequently $V(e_{T,h})$ converges to a finite value, which is the variance of the process about the ultimate forecast μ. For stationary models then, forecast error variances are bounded by the intrinsic variability of the series itself.

7.9   For the ARIMA(0,1,1) process, $\psi_j = 1 - \theta$, $j = 1, 2, \ldots$. Thus, we have

$$V(e_{T,h}) = \sigma^2 \left(1 + (h-1)(1-\theta)^2\right)$$

which is a linear function of h, so that forecast uncertainty increases with the forecast horizon at a linear rate. Similarly, the ARIMA(0,2,2) model has ψ-weights given by $\psi_j = 1 + \theta_2 + j(1 - \theta_1 - \theta_2)$, $j = 1, 2, \ldots$, and an h-step ahead forecast error variance of

$$V(e_{T,h}) = \sigma^2 \left(1 + (h-1)(1+\theta_2)^2 + \frac{1}{6}h(h-1)(2h-1)(1-\theta_1-\theta_2)^2 \right.$$
$$\left. + h(h-1)(1+\theta_2)(1-\theta_1-\theta_2) \right)$$

This is a cubic function of h so that forecast uncertainty may increase substantially as the forecast horizon increases.

7.10 These examples show how the degree of differencing (equivalently the order of integration) determines not only how successive forecasts are related to each other, but also the behavior of the associated error variances. Having obtained the forecast error variance $V(e_{T,h})$, a $100(1-\varsigma)\%$ forecast interval may be constructed as $f_{T,h} \pm z_{\varsigma/2}\sqrt{V(e_{T,h})}$, where $z_{\varsigma/2}$ is the $\varsigma/2$ percentage point of the standard normal distribution, for example, $z_{0.025} = 1.96$.

EXAMPLE 7.1 ARIMA Forecasting of the Spread

Example 3.2 fitted an AR(2) model to the United Kingdom interest rate spread, yielding parameter estimates $\hat{\phi}_1 = 1.192$, $\hat{\phi}_2 = -0.224$, and $\hat{\theta}_0 = 0.036$. With the last two observations being $x_{T-1} = 1.69$ and $x_T = 1.63$, forecasts are obtained as

$$f_{T,1} = 1.192x_T - 0.223x_{T-1} + 0.036 = 3.034$$
$$f_{T,2} = 1.192f_{T,1} - 0.224x_T + 0.036 = 1.580$$
$$f_{T,3} = 1.192f_{T,2} - 0.224f_{T,1} + 0.036 = 1.562$$

and so on. As h increases, the forecasts eventually tend to 1.195, the sample mean of the spread. The ψ-weights are given by:

$$\psi_1 = \phi_1 = 1.192$$
$$\psi_2 = \phi_1^2 + \phi_2 = 1.199$$
$$\psi_3 = \phi_1^3 + 2\phi_1\phi_2 = 1.163$$
$$\psi_4 = \phi_1^4 + 3\phi_1^2\phi_2 + \phi_2^2 = 1.119$$

and, hence:

$$\psi_h = 1.192\psi_{h-1} - 0.224\psi_{h-2}.$$

With $\hat{\sigma} = 0.394$, the forecast error variances are

$$V(e_{T,1}) = 0.394^2 = 0.155$$
$$V(e_{T,2}) = 0.394^2(1 + 1.192^2) = 0.377$$
$$V(e_{T,3}) = 0.394^2(1 + 1.192^2 + 1.199^2) = 0.602$$
$$V(e_{T,4}) = 0.394^2(1 + 1.192^2 + 1.19^2 + 1.163^2) = 0.814$$

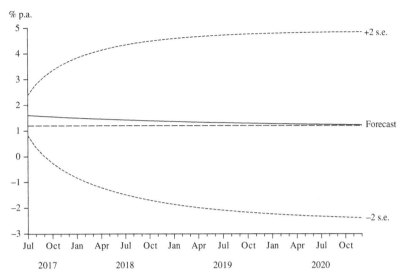

FIGURE 7.1   Forecasts of the United Kingdom interest rate spread: July 2017 to December 2020.

the forecast error variances eventually converging to the sample variance of the spread, 3.284.

Forecasts of the spread out to the end of 2020, accompanied by approximate 95% (2 standard error) forecast intervals, calculated as $f_{T,h} \pm 2\sqrt{V(e_{T,h})}$, are shown in Fig. 7.1, and clearly demonstrate both the slow convergence of the forecasts to the sample mean and the bounded nature of the forecast uncertainty.

If, on the other hand, we use the ARIMA(0,1,1) process of Example 4.1 to model the spread, with $\hat{\theta} = -0.204$ and $\hat{\sigma} = 0.398$ (and conveniently setting the insignificant drift to zero), then our forecasts are (using the final residual $\hat{a}_T = -0.081$):

$$f_{T,1} = 1.63 + 0.204 \times (-0.081) = 1.613$$

and, for $h > 1$,

$$f_{T,h} = f_{T,1} = 1.613$$

so that there is no tendency for the forecasts to converge to the sample mean or, indeed, to any other value. Furthermore, the forecast error variances are given by:

$$V(e_{T,h}) = 0.398^2 \left(1 + 1.204^2(h-1)\right) = 0.158 + 1.450(h-1) = -0.072 + 0.230h$$

which, of course, increase with h, rather than tending to a constant. This example thus illustrates, within the forecasting context, the radically different properties of ARMA models which have, on the one hand, a unit autoregressive root and, on the other, a root that is large but less than unity.

EXAMPLE 7.2 Forecasting Global Temperatures

In Example 4.3, an ARIMA(0,1,3) process was fitted to monthly global temperatures, which we now use to produce temperature forecasts out to 2020. Omitting the insignificant intercept, the fitted model is $\nabla x_t = (1 - 0.506B - 0.090B^2 - 0.119B^3)a_t$ with $\hat{\sigma} = 0.1236$, $\hat{a}_T = -0.020$, and $x_T = 0.585$. Extending the method of §7.4 in an obvious way, we obtain $f_{T,1} = 0.609$, $f_{T,2} = 0.619$, and $f_{T,h} = 0.621$ for $h > 2$. Fig. 7.2 shows these forecasts and their accompanying 95% forecast intervals: by the end of 2020 these intervals range from 0.12°C to 1.12°C, thus showing the high degree of uncertainty inherent in such forecasts, a consequence of the natural variability that exists in this series. Including the insignificantly positive intercept introduces a small upward trend into the forecasts, which increase to 0.642 by the end of the forecast period (with accompanying forecasting interval from 0.14°C to 1.14°C).

FORECASTING A TREND STATIONARY PROCESS

7.11 Let us now consider the trend stationary (TS) process

$$x_t = \beta_0 + \beta_1 t + \varepsilon_t \quad \phi(B)\varepsilon_t = \theta(B)a_t \tag{7.5}$$

The forecast of x_{T+h} made at time T is

$$f_{T,h} = \beta_0 + \beta_1(T + h) + g_{T,h}$$

where $g_{T,h}$ is the forecast of ε_{T+h}, which from (7.2) is given by:

$$g_{T,h} = E(\phi_1 \varepsilon_{T+h-1} + \phi_2 \varepsilon_{T+h-2} + \cdots + \phi_p x_{T+h-p} + a_{T+h}$$
$$- \theta_1 a_{T+h-1} - \cdots - \theta_q a_{T+h-q} | \varepsilon_T, \varepsilon_{T-1}, \ldots)$$

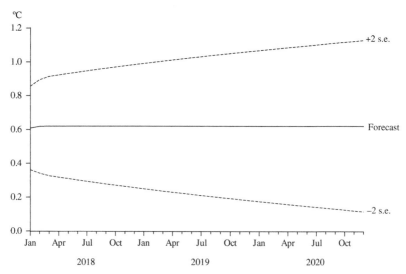

FIGURE 7.2 Forecasts of global temperatures: January 2018 to December 2020.

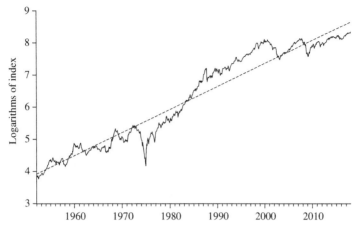

FIGURE 7.3 Logarithms of the *All Share* index with linear trend superimposed: 1952−2017.

Since ε_t is, by assumption, stationary, we know that $g_{T,h} \to 0$ as $h \to \infty$. Thus, for large h, $f_{T,h} = \beta_0 + \beta_1(T + h)$ and forecasts will be given simply by the extrapolated linear trend. For smaller h there will also be the component $g_{T,h}$, but this will dissipate as h increases. The forecast error will be

$$e_{T,h} = x_t - f_{T,h} = \varepsilon_{T+h} - g_{T,h}$$

and, hence, the uncertainty in any TS forecast is due solely to the error in forecasting the ARMA component. As a consequence, the forecast error variance is bounded by the sample variance of ε_t, this being in contrast to the error variances of the ARIMA(p,2,q) process and the ARIMA(p,1,q) with an intercept included, which, from §§**7.4−7.5**, also have forecasts that lie on a linear trend, but have *unbounded* error variances. In the simplest case in which ε_t is white noise, *all* forecasts of a TS process have the *same* error variance, σ^2.

7.12 Of course, the linear trend in (7.5) may be replaced with a breaking or nonlinear trend of the types discussed in Chapter 6, Breaking and Nonlinear Trends. Again, the uncertainty in any forecasts will be solely attributable to the error in forecasting the ARMA component, with the forecast error variance remaining bounded by the sample variance of the noise component.

EXAMPLE 7.3 Forecasting the *All Share* Index as a TS Process

A TS model fitted to (the logarithms of) the *All Share* index was estimated to be:

$$x_t = 3.914 + 0.0060t + \varepsilon_t$$

$$\varepsilon_t = 1.106\varepsilon_{t-1} - 0.118\varepsilon_{t-2} + a_t$$

That this is a misspecified model is clear from Fig. 7.3, which superimposes the fitted linear trend and reveals that there are highly persistent deviations of the series from the trend, confirmed by the largest autoregressive root being estimated to be 0.99. The artificiality of this example notwithstanding, extremely long horizon forecasts of x_{T+h} are given by $f_{T,h} = 3.914 + 0.0060(T + h)$, although shorter horizon forecasts will have appended to $f_{T,h}$ the forecast of the stationary AR(2) component $g_{T,h} = 1.106g_{T,h-1} - 0.118g_{T,h-2}$.

ENDNOTES

1. Throughout this chapter we use "forecast" rather than "predict." This is because in the modern literature on the econometrics of forecasting they have different, albeit subtle and rather deep, definitions. For a detailed discussion of these different definitions, see Clements and Hendry (1998, Chapter 2). Briefly, predictability is defined as a property of a random variable in relation to an information set (the conditional and unconditional distributions of the variable do not coincide). It is a necessary, but not sufficient, condition for forecastability, as the latter requires knowledge of what information is relevant and how it enters the causal mechanism.
2. A detailed exposition of forecasting from ARIMA models is provided by Box and Jenkins (1970, Chapter 5). A wide ranging and detailed discussion of forecasting economic time series is to be found in Granger and Newbold (1986).
3. See, for example, Box and Jenkins (1970, Appendix A5.1).

Chapter 8

Unobserved Component Models, Signal Extraction, and Filters

Chapter Outline

UNOBSERVED COMPONENT MODELS

8.1 A difference stationary, that is, $I(1)$, time series may always be decomposed into a stochastic nonstationary trend, or signal, component and a stationary noise, or irregular, component:

$$x_t = z_t + u_t \tag{8.1}$$

Such a decomposition can be performed in several ways. For instance, Muth's (1960) classic example assumes that the trend component z_t is a random walk

$$z_t = \mu + z_{t-1} + v_t$$

while u_t is white noise and independent of v_t, that is, $u_t \sim \mathrm{WN}\left(0, \sigma_u^2\right)$ and $v_t \sim \mathrm{WN}\left(0, \sigma_v^2\right)$, with $E(u_t v_{t-i}) = 0$ for all i. Thus, it follows that ∇x_t is the stationary process

$$\nabla x_t = \mu + v_t + u_t - u_{t-1} \tag{8.2}$$

which has an autocorrelation function that cuts off at lag one with coefficient

$$\rho_1 = -\frac{\sigma_u^2}{\sigma_u^2 + 2\sigma_v^2} \tag{8.3}$$

It is clear from (8.3) that $-0.5 \leq \rho_1 \leq 0$, the exact value depending on the relative sizes of the two variances, so that ∇x_t can be written as the MA(1) process:

$$\nabla x_t = \mu + e_t - \theta e_{t-1} \tag{8.4}$$

Applied Time Series Analysis. DOI: https://doi.org/10.1016/B978-0-12-813117-6.00008-9

where $e_t \sim \text{WN}(0, \sigma_e^2)$. On defining $\kappa = \sigma_v^2/\sigma_u^2$ to be the *signal-to-noise* variance ratio, the relationship between the parameters of (8.2) and (8.4) can be shown to be:

$$\theta = \frac{1}{2}\left((\kappa + 2) - (\kappa^2 + 4\kappa)^{1/2}\right), \quad \kappa = \frac{(1-\theta)^2}{\theta}, \quad \kappa \geq 0, \quad |\theta| < 1$$

and

$$\sigma_u^2 = \theta \sigma_e^2$$

Thus, $\kappa = 0$ corresponds to $\theta = 1$, so that the unit roots in (8.4) "cancel out" and the overdifferenced x_t is stationary, while $\kappa = \infty$ corresponds to $\theta = 0$, in which case x_t is a pure random walk. A test of the stationarity null of $\theta = 1$ has been set out in §**5.16**, which can, therefore, also be regarded as a test of the null $\sigma_v^2 = 0$, for if this is the case then z_t is a deterministic linear trend.

8.2   Models of the form of (8.1) are known as *unobserved component* (UC) models, a more general formulation for the components being:

$$\nabla z_t = \mu + \gamma(B)v_t$$

and

$$u_t = \lambda(B)a_t$$

(8.5)

where v_t and a_t are independent white noise sequences with finite variances σ_v^2 and σ_a^2, and where $\gamma(B)$ and $\lambda(B)$ are stationary polynomials having no common roots. It can be shown that x_t will then have the form:

$$\nabla x_t = \mu + \theta(B)e_t$$

(8.6)

where $\theta(B)$ and σ_e^2 can be obtained from:

$$\sigma_e^2 \frac{\theta(B)\theta(B^{-1})}{(1 - B)(1 - B^{-1})} = \sigma_v^2 \frac{\gamma(B)\gamma(B^{-1})}{(1 - B)(1 - B^{-1})} + \sigma_a^2 \lambda(B)\lambda(B^{-1})$$

(8.7)

From this we see that it is not necessarily the case that the parameters of the components can be identified from knowledge of the parameters of (8.6) alone: indeed, in general the components will not be identified. However, if z_t is restricted to be a random walk ($\gamma(B) = 1$), then the parameters of the UC model will be identified. This is clearly the case for Muth's model since σ_u^2 can be estimated by the lag one autocovariance of ∇x_t [the numerator of (8.3)] and σ_v^2 can be estimated from the variance of ∇x_t [the denominator of (8.3)] and the estimated value of σ_u^2.

8.3   This example illustrates, however, that even though the variances are identified, such a decomposition may not always be feasible, for it is unable to account for positive first-order autocorrelation in ∇x_t. To do so requires relaxing either the assumption that z_t is a random walk, so that the trend component contains both permanent and transitory movements, or the assumption that v_t and a_t are independent. If either of these assumptions are relaxed, the parameters of the Muth model will not be identified.

8.4 The assumption that the trend component, z_t, follows a random walk is not as restrictive as it may at first seem. Consider the Wold decomposition for ∇x_t:

$$\nabla x_t = \mu + \psi(B)e_t = \mu + \sum_{j=0}^{\infty} \psi_j e_{t-j} \tag{8.8}$$

Since $\psi(1) = \sum \psi_j$ is a constant, we may write:

$$\psi(B) = \psi(1) + C(B)$$

so that:

$$
\begin{aligned}
C(B) &= \psi(B) - \psi(1) \\
&= 1 + \psi_1 B + \psi_2 B^2 + \psi_3 B^3 + \cdots - \left(1 + \psi_1 + \psi_2 + \psi_3 + \cdots\right) \\
&= -\psi_1(1 - B) - \psi_2\left(1 - B^2\right) - \psi_3\left(1 - B^3\right) - \cdots \\
&= (1 - B)\left(-\psi_1 - \psi_2(1 + B) - \psi_3\left(1 + B + B^2\right) - \cdots\right)
\end{aligned}
$$

that is,

$$C(B) = (1 - B)\left(-\left(\sum_{j=1}^{\infty}\psi_j\right) - \left(\sum_{j=2}^{\infty}\psi_j\right)B - \left(\sum_{j=3}^{\infty}\psi_j\right)B^2 - \cdots\right) = \nabla\tilde{\psi}(B)$$

Thus,

$$\psi(B) = \psi(1) + \nabla\tilde{\psi}(B)$$

implying that:

$$\nabla x_t = \mu + \psi(1)e_t + \nabla\tilde{\psi}(B)e_t$$

This gives the decomposition due to Beveridge and Nelson (1981), with components

$$\nabla z_t = \mu + \left(\sum_{j=0}^{\infty}\psi_j\right)e_t = \mu + \psi(1)e_t \tag{8.9}$$

and

$$u_t = -\left(\sum_{j=1}^{\infty}\psi_j\right)e_t - \left(\sum_{j=2}^{\infty}\psi_j\right)e_{t-1} - \left(\sum_{j=3}^{\infty}\psi_j\right)e_{t-2} - \cdots = \tilde{\psi}(B)e_t$$

Since e_t is white noise, the trend component is, therefore, a random walk with rate of drift equal to μ and an innovation equal to $\psi(1)e_t$, which is therefore proportional to that of the original series. The noise component is clearly stationary, but since it is driven by the same innovation as the trend component, z_t and u_t must be *perfectly correlated*, in direct contrast to the Muth decomposition that assumes that they are independent. For example, the Beveridge–Nelson decomposition of the ARIMA(0,1,1) process (8.4) is:

$$\nabla z_t = \mu + (1 - \theta)e_t \tag{8.10}$$

$$u_t = \theta e_t \tag{8.11}$$

8.5 The relationship between the Beveridge–Nelson and Muth decompositions is exact. Rather than assuming u_t and v_t to be independent, suppose that $v_t = \alpha u_t$. Equating (8.2) and (8.4) then yields:

$$\nabla x_t = \mu + (1 + \alpha)u_t - u_{t-1} = \mu + e_t - \theta e_{t-1}$$

so that $e_t = (1 + \alpha)u_t$ and $\theta e_t = u_t$, thus recovering (8.11) and implying that $\theta = 1/(1 + \alpha)$. The trend (8.10) then becomes:

$$\nabla z_t = \mu + (1 - \theta)e_t = \mu + \frac{(1 - \theta)}{\theta}u_t = \mu + \alpha u_t = \mu + v_t$$

which recovers the Muth trend.

8.6 Following Newbold (1990), a straightforward way of estimating the Beveridge–Nelson components is to approximate the Wold decomposition (8.8) by an ARIMA(p,1,q) process by setting $\psi(B) = \theta(B)/\phi(B)$:

$$\nabla x_t = \mu + \frac{\theta(B)}{\phi(B)}e_t = \mu + \frac{\left(1 - \theta_1 B - \cdots - \theta_q B^q\right)}{\left(1 - \phi_1 B - \cdots - \phi_p B^p\right)}e_t \tag{8.12}$$

so that

$$\nabla z_t = \mu + \psi(1)e_t = \mu + \frac{\theta(1)}{\phi(1)}e_t = \mu + \frac{\left(1 - \theta_1 - \cdots - \theta_q\right)}{\left(1 - \phi_1 - \cdots - \phi_p\right)}e_t \tag{8.13}$$

Eq. (8.12) can also be written as

$$\frac{\phi(B)}{\theta(B)}\psi(1)\nabla x_t = \mu + \psi(1)e_t \tag{8.14}$$

and comparing (8.13) and (8.14) shows that

$$z_t = \frac{\phi(B)}{\theta(B)}\psi(1)x_t = \omega(B)x_t$$

The trend is, thus, a weighted average of current and past values of the observed series, with the weights summing to unity since $\omega(1) = 1$. The noise component is then given by:

$$u_t = x_t - \omega(B)x_t = (1 - \omega(B))x_t = \tilde{\omega}(B)x_t = \frac{\phi(1)\theta(B) - \theta(1)\phi(B)}{\phi(1)\theta(B)}x_t$$

Since $\tilde{\omega}(1) = 1 - \omega(1) = 0$, the weights for the noise component sum to zero. Using (8.12), this component can also be expressed as:

$$u_t = \frac{\phi(1)\theta(B) - \theta(1)\phi(B)}{\phi(1)\phi(B)\nabla} e_t \tag{8.15}$$

As u_t is stationary, the numerator of (8.15) can be written as $\phi(1)\theta(B) - \theta(1)\phi(B) = \nabla\varphi(B)$, since it must contain a unit root to cancel out the one in the denominator. As the order of the numerator is $\max(p, q)$, $\varphi(B)$ must be of order $r = \max(p, q) - 1$, implying that the noise has the ARMA (p,r) representation

$$\phi(B)u_t = \frac{\varphi(B)}{\phi(1)} e_t$$

For example, for the ARIMA(0,1,1) process (8.4), the components are:

$$z_t = (1 - \theta B)^{-1}(1 - \theta)x_t = \left(1 + \theta B + \theta^2 B^2 + \cdots\right)(1 - \theta)x_t = (1 - \theta)\sum_{j=0}^{\infty}\theta^j x_{t-j}$$

and

$$u_t = \frac{(1 - \theta B) - (1 - \theta)}{(1 - \theta B)}x_t = \frac{\theta(1 - B)}{(1 - \theta B)}x_t = \theta(1 - \theta B)^{-1}\nabla x_t = \theta\sum_{j=0}^{\infty}\theta^j x_{t-j}$$

Thus, the trend can be recursively estimated as:

$$\hat{z}_t = \theta\,\hat{z}_{t-1} + (1 - \theta)x_t \quad \hat{u}_t = x_t - \hat{z}_t$$

with starting values $\hat{z}_1 = x_1$ and $\hat{u}_1 = 0$.

8.7 In a more general context, it is possible for a time series x_t with Wold decomposition (8.8) to be written as (8.1) with z_t being a random walk and u_t being stationary and where the innovations of the two components are correlated to an arbitrary degree. However, only the Beveridge–Nelson decomposition is *guaranteed* to exist.

EXAMPLE 8.1 Beveridge–Nelson Decomposition of the *All Share* Index

The following ARIMA(2,1,2) model was found to adequately fit the logarithms of the *All Share* index:

$$\left(1 + 1.047B + 0.839B^2\right) \nabla x_t = 0.0057 + \left(1 + 1.155B + 0.884B^2\right) e_t$$

Thus,

$$\psi(1) = \frac{\theta(1)}{\phi(1)} = \frac{(1 + 1.155 + 0.884)}{(1 + 1.047 + 0.839)} = \frac{3.039}{2.886} = 1.053$$

and the Beveridge–Nelson trend is, thus,

$$\nabla z_t = 0.0057 + 1.053 e_t$$

or, equivalently,

$$z_t = -1.155z_{t-1} - 0.884z_{t-2} + 1.053x_t + 1.102x_{t-1} + 0.931x_{t-2}$$

Since,

$$\phi(1)\theta(B) - \theta(1)\phi(B) = -0.153 + 0.151B + 0.002B^2 = \nabla(-0.153 + 0.002B)$$

the noise component is, thus, the ARMA(2,1) process:

$$u_t = \frac{\varphi(B)}{\phi(1)\phi(B)} e_t = -1.047u_{t-1} - 0.839u_{t-2} - 0.053e_t - 0.0007e_{t-1}$$

SIGNAL EXTRACTION

8.8   Given a UC model of the form of (8.1) and models for z_t and u_t, it is often useful to provide estimates of these two unobserved components, a procedure that is known as *signal extraction*. A MMSE estimate of z_t, is an estimate $\hat{z}_t$ which minimizes $E(\zeta_t^2)$, where $\zeta_t = z_t - \hat{z}_t$ is the estimation error (cf. §7.2). From, for example, Pierce (1979), given an infinite sample of observations, denoted $\{x_t, -\infty \le t \le \infty\}$, such an estimator is:

$$\hat{z}_t = \nu_z(B)x_t = \sum_{j=-\infty}^{\infty} \nu_{zj}x_{t-j}$$

where the filter $\nu_z(B)$ is defined as:

$$\nu_z(B) = \frac{\sigma_v^2 \gamma(B)\gamma(B^{-1})}{\sigma_e^2 \theta(B)\theta(B^{-1})}$$

in which case the noise component can be estimated as:

$$\hat{u}_t = x_t - \hat{z}_t = (1 - \nu_z(B))x_t = \nu_u(B)x_t$$

For example, for the Muth model of a random walk overlaid with white noise:

$$\nu_z(B) = \frac{\sigma_v^2}{\sigma_e^2}(1-\theta B)^{-1}(1-\theta B^{-1})^{-1} = \frac{\sigma_v^2}{\sigma_e^2}\frac{1}{(1-\theta^2)}\sum_{j=-\infty}^{\infty}\theta^{|j|}B^j$$

so that, using $\sigma_v^2 = (1-\theta)^2\sigma_e^2$, obtained using (8.6), we have:

$$\hat{z}_t = \frac{(1-\theta)^2}{1-\theta^2}\sum_{j=-\infty}^{\infty}\theta^{|j|}x_{t-j}$$

Thus, for values of θ close to unity, $\hat{z}_t$ will be given by an extremely long moving average of future and past values of x. If θ is close to zero, however, $\hat{z}_t$ will be almost equal to the most recently observed value of x. From (8.3), large values of θ are seen to correspond to small values of the signal-to-noise variance ratio $\kappa = \sigma_v^2/\sigma_u^2$. When the noise component dominates, a long moving average of x values will provide the best estimate of the trend, while if the noise component is only small then the trend is essentially given by the current position of x.

8.9   The estimation error can be written as:

$$\zeta_t = z_t - \hat{z}_t = \nu_z(B)z_t - \nu_u(B)u_t$$

and Pierce (1979) shows that ζ_t will be stationary if z_t and u_t are generated by processes of the form of (8.4). In fact, ζ_t will follow the process:

$$\zeta_t = \theta_\zeta(B)\xi_t$$

where

$$\theta_\zeta = \frac{\gamma(B)\lambda(B)}{\theta(B)} \qquad \sigma_\xi^2 = \frac{\sigma_a^2 \sigma_v^2}{\sigma_e^2}$$

and $\xi_t \sim WN\left(0, \sigma_\xi^2\right)$.

For the Muth model ζ_t follows the AR(1) process

$$(1 - \theta B)\zeta_t = \xi_t$$

and the mean square error of the optimal signal extraction procedure is:

$$E\left(\zeta_t^2\right) = \frac{\sigma_a^2 \sigma_v^2}{\sigma_e^2\left(1 - \theta^2\right)}$$

8.10   As noted earlier, if we are given only a realization of x_t and its model, that is, (8.6), then component models for z_t and u_t are in general unidentified. If x_t follows the ARIMA(0,1,1) process

$$\nabla x_t = (1 - \theta B)e_t \tag{8.16}$$

then the most general signal-plus-*white*-noise UC model has z_t given by:

$$\nabla z_t = (1 - \Theta B)v_t \tag{8.17}$$

and for any Θ value in the interval $-1 \leq \Theta \leq \theta$ there exists values of σ_a^2 and σ_v^2 such that $z_t + u_t$ yields (8.16). It can be shown that setting $\Theta = -1$ minimizes the variance of both z_t and u_t, which is known as the *canonical decomposition* of x_t. Choosing this value implies that $\gamma(B) = 1 + B$, and we have:

$$\hat{z}_t = \frac{\sigma_v^2(1 + B)\left(1 + B^{-1}\right)}{\sigma_e^2(1 - \theta B)(1 - \theta B^{-1})}$$

and

$$(1 - \theta B)\zeta_t = (1 + B)\xi_t.$$

8.11   In this development, we have assumed that in estimating z_t the future as well as the past of x_t is available. In many applications, it is necessary to estimate z_t given only data on x_t up to $s = t - m$, for finite m. This includes the problems of signal extraction based either on current data ($m = 0$) or on recent data ($m < 0$), and the problem of forecasting the signal ($m > 0$). We, thus, need to extend the analysis to consider signal extraction given only the *semi-infinite* sample $\{x_s, \ s \leq t - m\}$. Pierce (1979) shows that, in this case, an estimate of z_t is given by:

$$\hat{z}_t^{(m)} = \nu_z^{(m)}(B)x_t$$

where

$$\nu_z^{(m)}(B) = \frac{(1-B)}{\sigma_e^2 \theta(B)} \left[\frac{\sigma_v^2 \gamma(B)\gamma(B^{-1})}{(1-B)\theta(B^{-1})} \right]_m$$

in which we use the notation

$$[h(B)]_m = \sum_{j=m}^{\infty} h_j B^j$$

Thus, for the Muth model we have

$$\nu_z^{(m)}(B) = \frac{\sigma_v^2(1-B)}{\sigma_e^2(1-\theta B)} \left[\frac{(1-B)^{-1}}{(1-\theta B^{-1})} \right]_m$$

and Pierce (1979) shows that this becomes, for $m \geq 0$,

$$\nu_z^{(m)}(B) = \frac{\sigma_v^2 B^m}{\sigma_e^2(1-\theta)} \sum_{j=0}^{\infty} (\theta B)^j = (1-\theta)B^m \sum_{j=0}^{\infty} (\theta B)^j$$

while, for $m < 0$,

$$\nu_z^{(m)}(B) = \theta^{-m}(1-\theta)B^m \sum_{j=0}^{\infty} (\theta B)^j + \frac{1}{(1-\theta B)} \sum_{j=0}^{-m-1} \theta^j B^{-j}$$

Thus, when either estimating z_t for the current observation ($m = 0$) or forecasting z_t ($m > 0$), we apply an exponentially weighted moving average to the observed series, beginning with the most recent data available, but not otherwise depending on the value of m. For $m < 0$, when we are estimating z_t based on some, but not all, of the available future observations of x_t, the filter comprises two parts: the same filter as in the $m \geq 0$ case applied to the furthest forward observation but with a declining weight (θ^{-m}) placed upon it, and a second term capturing the additional influence of the observed future observations.

8.12 UC models can also be analyzed within a *state space* framework, in which the Kalman filter plays a key role in providing both optimal forecasts and a method of estimating the unknown model parameters. In this framework, models such as the random-walk-plus-white noise are known as *structural models*, and a thorough discussion of the methodological and technical ideas underlying such formulations is contained in Harvey (1989) and Durbin and Koopman (2012), while Koopman et al. (1999) and Koopman et al. (2009) provide computer software: Chapter 17, State Space Models, discusses state space modeling in further detail.

FILTERS

8.13   The UC model (8.5) is also related to the *Hodrick–Prescott trend filter* (Hodrick and Prescott, 1997), which is a popular method of detrending economic time series. This filter is derived by minimizing the variation in the noise component $u_t = x_t - z_t$, subject to a condition on the "smoothness" of the trend component z_t. This smoothness condition penalizes acceleration in the trend, so that the minimization problem becomes that of minimizing the function:

$$\sum_{t=1}^{T} u_t^2 + \lambda \sum_{t=1}^{T} ((z_{t+1} - z_t) - (z_t - z_{t-1}))^2$$

with respect to z_t, $t = 0, 1, \ldots, T + 1$, where λ is a Lagrangean multiplier that can be interpreted as a smoothness parameter. The higher the value of λ, the smoother the trend is, so that in the limit, as $\lambda \to \infty$, z_t becomes a linear trend. The first-order conditions are:

$$0 = -2(x_t - z_t) + 2\lambda((z_t - z_{t-1}) - (z_{t-1} - z_{t-2})) - 4\lambda((z_{t+1} - z_t) - (z_t - z_{t-1}))$$
$$+ 2\lambda((z_{t+2} - z_{t+1}) - (z_{t+1} - z_t))$$

which may be written as:

$$x_t = z_t + \lambda(1-B)^2(z_t - 2z_{t+1} + z_{t+2}) = \left(1 + \lambda(1-B)^2 (1-B^{-1})^2\right)z_t$$

so that the Hodrick–Prescott (H–P) trend estimator is

$$\hat{z}_t(\lambda) = \left(1 + \lambda(1-B)^2(1-B^{-1})^2\right)^{-1} x_t \tag{8.18}$$

The MMSE trend estimator can be written using (8.7) as:

$$\hat{z}_t = \frac{\sigma_\nu^2 \gamma(B)\gamma\left(B^{-1}\right)}{\sigma_e^2 \theta(B)\theta(B^{-1})} x_t = \frac{\gamma(B)\gamma\left(B^{-1}\right)}{\gamma(B)\gamma(B^{-1}) + \left(\sigma_a^2/\sigma_\nu^2\right)\lambda(B)\lambda(B^{-1})} x_t$$

Comparing this with the H–P trend estimator (8.18) shows that, for the latter to be optimal in the MMSE sense, we must set

$$\gamma(B) = (1-B)^{-1}, \quad \lambda(B) = 1, \quad \delta = \frac{\sigma_a^2}{\sigma_\nu^2}$$

In other words, the underlying UC model must have the trend component $\nabla^2 z_t = \nu_t$ and u_t must be white noise.

8.14 Setting $\lambda = 100$ is often suggested when extracting a trend from an annual series. Theoretical and simulation analyses have, however, suggested using a much higher value when using annual data (see Harvey and Trimbur, 2008; Flaig, 2015, for example): other choices are discussed by Ravn and Uhlig (2002) and Maravall and del Rio (2007). For example, Ravn and Uhlig suggest that, if there are s periods per year (e.g., 12 if the data is observed monthly), then the smoothing parameter should be set at $\lambda = 1600(s/4)^m$, where m is set at either 2 or 4 (if the former this yields $\lambda = 100$ for annual data; if the latter then $\lambda = 6.25$).

However, if, as is likely in practice, the object of using an H−P filter has the purely descriptive aim of extracting a smooth trend component with a smoothly evolving growth rate, then some experimentation with different, and possibly high, values of λ is probably warranted.

8.15 In filtering terminology the H−P filter (8.18) is a *low-pass filter*. To understand this terminology, some basic concepts in filtering theory are useful. A *linear filter* of the observed series x_t may be defined as the two-sided weighted moving average:

$$y_t = \sum_{j=-n}^{n} a_j x_{t-j} = \left(a_{-n}B^{-n} + a_{-n+1}B^{-n+1} + \cdots + a_0 + \cdots + a_n B^n\right)x_t = a(B)x_t$$

Two conditions are typically imposed upon the filter $a(B)$: (1) that the filter weights either (a) sum to zero, $a(1) = 0$, or (b) sum to unity, $a(1) = 1$; and (2) that these weights are symmetric, $a_j = a_{-j}$ If condition (1,a) holds then $a(B)$ is a "trend-elimination" filter, whereas if (2,b) holds it will be a "trend-extraction" filter. If the former holds then $b(B) = 1 - a(B)$ will be the corresponding trend-extraction filter, having the same, but oppositely signed, weights as the trend-elimination filter $a(B)$ except for the central value, $b_0 = 1 - a_0$, thus ensuring that $b(B) = 1$.

8.16 The *frequency response function* of the filter is defined as $a(\omega) = \sum_j e^{-i\omega j}$ for a frequency $0 \leq \omega \leq 2\pi$. The *power transfer function* is then defined as:

$$|a(\omega)|^2 = \left(\sum_j a_j \cos\omega j\right)^2 + \left(\sum_j a_j \sin\omega j\right)^2$$

and the *gain* is defined as $|a(\omega)|$, measuring the extent to which the amplitude of the ω-frequency component of x_t is altered through the filtering operation. In general, $a(\omega) = |a(\omega)|e^{-i\theta(\omega)}$, where:

$$\theta(\omega) = \tan^{-1}\frac{\sum_j a_j \sin\omega j}{\sum_j a_j \cos\omega j}$$

is the *phase shift*, indicating the extent to which the ω−frequency component of x_t is displaced in time. If the filter is indeed symmetric then $a(\omega) = a(-\omega)$, so that $a(\omega) = |a(\omega)|$ and $\theta(\omega) = 0$, known as phase neutrality.

8.17 With these concepts, an "ideal" low-pass filter has the frequency response function:

$$a_L(\omega) = \begin{cases} 1 & \text{if } \omega < \omega_c \\ 0 & \text{if } \omega > \omega_c \end{cases} \tag{8.19}$$

Thus, $a_L(\omega)$ passes only frequencies lower than the cutoff frequency ω_c, so that just slow-moving, low-frequency components of x_t are retained. Low-pass filters should also be phase-neutral, so that temporal shifts are not induced by filtering. The ideal low-pass filter will take the form:

$$a_L(B) = \frac{\omega_c}{\pi} + \sum_{j=1}^{\infty} \frac{\sin\omega_c j}{\pi j}\left(B^j + B^{-j}\right)$$

In practice, low-pass filters will not have the perfect "jump" in $a_L(\omega)$ implied by (8.19). The H−P trend-extraction filter, that is, the one that provides an estimate of the trend component $\hat{\mu}_t = a_{H-P}(B)x_t$, where the weights are given by (8.18), has the frequency response function:

$$a_{H-P}(\omega) = \frac{1}{1 + 4\lambda(1 - \cos\omega)^2} \tag{8.20}$$

while the H−P trend-elimination filter, which provides the cycle estimate $\hat{\psi}_t = b_{H-P}(B)x_t = (1 - a_{H-P}(B))x_t$, has the frequency response function:

$$b_{H-P}(\omega) = 1 - a_{H-P}(\omega) = \frac{4\lambda(1 - \cos\omega)^2}{1 + 4\lambda(1 - \cos\omega)^2}$$

8.18 Rather than setting the smoothing parameter at an a priori value, such as $\lambda = 100$, it could also be set at the value that equates the gain to 0.5, that is, at the value that separates frequencies between those mostly associated with the trend and those mostly associated with the cycle. Since the H−P weights are indeed symmetric, the gain is given by (8.20), so equating this to 0.5 yields $\lambda = 1/4(1 - \cos\omega_{0.5})^2$, where $\omega_{0.5}$ is the frequency at which the gain is 0.5 (for more on this idea, see Kaiser and Maravall, 2005).

8.19 The ideal low-pass filter removes high-frequency components while retaining low-frequency components. A high-pass filter does the reverse, so that the complementary high-pass filter to (8.19) has $a_H(\omega) = 0$ if $\omega < \omega_c$ and $a_H(\omega) = 1$ if $\omega \geq \omega_c$. The ideal band-pass filter passes only frequencies in the range $\omega_{c,1} \leq \omega \leq \omega_{c,2}$, so that it can be constructed as the difference between two low-pass filters with cutoff frequencies $\omega_{c,1}$ and $\omega_{c,2}$. It will have the frequency response function $a_B(\omega) = a_{c,2}(\omega) - a_{c,1}(\omega)$, where $a_{c,2}(\omega)$ and $a_{c,1}(\omega)$ are the frequency response functions of the two low-pass filters, since this will give a frequency response of unity in the band $\omega_{c,1} \leq \omega \leq \omega_{c,2}$ and zero elsewhere. The weights of the band-pass filter will, thus, be given by

$a_{c,2,j} - a_{c,1,j}$, where $a_{c,2,j}$ and $a_{c,1,j}$ are the weights of the two low-pass filters, so that:

$$a_B(B) = \frac{w_{c,2} - w_{c,1}}{\pi} + \sum_{j=1}^{\infty} \frac{\sin w_{c,2} j - \sin w_{c,1} j}{\pi j} \left(B^j + B^{-j} \right) \tag{8.21}$$

8.20   As an example of the use of band-pass filters, a conventional definition of the economic business cycle emphasizes fluctuations of between one and a half and eight years (see Baxter and King, 1999), which leads to $w_{c,1} = 2\pi/8 = \pi/4$ and $w_{c,2} = 2\pi/1.5 = 4\pi/3$. Thus, a band-pass filter that passes only frequencies corresponding to these periods is defined as $y_t = a_{B,n}(B) x_t$ with weights:

$$a_{B,0} = a_{c,2,0} - a_{c,1,0} = \frac{4}{3} - \frac{1}{4} - \left(\zeta_{c,2,n} - \zeta_{c,1,n} \right)$$

$$a_{B,j} = a_{c,2,j} - a_{c,1,j} = \frac{1}{\pi j} \left(\sin \frac{4\pi j}{3} - \sin \frac{\pi j}{4} \right) - \left(\zeta_{c,2,n} - \zeta_{c,1,n} \right) \quad j = 1, \ldots, n$$

$$\tag{8.22}$$

where

$$\zeta_{c,i,n} = -\frac{\sum_{j=-n}^{n} a_{c,i,n}}{2n + 1} \quad i = 1, 2$$

The infinite length filter in (8.21) has been truncated to have only n leads and lags and the appearance of the $\zeta_{c,i,n}$ terms ensures that the filter weights sum to zero, so that $a_{B,n}(B)$ is a trend-elimination (i.e., cycle) filter. The filter in (8.22) is known as the Baxter–King (B–K) filter, with further extensions being provided by Christiano and Fitzgerald (2003).

8.21   The previously introduced filters all imply that the observed series is generated by heavily restricted ARIMA(0,d,q) processes. A rather less restrictive approach is to begin by assuming that the observed series has an ARIMA(p,d,q) representation and to then derive filters with the desired properties from this representation (see Proietti, 2009a,b, for technical details):

8.22   The H–P and B–K filters are often referred to as being ad hoc, in the sense here that they are invariant to the actual process generating x_t. This has the potential danger that such filters could produce a cyclical component, say, that might display cyclical features that are absent from the observed series, something that is known as the Slutsky–Yule effect. For example, it has been well documented that when the H–P filter is applied to a random walk, which obviously cannot contain any cyclical patterns, the detrended series can nevertheless display spurious cyclical behavior. The (ARIMA) model based filters are designed to overcome these limitations.

EXAMPLE 8.2 Fitting H−P Trends to Global Temperatures

Fig. 8.1 shows three H−P trends for monthly global temperatures, obtained using the smoothing parameter values $\lambda = 14,400$, $129,600$, and $500,000$ respectively. The Ravn−Uhlig rule with m equal to 2 and then 4 is used for the first two settings. These trends exhibit a good deal of "wriggling," whereas the largest setting

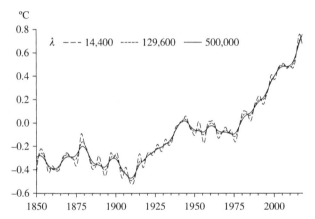

FIGURE 8.1   Alternative H−P trends for monthly global temperatures, 1850−2017. *H−P*, Hodrick−Prescott.

of $\lambda = 500,000$ (which was used for the H−P trend shown in Fig. 2.13) displays a considerably greater degree of smoothness and may, thus, be thought to be a better representation of an underlying trend movement.

EXAMPLE 8.3 Fitting an H−P Trend to British Real Per Capita GDP

Example 5.5 investigated the trend in the logarithms of British real per capita GDP for the period of 1822−1913. The top panel of Fig. 8.2 shows this series for the much longer period of 1270−1913 with an H−P trend calculated with $\lambda = 10,000$ superimposed. This trend looks to display a suitable degree of smoothness and this is confirmed by the annual trend growth rates shown in the bottom panel of Fig. 8.2. These are "smoothly varying" and show neatly two

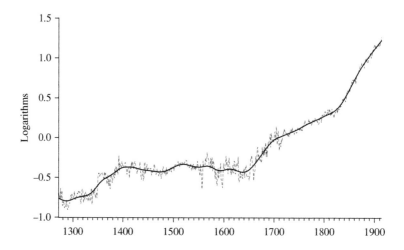

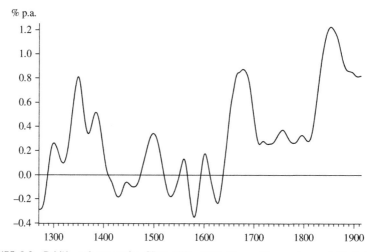

FIGURE 8.2   British real per capita GDP, 1270–1913. Top: with superimposed H–P trend with $\lambda = 10,000$; bottom: H–P trend annual growth rate. *H–P*, Hodrick–Prescott.

growth "takeoffs," the first in the middle of the 17th century and the second a century or so later with the onset of the industrial revolution.[1]

ENDNOTES

1. A detailed analysis of this important series (and others related to it) in the historiography of the British economy is provided by Crafts and Mills (2017), who also provide bounds for the trend growth rates using the approach of Giles (2011).

Chapter 9

Seasonality and Exponential Smoothing

Chapter Outline

SEASONAL PATTERNS IN TIME SERIES

9.1 In §§**2.16–2.17** we introduced the idea of seasonal patterns appearing in time series observed at frequencies greater than annual, typically monthly or quarterly. The presence of seasonality is often immediately apparent from a plot of the series (recall the quarterly United Kingdom beer sales series of Fig. 1.4), but it will also manifest itself in the sample autocorrelation function (SACF) of the appropriately differenced data. Fig. 9.1 shows the SACF of the first differences of beer sales, which is dominated by a pronounced seasonal pattern, and a similar effect is seen in Fig. 9.2, which shows the SACF for the square root of monthly England and Wales rainfall (recall §§**2.3–2.6** and Fig. 2.4). Clearly a seasonal pattern is a predictable feature of these series and is, therefore, susceptible to either modeling explicitly or to being removed by a suitable seasonal adjustment procedure, as in §§**2.16–2.17**.

MODELING DETERMINISTIC SEASONALITY

9.2 A simple model for seasonality was alluded to in §§**2.6–2.7**, which is to use a "seasonal mean" model in which there is a different mean for each season, that is, the model for x_t is:

$$x_t = \sum\nolimits_{i=1}^{m} \alpha_i s_{i,t} + \varepsilon_t \tag{9.1}$$

where the seasonal dummy variable $s_{i,t}$ takes the value 1 for the ith season and zero otherwise, there being m seasons in the year. Thus, for example, if the

Applied Time Series Analysis. DOI: https://doi.org/10.1016/B978-0-12-813117-6.00009-0
145

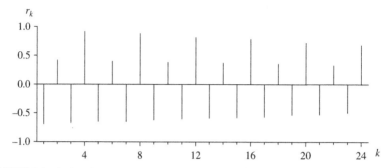

FIGURE 9.1 SACF of the first-difference of quarterly UK beer sales, 1997–2017.

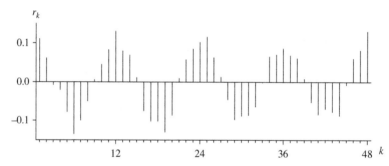

FIGURE 9.2 SACF of the square root of England and Wales monthly rainfall, 1875–2017.

data is monthly then $i = 1$ for January, etc., and $m = 12$. The noise ε_t may be modeled as an ARIMA process, say $\phi(B)\epsilon_t = \theta(B)a_t$, if required. The regression model (9.1) thus assumes that the seasonal pattern is *deterministic*, in the sense that the seasonal means α_i, $i = 1, \ldots, m$, remain constant through time.[1]

EXAMPLE 9.1 A Deterministic Seasonal Model for England and Wales Rainfall

The regression model (9.1) was fitted to the square root transformed monthly England and Wales rainfall series with ε_t taken to be white noise, an assumption that was found to be supported by diagnostic tests. Since a square root transformation of rainfall has been taken, the mean rainfall for month i is given by α_i^2, estimates of which are:

Jan	Feb	Mar	Apr	May	June	July	Aug	Sept	Oct	Nov	Dec
843	620	612	562	609	607	716	803	716	914	929	917

The seasonal pattern is both clear and perhaps surprising. The driest period is from February to June, which averages 602 mm per month, whereas the period from July through to January averages almost 40% more, being 834 mm.

Since there is no evidence that this simple model is misspecified, a further conclusion is that this seasonal pattern has remained constant throughout the entire sample period of over 140 years.

MODELING STOCHASTIC SEASONALITY

9.3 It would, however, be imprudent to rule out the possibility of an evolving seasonal pattern: in other words, the presence of *stochastic* seasonality. As in the modeling of stochastic trends, ARIMA processes have been found to do an excellent job in modeling stochastic seasonality, albeit in an extended form to that developed in previous chapters.

9.4 An important consideration when attempting to model a seasonal time series with an ARIMA model is to determine what sort of process will best match the SACFs and PACFs that characterize the data. Concentrating on the beer sales series, we have already noted the seasonal pattern in the SACF for ∇x_t shown in Fig. 9.1. In considering the SACF further, we note that the seasonality manifests itself in large positive autocorrelations at the seasonal lags $(4k, k \geq 1)$ being flanked by negative autocorrelations at the "satellites" $[4(k-1), 4(k+1)]$. The slow decline of these seasonal autocorrelations is indicative of *seasonal nonstationarity* and, analogous to the analysis of "nonseasonal nonstationarity," this may be dealt with by *seasonal differencing*, that is, by using the $\nabla_4 = 1 - B^4$ operator in conjunction with the usual ∇ operator. Fig. 9.3 shows the SACF of $\nabla \nabla^4$ transformed beer sales and this is now clearly stationary and, thus, potentially amenable to ARIMA identification.

9.5 In general, if we have a seasonal period of m then the seasonal differencing operator may be denoted as ∇_m. The nonseasonal and seasonal differencing operators may then be applied d and D times, respectively, so that a seasonal ARIMA model may take the general form

$$\nabla^d \nabla_m^D \phi(B) x_t = \theta(B) a_t \tag{9.2}$$

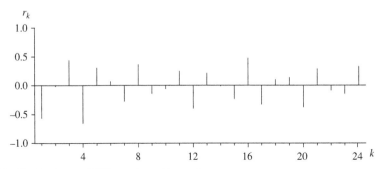

FIGURE 9.3 SACF of $\nabla \nabla^4$ transformed beer sales.

Appropriate forms of the $\theta(B)$ and $\phi(B)$ polynomials can then, at least in principle, be obtained by the usual methods of identification and/or model selection. Unfortunately, two difficulties are typically encountered. First, the PACFs of seasonal models are difficult both to derive and to interpret, so that conventional identification is usually based solely on the behavior of the appropriate SACF. Second, since the $\theta(B)$ and $\phi(B)$ polynomials need to account for the seasonal autocorrelation, at least one of them must be of minimum order m. This often means that the number of models which need to be considered in model selection procedures can become prohibitively large.

9.6   This difficulty is amply illustrated in Fig. 9.3. On the white noise null the standard error of a sample autocorrelation is 0.11, so that many of the values shown in the SACF are significantly different from zero, making the identification of a model of the type of (9.2) practically impossible and, if achieved, undoubtedly difficult to interpret. Box and Jenkins (1970, chapter 9) consequently developed an argument for using a restricted version of (9.2) which, they felt, could provide an adequate fit to many seasonal time series.

9.7   By way of introducing this model, consider the first 10 years of observations (1997−2006) on beer sales arranged in a year-by-quarter format, which emphasizes the fact that, in seasonal data, there are not one, but two, time intervals of importance.

	Q1	Q2	Q3	Q4
1997	7369	9464	9586	10,193
1998	7283	9748	8892	9837
1999	7215	9032	9315	10,265
2000	6852	9070	8865	9785
2001	6811	8972	8906	9939
2002	7137	9305	8820	9879
2003	7048	9286	9270	9896
2004	7318	9485	8795	10,043
2005	7090	9087	8995	9730
2006	6966	9500	8399	9582

These intervals correspond here to quarters and years and we would, therefore, expect two relationships to occur: (1) between observations for successive quarters in each year, and (2) between observations for the same quarters in successive years. This is clear in the data, where the seasonal effect implies that an observation for a particular quarter, say Q4, is related to the observations for previous Q4s.

9.8   The Q4 observations may then be linked by a model of the form:

$$\Phi(B^m)\nabla_m^D x_t = \Theta(B^m)\alpha_t \tag{9.3}$$

where $m = 4$ in the example and $\Phi(B^m)$ and $\Theta(B^m)$ are polynomials in B^m of orders P and Q respectively, that is,

$$\Phi(B^m) = 1 - \Phi_1 B^m - \Phi_2 B^{2m} - \cdots - \Phi_P B^{Pm}$$

$$\Theta(B^m) = 1 - \Theta_1 B^m - \Theta_2 B^{2m} - \cdots - \Theta_Q B^{Qm}$$

which satisfy standard stationarity and invertibility conditions. Now suppose that the same model holds for the observations from each quarter. This implies that all errors that correspond to a fixed quarter in different years are uncorrelated. However, the errors corresponding to adjacent quarters need not be uncorrelated, that is, the error series $\alpha_t, \alpha_{t-1}, \ldots$ may be autocorrelated. For example, beer sales in 2016Q4, while related to previous Q4 values, will also be related to the values in 2016Q3, 2016Q2, etc. These autocorrelations may be modeled by a second, nonseasonal, process:

$$\phi(B)\nabla^d \alpha_t = \theta(B)a_t \tag{9.4}$$

so that α_t is ARIMA(p, d, q) with a_t being a white noise process. Substituting (9.4) into (9.3) yields the general *multiplicative seasonal* model:

$$\phi_p(B)\Phi_P(B^m)\nabla^d \nabla_m^D x_t = \theta_q(B)\Theta_Q(B^m)a_t \tag{9.5}$$

The subscripts p, P, q, Q have been added for clarity so that the orders of the various polynomials may be emphasized and the ARIMA process in (9.5) is said to be of order $(p, d, q)(P, D, Q)_m$. A constant θ_0 can always be included in (9.5) and this will introduce a deterministic trend component into the model. A comparison with the "nonmultiplicative" model (9.2) shows that the $\theta(B)$ and $\phi(B)$ polynomials have been factored as:

$$\phi_{p+P}(B) = \phi_p(B)\Phi_P(B^m)$$

and

$$\theta_{q+Q}(B) = \theta_q(B)\Theta_Q(B^m)$$

9.9 Because the general multiplicative model (9.5) is rather complicated, explicit expressions for its ACF and PACF are difficult to provide. This led Box and Jenkins to consider a particularly simple case, in which an ARIMA (0,1,1) is used to link the x_ts one *year* apart:

$$\nabla_m x_t = (1 - \Theta B^m)\alpha_t$$

and a similar model is used to link α_ts one *observation* apart:

$$\nabla \alpha_t = (1 - \theta B)a_t$$

where, in general, θ and Θ will have different values. On combining the two equations we obtain the multiplicative ARIMA(0,1,1) (0,1,1)$_m$ model:

$$\nabla\nabla_m x_t = (1 - \theta B)(1 - \Theta B^m)\alpha_t \tag{9.6}$$

For invertibility, we require the roots of $(1 - \theta B)(1 - \Theta B^m)$ to satisfy the conditions $|\theta|, |\Theta| < 1$. The model (9.6) can be written as:

$$w_t = \left(1 - B - B^m + B^{m+1}\right)x_t = \left(1 - \theta B - \Theta B^m + \theta\Phi B^{m+1}\right)a_t$$

so that the autocovariances of w_t may be obtained from:

$$
\begin{aligned}
\gamma_k &= E(w_t w_{t-k}) \\
&= E(a_t - \theta a_{t-1} - \Theta a_{t-m} + \theta\Theta a_{t-m-1}) \\
&\quad \times (a_{t-k} - \theta a_{t-1-k} - \Theta a_{t-m-k} + \theta\Theta a_{t-m-1-k})
\end{aligned}
$$

these being

$$\gamma_0 = \left(1 + \theta^2\right)\left(1 + \Theta^2\right)\sigma^2$$

$$\gamma_1 = -\theta\left(1 + \Theta^2\right)\sigma^2$$

$$\gamma_{m-1} = \theta\Theta\sigma^2$$

$$\gamma_m = -\Theta\left(1 + \theta^2\right)\sigma^2$$

$$\gamma_{m+1} = \theta\Theta\sigma^2$$

with all the other γ_ks equal to zero. Hence, the ACF is:

$$\rho_1 = -\frac{\theta}{1 + \theta^2}$$

$$\rho_{m-1} = \frac{\theta\Theta}{(1 + \theta^2)(1 + \Theta^2)}$$

$$\rho_m = -\frac{\Theta}{1 + \Theta^2}$$

$$\rho_{m+1} = \rho_{m-1} = \rho_1\rho_m$$

and $\rho_k = 0$ otherwise.

9.10 On the assumption that the model is of the form of (9.6), the variances for the estimated sample autocorrelations at lags higher than $m + 1$ are given by:

$$V(r_k) = T^{-1}\left(1 + 2\left(r_1^2 + r_{m-1}^2 + r_m^2 + r_{m+1}^2\right)\right) \quad k > m + 1 \qquad (9.7)$$

Using this result in conjunction with the known form of the ACF will enable the ARIMA$(0, 1, 1)(0, 1, 1)_m$ model to be identified.[2] Of course, if the SACF follows a more complicated pattern, then other members of the ARIMA$(p, d, q)(P, D, Q)_m$ class will need to be considered.[3]

9.11 Forecasts for the ARIMA$(0,1,1)$ $(0,1,1)_m$ model may be computed using the approach outlined in §**7.2**, so that:

$$
\begin{aligned}
f_{T,h} = E(&x_{T+h-1} + x_{T+h-m} - x_{T+h-m-1} + a_{T+h} - \theta a_{T+h-1} \\
&- \Theta a_{T+h-m} + \theta\Theta a_{T+h-m-1} | x_T, x_{T-1}, \ldots)
\end{aligned}
$$

It can be shown that the ψ-weights in the process $x_t = \psi(B)a_t$, where:

$$\psi(B) = (1-B)^{-1}(1-B^m)^{-1}(1-\theta B)(1-\Theta B^m)$$

are given by:

$$\psi_{rm+1} = \psi_{rm+2} = \cdots = \psi_{(r+1)m-1} = (1-\theta)(r+1-r\Theta)$$

$$\psi_{(r+1)m} = (1-\theta)(r+1-r\Theta) + (1-\Theta)$$

and these may be used to calculate the h-step ahead forecast error variance as in (7.4).

EXAMPLE 9.2 Seasonal ARIMA Modeling of Beer Sales

The SACF for the $\nabla\nabla^4$ transformation of beer sales shown in Fig. 9.3 has $r_1 = -0.56$, $r_2 = -0.03$, $r_3 = 0.44$, $r_4 = -0.65$, and $r_5 = 0.30$. Since $r_2 \approx 0$ and $r_1 r_4 = 0.36$, these first five sample autocorrelations are, within reasonable sampling limits, consistent with the ACF of an ARIMA$(0, 1, 1)(0, 1, 1)_4$ airline model. Using (9.7) the standard error of the sample autocorrelations for lags greater than 5 is calculated to be 0.20. Only r_{16} exceeds two-standard errors, suggesting that this airline model could represent a satisfactory representation of the beer sales data. Fitting this model obtains[4]:

$$\nabla_1 \nabla_4 x_t = \left(1 - \frac{0.694}{(0.098)}B\right)\left(1 - \frac{0.604}{(0.110)}B^4\right)a_t \quad \hat\sigma = 271.9$$

The more general seasonal ARIMA model is estimated to be:

$$\nabla\nabla_4 x_t = \left(1 - \frac{0.802}{(0.072)}B - \frac{0.552}{(0.095)}B^4 + \frac{0.631}{(0.098)}B^5\right)a_t \quad \hat\sigma = 265.0$$

The multiplicative model imposes the nonlinear restriction $\theta_1\theta_4 + \theta_5 = 0$. The log-likelihoods of the two models are -547.76 and -545.64, leading to a likelihood ratio test statistic of 4.24, which is distributed as chi-square with one degree of freedom and so is not quite significant at the 2.5% level, although a Wald test does prove to be significant.

Using $\theta = 0.7$ and $\Theta = 0.6$ for simplicity, then the ψ-weights of the airline model are given, in general, by:

$$\psi_{4r+1} = \psi_{4r+2} = \psi_{4(r+1)-1} = 0.3(r+1-0.6r) = 0.3 + 0.12r$$

$$\psi_{4(r+1)} = 0.3(r+1-0.6r) + 0.4 = 0.7 + 0.12r$$

Thus,

$$\psi_1 = \psi_2 = \psi_3 = 0.3$$

$$\psi_4 = 0.7$$

$$\psi_5 = \psi_6 = \psi_7 = 0.42$$

$$\psi_8 = 0.82$$

$$\psi_9 = \psi_{10} = \psi_{11} = 0.54, \text{ etc.}$$

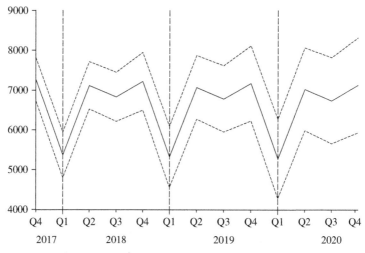

FIGURE 9.4   Airline model forecasts of beer sales out to 2020Q4 accompanied by two-standard error bounds.

Forecasts, with two-standard error bounds, for beer sales out to 2020Q4 are shown in Fig. 9.4, where their seasonal pattern is quite apparent. These forecasts show a slow decline for each quarter: the 2018Q1 forecast is 5370, the 2020Q1 forecast 5275, while the 2017Q4 forecast is 7266 compared to the 2020Q4 forecast of 7124. As expected, the forecast standard errors increase from 272 to 598 over the forecast horizon.

MIXED SEASONAL MODELS

9.12   The deterministic and stochastic seasonal models, (9.1) and (9.5), may be combined to form, on setting $d = D = 1$ for both simplicity and because these are the settings that are typically found,

$$x_t = \sum_{i=1}^m \alpha_i s_{i,t} + \frac{\theta_q(B)\Theta_Q(B^m)}{\phi_p(B)\Phi_P(B^m)\nabla\nabla_m} a_t \tag{9.8}$$

"Pure" stochastic seasonality simply requires that no seasonal dummies are significant in (9.8), i.e., that $\alpha_1 = \alpha_2 = \cdots = \alpha_m = 0$. Establishing whether there is "pure" deterministic seasonality is somewhat more complicated, for it requires both that the seasonal moving average polynomial $\Theta_Q(B^m)$ contains a seasonal unit root, i.e., that it can be factorized as $\Theta_Q(B^m) = \nabla_m \Theta_{Q-1}(B^m)$, so that the seasonal difference "cancels out," and also that $\Theta_{Q-1}(B^m) = \Phi_P(B^m)$, so that the seasonal polynomials in (9.8) also cancel out. Formally testing these hypotheses is quite complicated and will not be discussed here.[5]

SEASONAL ADJUSTMENT

9.13 In §**2.16** we introduced a decomposition of an observed time series into trend, seasonal, and irregular (or noise) components, focusing attention on estimating the seasonal component and then eliminating it to provide a *seasonally adjusted* series. Extending the notation introduced in (8.1), this implicit UC decomposition can be written as

$$x_t = z_t + s_t + u_t \qquad (9.9)$$

where the additional seasonal component s_t is assumed to be independent of both z_t and u_t. On obtaining an estimate of the seasonal component, $\hat{s}_t$, the seasonally adjusted series can then be defined as $x_t^a = x_t - \hat{s}_t$.

9.14 An important question is why we would wish to remove the seasonal component, rather than modeling it as an integral part of the stochastic process generating the data, as in fitting a seasonal ARIMA model, for example. A commonly held view is that the ability to recognize, interpret, or react to important nonseasonal movements in a series, such as turning points and other cyclical events, emerging patterns, or unexpected occurrences for which potential causes might be sought, may well be hindered by the presence of seasonal movements. Consequently, seasonal adjustment is carried out to simplify data so that they may be more easily interpreted by "statistically unsophisticated" users without this simplification being accompanied by too large a loss of information.

This qualifier is important because it requires that the seasonal adjustment procedure does not result in a "significant" loss of information. Although the moving average method introduced in §**2.16** is both intuitively and computationally simple, it may not be the best available method. Historically, seasonal adjustment methods have been categorized as either empirically- or model-based. The moving average method falls into the former category, as are the methods developed by statistical agencies, such as the sequence of procedures developed by the United States Bureau of the Census, the latest incarnation being known as X-13. Model-based methods employ signal extraction techniques based on ARIMA models fitted either to the observed series or to its components. The most popular of these methods is known as TRAMO/SEATS: see Gómez and Maravall (1996) and Mills (2013b). The distinction between empirical and model-based methods is, however, becoming blurred as X-13 also uses ARIMA models in its computations.[6]

EXPONENTIAL SMOOTHING

9.15 Returning to the two-component UC model, (8.1), where $x_t = z_t + u_t$, then a simple model for the signal or "level" z_t is to assume that its current value is an exponentially weighted moving average of current and past observations of x_t:

$$z_t = \alpha x_t + \alpha(1 - \alpha)x_{t-1} + \alpha(1-\alpha)^2 x_{t-2} + \cdots = \alpha \sum_{j=0}^{\infty} (1-\alpha)^j x_{t-j}$$
$$= \alpha\left(1 + (1 - \alpha)B + (1-\alpha)^2 B^2 + \cdots + (1-\alpha)^j B^j + \cdots\right)x_t$$

$$(9.10)$$

Since,[7]

$$1 + (1 - \alpha)B + (1-\alpha)^2 B^2 + \cdots + (1-\alpha)^j B^j + \cdots = (1 - (1-\alpha)B)^{-1}$$

Eq. (9.10) can be written as:

$$(1 - (1 - \alpha)B)z_t = \alpha x_t$$

or,

$$z_t = \alpha x_t + (1 - \alpha)z_{t-1} \qquad (9.11)$$

This shows that the current level, z_t, is a weighted average of the current observation, x_t, and the previous level, z_{t-1}, the weight being given by the "smoothing constant" α. Alternatively, (9.11) can be expressed in "error correction" form as:

$$z_t = z_{t-1} + \alpha(x_t - z_{t-1}) = z_{t-1} + \alpha e_t$$

so that the current level is updated from the previous level by a proportion of the current error $e_t = x_t - z_{t-1}$, the proportion again being given by the smoothing constant α.

9.16 Eq. (9.11) is the basic algorithm of *simple* (or *single*) *exponential smoothing*. Substituting (9.3) into (8.1) obtains:

$$\left(1 - \alpha(1 - (1-\alpha)B)^{-1}\right)x_t = u_t$$

This, in turn, may be written as $\nabla x_t = (1 - \theta B)a_t$ on setting $\theta = 1 - \alpha$ and $a_t = e_t/\theta$. Thus, simple exponential smoothing will be an optimal method of forecasting if x_t follows an ARIMA(0, 1, 1) process and the smoothing constant is set equal to $1 - \theta$. Indeed, it follows immediately that $f_{T,h} = z_T$ for all h, as was shown in §**7.4**.

Through its equivalence with the ARIMA(0, 1, 1) process, simple exponential smoothing will also be optimal for Muth's UC model of §**8.1** with level component given by $z_t = z_{t-1} + v_t$ (i.e., when there is no drift), where now the signal-to-noise variance ratio is related to the smoothing parameter by $\kappa = \alpha/(1 - \alpha)$.

9.17 Because the invertible region of an ARIMA(0, 1, 1) process is $-1 < \theta < 1$, this suggests that the range of the smoothing parameter is $0 < \alpha < 2$. Often a small value of α is found to work well, say $\alpha < 0.3$, but the smoothing constant may be estimated by minimizing the sum of squared one-step forecast errors, and this is now typically available in software routines.

9.18   Simple exponential smoothing is, therefore, a suitable forecasting procedure for a series in which a trend is absent. To capture a linear trend, the approach may be generalized by extending (9.11) to include a trend component,

$$
\begin{aligned}
z_t &= \alpha x_t + (1 - \alpha)(z_{t-1} + \tau_{t-1}) \\
&= z_{t-1} + \tau_{t-1} + \alpha e_t
\end{aligned}
\tag{9.12}
$$

where the error correction is now $e_t = x_t - z_{t-1} - \tau_{t-1}$, and defining a second updating equation for the trend τ_t:

$$
\begin{aligned}
\tau_t &= \beta(z_t - z_{t-1}) + (1 - \beta)\tau_{t-1} \\
&= \tau_{t-1} + \alpha\beta e_t
\end{aligned}
\tag{9.13}
$$

This pair of updating equations are together known as the *Holt–Winters* model.[8] Forecasts are given by:

$$
f_{T,h} = z_T + \tau_T h
\tag{9.14}
$$

and, therefore, lie on a "local" linear trend whose intercept and slope get updated each period by Eqs. (9.12) and (9.13). Using these recurrence relations, it can be shown that the Holt–Winters model is equivalent to the ARIMA$(0, 2, 2)$ process:

$$
\nabla^2 x_t = \left(1 - (2 - \alpha - \alpha\beta)B - (\beta - 1)B^2\right)a_t
$$

so that, in terms of the general process

$$
\nabla^2 x_t = (1 - \theta_1 B - \theta_2)a_t
\tag{9.15}
$$

the smoothing parameters are given by $\alpha = 1 + \theta_2$ and $\beta = (1 - \theta_1 - \theta_2)/(1 + \theta_2)$. Note that when $\alpha = \beta = 0$, then $\tau_t = \tau_{t-1} = \cdots = \tau$, say, and $z_t = z_{t-1} + \tau = z_0 + \tau t$, where z_0 is the initial value of the level component. Forecasts are then given by the "global" linear trend $f_{T,h} = z_0 + \tau(T + h)$. Moreover, in this case $\theta_1 = 2$ and $\theta_2 = -1$, so that:

$$
\nabla^2 x_t = \left(1 - 2B + B^2\right)a_t = \nabla^2 a_t
$$

which is equivalent to a trend stationary (TS) model for x_t.

9.19   A related approach is that of *double exponential smoothing*, which is defined by the pair of recursions:

$$
z_t = \gamma x_t + (1 - \gamma)z_{t-1}
$$

$$
\tau_t = \gamma(z_t - z_{t-1}) + (1 - \gamma)\tau_{t-1}
$$

so that only a single smoothing parameter is used.[9] Forecasts are computed using (9.14), so that they, again, follow a local linear trend with an intercept and slope that get updated every observation.

Double exponential smoothing is equivalent to the restricted ARIMA$(0, 2, 2)$ process

$$\nabla^2 x_t = (1 - (1 - \gamma)B)^2 a_t = \left(1 - 2(1 - \gamma)B + (1 - \gamma)^2 B^2\right) a_t$$

which places the restriction $\theta_1^2 + 4\theta_2 = 0$ on the parameters of (9.15). If $\alpha = \gamma(2 - \gamma)$ and $\beta = \gamma/(2 - \gamma)$, or equivalently that $\gamma^2 = \alpha\beta$ (i.e., that γ is the geometric mean of α and β), then Holt–Winters and double exponential smoothing are identical.

EXAMPLE 9.3 Forecasting Global Temperatures Using Exponential Smoothing

In Example 4.3, an ARIMA$(0, 1, 3)$ process without drift was fitted to monthly global temperatures, and in Example 7.2 this model was used to provide forecasts out to 2020. As $\hat{\theta}_2$ and $\hat{\theta}_3$, although significant, are both small when compared to $\hat{\theta}_1$, an ARIMA$(0, 1, 1)$ process should provide a decent fit to the series, and indeed it does, with $\hat{\theta} = 0.55$ and a root mean square error (RMSE) of 0.1255 [compared with 0.1236 for ARIMA$(0, 1, 3)$]. From the equivalence of simple exponential smoothing and the ARIMA$(0, 1, 1)$, we would expect the former model to produce a similar fit and forecasts for a smoothing parameter of $\alpha = 0.45$. Fitting the series by simple exponential smoothing and estimating α does indeed lead to this value for the smoothing parameter, an RMSE of 0.1257, and forecasts given by $f_{T,h} = z_T = 0.581$. These should be compared to the ARIMA$(0, 1, 3)$ forecasts obtained in Example 7.2, which, for $h > 2$, are equal to 0.621.

Acknowledging the possibility of a linear trend in global temperatures would require the use of either double exponential smoothing or Holt–Winters. The former estimates the single smoothing parameter to be $\gamma = 0.196$, accompanied by an RMSE of 0.1319. Interestingly, double exponential smoothing gives $z_T = 0.569$ and $\tau_T = -0.014$, so that, using (9.14), forecasts will contain a *negatively sloped,* albeit small, linear trend. Holt–Winters estimates the smoothing parameters as $\alpha = 0.45$ and $\beta = 0$, which implies that the trend component is a constant, so that $\tau_t = \tau_{t-1} = \cdots = \tau$, a value that is estimated by $x_2 - x_1 = 0.0005$. The Holt–Winters forecasts thus include a small positive linear trend which increases the forecasts from 0.582 to 0.599 by the end of the forecast period, December 2020. In either case, there is an absence of a significant positive drift in the forecasts, consistent with our earlier findings. Given that the RMSE of Holt–Winters was 0.1256, this implies that simple exponential smoothing is the most appropriate of these three techniques for forecasting monthly global temperatures.

9.20 Seasonality can easily be accommodated within the Holt–Winters framework. Based on (9.9), the *additive Holt–Winters* level updating equation (9.12) becomes

$$z_t = \alpha(x_t - s_{t-m}) + (1 - \alpha)(z_{t-1} + \tau_{t-1}) = z_{t-1} + \tau_{t-1}$$
$$+ \alpha(x_t - s_{t-m} - z_{t-1} - \tau_{t-1}) = z_{t-1} + \tau_{t-1} + \alpha e_t$$

The trend updating equation remains as (9.13) and there is an additional seasonal updating equation

$$s_t = \delta(x_t - z_t) + (1 - \delta)s_{t-m} = s_{t-m} + \delta(1 - \beta)e_t$$

Forecasts are then given by

$$f_{T,h} = z_T + \tau_T + s_{T+h-m}$$

These updating equations can be shown (Newbold, 1988) to be equivalent to the ARIMA model:

$$\nabla\nabla_m x_t = \theta_{m+1}(B)a_t \qquad (9.16)$$

where

$$\theta_1 = 1 - \alpha - \alpha\beta$$

$$\theta_2 = \cdots = \theta_{m-1} = -\alpha\beta$$

$$\theta_m = 1 - \alpha\beta - (1 - \alpha)\delta$$

$$\theta_{m+1} = -(1 - \alpha)(1 - \delta)$$

If $\beta = 0$, so that the trend is constant, then if $\theta_1\theta_m + \theta_{m+1} = 0$ as well, or equivalently $2 - 2\delta + \alpha\delta = 0$, (9.16) reduces to the ARIMA$(0, 1, 1)(0, 1, 1)_m$ airline model. Indeed, the airline model will also result if both $\alpha\beta$ and $\alpha\delta$ are negligibly small.

9.21 When modeling seasonal time series, it may be the case that the additive decomposition of (9.9) is felt to be inappropriate, for seasonal movements are often thought to be proportional to the level while the noise component still enters additively, that is, the decomposition takes the form:

$$x_t = z_t s_t + u_t$$

This, of course, rules out using a logarithmic transformation, which requires that all components enter multiplicatively. If this is the case then the *multiplicative Holt–Winters* model may be used, with the updating equations:

$$z_t = \alpha\left(\frac{x_t}{s_{t-m}}\right) + (1 - \beta)(z_{t-1} + \tau_{t-1}) = z_{t-1} + \tau_{t-1} + \frac{\alpha e_t}{s_{t-m}}$$

$$\tau_t = \beta(z_t - z_{t-1}) + (1 - \beta)\tau_{t-1} = \tau_{t-1} + \frac{\alpha\beta e_t}{s_{t-m}}$$

$$s_t = \delta\left(\frac{x_t}{z_t}\right) + (1 - \delta)s_{t-m} = s_{t-m} + \delta(1 - \alpha)\frac{e_t}{z_t}$$

Forecasts are then given by:

$$f_{T,h} = (z_T + \tau_T h)s_{T+h-m}$$

This model does not appear to have an equivalent ARIMA representation. Note that setting $\delta = 0$ in both the additive and multiplicative Holt−Winters models does *not* eliminate the seasonal component, it simply restricts the seasonal factors to be constant through time, since now $s_t = s_{t-m}$.

9.22 The exponential smoothing class of models has been extended and placed within a state space framework (see Chapter 17: State Space Models). The main extension has been to include "damping" effects into the trend specification: for example, (9.14) may be replaced with:

$$f_{T,h} = z_T + \tau_T \left(\phi + \phi^2 + \cdots + \phi^h \right)$$

where $0 < \phi < 1$ is a damping parameter which reduces the impact of the trend over the forecast horizon. The state space framework enables a variety of specifications to be placed in a consistent framework that allows for ready estimation and model and forecast comparison.[10]

EXAMPLE 9.4 Holt−Winters Seasonal Modeling of Beer Sales

In Example 9.2, an airline model and its unrestricted ARIMA counterpart was fitted to quarterly United Kingdom beer sales and forecasts were obtained out to 2020Q4. We now use both the additive and multiplicative Holt−Winters seasonal models to forecast this series. The smoothing parameters for the additive model were estimated to be $\alpha = 0.10$, $\beta = 0.79$, and $\delta = 0.33$. These imply an equivalent ARIMA model $\nabla\nabla_4 x_t = \theta_5(B)a_t$ with coefficients $\theta_1 = 0.82$,

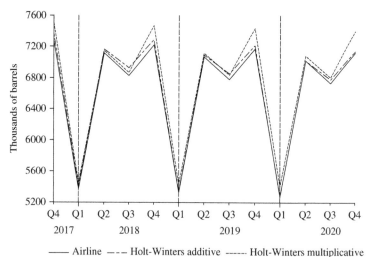

FIGURE 9.5 Airline and additive and multiplicative Holt−Winters forecasts of beer sales out to 2020Q4.

$\theta_2 = \theta_3 = -0.08$, $\theta_4 = 0.62$, and $\theta_5 = -0.60$, which are close to the fitted model's estimates of 0.80, 0, 0.55, and -0.62, respectively. Since these smoothing parameters imply that the airline restriction $\theta_1\theta_4 + \theta_5$ takes the value -0.09, and noting that $\alpha\beta = 0.08$ and $\alpha\delta = 0.03$, this suggests that the Holt–Winters additive forecasts should be similar to the airline model forecasts.

The multiplicative Holt–Winters smoothing parameters are estimated to be $\alpha = 0.10, \beta = 0.81$, and $\delta = 0$. While the level and trend parameters are essentially identical to their additive counterparts, a value for δ of zero implies that the seasonal component is constant. The airline model and the two Holt–Winters forecasts are shown in Fig. 9.5. The three sets of forecasts are quite close, with the airline model forecasts being smaller than their Holt–Winters counterparts.

Incorporating a damping factor into the trend yields an estimate of $\phi = 0.94$ for the additive model and 0.95 for the multiplicative model: such slow damping produces forecasts that are almost identical to their "undamped" counterparts.

ENDNOTES

1. An equivalent formulation of (9.1) is to use only $m-1$ dummies, but to also include an intercept, in which case the α_i coefficients have the interpretation of being seasonal deviations from the value taken by the intercept. Our preference is for the simpler and more direct interpretation afforded by (9.1), which also avoids having to choose which of the dummies to omit. Of course, including the full set of m dummies plus the intercept will lead to perfect collinearity between the regressors and a consequent inability to estimate the regression.

2. The ARIMA$(0, 1, 1)(0, 1, 1)_m$ model is often referred to as the "airline model," as Box and Jenkins first illustrated its use on airline travel data previously used by Brown (1963).

3. The ACFs for various low-order multiplicative seasonal models may be found in, for example, Box and Jenkins (1970, Appendix A9.1). For such models, the PACF can be thought of as a repetition of a combination of the autocorrelation and partial autocorrelation functions of the seasonal component about the seasonal partial values (see Hamilton and Watts, 1978). In general, the seasonal and nonseasonal moving average components introduce exponential decays and damped sine waves at the seasonal and nonseasonal lags, whereas with autoregressive processes the PACF cuts off.

4. On examining the residual ACF a significant autocorrelation of 0.27 is found at lag 8. Fitting an extended ARIMA$(0, 1, 1)(0, 1, 2)_4$ provides a marginally improved fit with the additional seasonal moving average term being just significant.

5. There is an important literature on testing for seasonal unit roots: see Choi (2015, chapter 6) for a comprehensive textbook treatment. Examples of mixed seasonal models using regional United Kingdom rainfall data are provided in Mills (2017b).

6. Details and software for all these methods are provided in *EViews 10*.

7. This uses the well-known series expansion $1 + y + y^2 + \cdots = (1-y)^{-1}$ for $|y| < 1$, with $y = (1-\alpha)B$.

8. Holt's original paper was published as a (U.S.) Office of Naval Research memorandum in 1957, but was republished as Holt (2004a), along with a short reflection by the author on the genesis of the method (Holt, 2004b). Holt's ideas gained much wider acceptance with the publication of Winters (1960), which tested the methods on sales data with such success that they became known as the Holt–Winters forecasting system.

9. This approach, developed independently of Holt, was formalized in Brown and Meyer (1961) and D'Esopo (1961), and given a book-length treatment in Brown (1963). Harrison (1965, 1967) provided the first synthesis of the exponential smoothing methodology, with later updates being given by Gardner (1985, 2006): see Mills (2011, pages 308−313) for a summary.

10. Hyndman et al. (2008) is a textbook development of this approach, which is too advanced to be discussed in any detail here. The ETS, which stands for *Error-Trend-Seasonal*, approach, as it has become known, is available in *EViews 10*, where details of its implementation may be found.

Chapter 10

Volatility and Generalized Autoregressive Conditional Heteroskedastic Processes

Chapter Outline

VOLATILITY

10.1 Following initial research on portfolio theory during the 1950s, volatility became an extremely important concept in finance, appearing regularly in models of, for example, asset pricing and risk management. Although there are various definitions of volatility, in the context of a time series it is generally taken to be a period in the evolution of the series that is associated with high variability or, equivalently, high variance. This was prompted by the observation that many time series, not just financial returns, appear to be characterized by alternating periods of relative tranquility in which variability is low and relative volatility where variability is considerably higher.

10.2 Much of the initial interest in volatility had to do with it not being directly observable, and several alternative measures were consequently developed to approximate it empirically.[1] In the early 1980s, it was proposed that volatility should be embedded within a formal stochastic model for the observed time series. This was prompted by the fact that, although some series appeared to be serially uncorrelated, they were certainly not independent through time. They, thus, had the potential to exhibit rich dynamics in their higher moments, these often being accompanied by interesting non-Gaussian distributional properties. Under such circumstances, attention should be focused on the characteristics of the higher moments of the series, rather than just on modeling the conditional mean.

Applied Time Series Analysis. DOI: https://doi.org/10.1016/B978-0-12-813117-6.00010-7
161

10.3 A straightforward way of doing this is to allow the variance (or typically, the conditional variance) of the process generating the series x_t to change either continuously or at certain discrete points in time. Although a stationary process must have a constant variance, certain conditional variances can change, so that although the unconditional variance $V(x_t)$ may be constant for all t, the conditional variance $V(x_t|x_{t-1}, x_{t-2}, \ldots)$, which depends on the realization of x_t, is able to alter from observation to observation.

10.4 A stochastic model having time-varying conditional variances may be defined by supposing that x_t is generated by the *product process*:

$$x_t = \mu + \sigma_t U_t \tag{10.1}$$

where U_t is a *standardized process*, so that $E(U_t) = 0$ and $V(U_t) = E(U_t^2) = 1$ for all t, and σ_t is a sequence of positive random variables such that:

$$V(x_t|\sigma_t) = E\big((x_t - \mu)^2|\sigma_t\big) = \sigma_t^2 E(U_t^2) = \sigma_t^2$$

σ_t^2 is, thus, the *conditional variance* and σ_t the *conditional standard deviation* of x_t.

Typically, $U_t = (x_t - \mu)/\sigma_t$ is assumed to be normal and independent of σ_t: we will further assume that it is strict white noise, so that $E(U_t U_{t-k}) = 0$ for $k \neq 0$. These assumptions imply that x_t has mean μ, variance:

$$E(x_t - \mu)^2 = E(\sigma_t^2 U_t^2) = E(\sigma_t^2)E(U_t^2) = E(\sigma_t^2)$$

and autocovariances

$$E(x_t - \mu)(x_{t-k} - \mu) = E(\sigma_t \sigma_{t-k} U_t U_{t-k}) = E(\sigma_t \sigma_{t-k})E(U_t U_{t-k}) = 0$$

so that it is white noise. However, note that both the squared and absolute deviations, $S_t = (x_t - \mu)^2$ and $M_t = |x_t - \mu|$, can be autocorrelated. For example,

$$\begin{aligned}
Cov(S_t, S_{t-k}) &= E(S_t - E(S_t))(S_{t-k} - E(S_t)) = E(S_t S_{t-k}) - (E(S_t))^2 \\
&= E(\sigma_t^2 \sigma_{t-k}^2)E(U_t^2 U_{t-k}^2) - (E(\sigma_t^2))^2 \\
&= E(\sigma_t^2 \sigma_{t-k}^2) - (E(\sigma_t^2))^2
\end{aligned}$$

so that

$$E(S_t^2) = E(\sigma_t^4) - (E(\sigma_t^2))^2$$

and the kth autocorrelation of S_t is

$$\rho_{k,S} = \frac{E(\sigma_t^2 \sigma_{t-k}^2) - (E(\sigma_t^2))^2}{E(\sigma_t^4) - (E(\sigma_t^2))^2}$$

This autocorrelation will only be zero if σ_t^2 is constant, in which case x_t can be written as $x_t = \mu + a_t$, where $a_t = \sigma U_t$ has zero mean and constant variance σ^2, which is just another way of defining a_t as white noise.

AUTOREGRESSIVE CONDITIONAL HETEROSKEDASTIC PROCESSES

10.5 Up until this point we have said nothing about how the conditional variances σ_t^2 might be generated. We now consider the case where they are a function of past values of x_t:

$$\sigma_t^2 = f(x_{t-1}, x_{t-2}, \ldots)$$

A simple example is:

$$\sigma_t^2 = f(x_{t-1}) = \alpha_0 + \alpha_1(x_{t-1} - \mu)^2 \tag{10.2}$$

where α_0 and α_1 are both positive to ensure that $\sigma_t^2 > 0$. With $U_t \sim \mathrm{NID}(0, 1)$ and independent of σ_t, $x_t = \mu + \sigma_t U_t$ is then conditionally normal,

$$x_t | x_{t-1}, x_{t-2}, \ldots \sim \mathrm{N}\left(\mu, \sigma_t^2\right)$$

so that

$$V(x_t | x_{t-1}) = \alpha_0 + \alpha_1(x_{t-1} - \mu)^2$$

If $0 < \alpha_1 < 1$ then the unconditional variance is $V(x_t) = \alpha_0/(1 - \alpha_1)$ and x_t is weakly stationary. It may be shown that the fourth moment of x_t is finite if $3\alpha_1^2 < 1$ and, if so, the kurtosis of x_t is given by $3(1 - \alpha_1^2)/(1 - 3\alpha_1^2)$. Since this must exceed 3, the unconditional distribution of x_t is fatter tailed than the normal. If this moment condition is not satisfied, then the variance of x_t will be infinite and x_t will not be weakly stationary.

10.6 This model is known as the *first-order autoregressive conditional heteroskedastic* [ARCH(1)] process and was originally introduced by Engle (1982, 1983). ARCH processes have proven to be extremely popular for modeling volatility in time series. A more convenient notation is to define $\varepsilon_t = x_t - \mu = U_t \sigma_t$, so that the ARCH(1) model can be written as:

$$\varepsilon_t | x_{t-1}, x_{t-2}, \ldots \sim \mathrm{NID}\left(0, \sigma_t^2\right)$$

$$\sigma_t^2 = \alpha_0 + \alpha_1 \varepsilon_{t-1}^2$$

On defining $\nu_t = \varepsilon_t^2 - \sigma_t^2$, the model can also be written as:

$$\varepsilon_t^2 = \alpha_0 + \alpha_1 \varepsilon_{t-1}^2 + \nu_t$$

Since $E(\nu_t | x_{t-1}, x_{t-2}, \ldots) = 0$, the model corresponds directly to an AR(1) model for the squared innovations ε_t^2. However, as $\nu_t = \sigma_t^2(U_t^2 - 1)$, the errors obviously have a time-varying variance.

10.7 A natural extension is to the ARCH(q) process, where (10.2) is replaced by:

$$\sigma_t^2 = f\left(x_{t-1}, x_{t-2}, \ldots, x_{t-q}\right) = \alpha_0 + \sum_{i=1}^{q} \alpha_i (x_{t-i} - \mu)^2$$

where $\alpha_i \geq 0$, $0 \leq i \leq q$. The process will be weakly stationary if all the roots of the characteristic equations associated with the ARCH parameters are less than unity. This implies that $\sum_{i=1}^{q} \alpha_i < 1$, in which case the unconditional variance is $V(x_t) = \alpha_0 / \left(1 - \sum_{i=1}^{q} \alpha_i\right)$. In terms of ε_t and σ_t^2, the conditional variance function is:

$$\sigma_t^2 = \alpha_0 + \sum_{i=1}^{q} \alpha_i \varepsilon_{t-i}^2$$

or, equivalently, on defining $\alpha(B) = \alpha_1 + \alpha_2 B + \cdots + \alpha_q B^{q-1}$,

$$\varepsilon_t^2 = \alpha_0 + \alpha(B)\varepsilon_{t-1}^2 + \nu_t$$

10.8 A practical difficulty with ARCH models is that, with q large, unconstrained estimation will often lead to violation of the nonnegativity constraints that must be placed on the α_is to ensure that the conditional variance σ_t^2 is always positive. In early applications of the model a rather arbitrary declining lag structure was imposed on the α_is to ensure that these constraints were met. To obtain more flexibility, a further extension, to the *generalized ARCH* (GARCH) process, was introduced by Bollerslev (1986). The GARCH(p,q) process has the conditional variance function:

$$\begin{aligned}
\sigma_t^2 &= \alpha_0 + \sum_{i=1}^{q} \alpha_i \varepsilon_{t-i}^2 + \sum_{i=1}^{p} \beta_i \sigma_{t-i}^2 \\
&= \alpha_0 + \alpha(B)\varepsilon_{t-1}^2 + \beta(B)\sigma_{t-1}^2
\end{aligned}$$

where $p > 0$ and $\beta_i \geq 0$, $i \leq 1 \leq p$. For the conditional variance of the GARCH(p,q) process to be well defined, all the coefficients in the corresponding ARCH(∞) model $\sigma_t^2 = \theta_0 + \theta(B)\varepsilon_t^2$ must be positive. Provided that $\alpha(B)$ and $\beta(B)$ have no common roots and that the roots of $1 - \beta(B)$ are all less than unity, this positivity constraint will be satisfied if, and only if, all the coefficients in $\theta(B) = \alpha(B)/(1 - \beta(B))$ are nonnegative. For the GARCH (1,1) process,

$$\sigma_t^2 = \alpha_0 + \alpha_1 \varepsilon_{t-1}^2 + \beta_1 \sigma_{t-1}^2$$

a model that has proved extremely popular for describing financial time series, these conditions simply require that all three parameters are nonnegative.

The equivalent form of the GARCH(p,q) process is

$$\varepsilon_t^2 = \alpha_0 + (\alpha(B) + \beta(B))\varepsilon_{t-1}^2 + \nu_t - \beta(B)\nu_{t-1} \tag{10.3}$$

so that ε_t^2 is ARMA(m,p), where $m = \max(p, q)$. This process will be weakly stationary if, and only if, the roots of $1 - \alpha(B) - \beta(B)$ are all less than unity, so that $\alpha(1) + \beta(1) < 1$.

10.9   If $\alpha(1) + \beta(1) = 1$ in (10.3) then $1 - \alpha(B) - \beta(B)$ will contain a unit root and we say that the model is *integrated* GARCH, or IGARCH. It is often the case that $\alpha(1) + \beta(1)$ is close to unity and, if so, a shock to the conditional variance will be *persistent* in the sense that it remains important for all future observations.

10.10   Although we have assumed that the distribution of ε_t is conditionally normal, this is not essential. For example, the distribution could be Student's t with unknown degrees of freedom υ that may be estimated from the data: for $\upsilon > 2$ such a distribution is leptokurtic and, hence, has thicker tails than the normal. Alternatively, the error distribution could be generalized exponential (GED) with parameter ς, which may again be estimated from the data. A normal distribution is characterized by $\varsigma = 2$, with $\varsigma < 2$ implying that the distribution is thick-tailed. Whatever the assumed error distribution, estimation will require nonlinear iterative techniques, and maximum likelihood estimation is available in many econometric packages.

10.11   The analysis has also proceeded on the further assumption that $\varepsilon_t = x_t - \mu_t$ is serially uncorrelated. A natural extension is to allow x_t to follow an ARMA(P,Q) process, so that the combined ARMA(P,Q)−ARCH (p,q) model becomes:

$$\Phi(B)(x_t - \mu) = \Theta(B)\varepsilon_t$$

$$\sigma_t^2 = \alpha_0 + \alpha(B)\varepsilon_{t-1}^2 + \beta(B)\sigma_{t-1}^2$$

TESTING FOR THE PRESENCE OF ARCH ERRORS

10.12   Let us suppose that an ARMA model for x_t has been estimated, from which the residuals e_t have been obtained. The presence of ARCH may lead to serious model misspecification if it is ignored. As with all forms of heteroskedasticity (i.e., nonconstant error variance), analysis assuming its absence will result in inappropriate parameter standard errors, these typically being too small. For example, ignoring ARCH will lead to the identification of ARMA models that tend to be overparameterized, as parameters that should be set to zero will show up as significant.

10.13 Methods for testing whether ARCH is present or not are, therefore, essential, particularly as estimation incorporating ARCH innovations requires complicated iterative techniques. Eq. (10.3) has shown that if ε_t is GARCH (p,q) then ε_t^2 is ARMA(m,p), where $m = \max(p, q)$, and standard ARMA theory follows through in this case. This implies that the squared residuals e_t^2 from the estimation of a pure ARMA process can then be used to identify m and p, and therefore q, in a similar fashion to the way the residuals themselves are used in conventional ARMA modeling. For example, the sample autocorrelations of e_t^2 have asymptotic variance T^{-1} and portmanteau statistics calculated from them are asymptotically χ^2 if the ε_t^2 are independent.

10.14 Formal tests are also available. A test of the null hypothesis that ε_t has a constant conditional variance against the alternative that the conditional variance is given by an ARCH(q) process, which is a test of $\alpha_1 = \cdots = \alpha_q = 0$ conditional upon $\beta_1 = \cdots = \beta_p = 0$, may be based on the Lagrange Multiplier (LM) principle. The test procedure is to run a regression of e_t^2 on $e_{t-1}^2, \ldots, e_{t-q}^2$ and to test the statistic $T \cdot R^2$ as a χ_q^2 variate, where R^2 is the squared multiple correlation coefficient of the regression. An asymptotically equivalent form of the test, which may have better small sample properties, is to compute the standard F test from the regression (these tests were introduced by Engle, 1982). The intuition behind this test is clear. If ARCH effects are absent from the data, then the variance is constant and variations in e_t^2 will be purely random. If ARCH effects are present, however, such variations will be predicted by lagged values of the squared residuals.

Of course, if the residuals themselves contain some remaining autocorrelation or, perhaps, some other form of nonlinearity, then it is quite likely that this test for ARCH will reject, since these misspecifications may induce autocorrelation in the squared residuals. We cannot simply assume that ARCH effects are necessarily present when the ARCH test rejects.

10.15 When the alternative is a GARCH(p,q) process, some complications arise. In fact, a general test of $p > 0$, $q > 0$ against a white noise null is not feasible, nor is a test of GARCH$(p + r_1, q + r_2)$ errors, where $r_1 > 0$ and $r_2 > 0$, when the null is GARCH(p,q). Furthermore, under this null, the LM test for GARCH(p,r) and ARCH$(p + r)$ alternatives coincide. What can be tested is the null of an ARCH(p) process against a GARCH(p,q) alternative (see Bollerslev, 1988).

10.16 Several modifications to the standard GARCH model result from allowing the relationship between σ_t^2 and ε_t to be more flexible than the quadratic relationship that has so far been assumed. To simplify the exposition, we shall concentrate on variants of the GARCH(1,1) process:

$$\sigma_t^2 = \alpha_0 + \alpha_1 \varepsilon_{t-1}^2 + \beta_1 \sigma_{t-1}^2 = \alpha_0 + \alpha_1 \sigma_{t-1}^2 U_{t-1}^2 + \beta_1 \sigma_{t-1}^2 \tag{10.4}$$

An early alternative was to model conditional standard deviations rather than variances (Schwert, 1989):

$$\sigma_t = \alpha_0 + \alpha_1|\varepsilon_{t-1}| + \beta_1\sigma_{t-1} = \alpha_0 + \alpha_1\sigma_{t-1}|U_{t-1}| + \beta_1\sigma_{t-1} \qquad (10.5)$$

This makes the conditional variance the square of a weighted average of absolute shocks, rather than the weighted average of squared shocks. Consequently, large shocks have a smaller effect on the conditional variance than in the standard GARCH model.

Rather than concentrating on the variance or standard deviation, a more flexible and general class of *power* GARCH models can be obtained by estimating an additional parameter (see Ding et al., 1993):

$$\sigma_t^\gamma = \alpha_0 + \alpha_1|\varepsilon_{t-1}|^\gamma + \beta_1\sigma_{t-1}^\gamma$$

10.17 An asymmetric response to shocks is made explicit in the *exponential* GARCH (EGARCH) model of Nelson (1991):

$$\log(\sigma_t^2) = \alpha_0 + \alpha_1 g\left(\frac{\varepsilon_{t-1}}{\sigma_{t-1}}\right) + \beta_1\log(\sigma_{t-1}^2) \qquad (10.6)$$

where

$$g\left(\frac{\varepsilon_{t-1}}{\sigma_{t-1}}\right) = \theta_1\frac{\varepsilon_{t-1}}{\sigma_{t-1}} + \left(\left|\frac{\varepsilon_{t-1}}{\sigma_{t-1}}\right| - E\left|\frac{\varepsilon_{t-1}}{\sigma_{t-1}}\right|\right)$$

The "news impact curve," $g(\cdot)$, relates conditional volatility, here given by $\log(\sigma_t^2)$, to "news," ε_{t-1}. It embodies an asymmetric response, since $\partial g/\partial\varepsilon_{t-1} = 1 + \theta_1$ when $\varepsilon_{t-1} > 0$ and $\partial g/\partial\varepsilon_{t-1} = 1 - \theta_1$ when $\varepsilon_{t-1} < 0$ (note that volatility will be at a minimum when there is no news, $\varepsilon_{t-1} = 0$). This asymmetry is potentially useful as it allows volatility to respond more rapidly to falls in x_t than to corresponding rises, which is an important stylized fact for many financial assets, and is known as the *leverage effect*. The EGARCH model also has the advantage that no parameter restrictions are needed to ensure that the variance is positive. It is easy to show that $g(\varepsilon_{t-1}/\sigma_{t-1})$ is strict white noise with zero mean and constant variance, so that $\log(\sigma_t^2)$ is an ARMA(1,1) process and will be stationary if $\beta_1 < 1$.

10.18 A model which nests (10.4)–(10.6) is the *nonlinear* ARCH model of Higgins and Bera (1992), a general form of which is:

$$\sigma_t^\gamma = \alpha_0 + \alpha_1 g^\gamma(\varepsilon_{t-1}) + \beta_1\sigma_{t-1}^\gamma$$

while an alternative is the threshold ARCH process:

$$\sigma_t^\gamma = \alpha_0 + \alpha_1 h^{(\gamma)}(\varepsilon_{t-1}) + \beta_1\sigma_{t-1}^\gamma$$

where

$$h^{(\gamma)}(\varepsilon_{t-1}) = \theta_1 |\varepsilon_{t-1}|^\gamma \mathbf{1}(\varepsilon_{t-1} > 0) + |\varepsilon_{t-1}|^\gamma \mathbf{1}(\varepsilon_{t-1} \leq 0)$$

$\mathbf{1}(\cdot)$ being the indicator function introduced in §**6.1**. If $\gamma = 1$, we have Zakoian's (1994) *threshold* ARCH (TARCH) model, while for $\gamma = 2$ we have the *GJR* model of Glosten et al. (1993), which allows a quadratic response of volatility to news but with different coefficients for good and bad news, although it maintains the assertion that the minimum volatility will result when there is no news.

10.19   An alternative formalization of the GARCH(1,1) model (10.4) has been proposed by Engle and Lee (1999), who define $\alpha_0 = \varpi(1 - \alpha_1 - \beta_1)$, where ϖ is the unconditional variance, or long-run volatility, to which the process reverts to:

$$\sigma_t^2 = \varpi + \alpha_1 \left(\varepsilon_{t-1}^2 - \varpi \right) + \beta_1 \left(\sigma_{t-1}^2 - \varpi \right)$$

This formalization may be extended to allow reversion to a varying level defined by q_t:

$$\sigma_t^2 = q_t + \alpha_1 \left(\varepsilon_{t-1}^2 - q_{t-1} \right) + \beta_1 \left(\sigma_{t-1}^2 - q_{t-1} \right)$$

$$q_t = \varpi + \xi(q_{t-1} - \varpi) + \zeta \left(\varepsilon_{t-1}^2 - \sigma_{t-1}^2 \right)$$

Here q_t is the permanent component of volatility, which converges to ϖ through powers of ξ, while $\sigma_t^2 - q_t$ is the transitory component, converging to zero via powers of $\alpha_1 + \beta_1$. This *component* GARCH model can also be combined with TARCH to allow asymmetries in both the permanent and transitory parts: this *asymmetric component* GARCH model automatically introduces asymmetry into the transitory equation.

There are many other variants to the basic GARCH model, but these typically require specialized software to estimate them and consequently are not discussed here.

FORECASTING FROM AN ARMA-GARCH MODEL

10.20   Suppose we have the ARMA(P,Q)-GARCH(p,q) model of §**10.11**:

$$x_t = \Phi_1 x_{t-1} + \cdots + \Phi_P x_{t-P} + \Theta_0 + \varepsilon_t - \Theta_1 \varepsilon_{t-1} - \cdots - \Theta_Q \varepsilon_{t-Q} \qquad (10.7)$$

$$\sigma_t^2 = \alpha_0 + \alpha_1 \varepsilon_{t-1}^2 + \cdots + \alpha_p \varepsilon_{t-p}^2 + \beta_1 \sigma_{t-1}^2 + \cdots + \beta_q \sigma_{t-q}^2 \qquad (10.8)$$

Forecasts of x_{T+h} can be obtained from the "mean equation" (10.7) in the manner outlined in §§**7.1**–**7.4**. When calculating forecast error variances, however, it can no longer be assumed that the error variance itself is constant. Thus, (7.4) must be amended to:

$$V(e_{t,h}) = \sigma_{T+h}^2 + \psi_1^2 \sigma_{T+h-1}^2 + \cdots + \psi_{h-1}^2 \sigma_{T+1}^2$$

with the σ_{T+h}^2 being obtained recursively from (10.8).

EXAMPLE 10.1 GARCH Models for the $-£ Exchange Rate

Table 10.1 presents the results of fitting various AR-GARCH models to the first differences of the $-£ exchange rate, ∇x_t. The choice of an AR(1) model for the conditional mean equation is based on our findings from Example 4.2. Assuming homoskedastic (GARCH(0,0)) errors produces the estimates in the first column of Table 10.1. The ARCH(1) statistic; the LM test for first-order ARCH, shows that there is strong evidence of conditional heteroskedasticity.

A GARCH(1,1) conditional variance is fitted in the second column, using the estimation technique of quasi-maximum likelihood, which enables standard errors to be adjusted for the presence of time-varying variances: see Bollerslev and Wooldridge (1992). Both GARCH parameters are significant, and the LM test for any neglected ARCH is insignificant. The GARCH parameters sum to just under unity, suggesting that shocks to the conditional variance are persistent. The autoregressive coefficient, although remaining significantly positive, is now even smaller in magnitude, confirming that the deviation from a "pure" random walk for the exchange rate has little economic content. The estimated "pure" GARCH(1,1) model is shown in the third column, with the omission of the autoregressive term being seen to have no effect on the remaining estimates of the model.[2]

If the lagged level of the exchange rate is added to the mean equation then this will provide a test of a unit root under GARCH(1,1) errors: doing so yields a coefficient estimate of -0.00001 with a t-statistic of just -0.26. The paradox found in Example 4.2 thus disappears: once the error is correctly specified as a GARCH process, there is no longer any tangible evidence against the hypothesis that the exchange rate is a random walk.

The conditional standard deviations from this model are shown in Fig. 10.1. Large values of $\hat{\sigma}_t$ are seen to match up with periods of high volatility in the

TABLE 10.1 $-£ Exchange Rate: GARCH Estimates: $\nabla x_t \sim$ AR(1)-GARCH(p,q)

	GARCH(0,0)	GARCH(1,1)	GARCH(1,1)
$\tilde{\Phi}_1$	0.0603 (0.0096)	0.0456 (0.0106)	–
$\tilde{\alpha}_0$		1.36 (0.066)	1.36 (0.066)
$\tilde{\alpha}_1$		0.068 (0.009)	0.068 (0.009)
$\tilde{\beta}_1$		0.921 (0.011)	0.921 (0.011)
$\tilde{\alpha}_1 + \tilde{\beta}_1$		0.989 (0.007)	0.989 (0.007)
ARCH(1)	165.6 [0.00]	0.8 [0.38]	1.2 [0.27]
$\mathcal{L}$	34237	35237	35230

Figures in ( ) are standard errors; Figures in [ ] are marginal significance levels. $\mathcal{L}$ is the log-likelihood. Estimates of α_0 are scaled by 10^6. *GARCH*, Generalized autoregressive conditional heteroskedastic; *ARCH*, autoregressive conditional heteroskedastic.

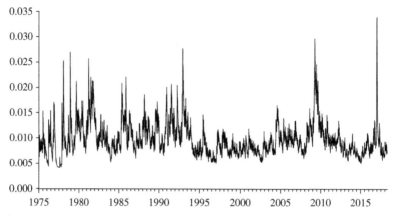

FIGURE 10.1   Conditional standard error of the $-£ exchange rate.

exchange rate, most notably around the United Kingdom's departure from the Exchange Rate Mechanism in September 1992; during the financial crisis of 2008–2009, in which the $-£ rate dropped by over a quarter in just a few months (recall Figs. 1.5 and 1.9); and in the aftermath of the Brexit referendum of June 2016. Note also the "asymmetric" nature of $\hat{\sigma}_t$: rapid increases are followed by much slower declines, thus, reflecting the persistence implied by the fitted models.

EXAMPLE 10.2   Forecasting the $-£ Exchange Rate

In Example 10.1 we found that the exchange rate could be modeled as:

$$x_t = x_{t-1} + \varepsilon_t$$

$$\sigma_t^2 = 1.36 \times 10^{-6} + 0.068\varepsilon_{t-1}^2 + 0.921\sigma_{t-1}^2$$

Forecasts of the exchange rate are given by $f_{T,h} = 1.351$ for all h, this being the end-December 2017 rate. Since a pure random walk has $\psi_i = 1$ for all i, the forecast error variances are given by:

$$V(e_{t,h}) = \sigma_{T,h}^2 + \sigma_{T,h-1}^2 + \cdots + \sigma_{T,1}^2$$

where, using the final residual $e_T = 0.0074$ and conditional error variance $\hat{\sigma}_T^2 = 0.0000482$,

$$\begin{aligned}
\sigma_{T,1}^2 &= 1.36 \times 10^{-6} + 0.068\varepsilon_T^2 + 0.921\sigma_T^2 \\
&= 1.36 \times 10^{-6} + 0.068 \times 0.0074^2 + 0.921 \times 0.0000482 \\
&= 0.0000495
\end{aligned}$$

$$\sigma_{T,j}^2 = 1.36 \times 10^{-6} + 0.921\sigma_{T,j-1}^2 \quad j \geq 2$$

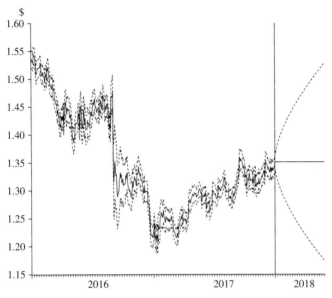

FIGURE 10.2 $-£ exchange rate, daily 2016−17 with two-standard error bounds and forecasts for a horizon of 100 days.

    Fig. 10.2 shows the exchange rate enclosed by two-conditional standard error bounds for 2016 and 2017 and with forecasts for 100 days ahead from the beginning of 2018. Note how the width of the bounds interval varies through time, most notably increasing during the large fall in the exchange rate after the Brexit referendum of June 2016. Note also how the conditional standard error bounds increase rapidly in the forecast period, so that the forecasts quickly become imprecise: the 100-step ahead forecast "interval" is 1.17−1.53 $−£.

ENDNOTES

1. Baillie (2006) and Mills and Markellos (2008, pages 157−162) provide short surveys of these "informal" measures of volatility. Since the impetus for modeling volatility came originally from analyzing financial markets, this area has seen the emergence of the *integrated* or *realized variance* nonparametric estimator of volatility: see, for example, Andersen et al. (2007) for a review of this growing literature.
2. Note that overfitting using GARCH(1,2) and GARCH(2,1) models proved unsuccessful. An improved fit was, however, obtained by estimating the model with GED errors and an IGARCH restriction, which reduces the estimate of the autoregressive coefficient even further to 0.019 with standard error 0.008.

Chapter 11

Nonlinear Stochastic Processes

Chapter Outline

MARTINGALES, RANDOM WALKS, AND NONLINEARITY

11.1 In §10.2 a distinction was drawn between serial uncorrelatedness and independence. Although this distinction lies at the heart of GARCH modeling, it is also of more general importance, manifesting itself in the concept of a *martingale*; a stochastic process that is a mathematical model of "fair play."[1] A martingale may be defined as a stochastic process x_t having the following properties:[2]

1. $E(|x_t|) < \infty$ for each t;
2. $E(x_t|x_s, x_{s-1}, \ldots) = x_s$.

Written as

$$E(x_t - x_s|x_s, x_{s-1}, \ldots) = 0, \quad s < t, \tag{11.1}$$

the martingale property implies that the MMSE forecast of a future increment of a martingale is zero. This property can be generalized to situations where:

$$E(x_t - x_s|x_s, x_{s-1}, \ldots) \geq 0, \quad s < t,$$

in which we have a *sub-martingale*, and to the case where this inequality is reversed, giving us a *super-martingale*.

11.2 The martingale given by (11.1) can be written equivalently as:

$$x_t = x_{t-1} + a_t,$$

where a_t is known as the martingale increment or *martingale difference*. When written in this form, x_t looks superficially identical to a random walk,

Applied Time Series Analysis. DOI: https://doi.org/10.1016/B978-0-12-813117-6.00011-9
173

where a_t is defined to be a stationary and uncorrelated sequence drawn from a fixed distribution, i.e., to be white noise (cf. §**4.6**).

Alternative definitions are, however, possible. For example, a_t could be defined to be *strict* white noise, so that it is both a stationary and independent sequence, rather than just being uncorrelated. Moreover, it is possible for a_t to be uncorrelated but not necessarily stationary. While the white noise assumptions rule this out, such behavior is allowed for martingale differences. This implies that there could be dependence between higher conditional moments—most notably, as we have seen in Chapter 10, Volatility and Generalized Autoregressive Conditional Heteroskedastic Processes, between conditional variances through time.

11.3 The possibility of this form of dependence leads naturally to the consideration of *nonlinear* stochastic processes capable of modeling such behavior. Nonlinearity can, however, be introduced in many ways, some of which may violate the martingale model. As an illustration, suppose that x_t is generated by the process $\nabla x_t = \eta_t$, with η_t being defined as:

$$\eta_t = a_t + \beta a_{t-1} a_{t-2}$$

where a_t is strict white noise. It follows immediately that η_t has zero mean, constant variance, and an autocorrelation function given by:

$$E\big(\eta_t \eta_{t-k}\big) = E\big(a_t a_{t-k} + \beta a_{t-1} a_{t-2} a_{t-k} + \beta a_t a_{t-k-1} a_{t-k-2}$$
$$+ \beta^2 a_{t-1} a_{t-2} a_{t-k-1} a_{t-k-2}\big)$$

For all $k \neq 0$, each of the terms in this expression has zero expectation, so that, as far as its second-order properties are concerned, η_t behaves just like an independent process. However, the MMSE forecast of a future observation, η_{t+1}, is not zero (the unconditional expectation), but the conditional expectation:

$$\hat{\eta}_{t+1} = E\big(\eta_{t+1} | \eta_t, \eta_{t-1}, \ldots\big) = \beta a_t a_{t-1}$$

It then follows that x_t is not a martingale, because:

$$E\big(x_{t+1} - x_t | \eta_t, \eta_{t-1}, \ldots\big) = \hat{\eta}_{t+1} \neq 0$$

and the nonlinear structure of the η_t process could be used to improve the forecasts of x_t over the simple "no-change" forecast associated with the martingale model.

11.4 Using the results of §§**3.30**–**3.32**, if $w_t = \nabla x_t$ is strict white noise then the asymptotic distribution (standardized by $\sqrt{T}$) of the sample autocorrelations calculated from a realization of w_t will be $N(0, 1)$, so that the random walk null would be rejected at the 5% significance level if, for example, $\sqrt{T}|r_1| > 1.96$.

If a set of sample autocorrelations are considered, say $r_1, \ldots, r_K$, then some will probably be significant even if the null is true: on average one out of 20 will be significant at the 5% level. As noted in §**3.32**, the portmanteau statistics $Q(K)$ of (3.13) may be used in these circumstances. On the random walk null, this statistic is distributed as χ_K^2, so that the null would be rejected for sufficiently high values. Note that this test does not require a specific alternative hypothesis: it may, thus, be regarded as a "diagnostic" test with, hopefully, some power against the null for a wide range of alternatives.

11.5 The portmanteau test does, however, require that the innovations to the random walk be strict white noise. If the innovations are merely uncorrelated, rather than independent, then this testing procedure will be unreliable. To show this, the strict white noise assumption on w_t may be relaxed to that of just satisfying the weak dependence conditions mentioned in §**5.12**. In this case, $\sqrt{T}r_1 \overset{a}{\sim} N(0, \tau^2)$, where:

$$\tau^2 = \sigma_w^{-4}\left(V(w_1 w_2) + 2\sum_{i=1}^{\infty} Cov(w_1 w_2, w_{i+1} w_{i+2})\right)$$

a result provided by Romano and Thombs (1996, Theorem 2.1). An example of such a process is $w_t = z_t z_{t-1}$, where z_t is itself zero mean strict white noise with $E(z_t^2) = \sigma_z^2$ and $E(z_t^4) < \infty$. In this case, Romano and Thombs show that, for all $i > 0$,

$$Cov(w_1 w_2, w_{i+1} w_{i+2}) = 0$$

$$V(w_1 w_2) = E\left(w_1^2 w_2^2\right) = \left(E\left(z_0^2\right)\right)^2 E\left(z_1^4\right) = \sigma_z^4 E\left(z_1^4\right)$$

and

$$\sigma_w^2 = E\left(w_t^2\right) = E\left(z_t^2 z_{t-1}^2\right) = \sigma_z^4$$

Thus,

$$\tau^2 = \frac{E\left(z_1^4\right)}{\sigma_z^4} > 1$$

For example, if z_t is standard normal, $\tau^2 = 3$ and, in general, τ^2 can be made arbitrarily large. Hence, a test of zero correlation based on, say, $\sqrt{T}|r_1| > 1.96$ will lead to a high probability of incorrectly rejecting the hypothesis of zero correlation.

11.6 Romano and Thombs (1996, Example 3.5) also show that, if w_t is not strict white noise, then $Q(K)$ is no longer asymptotically distributed as χ_K^2. For example, if $w_t = z_t z_{t-1}$, then $Q(K)$ is distributed as a weighted sum of independent χ_1^2 variates, leading to a rejection probability greater than the nominal significance level using the χ_K^2 distribution.

Consequently, Lobarto et al. (2001, 2002) propose modifying the portmanteau statistic to:

$$\tilde{Q}(K) = T \sum_{i=1}^{K} \left(\frac{r_i^2}{v_i} \right) \overset{a}{\sim} \chi_K^2$$

where

$$v_i = T^{-1} \sum_{t=i+1}^{T} \frac{(w_t - \overline{w})^2 (w_{t-i} - \overline{w})^2}{\hat{\sigma}_w^4}$$

They also propose further extensions based on considering the covariance matrix of the set of sample autocorrelations r_1, r_2, ..., r_K: see the mentioned references for details.

NONLINEAR STOCHASTIC MODELS

11.7 As discussed in §3.6, Wold's decomposition theorem allows us to represent every weakly stationary, purely nondeterministic, stochastic process as a linear combination of a sequence of uncorrelated random variables, as in (3.2). A stochastic process can then be considered nonlinear if it does not satisfy the assumptions underlying the decomposition, for example, if the representation is:

$$x_t - \mu = f(a_t, a_{t-1}, a_{t-2}, \ldots) \tag{11.2}$$

where $f(\cdot)$ is some arbitrary nonlinear function. However, the "curse of dimensionality" means that this representation is of little practical use. Consequently, as an approximation to $f(\cdot)$, consider a Taylor expansion of (11.2) around zero:

$$x_t - \mu = f(0, a_{t-1}, a_{t-2}) + a_t f'(0, a_{t-1}, a_{t-2}) + 0.5 a_t^2 f''(0, a_{t-1}, a_{t-2}) + \cdots$$

where f' and f'' are the first and second derivatives of f with respect to a_t. By dropping higher-order terms, we can express x_t in terms of its conditional moments. For example, by keeping only the first two terms, x_t can be expressed as a function of the conditional mean and variance, respectively. Simple forms of nonlinearity can also be obtained by assuming some low-order polynomial function for $f(\cdot)$: for example, the first-order nonlinear moving average (see Robinson, 1977).

$$x_t = a_t + \psi_1 a_{t-1}^2$$

Polynomial functions of lagged x_t can also be used (Jones, 1978), while another simple way of introducing nonlinearity is to allow x_t to respond in a different manner to innovations depending on their sign. For example,

Wecker (1981) introduced the asymmetric moving average process, whose first-order form is:

$$x_t = a_t + \theta a_{t-1} + \psi \, \mathbf{1}(a_{t-1} > 0)a_{t-1}$$

This model was extended to include both moving average and autoregressive components by Brännäs and De Gooijer (1994).

11.8   A wide variety of nonlinear models have been developed which allow for combinations of AR and MA terms and for deterministic or stochastic variations in their parameters through time. The most popular of these models will be described in subsequent sections.

BILINEAR MODELS

11.9   An important class of nonlinear model is the *bilinear*, which takes the general form

$$\phi(B)(x_t - \mu) = \theta(B)\varepsilon_t + \sum_{i=1}^{R}\sum_{j=1}^{S} \gamma_{ij} x_{t-i}\varepsilon_{t-j} \qquad (11.3)$$

Here $\varepsilon_t \sim SWN(0, \sigma_\varepsilon^2)$, where this notation is used to denote that the innovations ε_t are strict white noise. The second term on the right hand side of (11.3) is a bilinear form in ε_{t-j} and x_{t-i}, and this accounts for the nonlinear character of the model, for if all the γ_{ij} are zero, (11.3) clearly reduces to the familiar ARMA model. The bilinear model can be thought of as a higher-order Taylor approximation to the unknown nonlinear function $f(\cdot)$ than that provided by the Wold decomposition.

11.10   Little analysis has been carried out on this general bilinear form, but Granger and Andersen (1978) have analyzed the properties of several simple bilinear forms, characterized as:

$$x_t = \varepsilon_t + \gamma_{ij} x_{t-i}\varepsilon_{t-j}$$

If $i > j$ the model is called super-diagonal, if $i = j$ it is diagonal, and if $i < j$, it is sub-diagonal. If we define $\lambda = \gamma_{ij}\sigma$ then, for super-diagonal models, x_t has zero mean and variance $\sigma_\varepsilon^2/(1 - \lambda^2)$, so that $|\lambda| < 1$ is a necessary condition for stability.

Conventional identification techniques using the SACF of x_t would identify this series as white noise, but Granger and Andersen show that, in theory at least, the SACF of the squares of x_t would identify x_t^2 as an ARMA (i,j) process, so that we could distinguish between white noise and this bilinear model by analyzing x_t^2.

Diagonal models will also be stationary if $|\lambda| < 1$. If $i = j = 1$, x_t will be identified as MA(1), with $0 < \rho_1 < 0.1547$ (corresponding to $\lambda = \pm 0.605$), while x_t^2 will be identified as ARMA(1,1). However, if x_t actually was MA (1), then x_t^2 will also be MA(1), so that this result allows the bilinear model to be distinguished from the linear model. In general, the levels of a diagonal model will be identified as MA(i). Sub-diagonal models are essentially like super-diagonal models in that they appear to be white noise but generally have x_t^2 following an ARMA(i,j) process.

11.11 Charemza et al. (2005) discuss nonstationary generalizations of bilinear models that allow for unit roots. For example, they consider the following simple model:

$$x_t = (a + b\varepsilon_{t-1})x_{t-1} + \varepsilon_t \tag{11.4}$$

As shown by Granger and Andersen (1978), this process will be stationary if $a^2 + b^2\sigma_\varepsilon^2$. The process collapses to a random walk if $a = 1$ and $b = 0$. However, if we assume that b differs from zero, while $a = 1$, we can express the process in first differences as:

$$\nabla x_t = bx_{t-1}\varepsilon_{t-1} + \varepsilon_t \tag{11.5}$$

Assuming $x_0 = \varepsilon_0 = 0$, it can be shown that $E(x_t) = b\sigma_\varepsilon^2(t-1)$ and $E(\nabla x_t) = b\sigma_\varepsilon^2$. Although the process can produce mean reverting behavior, it is evident that it does not retain the desirable difference stationarity property of the random walk.

11.12 When $a = 1$, (11.4) can be considered to be a special case of the more general process,

$$x_t = \varphi_t x_{t-1} + \varepsilon_t$$

where φ_t is a random autoregressive coefficient with $E(\varphi_t) = 1$. Charemza et al. (2005) develop a simple t-ratio type test for detecting bilinearity in a unit root process. For small values of $b < 1/\sqrt{T}$, we can reasonably assume that $\nabla x_t \approx \varepsilon_t$ and the test regression can be formulated as:

$$\nabla x_t = bx_{t-1}\nabla x_{t-1} + u_t$$

The test statistic is simply the t-ratio of $\hat{b}$ in this regression estimated via OLS. Under the null of no bilinearity, i.e., $a = 1$ and $b = 0$, this test statistic is asymptotically normally distributed. The test regression can be augmented by a constant, drift or further autoregressive components in a straightforward manner by just adding the relevant terms. Charemza et al. suggest a two-step procedure: first test for a unit root and then test for bilinearity. This is consistent in the sense that the size of the unit root test is not affected by the possible detection of bilinearity in the second step.

11.13 Detailed analysis of the properties of bilinear models can be found in Granger and Andersen (1978) and Subba Rao and Gabr (1984). Most of the results are of considerable theoretical interest but are of little relevance in practice: for example, most of the conditions for stationarity and invertibility are too complicated to be used as constraints on the parameters in actual models.

11.14 Weiss (1986) provides a detailed comparison of the ARMA-ARCH model, given by Eqs. (10.7) and (10.8), with the bilinear model (11.3). At first sight, the models appear quite different: whereas the addition of the ARCH equation to the pure ARMA process (10.7) introduces nonlinearity by affecting the conditional variance, the addition of the bilinear terms contained in (11.3) alters the conditional mean of x_t. Weiss, however, argues that despite these different influences, the two processes can have similar properties with, for example, the bilinear process often being mistaken for an ARMA model with ARCH errors.

11.15 Why might this be? Suppose the true model for x_t is (11.3) but the ARMA model

$$\tilde{\phi}(B)(x_t - \tilde{\mu}) = \tilde{\theta}(B)\tilde{\varepsilon}_t$$

is fitted. The residual $\tilde{\varepsilon}_t$ is given by:

$$\tilde{\varepsilon}_t = \vartheta_1(B)\varepsilon_t + \vartheta_2(B)\sum_{i=1}^{R}\sum_{j=1}^{S}\gamma_{ij}x_{t-i}\varepsilon_{t-j}$$

where $\vartheta_1(B) = \phi^{-1}(B)\tilde{\theta}^{-1}(B)\tilde{\phi}(B)\theta(B)$ and $\vartheta_2(B) = \tilde{\phi}^{-1}(B)\tilde{\theta}^{-1}(B)\phi(B)$. On squaring this expression and taking conditional expectations, it is clear that $E(\tilde{\varepsilon}_t^2|x_{t-1}, x_{t-2}, \ldots)$ is not constant but will be a function of lagged ε_t^2, and hence may be thought to exhibit ARCH. For example, suppose the true model is:

$$x_t = \varepsilon_t + \gamma_{21}x_{t-1}\varepsilon_{t-1} \tag{11.6}$$

As $E(x_t) = 0$ and $E(x_t x_{t+i}) = 0$, $i > 0$, the use of traditional modeling techniques may identify the trivial ARMA model $x_t = \tilde{\varepsilon}_t$, where:

$$\tilde{\varepsilon}_t = \varepsilon_t + \gamma_{21}\varepsilon_{t-1}\tilde{\varepsilon}_{t-1}$$

Squaring this expression and taking expectations gives:

$$E(\tilde{\varepsilon}_t^2|x_{t-1}, x_{t-2}, \ldots) = \sigma_\varepsilon^2 + \gamma_{21}^2\sigma_\varepsilon^2\tilde{\varepsilon}_{t-1}^2$$

Now, the LM statistic for testing whether $\tilde{\varepsilon}_t$ is ARCH(1) is $T \cdot R^2$ from the regression of $\tilde{\varepsilon}_t^2$ on a constant and $\tilde{\varepsilon}_{t-1}^2$: given this expectation, such a statistic may well be large even if the correct model is really the bilinear process (11.3).

The correct LM statistic for testing $x_t = \tilde{\varepsilon}_t$ against the bilinear alternative (11.6) is, in fact, $T \cdot R^2$ from the regression of $\tilde{\varepsilon}_t$ on a constant, $\tilde{\varepsilon}_{t-1}^2$, and the additional regressor $\tilde{\varepsilon}_{t-1}$.

11.16 Attempts have been made to combine the bilinear model with ARCH errors, i.e., the bilinear process (11.3) with the ARCH specification (10.8): see, for example, Weiss (1986). This modeling procedure is, unfortunately, rather burdensome. If we just want a simple test for nonlinearity which is sensitive to both ARCH and bilinear alternatives, then Higgins and Bera (1988) proposed an easily computed simultaneous test for a joint ARCH and bilinear alternative. This is an LM test whose construction exploits the result that the individual LM tests for ARCH and bilinearity are additive, so that the joint test statistic is, thus, the sum of the individual test statistics. Moreover, because the two forms of nonlinearity are considered simultaneously, the LM test for bilinearity again has the standard $T \cdot R^2$ representation, being the test outlined previously.

11.17 Maravall (1983) considers an alternative form of bilinearity in which x_t is given by the ARMA process,

$$\phi(B)(x_t - \mu) = \theta(B)a_t$$

but where the *uncorrelated* innovation sequence is bilinear in a_t and the strict white noise sequence ε_t:

$$a_t = \varepsilon_t + \sum_{i=1}^{R} \sum_{j=1}^{S} \gamma_{ij} a_{t-i} \varepsilon_{t-j}$$

This may be interpreted as a bilinear model "forecasting white noise."

EXAMPLE 11.1 Is the \$–£ Exchange Rate Bilinear?

Given the above discussion, is it possible that the GARCH model fitted to the \$–£ exchange rate in Example 10.1 is a misspecification and the true process generating the series is of bilinear form? An obvious way to proceed is to consider the SACFs and PACFs of the differences and squared differences. Recall that in Example 4.2, it was found that the SACF of $\tilde{\varepsilon}_t = \nabla x_t$ was consistent with an AR(1) process. For $\tilde{\varepsilon}_t^2$, the first hundred sample autocorrelations are significantly positive, and many of the partial autocorrelations are as well, which suggests that an ARMA(1,1) process could be appropriate. This pair of findings is consistent with a diagonal bilinear model with $R = S = 1$. The LM test for such bilinearity, obtained from regressing $\tilde{\varepsilon}_t$ on $\tilde{\varepsilon}_{t-1}$ and $\tilde{\varepsilon}_{t-1}^2$, produces a $T \cdot R^2$ of 64.7, distributed as χ_1^2, thus indicating evidence in favor of bilinearity. Of course, this statistic is only strictly valid in the absence of ARCH, which we know exists. Construction of the ARCH adjusted statistic produces a value of 28.1, thus confirming the possible presence of bilinearity.

THRESHOLD AND SMOOTH TRANSITION AUTOREGRESSIONS

11.18   A popular class of nonlinear model is the *self-exciting threshold autoregressive* (SETAR) process, which allows for asymmetry by defining a set of piecewise autoregressive models whose switch points, or "thresholds," are generally unknown (see Tong and Lim, 1980; Tong, 1990; Teräsvirta, 2006):

$$x_t = \sum_{j=1}^{r} \left(\phi_{j,1} x_{t-1} + \cdots + \phi_{j,p} x_{t-p} + a_{j,t} \right) \mathbf{1} \left(c_{j-1} < x_{t-d} \leq c_j \right) \qquad (11.7)$$

Here d is the (integer-valued) delay parameter and $c_1 < c_2 < \cdots < c_{r-1}$ are the thresholds: the model is often denoted SETAR(r: p, d).[3] It is assumed that $a_{j,t} \sim WN\left(0, \sigma_j^2\right)$, $j = 1, \ldots, r$, so that the error variance is allowed to alter across the r "regimes." A popular version of (11.7) is the two-regime SETAR(2: p, d) model:

$$\begin{aligned} x_t = & \left(\phi_{1,1} x_{t-1} + \cdots + \phi_{1,p} x_{t-p} + a_{1,t} \right) \mathbf{1}(x_{t-d} \leq c_1) \\ & + \left(\phi_{2,1} x_{t-1} + \cdots + \phi_{2,p} x_{t-p} + a_{2,t} \right) (1 - \mathbf{1}(x_{t-d} \leq c_1)) \end{aligned}$$

An important feature of the SETAR model is its ability to generate "limit cycles": if (11.7) is extrapolated assuming that the error terms equal zero, then the extrapolated series displays oscillations of a given length that do not die out.

As previously stated, asymmetry may be captured by the regimes: for example, if x_{t-d} measures the phase of an economic business cycle, a two-regime SETAR could describe processes whose dynamic properties differ across expansions and recessions. If the transition variable x_{t-d} is replaced by its difference ∇x_{t-d}, then any asymmetry lies in the growth rate of the series so that, for example, increases in growth rates may be rapid but the return to a lower level of growth may be slow.

If the transition variable x_{t-d} is replaced by t then the model becomes an autoregression with $r - 1$ breaks at times $c_1, \ldots, c_{r-1}$.

11.19   The SETAR formulation requires that the shift from one regime to another is immediate. Allowing the shift to be smooth is accomplished by defining the *exponential autoregressive* (EAR) process:

$$x_t = \phi_1 x_{t-1} + \cdots + \phi_p x_{t-p} + G(\gamma, x_{t-d})\left(\varphi_1 x_{t-1} + \cdots + \varphi_p x_{t-p} \right) + a_t \quad (11.8)$$

where the transition function

$$G(\gamma, x_{t-d}) = \exp\left(-\gamma x_{t-d}^2 \right), \quad \gamma > 0$$

is symmetric around zero, where it takes the value unity, and as $|x_{t-d}| \to \infty$ so $G(\gamma, x_{t-d}) \to 0$. From (11.8), the EAR may be interpreted as a linear AR process with stochastic time-varying coefficients $\phi_i + G(\gamma, x_{t-d})\varphi_i$. "Pure" linearity is obtained when either $\gamma \to 0$ or $\gamma \to \infty$. This model, originally proposed by Haggan and Ozaki (1981), was subsequently extended by Teräsvirta (1994) to allow for asymmetry in the transition function by including a location parameter c:

$$G_E(\gamma, c, x_{t-d}) = \exp\left(-\gamma\left(x_{t-d} - c\right)^2\right) , \quad \gamma > 0 \qquad (11.9)$$

This is known as the *exponential smooth transition AR* [ESTAR(p, d)] model, while an alternative specification of the transition function produces the *logistic* STAR (LSTAR) model (cf. the ESTR and LSTR breaking trend models of §§**6.15–6.17**):

$$G_L(\gamma, c, x_{t-d}) = (1 + \exp(-\gamma(x_{t-d} - c)))^{-1}, \quad \gamma > 0 \qquad (11.10)$$

Note that when $\gamma = 0$, $G_L(\gamma, c, x_{t-d}) = 0.5$ and (11.8) reduces to a linear AR model, while if $\gamma \to \infty$ the LSTAR model approaches the SETAR, albeit with $\sigma_1 = \sigma_2$. If t replaces x_{t-d} in (11.9) then the resulting model is referred to as a *time-varying* autoregression, which enables testing for the null of parameter constancy in linear AR models, with smoothly changing parameters forming the alternative to the null: see Lin and Teräsvirta (1994).

11.20 Since the SETAR is a piecewise linear model it can be estimated by a variant of OLS. Teräsvirta (2006) provides details and discusses the weak stationarity and ergodicity conditions required for consistent estimation. Both ESTAR and LSTAR models can be estimated by nonlinear least squares (NLS) and ML techniques, although the properties of the ML estimator generally remain unknown. Numerical problems may arise, however, when the transition parameter γ is large, since then the transition is rapid and accurate estimation of this parameter requires many observations to lie in a small neighborhood of the location parameter c. Convergence of the optimization algorithm may be further exacerbated if γ is of a much higher order of magnitude than the other parameters. Teräsvirta (1994) suggests that, when the transition is known to be quick, γ can be fixed at an appropriately large value rather than being estimated imprecisely.

EXAMPLE 11.2 A SETAR Model for Sunspots

In Example 3.3 a restricted linear AR(9) model was fitted to the annual sunspot numbers (recall Table 3.4 where the estimates of this model are provided).

Tong and Lim (1980), in a paper containing the first detailed exposition of the SETAR model, used the sunspot numbers as an illustration of fitting the model and we update their analysis here. Using the same restricted AR(9) specification for each regime, a SETAR(3:9, 2) was identified and estimated, leading to:

$$x_t = -\ 4.874 + 1.953\ x_{t-1} - 0.720\ x_{t-2} + 0.214\ x_{t-9} + a_{1,t}, \quad x_{t-2} < 20.2$$
$$\quad\ \ (7.363) \qquad (0.141) \qquad\quad (0.512) \qquad\qquad (0.048)$$

$$x_t = 10.742 + 1.520\ x_{t-1} - 0.780\ x_{t-2} + 0.108\ x_{t-9} + a_{2,t}, \quad 20.2 \leq x_{t-2} < 94$$
$$\quad\ \ (6.686) \qquad (0.057) \qquad\quad (0.116) \qquad\qquad (0.033)$$

$$x_t = 8.783 + 0.787\ x_{t-1} - 0.193\ x_{t-2} + 0.046\ x_{t-9} + a_{3,t}, \quad 94 < x_{t-4}$$
$$\quad\ (7.134) \qquad (0.074) \qquad\quad (0.059) \qquad\qquad (0.069)$$

Here the transition variable is x_{t-2} and the regime thresholds are at 20.2 and 94, the three regimes containing 63, 131, and 115 observations respectively. The overall residual standard error is 20.413, which represents a 14% improvement over the linear model. Fig. 11.1 shows the fit of the SETAR for the latter part of

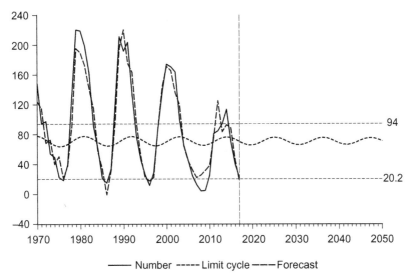

FIGURE 11.1 Sunspot number: SETAR fit and limit cycle. *SETAR*, Self-exciting threshold autoregressive.

the series from 1970 along with the computed limit cycle out to 2050. The limit cycle has a distinct period of 11 years, while the unusual behavior of sunspots over the last observed cycle from 2001 is clearly apparent.

EXAMPLE 11.3 An ESTAR Model for Long Interest Rates

As stated in Example 3.2, the United Kingdom interest rate spread is defined as the difference between long and short interest rates, the former being the yield on 20-year gilts. Fig. 11.2 shows the monthly change in this series, which

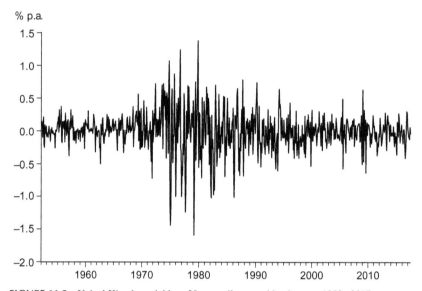

FIGURE 11.2 United Kingdom yield on 20-year gilts: monthly changes, 1952–2017.

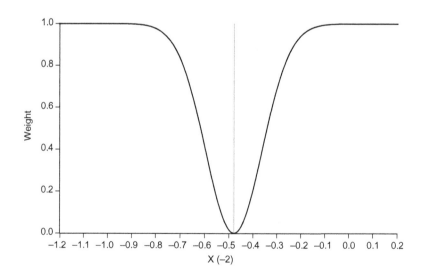

FIGURE 11.3 ESTAR weight function. *ESTAR*, Exponential smooth transition AR.

indicates that some form of nonlinearity may well be present. An ESTAR model fitted to this series produced:

$$x = \underset{(0.146)}{0.620}\, x_{t-1} + G_E(36.71, \, -0.48, x_{t-2})\left(-\underset{(0.148)}{0.350}x_{t-1} - \underset{(0.040)}{0.148}\, x_{t-2}\right) + a_t$$

The reason why this particular ESTAR(2, 2) specification was chosen will be discussed in Example 11.5. The midpoint of the transition is at -0.48% and the exponential transition function,

$$G_E(36.71, \, -0.48, x_{t-2}) = \exp\left(-36.71(x_{t-2}+0.48)^2\right)$$

is shown in Fig. 11.3, so that large changes in the gilt yield follow (with a delay of two months) a different AR(2) process to when the changes are more modest.

MARKOV-SWITCHING MODELS

11.21 Yet another way of introducing asymmetry is to consider "regime switching" models. Hamilton (1989, 1990), Engle and Hamilton (1990), and Lam (1990) all propose variants of a switching-regime Markov model, which can be regarded as a nonlinear extension of an ARMA process that can accommodate complicated dynamics, such as asymmetry and conditional heteroskedasticity. The setup is that of the UC model of §**8.1**, i.e., Eq. (8.1), where z_t now evolves as a two-state Markov process:

$$z_t = \alpha_0 + \alpha_1 S_t \qquad\qquad (11.11)$$

where

$$P(S_t = 1 | S_{t-1} = 1) = p$$

$$P(S_t = 0 | S_{t-1} = 1) = 1 - p$$

$$P(S_t = 1 | S_{t-1} = 0) = 1 - q$$

$$P(S_t = 0 | S_{t-1} = 0) = q$$

The noise component u_t is assumed to follow an AR(r) process $\phi(B)u_t = \varepsilon_t$, where the innovation sequence ε_t is strict white noise but $\phi(B)$ may contain a unit root, so that, unlike the conventional UC specification, u_t can be nonstationary. In fact, a special case of the conventional UC model results when $p = 1 - q$. The random walk component then has an innovation restricted to be a two-point random variable, taking the values 0 and 1 with probabilities q and $1 - q$ respectively, rather than a zero-mean random variable drawn from a continuous distribution, such as the normal.

11.22 The stochastic process for S_t is strictly stationary, having the AR(1) representation:

$$S_t = (1 - q) + \lambda S_{t-1} + V_t$$

where $\lambda = p + q - 1$ and where the innovation V_t has the conditional probability distribution

$$P(V_t = (1 - p)|S_{t-1} = 1) = p,$$
$$P(V_t = -p|S_{t-1} = 1) = 1 - p,$$
$$P(V_t = -(1 - q)|S_{t-1} = 0) = q,$$
$$P(V_t = q|S_{t-1} = 0) = 1 - q$$

This innovation is uncorrelated with lagged values of S_t, since

$$E(V_t|S_{t-j} = 1) = E(V_t|S_{t-j} = 0) = 0 \quad \text{for } j \geq 1$$

but it is not independent of such lagged values, as, for example,

$$E(V_t^2|S_{t-1} = 1) = p(1 - p),$$
$$E(V_t^2|S_{t-1} = 0) = q(1 - q)$$

The variance of the Markov process can be shown to be

$$\alpha_1^2 \frac{(1 - p)(1 - q)}{(2 - p - q)^2}$$

As this variance approaches zero, i.e., as p and q approach unity, so the random walk component (11.11) approaches a deterministic trend. If $\phi(B)$ contains no unit roots, x_t will approach a trend stationary process, whereas if $\phi(B)$ does contain a unit root, x_t approaches a difference stationary process.

11.23 ML estimates of the model are obtained by using (11.11) to write the noise component as

$$u_t = x_t - \alpha_0 - \alpha_1 S_t \tag{11.12}$$

Using (11.12), the innovations $\varepsilon_t = \phi(B)u_t$ can be expressed as

$$\varepsilon_t = \phi(B)(x_t - \alpha_0 - \alpha_1 S_t)$$

Assuming the innovations are normal, this expression can be utilized to calculate the log-likelihood function on noting that this can be decomposed as the sum of the conditional (on past observations) log-likelihoods. These conditional log-likelihoods depend on unobserved current and past realizations of the Markov states. A recursive relationship can be shown to hold between the conditional distribution of the states and the conditional likelihood of the observations and this can be exploited to obtain an algorithm for evaluating the log-likelihood function. Inferences about the unobserved components and states are then obtained as byproducts of this evaluation: details of the algorithm may be found in Hamilton (1989) and Lam (1990).

EXAMPLE 11.4 A Markov-Switching Model for the $-£ Exchange Rate

The two-state Markov process (11.11) with an AR(1) noise component $(1 - \phi B)u_t = \varepsilon_t$ was fitted to the daily $-£ exchange rate, with the probabilities estimated to be $\hat{p} = 0.963$ and $\hat{q} = 0.983$, which imply that the exchange rate stays in the first regime for an average duration of $(1 - \hat{p})^{-1} = 27$ days and in the second regime for an average duration of $(1 - \hat{q})^{-1} = 58$ days, the AR(1) process for the state being $S_t = 0.017 + 0.946 S_{t-1} + V_t$. The models for the two states are estimated to be:

$$S_t = 0: \quad x_t = \underset{(0.075)}{1.496,} \quad u_t = \underset{(0.0009)}{0.9972} \, u_{t-1} + \varepsilon_t, \quad \hat{\sigma}_\varepsilon = 0.015$$

$$S_t = 1: \quad x_t = \underset{(0.075)}{1.495,} \quad u_t = \underset{(0.0003)}{1.0006} \, u_{t-1} + \varepsilon_t, \quad \hat{\sigma}_\varepsilon = 0.007$$

The models are essentially identical in that both may be considered random walks, which, of course, is unsurprising. However, the variances of the innovations are rather different across the two regimes.

As a byproduct of the estimation algorithm, estimates of the state probabilities $P(S_t = 0)$ and $P(S_t = 1)$ may also be calculated, which enable us to provide some further insights into the two regimes. Fig. 11.4 plots the exchange rate

FIGURE 11.4 $-£ Exchange rate, daily 1975–2017, with regime indicator.

along with the indicator variable $p_t = \mathbf{1}(P(S_t = 0) \geq 0.5)$, which indicates when the exchange rate is more likely to be in the "high volatility" regime. This figure shows that there is a tendency to be in this regime when the exchange rate is changing rapidly, which accords well with the ARCH representation of the series in Example 10.1.

NEURAL NETWORKS

11.24 Neural networks (NNs) refer to a broad class of nonparametric models which have gained a good deal of popularity in recent years across a wide range of disciplines, including computer science, psychology, biology, linguistics, and pattern recognition (for a textbook treatment, see, for example, Haykin, 1999). These models originate from research in the cognitive sciences on emulating the structure and behavior of the human brain.

One of the most common types of NN is the multi-layered perceptron (MLP), which can be used for nonparametric regression and classification. These models are organized in three basic layers: the input layer of independent variables, the output layer of dependent variables, and one or more hidden layers in-between. An activation function regulates the dependencies between the elements of each layer. A univariate autoregressive MLP model with a single hidden layer can be represented as:

$$x_t = \sum_{i=1}^{p} \phi_i x_{t-i} + \sum_{j=1}^{q} \beta_j G\left(\sum_{i=1}^{p} \varphi_i x_{t-i}\right) + \varepsilon_t \qquad (11.13)$$

$G(\cdot)$ is the activation function and is a bounded nonlinear function that operates in an analogous manner to that of the transition functions used in STAR models. Several activation functions are employed in practice, with the most common being the hyperbolic tangent and the logistic. The second term in (11.13) refers to the hidden layer in the MLP. Obviously, (11.13) collapses to a standard AR(p) model when the activation function is linear. The residual term ε_t is usually assumed to be a white noise random variable.

11.25 The high flexibility, rich parameterization and nonlinear nature of NNs renders estimation particularly difficult (see White, 2006). One of the main problems is that NNs are highly susceptible to overfitting. Consequently, the estimation strategy of NNs is rather different to traditional linear model estimation in that it typically involves two steps: in-sample optimization (training or learning) with recurrent testing (cross-validation), and out-of-sample testing. The in-sample optimization is usually terminated prior to reaching the maximum possible performance, when the performance of the model in the cross-validation sample starts to deteriorate. In this way overfitting is avoided and a good forecasting performance in the testing sample is more likely. The estimation (training) algorithms used vary considerably and typically involve adjusting the direction of the negative gradient of some error criterion (e.g., mean squared or absolute error).

11.26 Several iterative methods have been proposed for solving the nonlinear estimation inherent in (11.13), and these are usually combined with additional constraints to ensure the smoothness of the estimated function. In the case of MLPs, most of these methods are based on variants of the back-propagation algorithm, which works backwards from the output layer and uses a gradient rule to vary biases and weights iteratively. The algorithm is sensitive to local minima in the error space and is, therefore, applied several times with different starting values.

An additional pitfall in MLP estimation concerns the selection of the appropriate model architecture: the number of hidden layers and the number of elements in each layer. One can either start with a small model and add hidden layers until performance is optimal, or start with an oversized model and prune small weights to reduce its size. Sometimes a preliminary optimization is undertaken to select a good set of starting values and model architecture and to reduce the computational burden. Model performance is often evaluated by information criteria.

11.27 A major problem with MLPs is their "black-box" property, since the parameters and structure of the model offer little intuition and conclusions can be drawn only implicitly via simulation or sensitivity analysis. Moreover, assessing the statistical significance of the parameters is problematic. Because of these various difficulties and the requirement for specialized software, examples of the fitting of NNs is not undertaken here.

NONLINEAR DYNAMICS AND CHAOS

11.28 So far, all the processes introduced in this chapter have the common aim of modeling *stochastic* nonlinearities in time series. This would seem the natural approach to take when dealing with stochastic time series processes, but a literature has also developed that considers the question of whether such series could have been generated, at least in part, by nonlinear *deterministic* laws of motion.

11.29 Research in the general area of nonlinear dynamics is concerned with the behavior of deterministic and stochastic nonlinear systems. Both applied and theoretical research has flourished over the past four decades across a variety of disciplines and an extensive overview of the research on nonlinear dynamics, albeit with a bias toward the natural sciences, is given by Hilborn (1997). The meaning of the term "nonlinear dynamics" seems to vary considerably across scientific disciplines and eras. For example, a popular interpretation, since the early 1980s, associates nonlinear dynamics with deterministic nonlinear systems and a specific dynamic behavior called *chaos*, although this term has itself been given several different interpretations.

11.30   This diversity of meanings is mainly a consequence of there being no formal and complete mathematical definition of a chaotic system (see, for example, Berliner, 1992). Broadly speaking, chaos is the mathematical condition whereby a simple (low-dimensional), nonlinear, dynamical system produces complex (infinite-dimensional or random-like) behavior. Even though these systems are deterministic, they are completely unpredictable in the long-run, due to "sensitive dependence on initial conditions," also known as Lyapunov instability. Chaotic systems also invariably have "fractal" or "self-similar" pictorial representations.

11.31   An example of a chaotic process is one that is generated by a deterministic difference equation

$$x_t = f\left(x_{t-1}, \ldots, x_{t-p}\right)$$

such that x_t does not tend to a constant or a (limit) cycle and has estimated covariances that are extremely small or zero. A simple example is provided by Brock (1986), where a formal development of deterministic chaos models is provided. Consider the difference equation,

$$x_t = f(x_{t-1}), \quad x_0 \in [0, 1]$$

where

$$f(x) = \begin{cases} x/\alpha & x \in [0, \alpha] \\ (1-x)/(1-\alpha) & x \in [\alpha, 1] \quad 0 < \alpha < 1 \end{cases}$$

Most realizations (or trajectories) of this difference equation generate the same SACFs as an AR(1) process for x_t with parameter $\phi = (2\alpha - 1)$. Hence, for $\alpha = 0.5$, the realization will be indistinguishable from white noise, even though it has been generated by a purely deterministic nonlinear process. Hsieh (1991) provides further discussion of this function, called a *tent map* because the graph of x_t against x_{t-1} (known as the *phase diagram*) is shaped like a "tent." Hsieh also considers other relevant examples of chaotic systems, such as the *logistic map*

$$x_t = 4x_{t-1}(1 - x_{t-1}) = 4x_{t-1} - 4x_{t-1}^2, \qquad 0 < x_0 < 1$$

This also has the same autocorrelation properties as white noise, although x_t^2 has an SACF consistent with an MA(1) process.

11.32   Are such models useful in practice? One must keep in mind that systematic research on chaos was first undertaken in the natural sciences, where nonlinear systems tend to be low-dimensional, either by experimental construction or from first principles, so chaos is a natural choice for explaining complex empirical behavior. This is because, in deterministic systems, the standard types of dynamic behavior are limited to fixed-point equilibria and limit cycles, and hence complexity can arise only in the presence of chaos or high-dimensionality. High-dimensional or "stochastic" chaos is then of little interest, since it is typically considered to be equivalent to randomness for all practical purposes.

Unfortunately, an analogous deduction is not possible for many nonscientific disciplines, such as finance, where it is generally accepted that financial markets and agents are inherently highly stochastic and evolving, and so there is no practical need to resort to chaos to explain complex behavior. Although chaos may have a prominent place in the study of deterministic low-dimensional dynamic behavior, it seems to have a limited and rather exotic role to play in the context of stochastic linear and nonlinear dynamics.

11.33 It is, therefore, not surprising that applications of chaos theory in, say, finance and economics have been far less popular and successful than in the natural sciences. Nevertheless, the interest in chaotic processes continues to persist, much of it being motivated by the ability of chaotic systems to produce complicated behavior without resorting to exogenous stochastic factors and shocks. An underlying hope has always been that the apparently stochastic behavior and long-run unpredictability of financial systems could be the product of a low-dimensional, and hence tractable, chaotic system.

11.34 Broadly speaking, research on chaos has taken two distinct directions. The first starts with a nonlinear deterministic theoretical model and demonstrates that specific configurations can produce chaotic behavior (see the selective review by Fernández-Rodríguez et al., 2005). For example, Brock (1988) considers some models of equilibrium asset pricing that might lead to chaos and complex dynamics. In these models, the idea that there should be no arbitrage profits in financial equilibrium is linked with the theory of economic growth to show how dynamics in the "dividend" process may be transmitted through the equilibrating mechanism to asset prices. These dynamics can be linear, nonlinear, or chaotic depending on the constraints imposed on the models.

Although several models of this type can produce "mathematical" chaos, especially in economics, empirical validation was never undertaken. Furthermore, the underlying strong assumptions regarding deterministic dynamic behavior are highly questionable (see Granger, 1992).

11.35 The second approach is model-free and uses nonparametric procedures to test observed time series for signs of chaotic behavior (see, for example, Fernández-Rodríguez et al., 2005; Kyrtsou and Serletis, 2006; Shintani and Linton, 2006, and the references contained therein). Although some studies claim to have found "empirical" chaos, such evidence cannot be considered as conclusive since the testing procedures used are susceptible to a variety of statistical problems, such as autocorrelation, small sample size, heteroskedasticity, and nonstationarity.

More importantly, all the evidence presented has been circumstantial, since no formal testing procedure has been developed for stochastic time series where chaos enters as the null hypothesis. Even if chaos was present in the data, estimating the unknown parameters of the underlying model would be practically impossible (Geweke, 1993).

Finally, the literature has not provided convincing arguments about the practical implications of chaos and the marginal benefits of assuming chaotic behavior. There has also been little empirical evidence of chaotic dynamics uncovered in time series from many areas, although much evidence of other types of stochastic nonlinearities. This evidence has been obtained from a variety of tests for nonlinearity, to which we now turn.

TESTING FOR NONLINEARITY

11.36 As the previous sections have demonstrated, there have been a wide variety of nonlinear processes proposed for modeling time series. We have, for example, compared ARCH and bilinear models, and in so doing have discussed LM tests for each. Nevertheless, given the range of alternative nonlinear models, it is not surprising that other tests for nonlinearity have also been proposed. Since the form of the departure from linearity is often difficult to specify a priori, many tests are diagnostic in nature, i.e., a clear alternative to the null hypothesis of linearity is not specified. This, of course, leads to difficulties in discriminating between the possible causes of any "nonlinear misspecification" that might be uncovered by such tests.

11.37 The detection of nonlinearity is further complicated by the fact that it has similar symptoms to other types of time series behavior. For example, Andersson et al. (1999) have shown that long memory may lead to spurious rejection of the linearity hypothesis. As demonstrated by Granger and Teräsvirta (1999) and Diebold and Inoue (2001), the opposite may also be true, since some nonlinear processes exhibit characteristics that might justify modeling via a long memory model.

11.38 A related approach considers testing and modeling nonlinearity within a long memory process (see, for example, Baillie and Kapetanios, 2007). Koop and Potter (2001) have shown that unpredictable structural instability in a time series may also produce erroneous evidence of threshold-type nonlinearity. An alarming finding by Ghysels et al. (1996) is that nonlinear transformations, such as the X11 seasonal adjustment procedure, that are routinely applied prior to time series modeling, may also induce nonlinear behavior. Equally, seasonal adjustments may smooth out structural shifts and switching between regimes (see Franses and Paap,

1999). Finally, as discussed by Van Dijk et al. (1999) and De Lima (1997), neglecting outliers and nonnormalities may also lead to spurious evidence of nonlinearity.

Despite these difficulties, testing for nonlinearity is usually an effort well spent, since the burden associated with the specification and estimation of nonlinear models is often substantial and complex.

11.39 Empirical applications and simulation studies (e.g., Lee et al., 1993; Barnett et al., 1997) have shown that no nonlinearity test dominates in all situations and that power varies with sample size and the characteristics of the underlying stochastic process. This means that, in practice, it is advisable to apply a variety of nonlinearity tests to the data to guide the model specification process.

11.40 Based on Volterra expansions, Ramsey (1969), Keenan (1985), and Tsay (1986b) provide regression-type tests of linearity against unspecified alternatives. These appear to have good power against the nonlinear moving average and bilinear alternatives, but possibly low power against ARCH models. In developing these tests, we assume that an AR(p) process has been fitted to the observed series x_t and that the residuals, e_t, and the fitted values, $\hat{x}_t = x_t - e_t$, have been calculated.

11.41 Ramsey's original *Regression Error Specification Test* (RESET) is constructed from the auxiliary regression

$$e_t = \sum_{i=1}^{p} \varphi_i x_{t-i} + \sum_{j=2}^{h} \delta_j \hat{x}_t^j + v_t$$

and is the F-test of the hypothesis H_0: $\delta_j = 0$, $j = 2,\ldots,h$. If $h = 2$, this is equivalent to Keenan's test, while Tsay augments the auxiliary regression with second-order terms:

$$e_t = \sum_{i=1}^{p} \varphi_i x_{t-i} + \sum_{i=1}^{p} \sum_{j=i}^{p} \delta_{ij} x_{t-i} x_{t-j} + v$$

in which the linearity hypothesis is H_0:$\delta_{ij} = 0$, for all i and j. These tests have LM interpretations and Tsay's test has power against a greater variety of nonlinear models than the RESET. A further extension is provided by Teräsvirta et al. (1993), in which the auxiliary regression becomes:

$$e_t = \sum_{i=1}^{p} \varphi_i x_{t-i} + \sum_{i=1}^{p} \sum_{j=i}^{p} \delta_{ij} x_{t-i} x_{t-j} + \sum_{i=1}^{p} \sum_{j=i}^{p} \sum_{k=j}^{p} \delta_{ijk} x_{t-i} x_{t-j} x_{t-k} + v_t$$

with the linearity hypothesis now being H_0:$\delta_{ij} = 0$, $\delta_{ijk} = 0$, for all i, j, and k. This is related to the NN test discussed by Lee et al. (1993) and appears to have better power.

11.42   A portmanteau test for nonlinearity developed by McLeod and Li (1983) is based on the Ljung−Box (1978) statistic calculated using the squared residuals obtained from a linear fit. The test exploits an idea of Granger and Andersen (1978), that if the residuals from an AR(p) fit are i.i.d., then the cross-product of their squares should have a correlation structure that is the same as that of the square of their cross products (see §**11.10**). Under the null hypothesis of linearity, the first m autocorrelations of the squared residuals are zero and the Ljung−Box portmanteau test statistic is distributed as χ^2_{m-p}. This test has good power against ARCH behavior and is asymptotically equivalent to the LM test developed by Engle (1982). As expected, the power of the test is sensitive to departures from normality.

11.43   When residuals from an ARMA-GARCH model are used, the test no longer follows a χ^2 distribution and must be corrected along the lines suggested by Li and Mak (1994). Pena and Rodriguez (2005) have proposed a simple extension of this test that employs information criteria in the selection of the optimal lag structure for the autoregressive models fitted to the squared residuals. The checking procedure works on the premise that if the optimal lag structure is nonzero, then it can be inferred that there are nonlinearities present in the data. Simulation evidence shows that when the BIC is used, this test performs favorably for a wide variety of nonlinear processes and sample sizes. However, it was found to have poor power against threshold nonlinear processes and certain types of heteroskedastic behavior.

11.44   Once evidence in favor of nonlinearity has been found, Hsieh (1989) has developed a test that can shed light on the type of nonlinearity present. More specifically, the test attempts to discriminate between two types of nonlinearity: "additive" and "multiplicative." In the former, nonlinearity enters solely through the conditional mean of the process:

$$e_t = g(x_{t-1}, \ldots, x_{t-k}, e_{t-1}, \ldots, e_{t-k}) + u_t$$

where $g(\cdot)$ is an arbitrary nonlinear function. This suggests that a bilinear, threshold, or smooth transition model may be appropriate. Multiplicative nonlinearity manifests itself through the conditional variance, thus pointing toward an ARCH-type model:

$$e_t = g(x_{t-1}, \ldots, x_{t-k}, e_{t-1}, \ldots, e_{t-k})u_t$$

The test exploits the fact that, unlike additive dependence, multiplicative dependence implies that

$$E(e_t | x_{t-1}, \ldots, x_{t-k}, e_{t-1}, \ldots, e_{t-k}) = 0 \tag{11.14}$$

Assuming $g(\cdot)$ is at least twice continuously differentiable, then it can be approximated via a Taylor expansion around zero. The test is based on the idea that the residuals u_t must be uncorrelated with the terms in this expansion under multiplicative dependence. The test is implemented by estimating the scaled third moment of the data:

$$r_{eee}(i,j) = \frac{T^{-1}\sum e_t e_{t-i} e_{t-j}}{\left(T^{-1}\sum e_t^2\right)^{1.5}}$$

Under the null hypothesis of multiplicative nonlinearity, $T^{0.5} r_{eee}(i,j)$ is asymptotically normally distributed with a variance that can be consistently estimated by:

$$\sigma^2 = \frac{T^{-1}\sum e_t^2 e_{t-i}^2 e_{t-j}^2}{\left(T^{-1}\sum e_t^2\right)^3}$$

As discussed by Hsieh (1989), the approach is related to that of Tsay (1986b), who tests jointly $r_{eee}(i,j)$ for $0 < i,j < k$. The difference is that Tsay's test assumes that e_t is i.i.d. while Hsieh's test assumes only that the expectation in (11.14) is zero under sufficient moment conditions. The former test thus captures any departures from linearity, while the latter rejects the null only in the presence of additive, but not multiplicative, nonlinearity.

11.45 Nonlinearity tests have also been based on the reversibility of a stochastic process. A stationary process is said to be time reversible if all its finite dimensional distributions are invariant to the reversal of time indices. In other words, if the probabilistic structure of a time series is identical whether going forward or backward in time then the series is time reversible, otherwise it is said to be irreversible. Sequences that are i.i.d. and stationary Gaussian, such as ARMA processes, will be time reversible. However, a linear, non-Gaussian process will, in general, be time irreversible. Ramsey and Rothman (1996) have proposed the TR test statistic, estimated for various lags k as:

$$TR(k) = \hat{B}_{2,1}(k) - \hat{B}_{1,2}(k)$$

where $\hat{B}_{2,1}(k)$ and $\hat{B}_{1,2}(k)$ are estimators of the *bicovariances* $E\left(x_t^2 x_{t-k}\right)$ and $E\left(x_t x_{t-k}^2\right)$, respectively. These can be estimated using the residuals from a linear fit as:

$$\hat{B}_{i,j}(k) = (T-k)^{-1} \sum_{t=k+1}^{T} e_t^i e_{t-k}^j \quad i,j = 1,\ 2$$

Although ARCH processes are irreversible, the TR test has no power against them since their bicovariances are zero. Under the null hypothesis of time reversibility, TR has an expected value of zero for all lags. When the process is i.i.d., TR is asymptotically normally distributed with variance,

$$V(TR(k)) = 2\frac{\left(\mu_4\mu_2 - \mu_3\right)}{T - k} - 2\frac{\mu_2^3(T - 2k)}{(T-k)^2}, \quad \mu_i = E\left(e_t^i\right).$$

As shown by Rothman (1992), the convergence to asymptotic normality is adequately fast even when the process is non i.i.d. and the test is applied to residuals from a linear fit with nonnormal errors. Rothman shows that the test has reasonable power against simple bilinear and SETAR models and that the distinct rejection pattern of the test can be utilized in the model identification process.

11.46 Nonparametric tests of serial independence have also attracted interest as a means of searching for nonlinearity (see Dufour, 1982). These include a wide variety of procedures, including sign, permutation, and rank tests for independence. Nonparametric approaches have also been developed to test against serial dependence of fixed order (see Pinske, 1998). Most of these nonparametric tests are based on the actual series, rather than on standardized residuals from some linear fit, and therefore, the applicability of their limit distributions for, say, AR residuals is mostly unknown.

11.47 A nonparametric test that has created considerable interest is the BDS (standing for Brock-Dechert-Scheinkman) statistic, based on the concept of the *correlation integral*: see, for example, Brock (1986), Brock et al. (1991), and Dechert (1996). The test is based on the idea that the evolution of the next values of any two blocks of observations, which are close in some metric, should also be close in the same metric. For an observed series x_t, the correlation integral $C_N(\ell, T)$ is defined as:

$$C_N(\ell, T) = \frac{2}{T_N(T_N - 1)} \sum_{t<s} I_t\left(x_t^N, x_s^N\right)$$

where

$$x_t^N = (x_t, x_{t+1}, \ldots, x_{t+N-1})$$

and

$$x_s^N = (x_s, x_{s+1}, \ldots, x_{s+N-1})$$

are called "N-histories," $I_t\left(x_t^N, x_s^N\right)$ equals one if $\left\| x_t^N - x_s^N \right\| < \ell$ and zero otherwise, $\| \cdot \|$ being the sup-norm, and $T_N = T - N + 1$.

The correlation integral is an estimate of the probability that any two N-histories, x_t^N and x_s^N, are within ℓ of each other. If the x_ts are strict white noise, then

$$C_N(\ell, T) \rightarrow C_1(\ell, T)^N, \quad \text{as } T \rightarrow \infty$$

and

$$w_N(\ell, T) = \frac{\sqrt{T}\left(C_N(\ell, T) - C_1(\ell, T)^N\right)}{\sigma_N(\ell, T)}$$

has a standard normal limiting distribution, where the expression for the variance $\sigma_N^2(\ell, T)$ may be found in, for example, Hsieh (1989, page 343). The BDS statistic $w_N(\ell, T)$ thus tests the null hypothesis that a series is strict white noise. It is a diagnostic test, since a rejection of this null is consistent with some type of dependence in the data, which could result from a linear stochastic system, a nonlinear stochastic system, or a nonlinear deterministic system. Additional diagnostic tests are, therefore, needed to determine the source of the rejection, but simulation experiments do suggest that the BDS test has power against simple linear deterministic systems as well as nonlinear stochastic processes.

11.48   Tests are also available for specific nonlinear alternatives. Tests against ARCH and bilinear alternatives have already been discussed in §§**11.15−11.16** and there is also a fully developed testing procedure against STAR models. From Teräsvirta (1994), an LM-type test statistic for the null of linearity against an LSTAR alternative can be constructed from the auxiliary regression,

$$e_t = \sum_{i=1}^{p} \varphi_i x_{t-i} + \sum_{i=1}^{p} \delta_{1j} x_{t-i} x_{t-d} + \sum_{i=1}^{p} \delta_{2j} x_{t-i} x_{t-d}^2 + \sum_{i=1}^{p} \delta_{3j} x_{t-i} x_{t-d}^3 + v_t$$

with the linearity hypothesis being $H_0 : \delta_{ij} = 0$, for all i and j. To test against an ESTAR alternative the same auxiliary regression is estimated, but without the fourth-order terms, i.e., we set $\delta_{3j} = 0$ a priori. This relationship between the two tests leads naturally to a method for discriminating between the two types of STAR models (see Teräsvirta, 1994, for details, and Example 11.5).

11.49   Of course, these tests assume that the delay parameter d is known. Typically, however, its value will be unknown and Teräsvirta suggests that it should be chosen on the basis of a sequence of LM tests for alternative values of d: we choose the value that minimizes the p-value of the individual tests in the sequence. The auxiliary regression can also be estimated with x_t rather than e_t as the dependent variable and this may be preferred as it provides a direct comparison with the AR(p) model under the null of linearity. Van Dijk et al. (2002) discuss some extensions to this testing procedure.

11.50   Further tests are discussed in Teräsvirta et al. (2011). It should be emphasized, however, that all these tests are designed to distinguish between linear and nonlinear *stochastic* dynamics. They are not, however, capable of distinguishing nonlinear stochastic dynamics from deterministic chaotic dynamics, although the rejection of linearity may, of course, motivate the investigation of chaotic models.

EXAMPLE 11.5 Nonlinearity Tests for the Long Interest Rate

The presence of nonlinearity in United Kingdom long interest rates can be assessed by subjecting the series to a variety of the tests previously discussed. An AR(2) process for the first-differences was found to be the most appropriate linear fit, estimated as

$$x_t = \underset{(0.035)}{0.304}\, x_{t-1} - \underset{(0.035)}{0.126}\, x_{t-2} + e_t$$

The RESET/Keenan test produces an F-statistic of 6.69, which is significant at the 1% level. Tsay's test statistic has an F-value of 2.32, this having a p-value of 0.07. The portmanteau statistic calculated using the squared residuals from the AR(2) fit is highly significant for all values of m, whereas the TR statistic for $k = 1$ and 2 are both insignificant. The BDS statistics from N up to 6 are all highly significant.

The tests for LSTAR for a delay d equal to 1 or 2 have p-values of 0.018 and 0.027, while the analogous ESTAR tests have p-values of 0.029 and 0.011, thus suggesting that an ESTAR(2,2) model should be considered, which explains the choice of model in Example 11.3.

FORECASTING WITH NONLINEAR MODELS

11.51   One-step ahead forecasting from nonlinear models is straightforward, but multistep forecasting may be complicated. If we have the simple nonlinear model, $x_t = g(x_{t-1}) + \varepsilon_t$ then the one-step ahead forecast is straightforwardly given by $f_{T,1} = g(x_T)$. However, the two-step ahead forecast is

$$f_{T,2} = E\left(x_{T+2}|x_T\right) = E(g(g(x_{T+1}) + \varepsilon_{T+1})) = \int_\varepsilon g(g(x_{T+1}) + \varepsilon_{T+1})dF(\varepsilon)$$

$$(11.15)$$

where $dF(\varepsilon)$ is the cumulative distribution function of ε_t. Numerical integration of (11.15) may prove difficult, particularly as the forecast horizon increases. If the error term is ignored, what Tong (1990) calls the "skeleton" forecast may be used: $f_{T,h} = g(x_{T+h-1}|x_T)$. This forecast will, however, be biased. Alternatively, the integral in (11.15) may be approximated by simulation or by bootstrapping the residuals of the fitted model.

Some nonlinear models do allow multistep forecasts to be obtained analytically and for further discussion on all these procedures, see Teräsvirta (2007).

ENDNOTES

1. The term martingale, which also denotes part of a horse's harness or a ship's rigging, refers in addition to a gambling system in which every losing bet is doubled, a usage that may be felt to be rather apposite when considering the behavior of financial data!
2. This is a rather informal definition which conditions only on the past history of the series. More formal and general definitions are available which use concepts from measure theory. The *Electronic Journal for History of Probability and Statistics* devotes an entire issue (Volume 5, Number 1, 2009) to "The Splendors and Miseries of Martingales."
3. A more general specification allows the orders of the autoregression to differ in each regime, producing the natural notation SETAR $(r:p_1, p_2, \ldots, p_r, d)$.

Chapter 12

Transfer Functions and Autoregressive Distributed Lag Modeling

Chapter Outline

TRANSFER FUNCTION-NOISE MODELS

12.1 The models that have been developed so far in this book have all been *univariate*, so that the current value of a time series depends, linearly or otherwise, only on past values of itself and, perhaps, a deterministic function of time. While univariate models are important in themselves, they also play a key role in providing a "baseline" to which *multivariate* models may be compared. We shall analyze several multivariate models over the next chapters, but our development begins with the simplest. This is the *single-input transfer function-noise* model, in which an *endogenous*, or *output*, variable y_t is related to a single *input*, or *exogenous*, variable x_t through the dynamic model[1]

$$y_t = \upsilon(B)x_t + n_t \tag{12.1}$$

where the lag polynomial $\upsilon(B) = \upsilon_0 + \upsilon_1 B + \upsilon_2 B^2 + \cdots$ allows x to influence y via a *distributed lag*: $\upsilon(B)$ is often referred to as the *transfer function* and the coefficients υ_i as the *impulse response weights*.

12.2 It is assumed that both input and output variables are stationary, perhaps after appropriate transformation. The relationship between the two is not, however, deterministic—rather, it will be contaminated by noise captured by the stochastic process n_t, which will generally be serially correlated. A crucial assumption made in (12.1) is that x_t and n_t are independent, so that past x's influence future y's but not vice-versa, so ruling out *feedback* from y to x.

12.3 In general, $\upsilon(B)$ will be of infinite order and, hence, some restrictions must be placed on the transfer function before empirical modeling of (12.1)

Applied Time Series Analysis. DOI: https://doi.org/10.1016/B978-0-12-813117-6.00012-0
201

becomes feasible. The typical way in which restrictions are imposed is analogous to the approximation of the linear filter representation of a univariate stochastic process by a ratio of low order polynomials in B, which leads to the familiar ARMA model (cf. §§3.25–3.27). More precisely, $v(B)$ may be written as the *rational distributed lag*

$$v(B) = \frac{\omega(B)B^b}{\delta(B)} \tag{12.2}$$

Here the numerator and denominator polynomials are defined as

$$\omega(B) = \omega_0 - \omega_1 B - \cdots - \omega_s B^s$$

and

$$\delta(B) = 1 - \delta_1 B - \cdots - \delta_r B^r$$

with the roots of $\delta(B)$ all assumed to be less than unity. The possibility that there may be a delay of b periods before x begins to influence y is allowed for by the factorization of the numerator in (12.2): if there is a contemporaneous relationship then $b = 0$.

12.4   The relationship between the impulse response weights v_i and the parameters $\omega_0, \ldots, \omega_s, \delta_1, \ldots, \delta_r$ and b can always be obtained by equating the coefficients of B^j in

$$\delta(B)v(B) = \omega(B)B^b$$

For example, if $r = 1$ and $s = 0$, so that

$$v(B) = \frac{\omega_0 B^b}{1 - \delta_1 B}$$

then

$$v_i = 0 \quad i < b$$

$$v_i = \omega_0 \quad i = b$$

$$v_i = \delta_1 v_{i-1} \quad i > b$$

Further examples are provided in Box and Jenkins (1970, Table 10.1) and Mills (1990, Table 13.1).

12.5   The noise process may be assumed to follow an ARMA (p, q) model:

$$n_t = \frac{\theta(B)}{\phi(B)} a_t$$

so that the combined transfer function-noise model can be written as

$$y_t = \frac{\omega(B)}{\delta(B)} x_{t-b} + \frac{\theta(B)}{\phi(B)} a_t \tag{12.3}$$

Box and Jenkins (1970, Chapter 11) develop an identification, estimation, and diagnostic checking procedure for single-input transfer function models of the form of (12.3). The identification stage uses the *cross-correlation function* between the output and input after they have both been transformed using the filter (i.e., ARMA model) that reduces x_t to white noise, which is known as *prewhitening*. Estimation and diagnostic checking use extensions of their univariate counterparts, although these are not necessarily straight-forward. There have also been several other identification techniques pro-posed over the years, most notably based on prewhitening the input and output using individual filters (ARMA models).

12.6   If identifying a univariate ARMA model is often considered to be an "art form," then identifying a transfer function in this way is even more so and, if there are multiple inputs, can become increasingly difficult, for the model is now:

$$y_t = \sum_{j=1}^{M} v_j(B)x_{j,t} + n_t = \sum_{j=1}^{M} \frac{\omega_j(B)B^{b_j}}{\delta_j(B)} x_{j,t} + \frac{\theta(B)}{\phi(B)} a_t \qquad (12.4)$$

where

$$\omega_j(B) = \omega_{j,0} - \omega_{j,1}B - \cdots - \omega_{j,s_j}B^{s_j}$$

and

$$\delta_j(B) = 1 - \delta_{j,1}B - \cdots - \delta_{j,r_j}B^{r_j}$$

The simplest way to proceed is to use the Box–Jenkins approach in a "piecemeal" fashion, identifying a set of single-input transfer functions between y and x_1, y and x_2, etc., and then combining them to identify the noise model, after which estimation and diagnostic checking can be attempted.

12.7   The problem here is that the sample cross-correlation functions between each prewhitened input and the correspondingly filtered output may be misleading if the x's are intercorrelated. In mitigation, if these input series have been differenced to induce stationarity then it is well known that such differencing will reduce intercorrelations between the series. It may then be the case that the stationary input series are only weakly related and, analogous to the situation of independent regressors in multiple regression analysis, this piecemeal approach to identification may often work quite well, particularly as joint estimation of the combined model and judicious use of diagnostic checking procedures may then enable an adequately speci-fied model to be obtained.

AUTOREGRESSIVE DISTRIBUTED LAG MODELS

12.8   Nevertheless, it would clearly be useful if an automatic model selec-tion procedure could be developed. This has not been done for the multiple input model (12.4), but if a restricted form of it is specified then such a procedure becomes feasible. This restricted form is known as the *autoregressive distributed lag*, or ARDL, model and is obtained by placing the following restrictions on (12.4):

$$\delta_1(B) = \cdots = \delta_M(B) = \phi(B) \quad \theta(B) = 1$$

so that the model is, on defining $\beta_j(B) = \omega_j(B)B^{b_j}$ and including an intercept,

$$\phi(B)y_t = \beta_0 + \sum_{j=1}^{M} \beta_j(B)x_{j,t} + a_t \qquad (12.5)$$

This is known as the ARDL($p, s_1, \ldots, s_M$) model and restricts all the autoregressive lag polynomials to be the same and excludes a moving average noise component, although this exclusion is not essential. These restrictions reduce the noise component to white noise through constraining the dynamics and enables (12.5) to be estimated by OLS, so that on selecting a maximum lag order of, say, m, goodness-of-fit statistics, such as information criteria, can be used to select the appropriate specification.

12.9 The ARDL representation (12.5) may be recast in a potentially useful way. Recalling the development of §**8.4**, each input polynomial may be decomposed as

$$\beta_j(B) = \beta_j(1) + \nabla \tilde{\beta}_j(B)$$

where

$$\tilde{\beta}_j(B) = \tilde{\beta}_{j,0} + \tilde{\beta}_{j,1} B + \tilde{\beta}_{j,2} B^2 + \cdots + \tilde{\beta}_{j,s_j-1} B^{s_j-1}$$

with

$$\tilde{\beta}_{j,i} = - \sum_{l=i+1}^{s_j} \beta_{j,l}$$

Consequently, (12.5) can be written as

$$y_t = \beta_0 + \sum_{i=1}^{p} \phi_i y_{t-i} + \sum_{j=1}^{M} \beta_j(1)x_{j,t} + \sum_{j=1}^{M} \tilde{\beta}_j(B)\nabla x_{j,t} + a_t \qquad (12.6)$$

Solving for y_t then yields

$$y_t = \theta_0 + \sum_{j=1}^{M} \theta_j x_{j,t} + \sum_{j=1}^{M} \tilde{\theta}_j(B)\nabla x_{j,t} + \varepsilon_t \qquad (12.7)$$

in which

$$\theta_0 = \phi^{-1}(1)\beta_0$$

$$\theta_j = \phi^{-1}(1)\beta_j(1)$$

$$\tilde{\theta}_j(B) = \phi^{-1}(B)\left(\tilde{\beta}_j(B) - \tilde{\phi}(B)\phi^{-1}(1)\beta_j(1)\right) \quad j = 1, \ldots, M$$

$$\varepsilon_t = \phi^{-1}(B)a_t$$

where

$$\tilde{\phi}(B) = \nabla^{-1}(\phi(B) - \phi(1))$$

has been used.

The representation (12.7) separates out the *long-run* relationships between the output and the inputs from short-run effects, but is not amenable to direct estimation. The estimate of the long-run relationship between y and x_j may be obtained from (12.6) and is given by

$$\hat{\theta}_j = \frac{\hat{\beta}_j(1)}{1 - \sum_{i=1}^p \hat{\phi}_i} = \frac{\hat{\beta}_{j,0} + \cdots + \hat{\beta}_{j,s_j}}{1 - \sum_{i=1}^p \hat{\phi}_i}$$

and an accompanying standard error may be computed accordingly.

Various other re-expressions of the ARDL model (12.5) are available and are discussed in detail in Banerjee et al. (1993, Chapter 2). One such transformation, known as the *error-correction* model, will be introduced and used extensively in Chapter 14, Error Correction, Spurious Regressions, and Cointegration.

EXAMPLE 12.1 An ARDL Model for UK Interest Rates

In Example 11.3 an ESTAR model was estimated for the monthly change in the United Kingdom long interest rate, which produced a modest improvement in fit over the linear AR(2) specification, estimated to be (with $DR20$ now denoting the change in the long rate):

$$DR20_t = \frac{0.304}{(0.035)} DR20_{t-1} - \frac{0.126}{(0.035)} DR20_{t-2} + \hat{a}_t \quad \hat{\sigma}_a = 0.279$$

We now fit an ARDL model with the change in the short interest rate, DRS, included as a single input. Setting the maximum lag order at $m = 4$, Fig. 12.1 shows the AIC values for the 20 possible ARDL models, from which an ARDL (2,1) is selected and which is estimated to be

$$DR20_t = \frac{0.227}{(0.036)} DR20_{t-1} - \frac{0.109}{(0.036)} DR20_{t-2} + \frac{0.297}{(0.021)} DRS_t - \frac{0.073}{(0.023)} DRS_{t-1} + \hat{a}_t$$

$$\hat{\sigma}_a = 0.249$$

The equivalent form of (12.6) is

$$DR20_t = \frac{0.227}{(0.036)} DR20_{t-1} - \frac{0.109}{(0.036)} DR20_{t-2} + \frac{0.224}{(0.028)} DRS_t + \frac{0.075}{(0.023)} \nabla DRS_t + \hat{a}_t$$

and the long-run parameter contained in (12.7) is then calculated to be

$$\hat{\theta} = \frac{0.224}{1 - 0.227 + 0.109} = \frac{0.254}{(0.028)}$$

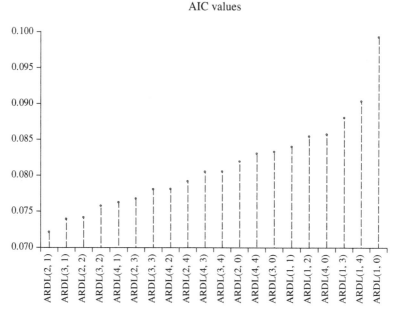

FIGURE 12.1 *AIC* values for ARDL models of short and long interest rates. *AIC*, Akaike Information criterion; *ARDL*, Autoregressive distributed lag.

The significance of both the contemporaneous and one-month lagged change in the short rate produces an 11% reduction in the residual standard error over the univariate model and shows that knowledge of changes in the short interest rate help to predict changes in the long interest rate.

EXAMPLE 12.2 ARDL Modeling of Global Temperatures

Fig. 12.2 shows global temperature and four possible "forcings"—total radiative forcing due to both anthropogenic and natural factors (excluding volcanic eruptions), radiative forcing due to volcanic stratospheric aerosols, and scaled indices of the Southern Oscillation and the Atlantic Multidecadal Oscillation—annually for the period of 1866–2015. From this figure, global temperature and total radiative forcing are clearly nonstationary, as would be expected, and unit root tests confirm they are both $I(1)$. Volcanic forcing and the two oceanic-atmospheric phenomena are, however, clearly stationary, as is also confirmed by unit root tests.

The ARDL model, (12.8), containing only stationary variables, was therefore considered, using obvious names for the variables to aid interpretation:

$$\nabla TEMP_t = \beta_0 + \sum_{i=1}^{m} \phi_i \nabla TEMP_{t-i} + \sum_{i=0}^{m} \beta_{1,i} \nabla TRF_{t-i} + \sum_{i=0}^{m} \beta_{2,i} VOLC_{t-i}$$
$$+ \sum_{i=0}^{m} \beta_{3,i} SO_{t-i} + \sum_{i=0}^{m} \beta_{4,i} AMO_{t-i} + a_t$$

$$(12.8)$$

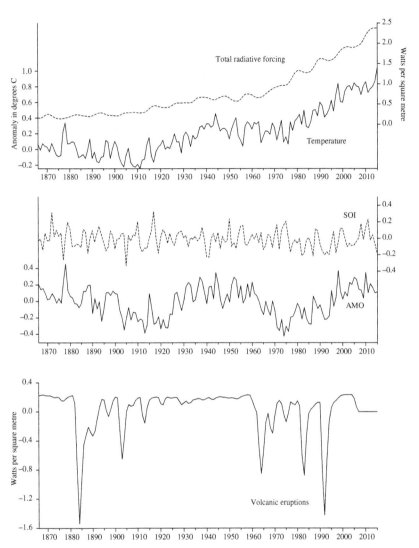

FIGURE 12.2 Climate data, annual 1866−2015. Top panel: temperature and total radiative forcing (excluding from volcanic eruptions); middle panel: Southern Oscillation index (SOI) and Atlantic Multidecadal Oscillation (AMO); bottom panel: radiative forcing from volcanic eruptions. *McDermott, G.R., 2017. Sceptic priors and climate policy. Working paper.; data downloaded from <https://github.com/grantmcdermott/sceptic-priors>.*

All the forcing variables may be considered to be exogenous and, on setting $m = 6$, an ARDL(3,2,0,1,4) model was selected, whose parameter estimates are shown in column (1) of Table 12.1. Various residual checks confirm the adequacy of this specification. Several of the parameter estimates are insignificant

TABLE 12.1 ARDL(3,2,0,1,4) Estimates of (12.8)

	Unrestricted ARDL (1)	Restricted (2)	Restricted (3)
$\hat{\beta}_0$	-0.002 (0.007)	$-$	$-$
$\hat{\phi}_1$	-0.519 (0.079)	-0.518 (0.071)	-0.520 (0.070)
$\hat{\phi}_2$	-0.350 (0.078)	-0.369 (0.066)	-0.370 (0.066)
$\hat{\phi}_3$	-0.333 (0.074)	-0.325 (0.067)	-0.324 (0.067)
$\hat{\beta}_{1,0}$	0.622 (0.483)	$-$	$-$
$\hat{\beta}_{1,1}$	-1.055 (0.761)	$-$	$-$
$\hat{\beta}_{1,2}$	1.160 (0.487)	0.560 (0.169)	0.561 (0.168)
$\hat{\beta}_{2,0}$	0.089 (0.022)	0.086 (0.021)	0.085 (0.021)
$\hat{\beta}_{3,0}$	-0.336 (0.058)	-0.342 (0.056)	-0.343 (0.056)
$\hat{\beta}_{3,1}$	-0.105 (0.066)	-0.107 (0.063)	-0.107 (0.063)
$\hat{\beta}_{4,0}$	0.379 (0.051)	0.382 (0.049)	0.385 (0.046)
$\hat{\beta}_{4,1}$	-0.239 (0.067)	-0.243 (0.058)	-0.241 (0.057)
$\hat{\beta}_{4,2}$	-0.017 (0.072)	$-$	$-$
$\hat{\beta}_{4,3}$	0.028 (0.069)	$-$	$-$
$\hat{\beta}_{4,4}$	-0.154 (0.061)	-0.147 (0.047)	-0.144 ($-$)
$\hat{\sigma}_a$	0.0696	0.0689	0.0687

ARDL, Autoregressive distributed lag.

and were, therefore, set to zero, with the restricted model estimates being shown in column (2). Written in the form of (12.6), this model is

$$\nabla TEMP_t = - \underset{(0.071)}{0.518} \nabla TEMP_{t-1} - \underset{(0.066)}{0.369} \nabla TEMP_{t-2} - \underset{(0.067)}{0.325} \nabla TEMP_{t-3}$$
$$+ \underset{(0.169)}{0.560} \nabla TRF_{t-2} + \underset{(0.021)}{0.086} VOLC_t - \underset{(0.082)}{0.449} SO_t + \underset{(0.063)}{0.107} \nabla SO_t$$
$$- \underset{(0.039)}{0.007} AMO_t + \underset{(0.058)}{0.243} \nabla AMO_t + \underset{(0.047)}{0.147} \nabla^4 AMO_t + \hat{a}_t$$

$$(12.9)$$

All the estimates are highly significant except for $\beta_4(1)$. Column (3) of Table 12.1 reports the estimates of the model when this coefficient is set to zero. With this restriction imposed, the model can be written in terms of the levels of each variable as

TABLE 12.2 ARDL(4,0,1,1) Estimates of (12.11)

	Unrestricted ARDL (1)	Restricted (2)
$\hat{\beta}_0$	− 0.046 (0.012)	− 0.046 (0.011)
$\hat{\phi}_1$	0.310 (0.080)	0.309 (0.078)
$\hat{\phi}_2$	0.083 (0.057)	0.094 (0.060)
$\hat{\phi}_3$	0.027 (0.063)	−
$\hat{\phi}_4$	0.133 (0.055)	0.144 (0.048)
$\hat{\beta}_{1,0}$	0.189 (0.483)	0.191 (0.032)
$\hat{\beta}_{2,0}$	0.050 (0.029)	0.048 (0.011)
$\hat{\beta}_{2,1}$	0.048 (0.029)	0.048 (−)
$\hat{\beta}_{3,0}$	− 0.307 (0.054)	− 0.305 (0.053)
$\hat{\beta}_{3,1}$	− 0.117 (0.061)	− 0.114 (0.060)
$\hat{\beta}_{4,0}$	0.390 (0.047)	0.393 (0.046)
$\hat{\beta}_{4,1}$	− 0.189 (0.012)	− 0.191 (0.056)
$\hat{\sigma}_a$	0.0659	0.0655

ARDL, Autoregressive distributed lag.

$$TEMP_t = - 0.520 TEMP_{t-1} - 0.370 TEMP_{t-2} - 0.324 TEMP_{t-3} + 0.561 TRF_{t-2}$$
$$+ 0.085 \sum_{i=0}^{\infty} VOLC_{t-i} - 0.343 SO_t - 0.450 \sum_{i=1}^{\infty} SO_{t-i}$$
$$+ 0.385 AMO_t + 0.144 \sum_{i=1}^{3} AMO_{t-i} + \text{constant}$$

$$(12.10)$$

The level of total radiative forcing, therefore, has a positive effect on temperatures, while it is the cumulative level of volcanic eruptions and the SO that effect temperatures; positively for the former and negatively for the latter. Because the long-run effect of the AMO on temperature change is zero, this index has only a transitory positive effect on temperature levels.

Of especial interest is the long-run coefficient on total radiative forcing, estimated to be

$$\hat{\theta}_1 = \frac{0.561}{1 + 0.520 + 0.370 + 0.324} = \frac{0.253}{(0.075)}$$

which has an accompanying 95% confidence interval of $0.1 < \theta_1 < 0.4$. The *transient climate response* (TCR) is defined as the warming produced after a doubling of CO_2 if CO_2 increases at a rate of 1% per annum, i.e., after 70 years. It may be calculated as $TCR = \hat{\theta}_1 \times F_{2\times}$, where $F_{2\times}$ is the change in forcing that results from such a doubling of CO_2. A value of $F_{2\times} = 3.71$ is the Intergovernmental Panel on Climate Change's (IPCC) best estimate of this parameter. Thus, TCR is estimated to be 0.94°C with a 95% confidence interval for the TCR of $0.4 < TCR < 1.5$. This is very much at the lower end of the range that the IPCC thinks is "most likely," this being $1.0°C-2.5°C$.

An alternative approach is to ignore the "$I(1)$-ness" of temperatures and total radiative forcing and to consider the "levels" model:

$$TEMP_t = \beta_0 + \sum_{i=1}^{m} \phi_i TEMP_{t-i} + \sum_{i=0}^{m} \beta_{1,i} TRF_{t-i} + \sum_{i=0}^{m} \beta_{2,i} VOLC_{t-i} + \sum_{i=0}^{m} \beta_{3,i} SO_{t-i} + \sum_{i=0}^{m} \beta_{4,i} AMO_{t-i} + a_t$$

(12.11)

Again setting $m = 6$, an ARDL(4,0,1,1,1) model was selected, whose estimates are shown in column (1) of Table 12.2. On noting that the coefficient estimates on $VOLC_t$ and $VOLC_{t-1}$ are almost identical, the restriction $\beta_{20} - \beta_{21} = 0$ was imposed, along with omitting the insignificant third-order lag on temperatures, and this restricted model is shown in column (2) of Table 12.2. Writing it in the form of (12.6), this model is

$$TEMP_t = -\frac{0.046}{(0.011)} + \frac{0.309}{(0.078)} TEMP_{t-1} + \frac{0.094}{(0.060)} TEMP_{t-2} + \frac{0.144}{(0.048)} TEMP_{t-4}$$
$$+ \frac{0.191}{(0.032)} TRF_t + \frac{0.096}{(0.022)} VOLC_t - \frac{0.048}{(-)} \nabla VOLC_t$$
$$- \frac{0.419}{(0.078)} SO_t + \frac{0.114}{(0.060)} \nabla SO_t + \frac{0.202}{(0.049)} AMO_t + \frac{0.191}{(0.056)} \nabla AMO_t + \hat{a}_t$$

This provides a slightly better fit than (12.9) and continues to pass all diagnostic checks. The long-run coefficient of total radiative forcing is now:

$$\hat{\theta}_1 = \frac{0.191}{1.0.309 - 0.094 - 0.144} = \frac{0.422}{(0.021)}$$

and this gives a 95% confidence interval for the TCR of $1.53°C < TCR < 1.61°C$. This is rather higher and much more precise than that obtained from (12.9) and lies in the central region of the IPCC's range of likely values of the TCR.

ENDNOTES

1. Other terms that are used are *dependent* for y_t and *independent* or *pre-determined* for x_t.

Chapter 13

Vector Autoregressions and Granger Causality

Chapter Outline

MULTIVARIATE DYNAMIC REGRESSION MODELS

13.1   In a natural extension to the ARDL model of the previous chapter, suppose that there are now *two* endogenous variables, $y_{1,t}$ and $y_{2,t}$, that may both be related to an exogenous variable x_t and its lags as well as to lags of each other. In the simplest case, such a model would be:

$$y_{1,t} = c_1 + a_{11}y_{1,t-1} + a_{12}y_{2,t-1} + b_{10}x_t + b_{11}x_{t-1} + u_{1,t}$$
$$y_{2,t} = c_2 + a_{21}y_{1,t-1} + a_{22}y_{2,t-1} + b_{20}x_t + b_{21}x_{t-1} + u_{2,t} \tag{13.1}$$

The "system" contained in Eq. (13.1) is known as a *multivariate dynamic regression*, a model treated in some detail in Spanos (1986, Chapter 24). Note that the "contemporaneous" variables, $y_{1,t}$ and $y_{2,t}$, are not included as regressors in the equations for $y_{2,t}$ and $y_{1,t}$, respectively, as this would lead to simultaneity and an identification problem, in the sense that the two equations making up (13.1) would then be statistically indistinguishable, there being the same variables in both. Of course, $y_{1,t}$ and $y_{2,t}$ may well be contemporaneously correlated, and any such correlation can be modeled by allowing the covariance between the innovations to be nonzero, so that $E(u_{1,t}u_{2,t}) = \sigma_{12}$ say, the variances of the two innovations then being $E(u_1^2) = \sigma_1^2$ and $E(u_2^2) = \sigma_2^2$.

13.2   The pair of equations in (13.1) may be generalized to a model containing n endogenous variables and k exogenous variables.[1] Gathering these together in the vectors $\mathbf{y'}_t = (y_{1,t}, y_{2,t}, \ldots, y_{n,t})$ and $\mathbf{x'}_t = (x_{1,t}, x_{2,t}, \ldots, x_{k,t})$,

Applied Time Series Analysis. DOI: https://doi.org/10.1016/B978-0-12-813117-6.00013-2

the general form of the multivariate dynamic regression model may be written as:

$$\mathbf{y}_t = \mathbf{c} + \sum_{i=1}^{p} \mathbf{A}_i \mathbf{y}_{t-i} + \sum_{i=0}^{q} \mathbf{B}_i \mathbf{x}_{t-i} + \mathbf{u}_t \tag{13.2}$$

where there is a maximum of p lags on the endogenous variables and a maximum of q lags on the exogenous variables. Here $\mathbf{c}' = (c_1, c_2, \ldots, c_n)$ is a $1 \times n$ vector of constants and $\mathbf{A}_1, \mathbf{A}_2, \ldots, \mathbf{A}_p$ and $\mathbf{B}_0, \mathbf{B}_1, \mathbf{B}_2, \ldots, \mathbf{B}_q$ are sets of $n \times n$ and $n \times k$ matrices of regression coefficients, respectively, such that

$$\mathbf{A}_i = \begin{bmatrix} a_{11,i} & a_{12,i} & \cdots & a_{1n,i} \\ a_{21,i} & a_{22,i} & \cdots & a_{2n,i} \\ \vdots & \vdots & & \vdots \\ a_{n1,i} & a_{n2,i} & \cdots & a_{nn,i} \end{bmatrix} \quad \mathbf{B}_i = \begin{bmatrix} b_{11,i} & b_{12,i} & \cdots & b_{1k,i} \\ b_{21,i} & b_{22,i} & \cdots & b_{2k,i} \\ \vdots & \vdots & & \vdots \\ b_{n1,i} & b_{n2,i} & \cdots & b_{nk,i} \end{bmatrix}$$

$\mathbf{u}'_t = (u_{1,t}, u_{2,t}, \ldots, u_{n,t})$ is a $1 \times n$ zero mean vector of innovations (or errors), whose variances and covariances can be gathered together in the symmetric $n \times n$ *error covariance* matrix

$$\Omega = E(\mathbf{u}_t \mathbf{u}'_t) = \begin{bmatrix} \sigma_1^2 & \sigma_{12} & \cdots & \sigma_{1n} \\ \sigma_{12} & \sigma_2^2 & \cdots & \sigma_{2n} \\ \vdots & & \vdots \\ \sigma_{1n} & \sigma_{2n} & \cdots & \sigma_n^2 \end{bmatrix}$$

It is assumed that these errors are mutually serially uncorrelated, so that $E(\mathbf{u}_t \mathbf{u}'_s) = \mathbf{0}$ for $t \neq s$, where $\mathbf{0}$ is an $n \times n$ null matrix.

13.3   The model (13.2) may be estimated by (multivariate) least squares if there are *exactly* p lags of the endogenous variables and q lags of the exogenous variables in each equation. If there are different lag lengths in the individual equations, then a systems estimator is required to obtain efficient estimates.[2]

VECTOR AUTOREGRESSIONS

13.4   Suppose the model (13.2) does not contain any exogenous variables, so that all the $\mathbf{B}_i$ matrices are zero, and that there are p lags of the endogenous variables in *every* equation:

$$\mathbf{y}_t = \mathbf{c} + \sum_{i=1}^{p} \mathbf{A}_i \mathbf{y}_{t-i} + \mathbf{u}_t \tag{13.3}$$

Because (13.3) is now simply a pth order autoregression in the vector $\mathbf{y}_t$ it is known as a *vector autoregression* (VAR(p)) of dimension n and, again, can be estimated by multivariate least squares.[3] It is assumed that all the series contained in $\mathbf{y}_t$ are stationary, which requires that the roots of the characteristic equation associated with (13.3),

$$A(B) = \mathbf{I}_n - \mathbf{A}_1 B - \cdots - \mathbf{A}_p B^p = \mathbf{0}$$

have moduli that are less than unity (bearing in mind that some of the np roots may appear as complex conjugates).

VARs have become extremely popular for modeling multivariate systems of time series because the absence of $\mathbf{x}_t$ terms precludes having to make any endogenous−exogenous classification of the variables, for such distinctions are often considered to be highly contentious.

GRANGER CAUSALITY

13.5 In the VAR (13.3) the presence of nonzero off-diagonal elements in the $\mathbf{A}_i$ matrices, $a_{rs,i} \neq 0$, $r \neq s$, implies that there are dynamic relationships between the variables, otherwise the model would collapse to a set of n univariate AR processes. The presence of such dynamic relationships is known as *Granger (-Sims) causality.*[4] The variable y_s *does not Granger-cause* the variable y_r if $a_{rs,i} = 0$ for all $i = 1, 2, \ldots, p$. If, on the other hand, there is at least one $a_{rs,i} \neq 0$ then y_s is said to *Granger-cause* y_r because if that is the case then past values of y_s are useful in forecasting the current value of y_r: Granger causality is, thus, a criterion of "forecastability." If y_r also Granger-causes y_s, the pair of variables are said to exhibit *feedback.*

13.6   Within a VAR(p), Granger causality running from y_s to y_r, which may be depicted as $y_s \rightarrow y_r$, can be evaluated by setting up the null hypothesis of *non-Granger causality* (y_s does not $\rightarrow y_r$), $H_0 : a_{rs,1} = \cdots = a_{rs,p} = 0$, and testing this with a Wald statistic; a multivariate extension of the standard F-statistic for testing a set of zero restrictions in a conventional regression model: see, for example, Mills (2014, §13.3).

13.7   The presence of nonzero off-diagonal elements in the error covariance matrix $\mathbf{\Omega}$ signals the presence of simultaneity. For example, $\sigma_{rs} \neq 0$ implies that $y_{r,t}$ and $y_{s,t}$ are contemporaneously correlated. It might be tempting to try and model such correlation by including $y_{r,t}$ in the equation for $y_{s,t}$ but, if this is done, then $y_{s,t}$ could equally well be included in the $y_{r,t}$ equation. As was pointed out in §**13.1**, this would lead to an identification problem, since the two equations would be statistically indistinguishable and the VAR could no longer be estimated. The presence of $\sigma_{rs} \neq 0$ is sometimes referred to as *instantaneous causality*, although we should be careful when interpreting this phrase, as *no* causal direction can be inferred from σ_{rs} being nonzero (recall the "correlation does not imply causation" argument found in any basic statistics text: see, e.g., Mills, 2014, §5.4).

DETERMINING THE LAG ORDER OF A VECTOR AUTOREGRESSION

13.8   To enable the VAR to become operational the lag order p, which will typically be unknown, needs to be determined empirically. A traditional way of selecting the lag order is to use a sequential testing procedure. Consider the model (13.3) with error covariance matrix $\Omega_p = E\left(\mathbf{u}_t \mathbf{u}_t'\right)$, where a p subscript is included to emphasize that the matrix is related to a VAR(p). An estimate of this matrix is given by:

$$\hat{\Omega}_p = (T-p)^{-1}\hat{\mathbf{U}}_p\hat{\mathbf{U}}_p'$$

where $\hat{\mathbf{U}}_p = (\hat{\mathbf{u}}_{p,1}', \ldots, \hat{\mathbf{u}}_{p,n}')'$ is the matrix of residuals obtained by OLS estimation of the VAR(p), $\hat{\mathbf{u}}_{p,r} = (\hat{u}_{r,p+1}, \ldots, \hat{u}_{r,T})'$ being the residual vector from the rth equation (noting that with a sample of size T, p observations will be lost through lagging). A likelihood ratio (LR) statistic for testing the order p against the order m, $m < p$, is

$$LR(p,m) = (T - np)\log\left(\frac{|\hat{\Omega}_m|}{|\hat{\Omega}_p|}\right) \sim \chi^2_{n^2(p-m)} \qquad (13.4)$$

Thus, if $LR(p,m)$ exceeds the α critical value of the χ^2 distribution with $n^2(p - m)$ degrees of freedom, then the hypothesis that the VAR order is m is rejected at the α level of significance in favor of the higher order p. The statistic uses the scaling factor $T - np$ rather than $T - p$ to account for possible small sample bias.

The statistic (13.4) may then be used sequentially beginning with a maximum value of p, $p_{\max}$ say, testing first $p_{\max}$ against $p_{\max} - 1$ using $LR(p_{\max}, p_{\max} - 1)$ and, if this statistic is not significant, then testing $p_{\max} - 1$ against $p_{\max} - 2$ using $LR(p_{\max} - 1, p_{\max} - 2)$, continuing until a significant test is obtained.

Alternatively, some type of information criterion can be minimized. These are essentially multivariate extensions of those initially introduced in §**3.35**: for example, the multivariate AIC and BIC criteria are defined as:

$$MAIC(p) = \log|\hat{\Omega}_p| + \left(2 + n^2p\right)T^{-1}$$

$$MBIC(p) = \log|\hat{\Omega}_p| + n^2pT^{-1}\ln T \quad p = 0, 1, \ldots, p_{\max}$$

13.9   After an order has been selected and the VAR fitted, checks on its adequacy need to be performed. These are analogues to the diagnostic checks used for univariate models introduced in §**3.34**, but with vector time series there is probably no substitute for detailed inspection of the residual correlation structure, including cross-correlations, for revealing subtle relationships that may indicate important directions for model improvement.

EXAMPLE 13.1 The Interaction of the United Kingdom Bond and Gilt Markets

Example 12.1 developed an ARDL model in which the change in the long United Kingdom interest rate, $\nabla R20_t$, was treated as endogenous and the change in the short interest rate, ∇RS_t, was assumed to be exogenous. It is important to understand that this exogeneity assumption may not be valid. These series may be thought of as being representative of the gilt and bond markets in the United Kingdom, which may interact in a dynamic fashion that could well involve a feedback from the gilt to the bond market, i.e., from long rates to short rates.

The interaction between the two markets may be investigated by first determining the order of the two-dimensional VAR for $y_t = (\nabla RS_t, \nabla R20_t)'$. Table 13.1 shows various statistics for doing this for a maximum setting of $p_{max} = 4$. The LR and MAIC statistics select an order of two while the MBIC selects an order of

TABLE 13.1 Lag Length Determination Statistics for the VAR Fitted to United Kingdom Interest Rates

p	$\mathcal{L}(p)$	$LR(p, p-1)$	MAIC	MBIC
0	-535.4	–	1.376	1.388
1	-470.9	128.4	1.221	1.257^a
2	-464.4	13.0^a	1.215^a	1.274
3	-463.6	1.6	1.223	1.307
4	-462.9	1.3	1.232	1.339

$LR(p, p-1) \sim \chi^2(4)$: $\chi^2_{0.05}(4) = 9.5$. VAR, Vector autoregression.
^{a}Selected value.

one, although the VAR(1) fit leaves a significant second-order residual autocorrelation in the $\nabla R20$ equation. An order of two was, therefore, chosen with the fitted VAR(2) being:

$$\begin{bmatrix} \nabla RS_t \\ \nabla R20_t \end{bmatrix} = \begin{bmatrix} \underset{(0.040)}{0.218} & \underset{(0.061)}{0.279} \\ \underset{(0.026)}{-0.011} & \underset{(0.040)}{0.313} \end{bmatrix} \begin{bmatrix} \nabla RS_{t-1} \\ \nabla R20_{t-1} \end{bmatrix} + \begin{bmatrix} \underset{(0.039)}{0.021} & \underset{(0.062)}{-0.067} \\ \underset{(0.026)}{0.022} & \underset{(0.040)}{-0.140} \end{bmatrix} \begin{bmatrix} \nabla RS_{t-2} \\ \nabla R20_{t-2} \end{bmatrix} + \begin{bmatrix} \hat{u}_{1,t} \\ \hat{u}_{2,t} \end{bmatrix}$$

The intercept vector c has been excluded from the model as, consistent with Example 12.1, it was found to be insignificant. Various checks on the residuals of the VAR(2) failed to uncover any model inadequacy.

Within the estimated AR(2) model, the Granger causality Wald statistics test $a_{12,1} = a_{12,2} = 0$ for the null $\nabla R20$ does not $\rightarrow \nabla RS$, and $a_{21,1} = a_{21,2} = 0$ for the null ∇RS does not $\rightarrow \nabla$R20. These statistics are 20.87 and 0.83, respectively, and reveal that the long rate Granger-causes the short rate, but that there is *no* feedback: movements in the gilt market thus lead, and so help to forecast, movements in the bond market.

This result contradicts the ARDL model of Example 12.1, in which it was *assumed* that movements in the bond market influenced the gilt market. Note, however, that the ARDL model allowed the contemporaneous value of ∇RS$_t$ to appear as a regressor, which is precluded in the VAR. Nevertheless, it would be expected that the covariance (correlation) between the residuals of the VAR would be positive and substantial. The correlation is, in fact, 0.45, confirming that there are strong contemporaneous movements in the two markets, as might be expected.

VARIANCE DECOMPOSITIONS AND INNOVATION ACCOUNTING

13.10   While the estimated coefficients of a VAR(1) are relatively easy to interpret, this quickly becomes problematic for higher order VARs because not only do the number of coefficients increase rapidly (each additional lag introduces a further n^2 coefficients), but many of these coefficients will be imprecisely estimated and highly intercorrelated, so becoming statistically insignificant. This can be seen in the estimated VAR(2) of Example 13.1, where only $\hat{a}_{22,2}$ in $\hat{\mathbf{A}}_2$ is significant.

13.11   This has led to the development of several techniques for examining the "information content" of a VAR that are based on the *vector moving average representation* (VMA) of $\mathbf{y}_t$. Suppose that the VAR is written in lag operator form as

$$\mathbf{A}(B)\mathbf{y}_t = \mathbf{u}_t$$

where, as in §**13.4**,

$$\mathbf{A}(B) = \mathbf{I}_n - \mathbf{A}_1 B - \cdots - \mathbf{A}_p B^p$$

is a matrix polynomial in B. Analogous to the univariate case (recall §§**3.8**–**3.9**), the (infinite order) VMA representation is

$$\mathbf{y}_t = \mathbf{A}^{-1}(B)\mathbf{u}_t = \mathbf{\Psi}(B)\mathbf{u}_t = \mathbf{u}_t + \sum_{i=1}^{\infty} \mathbf{\Psi}_i \mathbf{u}_{t-i} \qquad (13.5)$$

where

$$\mathbf{\Psi}_i = \sum_{j=1}^{i} \mathbf{A}_j \mathbf{\Psi}_{i-j} \quad \mathbf{\Psi}_0 = \mathbf{I}_n \quad \mathbf{\Psi}_i = \mathbf{0} \quad i < 0$$

this recursion being obtained by equating coefficients of B in $\mathbf{\Psi}(B)\mathbf{A}(B) = \mathbf{I}_n$.

13.12 The $\mathbf{\Psi}_i$ matrices can be interpreted as the *dynamic multipliers* of the system, since they represent the model's response to a unit shock in each of the variables. The response of y_r to a unit shock in y_s (produced by $u_{s,t}$ taking the value unity rather than its expected value of zero) is, therefore, given by the *impulse response function*, which is the sequence $\psi_{rs,1}, \psi_{rs,2}, \ldots,$ where $\psi_{rs,i}$ is the rsth element of the matrix $\mathbf{\Psi}_i$.

Since $\mathbf{\Omega}_p = E(\mathbf{u}_t \mathbf{u}'_t)$ is not required to be diagonal, the components of $\mathbf{u}_t$ may be contemporaneously correlated. If these correlations are high, simulation of a shock to y_s, while all other components of $\mathbf{u}_t$ are held constant, could be misleading, as there is no way of separating out the response of y_r to a y_s shock from its response to other shocks that are correlated with $u_{s,t}$. However, if we define the lower triangular matrix $\mathbf{S}$ such that $\mathbf{S}\mathbf{S}' = \mathbf{\Omega}_p$ and define $\mathbf{v}_t = \mathbf{S}^{-1}\mathbf{u}_t$, then $E(\mathbf{v}_t \mathbf{v}'_t) = \mathbf{I}_n$ and the transformed errors $\mathbf{v}_t$ are orthogonal to each other (this is known as a *Cholesky decomposition*). The VMA representation can then be renormalized into the *recursive* form:

$$\mathbf{y}_t = \sum_{i=0}^{\infty} (\mathbf{\Psi}_i \mathbf{S})(\mathbf{S}^{-1}\mathbf{u}_{t-i}) = \sum_{i=0}^{\infty} \mathbf{\Psi}_i^O \mathbf{v}_{t-i}$$

where $\mathbf{\Psi}_i^O = \mathbf{\Psi}_i \mathbf{S}$ (so that $\mathbf{\Psi}_0^O = \mathbf{\Psi}_0 \mathbf{S}$ is lower triangular). The impulse response function of y_r to a y_s shock is then given by the sequence $\psi_{rs,0}^O, \psi_{rs,1}^O, \psi_{rs,2}^O, \ldots,$ where each impulse response can be written compactly as:

$$\psi_{rs,i}^O = \mathbf{e}'_r \mathbf{\Psi}_i \mathbf{S} \mathbf{e}_s \tag{13.6}$$

Here $\mathbf{e}_s$ is the $n \times 1$ selection vector containing unity as the sth element and zero elsewhere. This sequence is known as the *orthogonalized impulse response function*. The (*accumulated*) *long-run response* is then:

$$\psi_{rs}^O(\infty) = \sum_{i=0}^{\infty} \mathbf{e}'_r \mathbf{\Psi}_i \mathbf{S} \mathbf{e}_s \tag{13.7}$$

The entire set of long-run responses may then be gathered together in the matrix

$$\mathbf{\Psi}^O(\infty) = \sum_{i=0}^{\infty} \mathbf{\Psi}_i \mathbf{S} = \mathbf{\Psi}(1)\mathbf{S}$$

13.13 The uncorrelatedness of the $\mathbf{v}_t$s allows the error variance of the h-step ahead forecast of y_r to be decomposed into components "accounted" by these innovations, a technique thus known as *innovation accounting*, a term coined by Sims (1981). For example, the proportion of the h-step ahead forecast error variance of y_r accounted by the orthogonalized innovations to y_s is given by:

$$V_{rs,h}^O = \frac{\sum_{i=0}^{h} \left(\psi_{rs,h}^O\right)^2}{\sum_{i=0}^{h} \mathbf{e}'_r \mathbf{\Psi}_i \mathbf{\Omega}_p \mathbf{\Psi}'_i \mathbf{e}_r} = \frac{\sum_{i=0}^{h} (\mathbf{e}'_r \mathbf{\Psi}_i \mathbf{S} \mathbf{e}_s)^2}{\sum_{i=0}^{h} \mathbf{e}'_r \mathbf{\Psi}_i \mathbf{\Omega}_p \mathbf{\Psi}'_i \mathbf{e}_r}$$

For large h, this *orthogonalized forecast error variance decomposition* allows the isolation of those relative contributions to variability that are, intuitively, "persistent."

The technique of orthogonalization does, however, have an important disadvantage, for the choice of the $\mathbf{S}$ matrix is not unique, so that different orderings of the variables will alter the $\psi_{rs,i}^O$ coefficients and, hence, the impulse response functions and variance decompositions. The extent of these changes will depend on the size of the contemporaneous correlations between the innovations.

13.14 Apart from comparing the impulse responses and variance decompositions for alternative orderings of the variables, one solution to this problem is to use Pesaran and Shin's (1997) *generalized impulse responses*, defined by replacing $\mathbf{S}$ in (13.6) with $\sigma_r^{-1} \mathbf{\Omega}_p$:

$$\psi_{rs,i}^G = \sigma_r^{-1} \mathbf{e}'_r \mathbf{\Psi}_i \mathbf{\Omega}_p \mathbf{e}_s$$

The generalized impulse responses are invariant to the ordering of the variables, are unique, and fully account for the historical patterns of correlations observed amongst the different shocks. The orthogonalized and generalized impulse responses coincide only when $\mathbf{\Omega}_p$ is diagonal, and in general, are only the same for $s = 1$.

EXAMPLE 13.2 Variance Decomposition and Innovation Accounting for the Bond and Gilt Markets

From Example 13.1, the VAR(2) fitted to $\mathbf{y}_t = (\nabla RS_t, \nabla R20_t)'$ has

$$\hat{\mathbf{A}}_1 = \begin{bmatrix} 0.218 & 0.279 \\ -0.012 & 0.313 \end{bmatrix} \quad \hat{\mathbf{A}}_2 = \begin{bmatrix} 0.021 & -0.067 \\ 0.022 & -0.140 \end{bmatrix}$$

The VMA representation (13.5) then has coefficient matrices given by:

$$\mathbf{\Psi}_i = \mathbf{A}_1 \mathbf{\Psi}_{i-1} + \mathbf{A}_2 \mathbf{\Psi}_{i-2}$$

so that

$$\Psi_1 = A_1 \Psi_0 \qquad = \begin{bmatrix} 0.218 & 0.279 \\ -0.012 & 0.313 \end{bmatrix}$$

$$\Psi_2 = A_1 \Psi_1 + A_2 \Psi_0 \quad = \begin{bmatrix} 0.218 & 0.279 \\ -0.012 & 0.313 \end{bmatrix}^2 + \begin{bmatrix} 0.021 & -0.067 \\ 0.022 & -0.149 \end{bmatrix}$$

$$= \begin{bmatrix} 0.065 & 0.081 \\ 0.016 & -0.045 \end{bmatrix}$$

$$\Psi_3 = A_1 \Psi_2 + A_2 \Psi_1 \quad = \begin{bmatrix} 0.024 & -0.010 \\ 0.011 & -0.053 \end{bmatrix}$$

$$\vdots$$

The estimated error covariance matrix is

$$\hat{\Omega}_2 = \begin{bmatrix} 0.183 & 0.054 \\ 0.054 & 0.078 \end{bmatrix}$$

so that the contemporaneous correlation between the innovations is 0.46, thus necessitating orthogonalization. The Cholesky decomposition of $\hat{\Omega}_2$ for the ordering ∇RS, $\nabla R20$ is

$$S = \begin{bmatrix} 0.428 & 0 \\ 0.127 & 0.249 \end{bmatrix} = \Psi_0^O$$

with

$$S^{-1} = \begin{bmatrix} 2.336 & 0 \\ -1.191 & 4.015 \end{bmatrix}$$

Thus,

$$\Psi_1^O = \Psi_1 S = \begin{bmatrix} 0.128 & 0.069 \\ 0.035 & 0.078 \end{bmatrix}$$

$$\Psi_2^O = \Psi_2 S = \begin{bmatrix} 0.038 & 0.020 \\ 0.001 & -0.011 \end{bmatrix}$$

$$\Psi_3^O = \Psi_3 S = \begin{bmatrix} 0.009 & -0.002 \\ -0.002 & -0.013 \end{bmatrix}$$

$$\vdots$$

The orthogonalized impulse response functions are then, for $y_1 = \nabla RS$ and $y_2 = \nabla R20$,

$$\psi_{12,0}^O = 0, \quad \psi_{12,1}^O = \begin{bmatrix} 1 & 0 \end{bmatrix} \begin{bmatrix} 0.128 & 0.069 \\ 0.035 & 0.078 \end{bmatrix} \begin{bmatrix} 0 \\ 1 \end{bmatrix} = 0.069, \quad \psi_{12,2}^O = 0.021, \quad \dots$$

$$\psi_{21,0}^O = 0.013 \quad \psi_{21,1}^O = \begin{bmatrix} 0 & 1 \end{bmatrix} \begin{bmatrix} 0.131 & 0.069 \\ 0.035 & 0.078 \end{bmatrix} \begin{bmatrix} 1 \\ 0 \end{bmatrix} = 0.035, \quad \psi_{21,2}^O = 0.001, \quad \dots$$

These response functions, along with their accumulations, are shown in Fig. 13.1. Also shown are their counterparts when the ordering is reversed. There is a considerable difference between the two, showing clearly how a sizeable

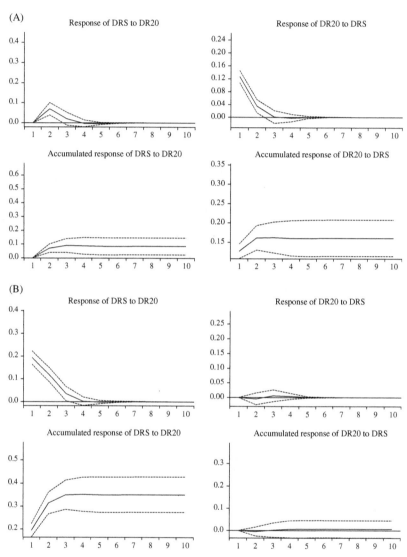

FIGURE 13.1 (A) Impulse response function and accumulated response for Cholesky ordering DRS, DR20 with two-standard error bounds; (B) Impulse response function and accumulated response for Cholesky ordering DR20, DRS with two-standard error bounds. DRS = ∇RS, DR20 = ∇R20.

contemporaneous correlation between the innovations can alter the impulse responses. Nevertheless, the response of ∇RS to an innovation in ∇R20 is clearly complete within six months and there is a smooth convergence of the accumulated response to a new positive "level." The response of ∇R20 to an ∇RS innovation is small when ∇R20 is ordered first.

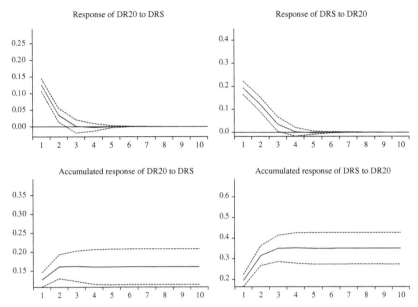

FIGURE 13.2 Generalized impulse response function and accumulated responses with two-standard error bounds.

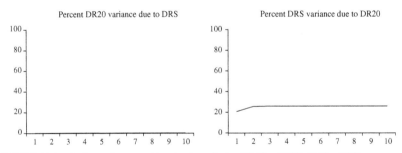

FIGURE 13.3 Variance decomposition for the ordering DR20 = ∇R20, DRS = ∇RS.

Fig. 13.2 shows the generalized impulse response functions. The generalized responses for ∇RS are similar to the orthogonalized responses when ∇R20 is first in the ordering and vice versa for ∇R20 itself. Fig. 13.3 shows the associated variance decompositions when ∇R20 is first in the ordering. These show that innovations to ∇R20 explain around 25% of the variation in ∇RS, but that innovations to ∇RS explain none of the variation in ∇R20.

STRUCTURAL VECTOR AUTOREGRESSIONS

13.15 The "noninvariance property" of VARs has generated much detailed analysis and criticism of the variance decomposition methodology, mainly focusing on the inability of VARs to be regarded as "structural" in the traditional econometric sense, so that shocks cannot be uniquely identified with a specific variable unless prior identifying assumptions are made, without which the computed impulse response functions and variance decompositions would be invalid. The triangular "recursive" structure of **S** has been criticized for being *atheoretical*, and has led to the development of other sets of identifying restrictions that are based more explicitly on theoretical considerations using the *structural VAR* (SVAR) approach: see Cooley and LeRoy (1985); Blanchard (1989); and Blanchard and Quah (1989).

13.16 The Cholesky decomposition of §**13.12** can be written as $\mathbf{u}_t = \mathbf{S}\mathbf{v}_t$ with $\mathbf{SS}' = \mathbf{\Omega}_p$ and $E(\mathbf{v}_t\mathbf{v}'_t) = \mathbf{I}_n$. A more general formulation is:

$$\mathbf{A}\mathbf{u}_t = \mathbf{B}\mathbf{v}_t$$

so that

$$\mathbf{BB}' = \mathbf{A}\mathbf{\Omega}_p\mathbf{A}' \tag{13.8}$$

Since both **A** and **B** are $n \times n$ matrices, they contain $2n^2$ elements, but the symmetry of the matrices on either side of (13.8) imposes $n(n + 1)/2$ restrictions. A further $2n^2 - n(n + 1)/2 = n(3n - 1)/2$ restrictions, at least, must then be imposed to complete the identification of **A** and **B**. These will typically be specific values for some of the elements: for example, if $n = 3$ then defining

$$\mathbf{A} = \begin{bmatrix} a_{11} & 0 & 0 \\ a_{21} & a_{22} & 0 \\ a_{31} & a_{32} & a_{33} \end{bmatrix} \quad \mathbf{B} = \begin{bmatrix} 1 & 0 & 0 \\ 0 & 1 & 0 \\ 0 & 0 & 1 \end{bmatrix}$$

imposes 12 restrictions in the form required to obtain the Cholesky decomposition. Equally, the system with

$$\mathbf{A} = \begin{bmatrix} 1 & 0 & 0 \\ a_{21} & 1 & 0 \\ a_{31} & a_{32} & 1 \end{bmatrix} \quad \mathbf{B} = \begin{bmatrix} b_{11} & 0 & 0 \\ 0 & b_{22} & 0 \\ 0 & 0 & b_{33} \end{bmatrix}$$

will also be identified, the coefficients on the diagonal of **B** giving the standard deviations of the "unnormalized" structural innovations.

13.17 An alternative form of restriction is also possible. The long-run impulse response may be written, on generalizing (13.7), as

$$\psi_{rs}(\infty) = \sum_{i=0}^{\infty} \mathbf{e}'_r \mathbf{\Psi}_i \mathbf{A}^{-1} \mathbf{B} \mathbf{e}_s$$

or, in matrix form,

$$\mathbf{\Psi}(\infty) = \sum_{i=0}^{\infty} \mathbf{\Psi}_i \mathbf{A}^{-1}\mathbf{B} = \mathbf{\Psi}(1)\mathbf{A}^{-1}\mathbf{B}$$

Restrictions may be imposed on the elements of $\mathbf{\Psi}(\infty)$, typically that they take on zero values: for example, setting $\psi_{rs}(\infty) = 0$ restricts the long-run response of y_r to a y_s shock to be zero.

EXAMPLE 13.3 Quenouille's Hog Series Example Revisited

The first empirical analysis of a multivariate time series was provided by Quenouille (1957, Chapter 8), who analyzed five annual United States time series from 1867 to 1948. The series were: the number and price of hogs ($y_{1,t}$ and $y_{2,t}$), the price and supply of corn ($y_{3,t}$ and $y_{4,t}$), and the farm wage rate ($y_{5,t}$). Exact definitions of each of these variables are given in Quenouille (1957, Section 8.1), which also provides the actual data in Table 8.1a. These five series are shown in Fig. 13.4. Although there are some indications of nonstationarity in the individual series, we shall follow Quenouille and include a linear trend in

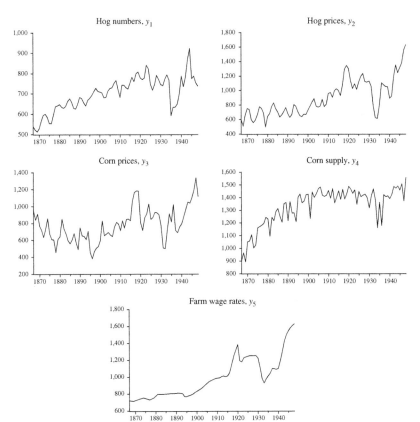

FIGURE 13.4 Quenouille's data set: annual, 1867–1948.

TABLE 13.2 Lag Length Determination Statistics for the VAR Fitted to the Quenouille Data

p	$\mathcal{L}(p)$	$LR(p, p-1)$	MAIC	MBIC
0	-2211.3	–	58.45	58.76
1	-2002.2	379.5	53.61	54.69[a]
2	-1954.2	81.0	53.00	54.84
3	-1928.6	39.7	52.99	55.80
4	-1892.9	50.8[a]	52.71[a]	56.08
5	-1872.2	26.7	52.82	56.96
6	-1846.0	30.4	52.79	57.70

$LR(p, p-1) \sim \chi^2(25)$: $\chi^2_{0.05}(25) = 37.7$. VAR, Vector autoregression.
[a]Selected value.

the VAR specification (although he approached the modeling using a rather different framework):

$$\mathbf{y}_t = \mathbf{c} + \mathbf{d}t + \sum_{i=1}^{p} \mathbf{A}_i \mathbf{y}_{t-i} + \mathbf{u}_t$$

where $\mathbf{d}' = (d_1, d_2, \ldots, d_n)$ is a $1 \times n$ vector of constants giving the trend terms for each individual equation in the VAR. The various criteria for selecting the lag length p for a maximum setting of $p_{max} = 6$ are shown in Table 13.2. The LR test sequence and the MAIC both select a lag length of four while the MBIC selects a lag length of two. Fig. 13.5 shows the residual cross-correlation functions for the longer setting and these reveal little evidence of model misspecification, while the estimated coefficient matrix for the fourth lag is:

$$\hat{\mathbf{A}}_4 = \begin{bmatrix} -0.123 & 0.138^* & 0.126^* & 0.092 & -0.085^* \\ {\scriptstyle(0.117)} & {\scriptstyle(0.042)} & {\scriptstyle(0.057)} & {\scriptstyle(0.063)} & {\scriptstyle(0.091)} \\ -0.126 & 0.108 & -0.359^* & -0.213 & -0.203^* \\ {\scriptstyle(0.309)} & {\scriptstyle(0.110)} & {\scriptstyle(0.150)} & {\scriptstyle(0.166)} & {\scriptstyle(0.240)} \\ -0.201 & 0.019 & -0.032 & -0.471 & 0.271^* \\ {\scriptstyle(0.623)} & {\scriptstyle0.022} & {\scriptstyle(0.304)} & {\scriptstyle(0.335)} & {\scriptstyle(0.485)} \\ 0.515 & 0.113 & -0.094 & 0.463^* & -0.656^* \\ {\scriptstyle(0.366)} & {\scriptstyle(0.130)} & {\scriptstyle(0.178)} & {\scriptstyle(0.196)} & {\scriptstyle(0.284)} \\ 0.196 & 0.040 & -0.146^* & -0.158^* & -0.246^* \\ {\scriptstyle(0.159)} & {\scriptstyle(0.057)} & {\scriptstyle(0.078)} & {\scriptstyle(0.085)} & {\scriptstyle(0.124)} \end{bmatrix}$$

As there are eight coefficients that are significantly different from zero at the 10% level (denoted by asterisks), a lag length of four rather than two is clearly appropriate.[5]

The inclusion of a trend is significant in the $y_{5,t}$ equation but not in any of the others, and the 20 characteristic roots of the VAR(4), obtained by solving the equation

Residual cross-correlation functions with 2 Standard Error Bounds

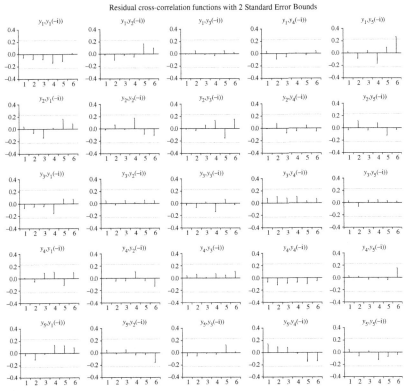

FIGURE 13.5 Residual cross-correlation functions from VAR(4) fit. *VAR*, Vector autoregression.

$$\hat{A}(B) = I_n - \hat{A}_1 B - \cdots - \hat{A}_4 B^4 = 0$$

and shown graphically in Fig. 13.6, all have modulus less than unity, thus, satisfying the stationarity condition.

The Granger causality statistics may conveniently be represented as Table 13.3. The first two rows show that hog numbers and prices are Granger-caused by all the variables in the system, so that there is feedback between the hog population and hog prices. The supply of corn, on the other hand, is exogenous, as there are no significant statistics in the fourth row. From the third row, it is seen that corn supply Granger-causes corn prices, and from the fifth row this variable also causes wage rates, as does the price of corn. Wage rates are not, however, affected by the hog population or hog prices.

The residual correlation matrix is reported as Table 13.4 and shows that there are four large contemporaneous correlations (the standard error to be attached to these correlations is approximately 0.11). Since there appear to be no grounds for choosing one Cholesky ordering over another, this suggests that the

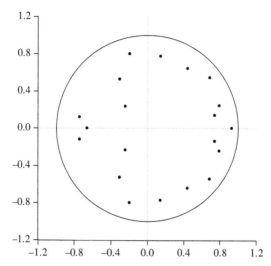

FIGURE 13.6 Roots of the characteristic equation associated with the VAR(4) fit.

TABLE 13.3 Granger Causality Test Statistics for the Quenouille Data

	y_1	y_2	y_3	y_4	y_5
$y_i \nrightarrow y_1$	–	74.0ᵃ [.000]	38.6ᵃ [.00]	62.3ᵃ [.00]	10.8ᵃ [.03]
$y_i \nrightarrow y_2$	12.1ᵃ [.02]	–	50.0ᵃ [.00]	23.5ᵃ [.00]	11.8ᵃ [.02]
$y_i \nrightarrow y_3$	0.5 [.97]	1.8 [.97]	–	18.9ᵃ [.00]	1.0 [.91]
$y_i \nrightarrow y_4$	3.0 [.55]	3.1 [.54]	4.1 [.39]	–	8.8 [.7]
$y_i \nrightarrow y_5$	7.8 [.10]	7.4 [.12]	66.6ᵃ [.00]	36.5ᵃ [.00]	–

Figure in brackets are p-values.
ᵃSignificance at 5%.

information contained in this matrix may be used to place restrictions in a SVAR. With $n = 5$ there must be at least 35 restrictions placed on the 50 coefficients contained in the **A** and **B** matrices of (13.8). We may conveniently choose **B** to be a diagonal matrix in which the diagonal elements have then the interpretation of being the standard deviations of the structural shocks. Given the pattern of the residual correlation matrix, **A** may be chosen to be the lower triangular matrix:

TABLE 13.4 Contemporaneous Residual Correlation Matrix

	y_1	y_2	y_3	y_4	y_5
y_1	1				
y_2	-0.21	1			
y_3	0.13	-0.03	1		
y_4	-0.01	0.08	-0.60	1	
y_5	-0.07	0.35	0.23	0.08	1

$$
\mathbf{A} = \begin{bmatrix}
1 & 0 & 0 & 0 & 0 \\
a_{21} & 1 & 0 & 0 & 0 \\
0 & 0 & 1 & 0 & 0 \\
0 & 0 & a_{43} & 1 & 0 \\
0 & a_{52} & a_{53} & 0 & 1
\end{bmatrix}
$$

These settings impose 41 restrictions, so that there are six overidentifying restrictions. This *structural factorization* was then estimated as:

$$
\mathbf{A} = \begin{bmatrix}
1 & 0 & 0 & 0 & 0 \\
\underset{(0.29)}{0.56} & 1 & 0 & 0 & 0 \\
0 & 0 & 1 & 0 & 0 \\
0 & 0 & \underset{(0.05)}{0.35} & 1 & 0 \\
0 & \underset{(0.05)}{-0.18} & \underset{(0.03)}{-0.06} & 0 & 1
\end{bmatrix}
$$

$$
\mathbf{B} = \begin{bmatrix}
\underset{(1.59)}{19.88} & 0 & 0 & 0 & 0 \\
0 & \underset{(4.09)}{51.09} & 0 & 0 & 0 \\
0 & 0 & \underset{(8.46)}{105.69} & 0 & 0 \\
0 & 0 & 0 & \underset{(3.98)}{49.68} & 0 \\
0 & 0 & 0 & 0 & \underset{(1.96)}{24.40}
\end{bmatrix}
$$

The overidentifying restrictions may be tested for their validity with an LR test. This produces a test statistic of 8.9, which is distributed as $\chi^2(6)$ and has a p-value of .18, so that these overidentifying restrictions are acceptable. Fig. 13.7 shows the accumulated 10-year impulse responses of each of the five variables to the five shocks, while Fig. 13.8 shows the accompanying variance

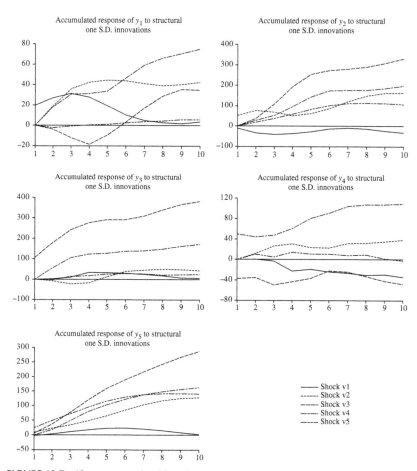

FIGURE 13.7 10-year accumulated impulse responses to short-run restricted structural shocks.

decompositions. In the "long-run," the hog population $y_{1,t}$ only feeds back onto the supply of corn $y_{4,t}$, interestingly in a negative fashion. Wage rates only have a long-run (positive) effect on hog prices $y_{2,t}$. The largest long-run responses are corn prices ($y_{3,t}$) and corn supply on hog prices and wage rates.

As an example of using long-run restrictions in the SVAR, we considered, based on the behavior of the impulse responses shown in Fig. 13.8, the following restricted long-run impulse response matrix:

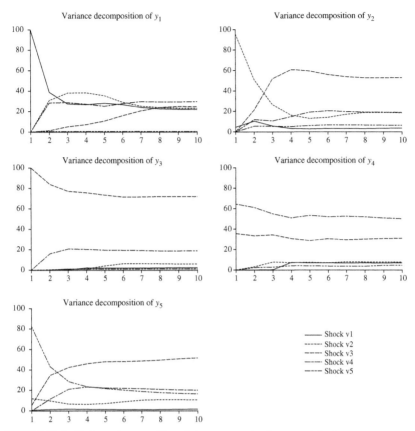

FIGURE 13.8   Variance decomposition of short-run restricted structural shocks.

$$
\Psi(\infty) = \begin{bmatrix}
0 & \psi_{12}(\infty) & \psi_{13}(\infty) & \psi_{14}(\infty) & 0 \\
0 & \psi_{22}(\infty) & \psi_{23}(\infty) & 0 & \psi_{25}(\infty) \\
\psi_{31}(\infty) & 0 & \psi_{33}(\infty) & 0 & \psi_{35}(\infty) \\
\psi_{41}(\infty) & 0 & 0 & \psi_{44}(\infty) & 0 \\
0 & 0 & \psi_{53}(\infty) & \psi_{54}(\infty) & \psi_{55}(\infty)
\end{bmatrix}
$$

With **A** set to the identity matrix, the number of zero long-run accumulated impulse responses imposed on $\Psi(\infty)$ is sufficient for identification. Fig. 13.9 shows the 10-year accumulated impulse responses so obtained and these are rather different from those shown in Fig. 13.8. This emphasizes how different

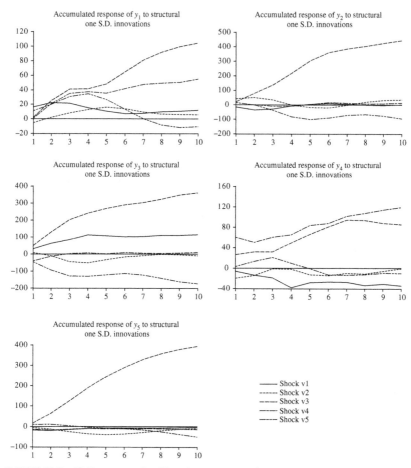

FIGURE 13.9 10-Year accumulated impulse responses to long-run restricted structural shocks.

assumptions about the relationships between innovations and structural shocks can lead to different impulse response functions, so that such analyses should be undertaken with considerable care and using as much information about the likely interaction of the variables making up the VAR as is available, which admittedly may not be a great deal.

ENDNOTES

1. The concepts of endogeneity and exogeneity being used here are the simplest possible: essentially a variable is termed endogenous if it is determined within the model, exogenous if it is determined outside of the model. These terms are deliberately kept loose but there are various tighter definitions in use for the models being discussed here. For an introductory text book discussion of these concepts, see Mills and Markellos (2008, Chapter 8.6); for more detailed treatment, see Hendry (1995).

2. When the lag lengths p and q are the same across all equations then each of the equations will contain identical regressors. The model is then of a special type that can be efficiently estimated by OLS applied to each equation separately, known as multivariate least squares. When the lag lengths differ across equations this result no longer holds and a systems estimator must be used. A natural estimator is then Zellner's (1962) *seemingly unrelated least squares*.

3. The VAR was brought to the attention of economists by Sims (1980), although a more general model, the vector ARMA, had been introduced into the statistical literature over twenty years earlier by Quenouille (1957).

4. The seminal papers on causality are Granger (1969) and Sims (1972). Although Granger provided an illustrative example to show the potential usefulness of the concept, he couched causality in a cross-spectral framework, which is generally unappealing to many economists, who were his prime audience, although the concept has much wider applicability. Neither did he develop an estimation and testing methodology. An appreciation of the concept's importance, thus, had to wait until a time domain approach to estimation and testing was developed, and this was provided soon after by Sims, who certainly helped to further popularize the concept by choosing as an example the then "hot" economic topic of the causal links between money and income.

   Granger fully recognized that a precursor of his causality framework had been proposed over a decade earlier in Wiener (1956) and he typically referred to it as Wiener−Granger causality. For a detailed treatment of the concept, see Mills (2013a, Chapter 9).

5. The other estimated lag coefficient matrices are not reported as they convey little information as to the properties of the fitted VAR.

Chapter 14

Error Correction, Spurious Regressions, and Cointegration

Chapter Outline

THE ERROR CORRECTION FORM OF AN AUTOREGRESSIVE DISTRIBUTED LAG MODEL

14.1   The simplest case of the ARDL (autoregressive distributed lag) model introduced in §**12.7** is the ARDL$(1, 1)$:

$$y_t = \beta_0 + \phi y_{t-1} + \beta_{1,0} x_t + \beta_{1,1} x_{t-1} + a_t \tag{14.1}$$

Suppose now that we recast this ARDL by writing it as

$$\nabla y_t = \beta_0 - (1 - \phi) y_{t-1} + \left(\beta_{1,0} + \beta_{1,1} \right) x_{t-1} + \beta_{1,0} \nabla x_t + a_t$$

or

$$\nabla y_t = \beta_{1,0} \nabla x_t - (1 - \phi) \left(y_{t-1} - \frac{\beta_0}{1 - \phi} - \frac{\beta_{1,0} + \beta_{1,1}}{1 - \phi} x_{t-1} \right) + a_t$$

i.e., as

$$\nabla y_t = \beta_{1,0} \nabla x_t - (1 - \phi)(y_{t-1} - \theta_0 - \theta_1 x_{t-1}) + a_t \tag{14.2}$$

This representation of the ARDL expresses the *current change* in the endogenous variable, ∇y_t, as a linear function of the *current change* in the exogenous variable ∇x_t and a proportion $1 - \phi$ of the *previous discrepancy* (or *error*) from the long-run "equilibrium" relationship $y = \theta_0 + \theta_1 x$. The representation (14.2) is known as the *error-correction model* or ECM. If the parameters of the equilibrium relationship are unknown, then they may be estimated either by using nonlinear least squares on (14.2) or by expressing the ECM as

$$\nabla y_t = \beta_0 + \beta_{1,0} \nabla x_t + \gamma(y_{t-1} - x_{t-1}) + \delta x_{t-1} + a_t \tag{14.3}$$

Applied Time Series Analysis. DOI: https://doi.org/10.1016/B978-0-12-813117-6.00014-4
233

which may be estimated directly by OLS and where a comparison of (14.3) with (14.2) shows that

$$\theta_0 = -\frac{\beta_0}{\gamma} \quad \theta_1 = \frac{\gamma - \delta}{\gamma}$$

The ECM was introduced originally by Sargan (1964) and further analyzed by, for example, Davidson et al. (1978). It may readily be extended to the general ARDL$(p, s_1, \ldots, s_M)$ model. Denoting the error correction as

$$ec_t = y_t - \theta_0 - \sum_{j=1}^{M} \theta_j x_{j,t}$$

then (14.2) generalizes to

$$\nabla y_t = \beta_0 - \phi(1)ec_{t-1} + \phi^*(B)\nabla y_{t-1} + \sum_{j=1}^{M} \tilde{\beta}_j(B)\nabla x_{j,t-1}$$
$$+ \sum_{j=1}^{M} \beta_j(B)\nabla x_{j,t} + a_t \tag{14.4}$$

where

$$\phi^*(B) = \sum_{i=1}^{p} \phi_i B^i = \phi(B) - 1$$

SPURIOUS REGRESSIONS

14.2 As in Chapter 12, Transfer Functions and Autoregressive Distributed Lag Modeling, it has been implicitly assumed that all the variables entering the ARDL/ECM are stationary, so that any nonstationary series have been appropriately differenced beforehand. What would happen if nonstationary variables were not prior differenced but were entered as levels? That there is a theoretical issue is clearly apparent. The standard proof of the consistency of OLS when there are stochastic regressors, as there are here, relies on the assumption that the probability limit of $T^{-1}X'X$, where X is a matrix containing the data on the explanatory variables, tends to a fixed matrix; i.e., the matrix of expectations of sums of squares and cross-products of the data tends to a matrix of constants (see, for example, Mills, 2013a, §§6.3−6.4). In other words, as the sample size T increases, the sample moments of the data settle down to their population values. For there to be fixed population moments to which these sample moments converge, the data must be stationary. If it was not, then, as in the case of integrated series, the data may display a tendency to increase in magnitude over time, so that there are no fixed values in the matrix of expectations of sums of squares and cross-products of these data.

14.3 What, though, are the practical implications of regressing nonstationary time series? This was a question considered in a famous paper by Granger and Newbold (1974), who began by focusing attention on the then widespread practice in the applied econometrics literature of reporting time series regressions with an apparently high degree of fit, as measured by the coefficient of multiple correlation, R^2, accompanied by extremely low values of Durbin and Watson's (1950, 1951) dw statistic testing for autocorrelated errors. Under the null hypothesis of white noise errors, $dw = 2$, whereas under the alternative of positively autocorrelated errors, $dw < 2$, and, in the limit, when the errors follow a random walk, $dw = 0$. Thus, if the dw statistic is small, there must be a considerable degree of positive autocorrelation in the residuals, bordering on nonstationarity.

14.4 Granger and Newbold considered the following data generation process (DGP):

$$y_t = \phi y_{t-1} + u_t \quad u_t \sim \text{i.i.d.}\left(0, \sigma_u^2\right) \tag{14.5a}$$

$$x_t = \phi^* x_{t-1} + v_t \quad v_t \sim \text{i.i.d.}\left(0, \sigma_v^2\right) \tag{14.5b}$$

$$E(u_t v_s) = 0 \text{ for all } t, s \quad E(u_t u_{t-k}) = E(v_t v_{t-k}) = 0 \text{ for all } k \neq 0$$

i.e., that y_t and x_t are uncorrelated first-order autoregressive processes. Since x_t neither affects or is affected by y_t, it should be hoped that the coefficient β_1 in the regression model

$$y_t = \beta_0 + \beta_1 x_t + \varepsilon_t \tag{14.6}$$

would converge in probability to zero, reflecting the lack of any relationship between the two series, as would the R^2 statistic from this regression.

14.5 A point not often recognized is that in (14.6) both the null hypothesis $\beta_1 = 0$, which implies that $y_t = \beta_0 + \varepsilon_t$, and the alternative $\beta_1 \neq 0$ will in general lead to false models, since the true DGP, given by (14.5), is not nested within (14.6). For example, the null $\beta_1 = 0$ implies that y_t is white noise under the assumptions of OLS regression, which is only the case if $\phi = 0$. Nevertheless, if y_t and x_t are stationary autocorrelated processes $(-1 < \phi, \phi^* < 1)$, then the OLS-estimated regression coefficient $\hat{\beta}_1$ and its associated t-statistic $(t = |\hat{\beta}_1|/se(\hat{\beta}_1))$ will both converge to zero as $T \to \infty$, although the t-test would over-reject, i.e., with stationary series, regression of a set of variables independent of the "dependent" variable produces coefficients that converge to zero.

TABLE 14.1 Statistics Obtained by Regressing Two Independent Random Walks, i.e., (14.6)

A. *t*-Statistics

t	0–2	2–4	4–6	6–8	8–10	10–12	12–14	14–16	16–18	>18
Frequency	325	281	178	98	67	27	15	3	4	2

B. R^2 Statistics

R^2	0–0.1	0.1–0.2	0.2–0.3	0.3–0.4	0.4–0.5	0.5–0.6	0.6–0.7	0.7–0.8	0.8–0.9	0.9–1
Frequency	366	172	132	90	70	73	55	32	10	0

C. *dw* Statistics

dw	0–0.2	0.2–0.4	0.4–0.6	0.6–0.8	0.8–1.0	1.0–1.2
Frequency	283	412	203	66	27	9

In finite samples, however, problems remain. Granger and Newbold showed that if both ϕ and ϕ^* are large, in the region of 0.9 say, then the expected value of R^2 will be around 0.5, thus implying that a reasonably high value of this statistic should not be taken as evidence of there being significant relationships between autocorrelated series. Often, a high value of R^2 would also be accompanied by a low value of dw, so that Granger and Newbold argued that the inequality $R^2 > dw$ might well arise from an attempt to fit regressions relating the levels of independent but autocorrelated time series.

14.6   More serious problems arise when regressions are fitted to independent random walks, i.e., when $\phi = \phi^* = 1$ in Eq. (14.5a,b). Panel (A) of Table 14.1 shows the frequency distribution of $t = \left|\hat{\beta}_1\right|/se\left(\hat{\beta}_1\right)$, obtained from the regressions of 1000 simulations of pairs of independent random walks, each of length $T = 50$, with starting values $y_0 = x_0 = 0$ and each with standard normal innovations. Panel (B) shows the frequency distribution of the R^2 statistics obtained from each of these 1000 regressions, while panel (C) shows the frequency distribution of the dw statistics.

Using a traditional t-test at the 5% significance level (so that the critical t-value is approximately 2), the (correct) null hypothesis of no relationship between the two series ($\beta_1 = 0$) would be incorrectly rejected two-thirds of the time (675 times out of 1000). If $\hat{\beta}_1/se\left(\hat{\beta}_1\right)$ was distributed as standard normal then the expected value of t may be shown to be $\sqrt{22}/\pi = 0.8$, but the average value of the t-statistics in Table 14.1 is 3.94, suggesting that the standard deviation of $\hat{\beta}_1$ is being underestimated by a factor of around 5. Thus, instead of using a critical t-value of 2, a value in excess of 10 should be used when deciding whether an estimated coefficient is significant or not at the 5% level (there are, in fact, 51 t-statistics greater than 10 reported in Table 14.1).

The average value of R^2 is 0.24 with almost two-thirds (634 out of 1000) of the values being greater than 0.2. The average value of the dw statistic is 0.34 with a maximum value of 1.17, which is some way below even the 1% critical value of 1.32, so that this statistic flags the problem of residual autocorrelation in every one of the 1000 regressions, as indeed should be hoped. The inequality $R^2 > dw$ is found to hold in almost a third of the regressions.

14.7   In further simulations, Granger and Newbold extended the DGP to include multiple regressors and ARIMA(0,1,1) innovations, and found that the results of Table 14.1 were repeated. Indeed, as the number of independent random walks was increased, so did the proportion of times the null of no relationship was rejected at conventional significance levels. Granger and Newbold, thus, argued that regressions using integrated time series were likely to be *spurious*, in that they would typically produce an apparently significant relationship even when the variables were unrelated to each other.

14.8 These essentially empirical conclusions were given an analytical foundation by Phillips (1986). Using the DGP (14.5a,b), but with more general assumptions concerning the innovations u_t and v_t (essentially the weak dependency conditions alluded to in **§5.12**), Phillips showed that neither $\hat{\beta}_0$ nor $\hat{\beta}_1$ converged in probability to constants as $T \to \infty$. Moreover, $\hat{\beta}_1$ had a nondegenerate limiting distribution, so that different arbitrarily large samples would yield randomly differing estimates of β_1. The distribution of $\hat{\beta}_0$ actually diverges, so that estimates are likely to get further and further away from the true value as the sample size increases. The uncertainty about the regression (14.6) stemming from its spurious nature thus persists asymptotically, being a consequence of the sample moments of y_t and x_t (and their joint sample moments) not converging to constants but, upon appropriate standardization, to random variables.

14.9 Phillips then showed that the conventional t-ratio on $\hat{\beta}_1$ (similarly for $\hat{\beta}_0$) does not have a t-distribution: in fact, it does not have *any* limiting distribution, for it diverges as $T \to \infty$ so that there are *no* asymptotically correct values for these tests. The rejection rate when these tests use a critical value given by conventional asymptotic theory (such as 1.96) will, thus, continue to increase with sample size.

The R^2 statistic has a nondegenerate limiting distribution and dw converges to zero as $T \to \infty$. Low values for this statistic and moderate values of R^2 are, therefore, to be expected in spurious regressions, such as (14.6), with data generated as integrated processes.

14.10 In fact, an early analysis of spurious or *nonsense* regressions, as was termed, was carried out almost a half-century before Granger and Newbold by Yule (1926). Yule also used simulations but focused on the distributions of correlation, rather than regression, coefficients (of course, one is just a scaled version of the other in bivariate models). His analysis remains noteworthy, however, and considers three situations: (1) both variables are $I(0)$ and i.i.d.; (2) both variables are $I(1)$ and their differences are i.i.d.; and (3) both variables are $I(2)$ and their second differences are i.i.d.

Figs. 14.1−14.3 show distributions of correlation coefficients for 1000 simulations of pairs of variables of length $T = 100$. Case (1) is shown in Fig. 14.1, which gives the distribution of the correlation coefficient r_{uv} between two independent, standard normal white noises u_t and v_t. This correlation is well behaved and has a symmetric, nearly Gaussian, distribution centred on zero but bounded by ± 1. Case (2) is shown in Fig. 14.2. Here the correlation coefficient is r_{yx}, where $y_t = y_{t-1} + u_t$ and $x_t = x_{t-1} + v_t$ are independent random walks. The distribution of r_{yx} is closer to a semiellipse with excess frequency at both ends of the distribution. Consequently, values of r_{yx} well away from zero are far more likely here than in case (1). Fig. 14.3 shows case (3) for the correlation r_{zw}, where

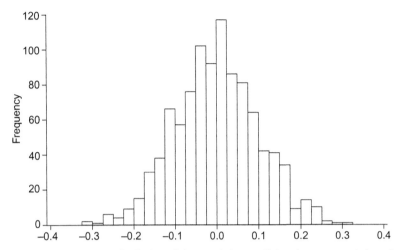

FIGURE 14.1 Frequency distribution of the correlation coefficient between two independent $I(0)$ series.

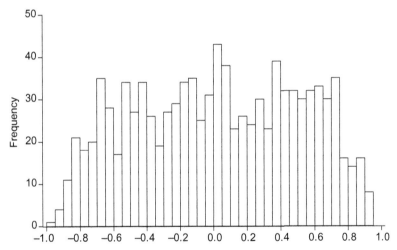

FIGURE 14.2 Frequency distribution of the correlation coefficient between two $I(1)$ series with independent first differences.

$z_t = z_{t-1} + y_t = 2z_{t-1} - z_{t-2} + u_t$ and $w_t = w_{t-1} + x_t = 2w_{t-1} - w_{t-2} + v_t$. The distribution of r_{zw} is U-shaped so that the most likely correlations between two such $I(2)$ unrelated series are ± 1, precisely the values that would occur if the two series were *perfectly* correlated.

14.11 If a test statistic, based on a correlation coefficient, assumes the distribution to be the one applying to case (1) when, in fact, the correct

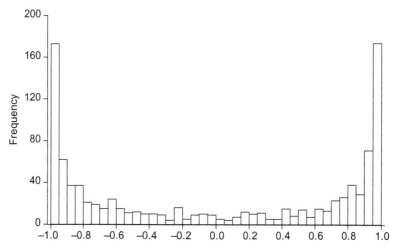

FIGURE 14.3 Frequency distribution of the correlation coefficient between two $I(2)$ series with independent second differences.

distribution is the one that applies to case (2), the frequency with which the null hypothesis of independence is rejected will greatly exceed the nominal size of the test, which is given by the expected number of rejections if (1) were true. Case (3) is even worse, with the least likely outcome being the discovery of the truth, for there is almost no chance of finding $r_{zw} \cong 0$ even though the population value expected under the null is zero. Indeed, the most likely sample value is $r_{zw} = \pm 1$.

14.12 Figs. 14.1−14.3 thus show the inferential difficulties arising from spurious correlations generated by regressing independent series of the *same order of integration* on each other. Difficulties also arise in regressions of an $I(2)$ on an $I(1)$ series (or vice versa), with Fig. 14.4 showing the distribution of r_{zx}, which is also U-shaped.

Less serious problems occur in regressions of an $I(1)$ on an $I(0)$ series (or vice versa). As shown in Fig. 14.5, the distribution of r_{yv} is similar in shape to that of r_{uv}. The reason for this is that when an $I(0)$ series is regressed on an $I(1)$ series, the only way that OLS can make the regression consistent and minimize the sum of squares is to drive the coefficient on the $I(1)$ variable (equivalently the correlation) to zero. Such possibilities do not arise when both series are integrated.

14.13 Could the spurious regression problems associated with nonstationary regressors be alleviated by including a time trend in the regression, i.e., by replacing (14.6) with

$$y_t = \beta_0 + \beta_1 x_t + \theta t + \varepsilon_t \tag{14.7}$$

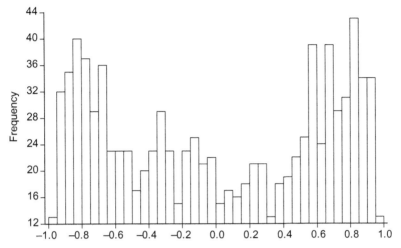

FIGURE 14.4   Frequency distribution of the correlation coefficient between an $I(1)$ and an $I(2)$ series with independent first differences and second differences, respectively.

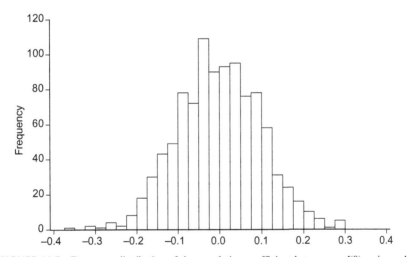

FIGURE 14.5   Frequency distribution of the correlation coefficient between an $I(0)$ series and an $I(1)$ series with independent first differences.

It would appear not, for $\hat{\beta}_1$ continues to have a nondegenerate distribution asymptotically (i.e., it does not converge to zero), and tests of $\beta_1 = 0$ diverge in distribution, tending to result in a false rejection of this null hypothesis (these results were provided by Durlauf and Phillips, 1988). Consequently, the spurious regression problem is not resolved by attempting to remove deterministic trends from the data.

14.14 What, then, should be done to resolve the spurious regression problem? After a further and extended simulation analysis, Granger and Newbold (1977) recommended the approach implicitly adopted in Chapter 12, Transfer Functions and Autoregressive Distributed Lag Modeling; that of appropriately differencing the nonstationary regressors. Although they did not consider it to be a "surefire universal solution," they did think that differencing would be useful when the nonstationary series were rather smooth, with large and positive low-order autocorrelations—in other words, close to being random walks.

14.15 Of course, the potentially spurious regression (14.6) contains just the contemporaneous exogenous variable, x_t, as a regressor and so may be regarded as the particularly simple ARDL(0,0) model. What would happen if a more general ARDL model was fitted to a pair of independent $I(1)$ processes? This was the question, in effect, posed by Hendry (1977), focusing on the ARDL(1,1) of (14.1). Table 14.2 shows the frequency distributions of the t-statistics testing the nulls $\beta_0 = 0$ and $\beta_1 = 0$, denoted t_0 and t_1 respectively, using the same DGP and simulation setup as employed in §**14.6**. As in that experiment, the means of these test statistics should be approximately 0.8 and they are, in fact, found to be 0.80 and 0.83, respectively. Moreover, 4.8% and 6.4% of the two distributions take on values greater than 2, so these findings are exactly what one would expect from a well-specified regression in which y_t and x_t are unrelated to each other.

Fig. 14.6 shows the frequency distributions of $\hat{\beta}_0$, $\hat{\beta}_1$, and $\hat{\phi}$. These are consistent with what we would expect under the DGP (14.5): both coefficients on the exogenous variable are estimated to be small and, given the accompanying t-statistics from Table 14.2, invariably insignificantly different from zero. The coefficient on y_{t-1}, on the other hand, is typically estimated to be close to unity (note that it is well known that $\hat{\phi}$ is biased downward in estimated ARDL models). Fig. 14.7 provides the frequency distributions of R^2 and dw: the former tends to be quite large (its average value is 0.82), while the latter is distributed symmetrically around an average value of 1.93 (dw is also biased downward from 2, due to the bias in estimating $\hat{\phi}$). It is clear that, within the bounds of sampling variation, a random walk model for y_t would typically emerge from estimating an ARDL(1,1) under the DGP (14.5).

ERROR CORRECTION AND COINTEGRATION

14.16 An equivalent way of expressing the spurious nature of (14.6) is to note that the error, $\varepsilon_t = y_t - \beta_0 - \beta_1 x_t$, may, under the DGP (14.5), be regarded as a linear combination of $I(1)$ processes and should therefore be $I(1)$ as well, thus invalidating all least squares regression theory. While this would appear, on the face of it, to be an eminently sensible argument, it

TABLE 14.2 Statistics Obtained by Fitting an ARDL(1,1) Model to Two Independent Random Walks

t-Statistics							
t_0	0–0.5	0.5–1.0	1.0–1.5	1.5–2.0	2.0–2.5	2.5–3.0	>3.0
Frequency	380	303	186	83	31	12	5
t_1	0–0.5	0.5–1.0	1.0–1.5	1.5–2.0	2.0–2.5	2.5–3.0	>3.0
Frequency	388	267	194	87	43	16	5

ARDL, Autoregressive distributed lag.

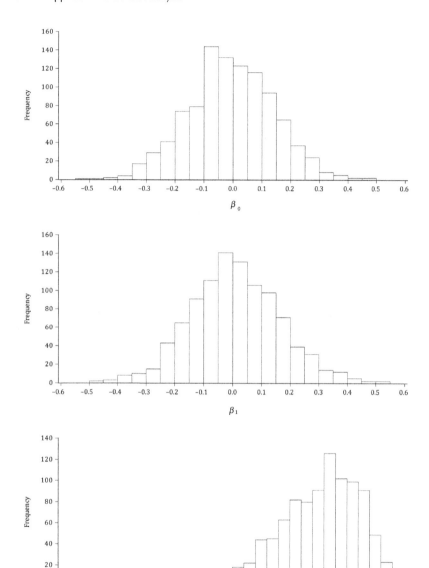

FIGURE 14.6 Frequency distributions of coefficients from the simulated ARDL(1,1) model. *ARDL*, Autoregressive distributed lag.

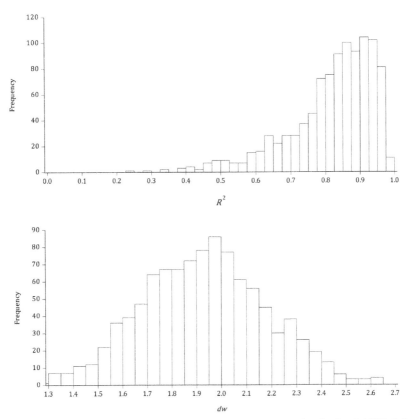

FIGURE 14.7 Frequency distributions of summary statistics from the simulated ARDL(1,1) model. *ARDL,* Autoregressive distributed lag.

turns out that it is not always true, for it is possible for a linear combination of $I(1)$ processes to actually be $I(0)$.

14.17 More generally, if $y_t \sim I(d)$ and $x_t \sim I(d)$ then the linear combination

$$e_t = y_t - ax_t \qquad (14.8)$$

will usually be $I(d)$ as well. It is possible, however, that e_t may be integrated of a lower order, say $I(d-b)$, where $b > 0$, in which case a special constraint operates on the long-run components of the two series. If $d = b = 1$, so that y_t and x_t are both $I(1)$ and, hence, dominated by "permanent" components (recall §5.1), e_t will be $I(0)$ and, hence, will have only transitory components: y_t and ax_t must, therefore, have long-run components that cancel out to produce e_t. In such circumstances, y_t and x_t are said to be *cointegrated,* although it must be emphasized that it will *not* generally be true that there will exist an a that makes $e_t \sim I(0)$ or, in general, $I(d-b)$.[1]

14.18   The idea of cointegration can be related to the concept of *long-run equilibrium* (recall §**14.1**), which can be illustrated by the bivariate relationship $y_t = ax_t$ or

$$y_t - ax_t = 0$$

Thus e_t in (14.8) measures the extent to which the "system" is out of equilibrium and can, therefore, be termed the "equilibrium error." Assuming that $d = b = 1$, so that y_t and x_t are both $I(1)$, the equilibrium error will then be $I(0)$, and e_t will rarely drift far from zero and will often cross the zero line (again recall §**5.1**). In other words, equilibrium will occasionally occur, at least to a close approximation, whereas if y_t and x_t are not cointegrated, so that $e_t \sim I(1)$, the equilibrium error will wander widely and zero crossings would be rare, suggesting that, under these circumstances, the concept of equilibrium has no practical implications.

14.19   Can the concept of cointegration be linked to the analysis of spurious regressions? Consider again (14.5), but now relax the independence condition, i.e., let $E(u_t v_t) = \sigma_{uv}$, say, and define the (contemporaneous) innovation covariance matrix

$$\Sigma = \begin{bmatrix} \sigma_u^2 & \sigma_{uv} \\ \sigma_{uv} & \sigma_v^2 \end{bmatrix}$$

For least squares theory to operate on (14.6), we require that Σ be non-singular. If, however, it is singular then

$$|\Sigma| = \sigma_u^2 \sigma_v^2 - \sigma_{uv}^2 = 0$$

This implies that $\Sigma \begin{pmatrix} 1 & -a \end{pmatrix} = \mathbf{0}$, where $a = \sigma_{uv}/\sigma_v^2$. Singularity of Σ turns out to be a necessary condition for y_t and x_t to be cointegrated, since in this case $|\Sigma| = 0$ implies that the "long-run" correlation between the innovations u_t and v_t, given by $\rho_{uv} = \sigma_{uv}/\sigma_u \sigma_v$, is unity (Phillips, 1986). For $\rho_{uv} < 1$, y_t and x_t are not cointegrated and when $\rho_{uv} = 0$, so that u_t and v_t are independent, we have Granger and Newbold's spurious regression.

14.20   Cointegration and error correction are also intimately linked. The equilibrium error (14.8), which will be $I(0)$ if y_t and x_t are both $I(1)$ and cointegrated, is exactly of the form ec_t that enters with a lag in the ECM (14.4). Consequently, if y_t and $x_{1,t}, x_{2,t}, \ldots, x_{M,t}$ are all $I(1)$ and if y is cointegrated with the x's such that

$$e_t = y_t - a_1 x_{1,t} - \cdots - a_M x_{M,t} \sim I(0)$$

then there will exist an ECM of the form of (14.4), a result that is known as *Granger's Representation Theorem*, which is proved in a more general framework by Engle and Granger (1987): see §**15.5**.

14.21 When there is cointegration between y_t and x_t, then the *cointegrating regression* (14.6) exhibits some interesting properties. If x_t does not contain a drift then the OLS estimate of β_1 is *super-consistent*, in that $\hat{\beta}_1$ converges to β_1 at the rate T rather than at the rate $T^{1/2}$, as in the standard regression case. OLS will, thus, estimate the cointegrating parameter precisely. However, the distribution of $\hat{\beta}_1$ will be skewed and the associated t-ratio will not be asymptotically normal.

The assumption that x_t does not contain a drift is not innocuous, however, for if it does contain a drift then normality of the distribution of $\hat{\beta}_1$ is recovered. Interestingly, if there are a set of regressors $x_{1,t}, x_{2,t}, \ldots, x_{M,t}$, some of which may have drifts, then super-consistency of the cointegration parameters continues to hold, but the limiting joint distribution of the estimators is both nonnormal and singular, since the regressors will be perfectly correlated asymptotically. This is because an $I(1)$ variable with drift can always be expressed as the sum of a time trend and an $I(1)$ variable without drift, e.g., as

$$\nabla x_t = \pi + v_t = x_0 + \pi t + \nabla \tilde{x}_t, \quad \nabla \tilde{x}_t = v_t$$

so that the correlation between two such variables will be dominated by their trends rather than by the driftless $I(1)$ components and will reach unity asymptotically.

TESTING FOR COINTEGRATION

14.22 Given the crucial role that cointegration plays in regression models with integrated variables, it is clearly important to test for its presence. Tests may be based on the residuals from the cointegrating regression, i.e.,

$$\hat{e}_t = y_t - \hat{\beta}_0 - \hat{\beta}_1 x_{1,t} - \cdots - \hat{\beta}_M x_{M,t} \tag{14.9}$$

Such residual-based procedures seek to test a null hypothesis of *no* cointegration by using the unit root tests developed in §§**5.4**−**5.10** applied to $\hat{e}_t$ (see Engle and Granger, 1987: these test statistics are denoted *EG* to distinguish them from the conventional Dickey−Fuller tests).

A problem here is that, since $\hat{e}_t$ is derived as a residual from a regression in which the cointegrating parameters are estimated, and since if the null of non-cointegration was true such estimates would not be identified, using the conventional τ_μ critical values would reject the null too often, because OLS will seek the set of cointegrating parameters that minimizes the residual variance and are, hence, most likely to result in a stationary residual series.

An additional factor that influences the critical values is the number of regressors M. For example, the large T 5% critical τ_μ value when $M = 1$ is -3.37, while if $M = 5$ it is -4.71 (recall from §**5.6** that the usual 5% critical τ_μ value is -2.86). As with conventional unit root tests, different sets of critical values are used if there is no constant in the cointegrating regression or if there is both a constant and a trend (corresponding to the τ and τ_τ variants; nonparametric tests analogous to those of §5.12 may also be constructed (see Phillips and Ouliaris, 1990).

14.23 Of course, all the variables appearing in the cointegrating regression (14.9) must be $I(1)$, so that this assumption needs to be checked by subjecting the $M + 1$ variables to pretests for a unit root. These tests clearly have the potential to mislead when attempting to classify the integration properties of the variables. Pesaran et al. (2001, henceforth PSS), in contrast, propose a "bounds" test for cointegration, based on the ARDL model, that is robust to whether the variables are $I(0)$, $I(1)$, or mutually cointegrated. The *conditional error correction* (CEC) form of an ARDL model is, with a time trend included,

$$
\nabla y_t = \alpha_0 + \alpha_1 t - \phi(1)y_{t-1} + \sum_{j=1}^{M} \beta_j(1)x_{j,t-1}
$$

$$
+ \phi^*(B)\nabla y_{t-1} + \sum_{j=0}^{M} \gamma_j(B)\nabla x_{j,t} + a_t
$$

(14.10)

where $\gamma_j(B) = \beta_j(1) + \tilde{\beta}_j(B)$. The null of no long-run relationship (non-cointegration) is then $\phi(1) = \beta_1(1) = \cdots = \beta_M(1) = 0$, which may be tested using a standard F- or Wald statistic. PSS provide two sets of asymptotic critical values corresponding to the polar cases of all variables being purely $I(0)$ or purely $I(1)$. When the test statistic is below the lower critical value, the null is not rejected, and it is concluded that cointegration is not possible. If the test statistic is above the upper critical value, the null can be rejected, and it may be concluded that cointegration is possible. If, however, the test statistic falls between the lower and upper critical values the test is inconclusive and additional analysis and testing is required.

14.24 Although (14.10) is the general form of the CEC, there are several ways in which the constant and trend can enter the error correction. For example, both could be omitted from (14.10), so that $\alpha_0 = \alpha_1 = 0$ and the CEC can be written:

$$
\nabla y_t = - \phi(1)\left(y_{t-1} - \sum_{j=1}^{M} \frac{\beta_j(1)}{\phi(1)} x_{j,t-1} \right) + \phi^*(B)\nabla y_{t-1} + \sum_{j=1}^{M} \gamma_j(B)\nabla x_{j,t} + a_t
$$

i.e., as

$$
\nabla y_t = - \phi(1)ec_{t-1} + \phi^*(B)\nabla y_{t-1} + \sum_{j=1}^{M} \gamma_j(B)\nabla x_{j,t} + a_t
$$

where

$$ec_t = y_t - \sum_{j=1}^{M} \frac{\beta_j(1)}{\phi(1)} x_{j,t}$$

is the error correction. If just the trend is omitted from (14.10) then the CEC becomes either

$$\nabla y_t = \alpha_0 - \phi(1) \left(y_{t-1} - \sum_{j=1}^{M} \frac{\beta_j(1)}{\phi(1)} x_{j,t-1} \right) + \phi^*(B) \nabla y_{t-1}$$

$$+ \sum_{j=1}^{M} \gamma_j(B) \nabla x_{j,t} + a_t$$

or

$$\nabla y_t = - \phi(1) \left(y_{t-1} - \frac{\alpha_0}{\phi(1)} - \sum_{j=1}^{M} \frac{\beta_j(1)}{\phi(1)} x_{j,t-1} \right) + \phi^*(B) \nabla y_{t-1}$$

$$+ \sum_{j=1}^{M} \gamma_j(B) \nabla x_{j,t} + a_t$$

in which the constant is restricted to appear only in the error correction. Alternatively, both the constant and trend may be restricted to appear only in the error correction:

$$\nabla y_t = - \phi(1) \left(y_{t-1} - \frac{\alpha_0}{\phi(1)} - \frac{\alpha_1}{\phi(1)} (t-1) - \sum_{j=1}^{M} \frac{\beta_j(1)}{\phi(1)} x_{j,t-1} \right)$$

$$+ \phi^*(B) \nabla y_{t-1} + \sum_{j=1}^{M} \gamma_j(B) \nabla x_{j,t} + a_t$$

Different sets of critical values are required and are provided by PSS for these alternative specifications of the error correction.

EXAMPLE 14.1 Are United Kingdom Interest Rates Cointegrated?

In Example 12.1, an ARDL model was fitted to the *changes* in United Kingdom long and short interest rates. Since both R20 and RS are $I(1)$ processes it is possible that they may be cointegrated. Two cointegrating regressions may be calculated here, for there seems to be no compelling reason to select one interest rate rather than the other as the "dependent" variable:

$$\hat{e}_{1,t} = R20_t - \hat{\beta}_0 - \hat{\beta}_1 RS_t$$

and

$$\hat{e}_{2,t} = RS_t - \hat{\beta}_0' - \hat{\beta}_1' R20_t$$

These lead to the ADF-type regressions

$$\nabla \hat{e}_{1,t} = - \underset{(0.007)}{0.026} \hat{e}_{1,t-1} + \underset{(0.035)}{0.205} \nabla \hat{e}_{1,t-1}$$

and

$$\nabla \hat{e}_{2,t} = - \underset{(0.008)}{0.031} \hat{e}_{2,t-1} + \underset{(0.035)}{0.226} \nabla \hat{e}_{2,t-1}$$

From these the Engle–Granger cointegration test statistics $EG_1 = -3.58$ and $EG_2 = -4.03$ are obtained. Since these have p-values of .017 and .004, respectively, the null of non-cointegration is conclusively rejected in favor of R20 and RS being cointegrated.[2]

Alternatively, two bounds tests may be computed. An ARDL(2,1) was selected for RS, leading to the CEC

$$\nabla RS_t = - \underset{(0.007)}{0.030} ec_{t-1} + \underset{(0.030)}{0.262} \nabla RS_{t-1} + \underset{(0.047)}{0.719} \nabla R20_t + \hat{a}_{2,t}$$

Neither a constant nor a trend are included as both were found to be insignificant. The F-statistic for testing the joint null $\phi(1) = \beta(1) = 0$ is 8.15, which exceeds the 1% critical value of 6.02 for $I(1)$ variables, while the t-statistic just testing $\phi(1) = 0$ is -4.04, which also exceeds (is more negative than) the 1% critical value of -3.22 for $I(1)$ variables, thus providing a strong rejection of the non-cointegration null.

An ARDL(3,2) was selected for R20, leading to the CEC:

$$\nabla R20_t = - \underset{(0.004)}{0.010} ec_{t-1} + \underset{(0.036)}{0.230} \nabla R20_{t-1} - \underset{(0.032)}{0.109} \nabla R20_{t-2}$$
$$+ \underset{(0.021)}{0.302} \nabla RS_t - \underset{(0.023)}{0.079} \nabla RS_{t-1} + \hat{a}_{1,t}$$

Here the F-statistic is only 2.78, which is smaller than the 5% critical value of 3.15 for $I(0)$ variables, although the t-statistic is -2.36, which is significant at the 10% level for $I(1)$ variables, the critical value being -2.28. Notwithstanding these conflicting results, it nevertheless seems safe to conclude that United Kingdom interest rates are indeed cointegrated.

ESTIMATING COINTEGRATING REGRESSIONS

14.25 Having found that y_t cointegrates with $x_{1,t}, \ldots, x_{M,t}$, the parameters in the cointegrating regression

$$y_t = \beta_0 + \beta_1 x_{1,t} + \cdots + \beta_M x_{M,t} + e_t \tag{14.11}$$

then need to be estimated. Although OLS estimation produces superconsistent estimates of the parameters, they nevertheless have biased and asymmetric sampling distributions even asymptotically. This is a consequence of the potential simultaneity between y_t and the $x_{j,t}$ as well as autocorrelation in e_t, which is endemic given that the error is only required to be $I(0)$ rather than white noise. OLS estimates and accompanying standard errors, therefore, provide an unreliable basis on which to form inferences about the cointegrating parameters.

The *fully modified OLS* (FM-OLS) estimator of Phillips and Hansen (1990) introduces a semiparametric correction to OLS which eliminates this bias and asymmetry: see, for example, Mills and Markellos (2008, Chapter 9.4) for technical details.[3] *Dynamic OLS* (DOLS), on the other hand, deals with these problems by including leads and lags of $\nabla x_{j,t}$, and possibly lags of ∇y_t, as additional regressors in (14.10) so that standard OLS may continue to be used, i.e.,

$$y_t = \beta_0 + \sum_{j=1}^{M} \beta_{j,t} x_{j,t} + \sum_{i=1}^{p} \gamma_i \nabla y_{t-i} + \sum_{j=1}^{M} \sum_{i=-p_1}^{p_2} \delta_{j,i} \nabla x_{j,t-i} + e_t$$

(14.12)

An estimate of the cointegrating relationship is also provided by the error correction term in the appropriate form of the CEC set out in §**14.23**: e.g., if there is no intercept or trend in the CEC (14.10) then

$$ec_t = y_t - \sum_{j=1}^{M} \frac{\beta_j(1)}{\phi(1)} x_{j,t}$$

will provide estimates of the cointegrating parameters.

EXAMPLE 14.2 Estimating a Cointegrating Relationship Between United Kingdom Interest Rates

The OLS estimated cointegration regressions used in computing the EG cointegration test statistics are

$$R20_t = \frac{2.438}{(0.111)} + \frac{0.799}{(0.015)} RS_t + \hat{e}_{1,t}$$

and

$$RS_t = -\frac{1.005}{(0.155)} + \frac{0.974}{(0.019)} R20_t + \hat{e}_{2,t}$$

Through the super-consistency property of OLS, the slope estimates are precisely estimated, but they are asymptotically biased. The semiparametrically corrected FM-OLS estimates are

$$R20_t = \frac{2.321}{(0.284)} + \frac{0.817}{(0.039)} RS_t + \hat{e}_{1,t}$$

and

$$RS_t = -\frac{0.989}{(0.385)} + \frac{0.973}{(0.047)} R20_t + \hat{e}_{2,t}$$

and have slightly different point estimates, but much larger standard errors. The DOLS estimates are, with the settings $p = 0$, $p_1 = p_2 = 1$

$$R20_t = \frac{2.383}{(0.286)} + \frac{0.808}{(0.039)} RS_t + \sum_{i=-1}^{1} \hat{\delta}_i \nabla RS_{t-i} + \hat{e}_{1,t}$$

and

$$RS_t = -\frac{0.989}{(0.389)} + \frac{0.973}{(0.048)} R20_t + \sum_{i=-1}^{1} \hat{\delta}_i \nabla R20_{t-i} + \hat{e}_{2,t}$$

which are similar to the FM-OLS estimates. From the CECs presented in Example 14.1, the estimates of the cointegrating relationships are, on allowing an intercept to appear in the error correction,

$$R20_t = \frac{0.883}{(0.169)} RS_t + \frac{1.763}{(1.237)} + ec_{1,t}$$

$$RS_t = \frac{0.936}{(0.128)} R20_t - \frac{0.674}{(1.043)} + ec_{2,t}$$

Using standard t-tests, the FM-OLS, DOLS, and CEC estimates of β_1' are insignificantly different from unity, and neither is the CEC estimate of β_1. If these parameters are set equal to this value, then the error correction becomes

$$ec_t = R20_t - RS_t - \beta_0 = SPREAD_t - \beta_0$$

Thus, the data is compatible with R20 and RS both being $I(1)$ and cointegrated with a parameter of unity, so that the error correction is the deviation of the spread from its equilibrium value. Recall from Example 5.1 that the spread has previously been found to be $I(0)$, as it must be to become an error correction. Using the spread in the error correction leads to the following estimated models:

$$\nabla R20_t = -\frac{0.013}{(0.005)}\left(SPREAD_{t-1} - \frac{1.017}{(0.710)}\right) + \frac{0.303}{(0.021)}\nabla RS_t - \frac{0.080}{(0.023)}\nabla RS_{t-1}$$
$$+ \frac{0.232}{(0.036)}\nabla R20_{t-1} - \frac{0.108}{(0.032)}\nabla R20_{t-2} + \hat{a}_{1,t}$$

$$\hat{\sigma}_a = 0.249$$

and

$$\nabla RS_t = \frac{0.030}{(0.008)}\left(SPREAD_{t-1} - \frac{1.145}{(0.446)}\right) + \frac{0.719}{(0.047)}\nabla R20_t$$
$$+ \frac{0.261}{(0.030)}\nabla RS_{t-1} + \hat{a}_{2,t}$$

$$\hat{\sigma}_a = 0.428$$

In this latter model the lagged spread enters significantly and so provides an improvement over the model fitted to just differences of the interest rates in Example 12.1. Note also that the intercept in the error correction term of the CEC for RS is now significant and is estimated to be 1.145, close to the "equilibrium level" found when fitting an AR(2) process to the spread in Example 3.2.

EXAMPLE 14.3 Error Correction Modeling of Global Temperatures

In Example 12.1, two ARDL models were fitted to global temperatures and various forcing variables. Since temperature and total radiative forcing were both found to be $I(1)$ from unit root pretests, while volcanic stratospheric aerosols and the SO and AMO indices were found to be $I(0)$, Eq. (12.8) was defined in terms of the differences of temperature and total radiative forcing, so that all variables are entered as $I(0)$ processes. Eq. (12.11), on the other hand, ignored the different orders of integration, with all variables being entered in levels. This led to a major difference in the estimate of the important transient climate response (TCR), which is defined as a multiple (3.71) of the long-run coefficient on total radiative forcing. From (12.8), the TCR was estimated to be 0.94°C with a 95% confidence interval running from 0.4 to 1.5°C, whereas from (12.11), the TCR was estimated to be 1.57°C with a confidence interval running from 1.53 to 1.61°C.

The bounds test calculated from the unrestricted version of (12.11) for a restricted intercept and no trend produced an F-statistic of 11.64, which far exceeds the 1% critical value of 4.37 and so conclusively rejects the null of no long-run relationship between temperature and the forcing variables. The implied error correction was then estimated to be

$$ec_t = \text{TEMP}_t + \underset{(0.021)}{0.010} - \underset{(0.021)}{0.422} \text{TRF}_t - \underset{(0.064)}{0.218} \text{VOLC}_t$$
$$+ \underset{(0.234)}{0.947} \text{SO}_t - \underset{(0.080)}{0.450} \text{AMO}_t$$

which yields the same estimate and confidence interval for the long-run coefficient on total radiative forcing as (12.11). Alternatively, only temperature and total radiative forcing may be allowed to enter the error correction, so implicitly assuming that the other forcings are $I(0)$ and have no long-run effect on temperature. In this case, the F-statistic is 11.75 with a 1% critical value of 5.58, and the estimate of the long-run coefficient is unchanged. These findings provide further evidence that the TCR is precisely estimated at around 1.6°C.

ENDNOTES

1. The concept of cointegration was initially developed by Granger (1981) and extended in Granger and Weiss (1983) before being introduced to a wider audience by the extremely influential Engle and Granger (1987), which has become one of the most highly cited articles in economics. See Mills (2013a, Chapter 10) for more detailed historical discussion and analysis.
2. The nonparametric test of Phillips and Ouliaris (1990) gives statistics of -3.38 and -3.90, respectively, with p-values of .030 and .007.
3. A similar approach is taken in the *canonical cointegrating regression* method of Park (1992).

Chapter 15

Vector Autoregressions With Integrated Variables, Vector Error Correction Models, and Common Trends

Chapter Outline

VECTOR AUTOREGRESSIONS WITH INTEGRATED VARIABLES

15.1 Having analyzed the impact of $I(1)$ variables, and hence the possibility of cointegration, on single-equation autoregressive distributed lag models in Chapter 14, Error Correction, Spurious Regressions, and Cointegration, the implications of allowing vector autoregressions to contain $I(1)$ variables clearly require discussing. Consider, then, the n-variable VAR(p) of §**13.11**,

$$A(B)\boldsymbol{y}_t = \boldsymbol{c} + \boldsymbol{u}_t \qquad (15.1)$$

where, as in §**13.2**, $E(\boldsymbol{u}_t) = \boldsymbol{0}$ and

$$E(\boldsymbol{u}_t\boldsymbol{u}_s) = \begin{cases} \boldsymbol{\Omega}_p & t = s \\ \boldsymbol{0} & t \neq s \end{cases}$$

Using the matrix generalization of the "Beveridge—Nelson" decomposition of §**8.4**, the matrix polynomial

Applied Time Series Analysis. DOI: https://doi.org/10.1016/B978-0-12-813117-6.00015-6

$$A(B) = I_n - \sum_{i=1}^{p} A_i B^i$$

can always be written, for $p > 1$, as

$$A(B) = (I_n - AB) - \Phi(B)B\nabla$$

where

$$A = \sum_{i=1}^{p} A_i$$

and

$$\Phi(B) = \sum_{i=1}^{p-1} \Phi_i B^{i-1}, \quad \Phi_i = -\sum_{j=i+1}^{p} A_j$$

The Φ_i matrices can be obtained recursively from $\Phi_1 = -A + A_1$ as $\Phi_i = \Phi_{i-1} + A_i$, $i = 2, \ldots, p-1$. With this decomposition of $A(B)$, (15.1) can always be written as

$$(I_n - AB - \Phi(B)\nabla)y_t = c + u_t$$

or

$$y_t = c + \Phi(B)\nabla y_{t-1} + Ay_{t-1} + u_t$$

An equivalent representation is

$$\nabla y_t = c + \Phi(\mathbf{B})\nabla y_{t-1} + \Pi y_{t-1} + u_t \tag{15.2}$$

where

$$\Pi = A - I_n = -A(1)$$

is known as the *long-run matrix*. The representation (15.2) is the multivariate counterpart of the ADF regression (recall Example 5.1), and it should be emphasized that it is a purely *algebraic* transformation of (15.1), as no assumptions about the properties of y_t have been made up to this point.

15.2   Consider first the case where $A = I_n$, so that $\Pi = 0$ and ∇y_t follows the VAR($p - 1$)

$$\nabla y_t = c + \Phi(B)\nabla y_{t-1} + u_t \tag{15.3}$$

where y_t is an $I(1)$ process and a VAR in the first differences ∇y_t, as in (15.3), is the appropriate specification.

15.3   There are some interesting and important results that follow from the relationships existing between Eqs. (15.1) and (15.3). From the recursions of

§**15.1** there is seen to be a direct link between the coefficient matrices of (15.1) and (15.2):

$$A_p = - \Phi_{p-1}$$

$$A_i = \Phi_i - \Phi_{i-1}, \quad i = 2, \ldots, p - 1$$

$$A_1 = \Pi + I_n + \Phi_1$$

It can then be shown (see, for example, Hamilton, 1994, Chapter 18.2) that irrespective of the order of integration of y_t, t-tests on individual coefficients of A_i are asymptotically valid, as are F-tests of linear combinations of the A_i other than the "unit root" combination $A_1 + A_2 + \cdots + A_p$. Likelihood ratio tests for determining lag order are also asymptotically valid, as is the use of information criteria. What are not valid, however, are Granger-causality tests, which turn out not to have the usual χ^2 limiting distribution. These results hold irrespective of whether the variables in y_t have drifts or not.

VECTOR AUTOREGRESSIONS WITH COINTEGRATED VARIABLES

15.4 The condition $A = I_n$ implies that

$$|\Pi| = |A_1 + \cdots + A_p - I_n| = 0 \tag{15.4}$$

that is, that the long-run matrix is singular and must, therefore, have a rank that is less than n. The VAR (15.1) is then said to contain *at least one* unit root. Note, however, that (15.4) does not necessarily imply that $A = I_n$ and it is this fact that leads to cointegrated VARs (CVARs). Thus, suppose that (15.4) holds, so that the long-run matrix Π is singular and $|\Pi| = 0$, but $\Pi \neq 0$ and $A \neq I_n$. Being singular, Π will thus have reduced rank, say r, where $0 \leq r \leq n$. In such circumstances, Π can be expressed as the product of two $n \times r$ matrices α and β such that $\Pi = \beta\alpha'$.

To see why this is the case, note that α' can be defined as the matrix containing the r linearly dependent rows of Π, so that Π must be able to be written as a linear combination of α':β is then the matrix of coefficients that are needed to do this. These r linearly independent rows of Π, when written as the rows of $\alpha' = (\alpha_1, \ldots, \alpha_r)'$, are known as the *cointegrating vectors* and Π will contain only $n - r$ unit roots, rather than the n unit roots that it would contain if $\Pi = 0$, which would be the case if $r = 0$.

15.5 Why are the rows of α' known as cointegrating vectors? Substituting $\Pi = \beta\alpha'$ into (15.2) yields

$$\nabla y_t = c + \Phi(B)\nabla y_{t-1} + \beta\alpha' y_{t-1} + u_t \tag{15.5}$$

The assumption that $y_t \sim I(1)$ implies that, since $\nabla y_t \sim I(0)$, it must be the case that $A_1 = \Pi + I_n + \Phi_1$ to ensure that both sides of (15.5) "balance," i.e., they are of the same order of integration. In other words, α' is a matrix whose rows, when post-multiplied by y_t, produce *stationary* linear combinations of y_t: the r linear combinations $\alpha_1'y_t, \ldots, \alpha_r'y_t$ are all stationary and can, thus, play the role of cointegrating relationships.

15.6 Consequently, if y_t is cointegrated with cointegrating rank r, then it can be represented as the *vector error correction model* (VECM)

$$\nabla y_t = c + \Phi(B)\nabla y_{t-1} + \beta e_{t-1} + u_t \tag{15.6}$$

where $e_t = \alpha'y_t$ contains the r stationary *error corrections*. This is known as *Granger's Representation Theorem* and is clearly the multivariate extension and generalization of (14.4).

15.7 Several additional points are worth mentioning. The parameter matrices α and β are not uniquely identified, since for any nonsingular $r \times r$ matrix ξ, the products $\beta\alpha'$ and $\beta\xi(\xi^{-1}\alpha')$ will both equal Π. Some normalization is, therefore, typically imposed—setting some elements of α to unity is often the preferred choice.

If $r = 0$, then we have already seen in §**15.2** that the model becomes the VAR($p - 1$) (15.3) in the first differences ∇y_t. If, on the other hand, $r = n$, then Π is of full rank and is nonsingular, and y_t will contain *no* unit roots and will be $I(0)$, so that a VAR(p) in the levels of y_t is appropriate from the outset.

The error corrections e_t, although stationary, are not restricted to having zero means, so that, as (15.6) stands, growth in y_t can come about via both the error correction e_t and the "autonomous" drift component c. How this intercept, and perhaps a trend, are treated in (15.6) is important in determining the appropriate estimation procedure and the set of critical values used for inference (cf. the alternative forms of the conditional error correction (CEC) in §**14.23**). Banerjee et al. (1993, chapter 5) and Mills and Markellos (2008, chapter 9) provide detailed treatments of the alternative ways in which intercepts and trends may enter VECMs and the implications of doing so: an introductory discussion is provided in §**15.10**.

EXAMPLE 15.1 A Simple Example of the Algebra of VECMs

Let us assume that $p = n = 2$ so that we have a VAR(2) in the variables y_1 and y_2, with intercepts and trends omitted for simplicity:

$$y_{1,t} = a_{11,1}y_{1,t-1} + a_{12,1}y_{2,t-1} + a_{11,2}y_{1,t-2} + a_{12,2}y_{2,t-2} + u_{1,t}$$

$$y_{2,t} = a_{21,1}y_{1,t-1} + a_{22,1}y_{2,t-1} + a_{21,2}y_{1,t-2} + a_{22,2}y_{2,t-2} + u_{2,t}$$

The various coefficient matrices required for (15.2) are

$$A_1 = \begin{bmatrix} a_{11,1} & a_{12,1} \\ a_{21,1} & a_{22,1} \end{bmatrix} \quad A_2 = \begin{bmatrix} a_{11,2} & a_{12,2} \\ a_{21,2} & a_{22,2} \end{bmatrix}$$

$$A = A_1 + A_2 = \begin{bmatrix} a_{11,1} + a_{11,2} & a_{12,1} + a_{12,2} \\ a_{21,1} + a_{21,2} & a_{22,1} + a_{22,2} \end{bmatrix} = \begin{bmatrix} a_{11} & a_{12} \\ a_{21} & a_{22} \end{bmatrix}$$

$$\Pi = A - I_2 = \begin{bmatrix} \pi_{11} & \pi_{12} \\ \pi_{21} & \pi_{22} \end{bmatrix} = \begin{bmatrix} a_{11} - 1 & a_{12} \\ a_{21} & a_{22} - 1 \end{bmatrix}$$

The singularity condition on the long-run matrix Π is

$$|\Pi| = 0 = \pi_{11}\pi_{22} - \pi_{12}\pi_{21}$$

which implies that

$$\Pi = \begin{bmatrix} \pi_{11} & \pi_{12} \\ (\pi_{22}/\pi_{12})\pi_{11} & (\pi_{22}/\pi_{12})\pi_{12} \end{bmatrix}$$

and

$$\beta = \begin{bmatrix} 1 \\ \pi_{22}/\pi_{12} \end{bmatrix} \quad \alpha' = \begin{bmatrix} \pi_{11} & \pi_{12} \end{bmatrix}$$

Equivalently, on normalizing using $\xi = \pi_{11}$,

$$\beta = \begin{bmatrix} \pi_{11} \\ (\pi_{22}/\pi_{12}) \end{bmatrix} \quad \alpha' = \begin{bmatrix} 1 & \pi_{12}/\pi_{11} \end{bmatrix}$$

The VECM (15.6) is then, on noting that, with $p = 2$, $\Phi(B) = \Phi_1 = -A + A_1 = -A_2$,

$$\nabla y_t = -A_2 \nabla y_{t-1} + \beta \alpha' y_{t-1} + u_t$$

or

$$\begin{bmatrix} \nabla y_{1,t} \\ \nabla y_{2,t} \end{bmatrix} = -\begin{bmatrix} a_{11,2} & a_{12,2} \\ a_{21,2} & a_{22,2} \end{bmatrix} \begin{bmatrix} \nabla y_{1,t-1} \\ \nabla y_{2,t-1} \end{bmatrix} + \begin{bmatrix} \pi_{11} \\ (\pi_{22}/\pi_{12}) \end{bmatrix} \begin{bmatrix} \pi_{11} & \pi_{12} \end{bmatrix} \begin{bmatrix} y_{1,t-1} \\ y_{2,t-1} \end{bmatrix} + \begin{bmatrix} u_{1,t} \\ u_{2,t} \end{bmatrix}$$

Written equation by equation, this is

$$\nabla y_{1,t} = -a_{11,2}\nabla y_{1,t-1} - a_{12,2}\nabla y_{2,t-1} + \pi_{11}e_{t-1} + u_{1t}$$

$$\nabla y_{2,t} = -a_{21,2}\nabla y_{1,t-1} - a_{22,2}\nabla y_{2,t-1} + \left(\frac{\pi_{22}}{\pi_{12}}\right)\pi_{11}e_{t-1} + u_{2t}$$

where

$$e_t = y_{1,t} - \left(\frac{\pi_{12}}{\pi_{11}}\right)y_{2,t}$$

is the single error correction. The various π_{rs} coefficients can themselves be expressed in terms of the $a_{rs,i}$ coefficients, $r, s, i = 1, 2$, if desired.

ESTIMATION OF VECTOR ERROR CORRECTION MODELS AND TESTS OF COINTEGRATING RANK

15.8 Estimation of the VECM (15.5) is nonstandard because the α and β matrices enter in nonlinear fashion as the product $\beta\alpha'$. Without going into unnecessary technical details, ML estimates are obtained in the following way. Consider again (15.5) but now written as:

$$\nabla y_t = c + \sum_{i=1}^{p-1} \Phi_i \nabla y_{t-i} + \beta\alpha' y_{t-1} + u_t \tag{15.7}$$

The first step is to estimate (15.7) under the restriction $\beta\alpha' = 0$. As this is simply the "differenced VAR" (15.3), OLS estimation will yield the set of residuals $\hat{u}_t$, from which we may calculate the sample covariance matrix

$$S_{00} = T^{-1} \sum_{t=1}^{T} \hat{u}_t \hat{u}_t'$$

The second step is to estimate the multivariate regression

$$y_{t-1} = d + \sum_{i=1}^{p-1} \Xi_i \nabla y_{t-i} + v_t$$

by OLS, and use the residuals $\hat{v}_t$ to calculate the covariance matrices

$$S_{11} = T^{-1} \sum_{t=1}^{T} \hat{v}_t \hat{v}_t'$$

and

$$S_{10} = T^{-1} \sum_{t=1}^{T} \hat{u}_t \hat{v}_t' = S_{01}$$

These two regressions partial out the effects of the lagged differences $\nabla y_{t-1}, \ldots, \nabla y_{t-p+1}$ from ∇y_t and y_{t-1}, leaving us to concentrate on the relationship between these two variables, which is parameterized by $\beta\alpha'$. The vector α is then estimated by the r linear combinations of y_{t-1} which have the largest squared partial correlations with ∇y_t: this is known as a *reduced rank regression*.

15.9 More precisely, this procedure maximizes the likelihood of (15.7) by treating it as a generalized eigenvalue problem and solving a set of equations of the form:

$$\left(\lambda_i S_{11} - S_{10} S_{00}^{-1} S_{01}\right) v_i = 0 \quad i = 1, \ldots, n \tag{15.8}$$

where $\lambda_1 \geq \lambda_2 \geq \cdots \geq \lambda_n \geq 0$ are the set of eigenvalues and $V = (v_1, v_2, \ldots, v_n)$ contains the set of associated eigenvectors, subject to the normalization

$$V' S_{11} V = I_n$$

The ML estimate of α is then given by the eigenvectors corresponding to the r largest eigenvalues:

$$\hat{\alpha} = (v_1, v_2, \ldots, v_r)$$

and the ML estimate of β is consequently calculated as $\hat{\beta} = S_{01} \hat{\alpha}$, which is equivalent to the estimate of β that would be obtained by substituting $\hat{\alpha}$ into (15.7) and estimating by OLS, which also provides ML estimates of the remaining parameters in the model.

15.10 This procedure can be straightforwardly adapted when a trend is included in (15.7) and when various restrictions are placed upon the intercept and trend coefficients. This involves adjusting the first- and second-step regressions to accommodate these alterations. Consider again the levels VAR (15.1) with a linear trend included:

$$A(B)y_t = c + dt + u_t \tag{15.9}$$

Quite generally, the intercept and trend coefficients may be written as:

$$c = \beta \gamma_1 + \beta_\perp \gamma_1^* \quad d = \beta \gamma_2 + \beta_\perp \gamma_2^*$$

where $\beta_\perp$ is an $n \times (n-r)$ matrix known as the *orthogonal complement* of β, defined such that $\beta_\perp' \beta = 0$, γ_1 and γ_2 are $r \times 1$ vectors, and γ_1^* and γ_2^* are $(n-r) \times 1$ vectors. It then follows that

$$\beta' c = \beta' \beta \gamma_1 + \beta' \beta_\perp \gamma_1^* = \beta' \beta \gamma_1$$

and, similarly, $\beta' d = \beta' \beta \gamma_2$. The associated VECM can then be written as

$$\nabla y_t = \Phi(B) \nabla y_{t-1} + \beta_\perp \left(\gamma_1^* + \gamma_2^* t \right) + \beta \left(\gamma_1 + \gamma_2(t-1) + e_{t-1} \right) + u_t$$

The trend will be restricted to the error correction if $\beta_\perp \gamma_2^* = 0$, that is, if $d = \beta \gamma_2$. Similarly, the intercept will be restricted to the error correction if $\beta_\perp \gamma_1^* = 0$ ($c = \beta \gamma_1$). Thus, the "trend included" error correction may be defined as $e_t^* = e_t + \gamma_1 + \gamma_2 t$.

15.11 Of course, ML estimation is based upon a known value of the cointegrating rank r, but in practice this value will be unknown. Fortunately, the set of Eq. (15.8) also provides a method of determining the value of r. If $r = n$ and Π is unrestricted, the maximized log likelihood is given by:

$$\mathcal{L}(n) = K - \left(\frac{T}{2} \right) \sum_{i=1}^{n} \log(1 - \lambda_i)$$

where

$$K = -\left(\frac{T}{2}\right)(n(1 + 2\log2\pi) + \log|S_{00}|)$$

For a given value of $r < n$, only the first r eigenvalues should be positive, and the restricted log likelihood is

$$\mathcal{L}(r) = K - \left(\frac{T}{2}\right)\sum_{i=1}^{r}\log(1 - \lambda_i)$$

An LR test of the hypothesis that there are r cointegrating vectors against the alternative that there are n is then given by:

$$\eta_r = 2(\mathcal{L}(n) - \mathcal{L}(r)) = -T\sum_{i=r+1}^{n}\log(1 - \lambda_i)$$

This is known as the *trace statistic* and testing proceeds in the sequence $\eta_0, \eta_1, \ldots, \eta_{n-1}$. A cointegrating rank of r is selected if the *last* significant statistic is η_{r-1}, which thereby rejects the hypothesis of $n - r + 1$ unit roots in $\mathbf{\Pi}$. The trace statistic measures the importance of the adjustment coefficients β on the eigenvectors to be potentially omitted.

15.12   An alternative test is to assess the significance of the largest eigenvalue with

$$\zeta_r = -T\log(1 - \lambda_{r+1}) \quad r = 0, 1, \ldots, n - 1$$

which is known as the *maximal-eigenvalue* or *λ-max statistic*. Both η_r and ζ_r have nonstandard limiting distributions that are generalizations of the Dickey–Fuller unit root distributions. The limiting distributions depend on n and on the restrictions imposed on the behavior of the constant and trend appearing in the VECM (cf. §**15.10**).

These tests are often referred to as *Johansen system cointegration tests*: see, for example, Johansen (1988, 1995), in which this approach was first proposed and subsequently developed.

EXAMPLE 15.2 A VECM Representation of United Kingdom Long and Short Interest Rates

Example 13.1 estimated a VAR(2) for $\nabla\mathbf{y}_t = (\nabla RS_t, \nabla R20_t)'$. Given that Example 14.1 has demonstrated that the two interest rates are cointegrated, we now investigate a VECM for the levels vector $\mathbf{y}_t = (RS_t, R20_t)'$. From §**15.3**, lag order determination statistics remain appropriate for the levels VAR even if, as has been found, the two interest rates are both $I(1)$. Thus, from Table 15.1, a lag order of $p = 3$ is selected.

Since $n = 2$, setting the cointegrating rank as $r = 0$ would imply that there was no cointegration and the representation would be that found in Example

TABLE 15.1 Lag Length Determination Statistics for $y_t = (RS_t, R20_t)'$

p	$\mathcal{L}$	$LR(p, p-1)$	MAIC	MBIC
0	-3650.3	–	9.365	9.377
1	-530.2	6216.12	1.375	1.411
2	-462.4	134.82	1.211	1.271^a
3	-455.9	12.76^a	1.205^a	1.289
4	-455.4	0.98	1.214	1.321
5	-454.4	2.11	1.221	1.353
6	-451.6	5.41	1.225	1.380

$LR(p, p-1) \sim \chi^2(4)$: $\chi^2_{0.05}(4) = 9.49$. *MAIC*, multivariate AIC criterion; *MBIC*, multivariate BIC criterion.
^{a}*Denotes selected value.*

13.1; a VAR(2) in the differences ∇RS and $\nabla R20$. If $r = 1$ there will be a single cointegrating vector with the error correction $e_t = \alpha_1 RS_t + \alpha_2 R20_t + \alpha_0$, where an intercept is included. If $r = 2$ then there are no unit roots and a VAR(3) in levels is appropriate.

Including c in (15.1), allowing an intercept in the cointegrating vector and estimating by ML obtains the eigenvalues $\lambda_1 = 0.0202$ and $\lambda_2 = 0.0014$, using which the trace statistics $\eta_0 = 17.13$ and $\eta_1 = 1.12$ and maximum eigenvalue statistics $\zeta_0 = 16.01$ and $\zeta_1 = 1.12$ are calculated. The η_0 and ζ_0 statistics reject the null hypothesis of $r = 0$ in favor of $r > 0$ with p-values of .03, but the η_1 and ζ_1 statistics, which, by definition, are equal in this example, cannot reject the null of $r = 1$ in favor of $r = 2$, the p-values being .29. We are, thus, led to the conclusion that RS and R20 are indeed cointegrated, implying that using a VAR in the first differences to model $y_t = (RS_t, R20_t)'$ constitutes a misspecification.

ML estimation of the implied VECM obtains these estimates, written in individual equation form for convenience (no intercepts were included in the individual equations as, consistent with previous analyses, they were found to be insignificant):

$$\nabla RS_t = \underset{(0.040)}{0.227} \nabla RS_{t-1} + \underset{(0.039)}{0.039} \nabla RS_{t-2} + \underset{(0.061)}{0.270} \nabla R20_{t-1} - \underset{(0.062)}{0.079} \nabla R20_{t-2}$$
$$+ \underset{(0.008)}{0.026} e_{t-1} + \hat{u}_{1,t}$$

$$\nabla R20_t = - \underset{(0.026)}{0.013} \nabla RS_{t-1} + \underset{(0.026)}{0.020} \nabla RS_{t-2} + \underset{(0.040)}{0.315} \nabla R20_{t-1} - \underset{(0.040)}{0.139} \nabla R20_{t-2}$$
$$- \underset{(0.005)}{0.004} e_{t-1} + \hat{u}_{2,t}$$

$$e_t = R20_t - \underset{(0.122)}{1.044} RS_t - \underset{(0.886)}{0.898}$$

IDENTIFICATION OF VECTOR ERROR CORRECTION MODELS

15.13 The error correction in Example 15.2 has been normalized by setting $\alpha_2 = 1$. With one cointegrating vector ($r = 1$), imposing one restriction is sufficient to *identify* the cointegrating vector. More generally, the assumption that the rank of Π is r implicitly imposes $(n-r)^2$ restrictions on its n^2 coefficients, leaving $n^2 - (n-r)^2 = 2nr - r^2$ free parameters. The two $n \times r$ matrices, α and β, involve $2nr$ parameters, so that identifying $\Pi = \beta\alpha'$ requires a total of r^2 restrictions.

If, for the moment, the identifying restrictions are imposed only on the α matrix, if they are linear, and if there are no cross-cointegrating vector restrictions, then these restrictions can be written for the ith cointegrating vector as $R_i\alpha_i = a_i$, where R_i and a_i are an $r \times n$ matrix and an $r \times 1$ vector, respectively. A necessary and sufficient condition for α to be uniquely identified is that the rank of each $R_i\alpha_i$ is r, while the necessary condition is that there must be r restrictions placed on each of the r cointegrating vectors.[1] Note that the identification of α, and hence Π, is achieved solely through restrictions on α itself. Long-run relationships cannot be identified through restrictions on the short-run dynamics: consequently, the Φ_i coefficients in (15.6) may be estimated freely.

15.14 If the number of restrictions imposed on α is k, then setting k equal to r^2 constitutes *exact identification*. The imposition of r restrictions on each of the r cointegrating vectors does not alter the likelihood $\mathcal{L}(r)$, so that, while their imposition enables a unique estimate of α to be obtained, the validity of the restrictions cannot be tested. Typically, r restrictions are obtained by normalization, and if $r = 1$ then this is all that is required, as was the case in Example 15.2. For $r > 1$, a further $r^2 - r$ restrictions are needed ($r - 1$ on each equation), and this forms the basis for Phillips' (1991) *triangular representation*. This writes α as

$$\alpha' = \begin{bmatrix} I_r & -\Gamma \end{bmatrix}$$

where Γ is an $r \times (n - r)$ matrix. The r^2 just-identifying restrictions are, thus, made up of r normalizations and $r^2 - r$ zero restrictions, corresponding to solving $\alpha'y_t$ for the first r components of y_t.

15.15 When $k > r^2$, there are $k - r^2$ *overidentifying* restrictions. If $\mathcal{L}(r:q)$ denotes the log-likelihood after the imposition of the $q = k - r^2$ overidentifying restrictions, then the validity of these restrictions can be tested using the LR statistic $2(\mathcal{L}(r) - \mathcal{L}(r:q))$, which is asymptotically distributed as $\chi^2(q)$.

15.16 Restrictions may also be placed on β and may link α and β. One source of restrictions is to consider hypotheses concerning the *weak exogeneity* of some of the variables. Suppose we make the partition $y_t = \left(x'_t, z'_t\right)'$, where x_t and z_t are $n_1 \times 1$ and $n_2 \times 1$ vectors with $n_1 + n_2 = n$, and write the VECM (15.7) as the pair of "marginal" models

$$\nabla x_t = c_1 + \sum_{i=1}^{p-1} \Phi_{1,i} \nabla y_{t-i} + \beta_1 \alpha' y_{t-1} + u_{1,t} \qquad (15.10a)$$

$$\nabla z_t = c_2 + \sum_{i=1}^{p-1} \Phi_{2,i} \nabla y_{t-i} + \beta_2 \alpha' y_{t-1} + u_{2,t} \qquad (15.10b)$$

where

$$\Phi_i = \begin{bmatrix} \Phi_{1,i} \\ \Phi_{2,i} \end{bmatrix} \quad i = 1, \ldots, m-1 \quad \beta = \begin{bmatrix} \beta_1 \\ \beta_2 \end{bmatrix} \quad u_t = \begin{bmatrix} u_{1,t} \\ u_{2,t} \end{bmatrix}$$

are conformable partitions. The condition for z_t to be weakly exogenous for (α, β_1) is $\beta_2 = 0$, in which case the error correction $e_t = \alpha' y_t$ does not enter the marginal model for z_t.[2]

Such weak exogeneity hypotheses may be tested by including the n_2 zero restrictions on β, that is, under the null hypothesis, $\beta = \begin{bmatrix} \beta_1 & 0 \end{bmatrix}'$, in the q overidentifying restrictions of the LR test previously outlined in §15.15.

EXAMPLE 15.3 Tests on the VECM of United Kingdom Interest Rates

As well as the normalization $\alpha_2 = 1$, which is enough to just-identify the cointe-grating vector of the VECM in Example 15.2, two further restrictions are sug-gested by the estimated coefficients of the model. The first is $\alpha_1 = -1$, since $\hat{\alpha}_1$ is insignificantly different from this value. This restriction defines the error cor-rection to be the deviation of the spread from its equilibrium value, as was found in the ARDL model fitted in Example 14.2. Second, the error correction term in the equation for $\nabla R20$ is insignificantly different from zero, thus raising the ques-tion of whether R20 might be weakly exogenous. In the notation of §15.15, $n_1 = n_2 = 1$, $\beta = \begin{bmatrix} \beta_1 & \beta_2 \end{bmatrix}$ and we wish to test the hypothesis $\beta_2 = 0$ to establish the weak exogeneity of R20.

As there are two overidentifying restrictions, the LR test is $2(\mathcal{L}(1) - \mathcal{L}(1:2)) = 0.67 \sim \chi^2(2)$, which has a p-value of just .71, so that the restrictions are satisfied. Estimation of the restricted model yields

$$\nabla RS_t = \underset{(0.040)}{0.227} \nabla RS_{t-1} + \underset{(0.040)}{0.039} \nabla RS_{t-2} + \underset{(0.061)}{0.270} \nabla R20_{t-1} - \underset{(0.062)}{0.080} \nabla R20_{t-2}$$
$$+ \underset{(0.008)}{0.030} e_{t-1}^R + \hat{u}_{1,t}$$

$$\nabla R20_t = -\underset{(0.026)}{0.013} \nabla RS_{t-1} + \underset{(0.026)}{0.020} \nabla RS_{t-2} + \underset{(0.040)}{0.315} \nabla R20_{t-1}$$
$$- \underset{(0.040)}{0.138} \nabla R20_{t-2} + \hat{u}_{2,t}$$

where the restricted error correction

$$e_t^R = R20_t - RS_t - \underset{(0.454)}{1.191}$$

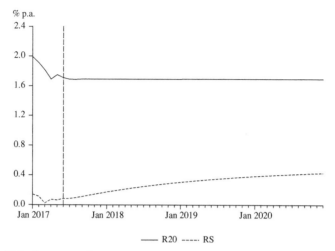

FIGURE 15.1 Interest rate forecasts to December 2020.

only enters the ∇RS equation. Note also that both $\hat{\phi}_{1,21}$ and $\hat{\phi}_{2,21}$ are insignificantly different from zero so that R20 can, in fact, be regarded as *strongly exogenous*, there being no feedback from short rates to long rates.

Forecasts of future values of interest rates may be obtained in the manner described in Chapter 7, An Introduction to Forecasting With Univariate Models, on an equation by equation basis. Fig. 15.1 shows forecasts of R20 and RS out to the end of 2020. The forecasts are shown to quickly stabilize and at the end of the forecast period are 1.694% and 0.426%, respectively, the difference in these rates, 1.268%, being close to the equilibrium value of the spread.

STRUCTURAL VECTOR ERROR CORRECTION MODELS

15.17 Following Johansen and Juselius (1994), a "structural VECM" may be written as

$$\Gamma_0 \nabla y_t = \sum_{i=1}^{p-1} \Gamma_i \nabla y_{t-i} + \Theta \alpha' y_{t-1} + v_t \qquad (15.11)$$

which is related to the "reduced form" VECM

$$\nabla y_t = \sum_{i=1}^{p-1} \Phi_i \nabla y_{t-i} + \beta \alpha' y_{t-1} + u_t$$

through

$$\Gamma_i = \Gamma_0 \Phi_i \quad i = 1, \ldots, p-1$$
$$\Gamma_0 \beta = \Theta \quad v_t = \Gamma_0 u_t$$

so that

$$E\left(\nu_t\nu_t'\right) = \Gamma_0\Omega_p\Gamma_0'$$

Note that this framework assumes that the cointegrating vectors have already been identified (and their parameters set), so that identification of the "short-run" structure, that is, the set of parameters $\Gamma_0, \Gamma_1, \ldots, \Gamma_{p-1}, \Theta$, is carried out conditionally on the form of α. This can be done using conventional methods and will typically proceed in an exploratory fashion as little will usually be known a priori about the short-run structure.

EXAMPLE 15.4 A Structural VECM for United Kingdom Interest Rates

We know from Example 14.1 that $\nabla R20_t$ and ∇RS_t are contemporaneously correlated and this is confirmed by a correlation of 0.46 between the residuals $\hat{u}_{1,t}$ and $\hat{u}_{2,t}$ of the VECM of Example 15.3. Thus, Γ_0, which here is 2×2, must be non-diagonal and so a structural VECM may be constructed. With $p = 3$, the matrices in (15.10a,b) take the form:

$$\Gamma_0 = \begin{pmatrix} 1 & \gamma_{12,0} \\ \gamma_{21,0} & 1 \end{pmatrix} \quad \Gamma_1 = \begin{pmatrix} \gamma_{11,1} & \gamma_{12,1} \\ \gamma_{21,1} & \gamma_{22,1} \end{pmatrix} \quad \Gamma_2 = \begin{pmatrix} \gamma_{11,2} & \gamma_{12,2} \\ \gamma_{21,2} & \gamma_{22,2} \end{pmatrix} \quad \Psi = \begin{bmatrix} \psi_1 \\ \psi_2 \end{bmatrix}$$

While two normalization restrictions have been imposed on Γ_0, a further restriction is required for the equation system to be identified. Two possibilities are available: either $\gamma_{12,0} = 0$ or $\gamma_{21,0} = 0$. Table 15.2 reports the model estimates under each of these identifications. Under the first identification, three coefficients are estimated to be insignificantly different from zero and a joint test of these three zero restrictions produces a test statistic that has a p-value of just .57. The so restricted model is:

$$\nabla RS_t = \underset{(0.038)}{0.229} \nabla RS_{t-1} + \underset{(0.059)}{0.253} \nabla R20_{t-1} + \underset{(0.008)}{0.026} e_{t-1}^R + \hat{v}_{1,t}$$

$$\nabla R20_t = \underset{(0.021)}{0.302} \nabla RS_t - \underset{(0.023)}{0.080} \nabla RS_{t-1} + \underset{(0.036)}{0.232} \nabla R20_{t-1} - \underset{(0.032)}{0.108} \nabla R20_{t-2}$$
$$- \underset{(0.005)}{0.013} e_{t-1}^R + \hat{v}_{2,t}$$

Under the second identifying restriction there are six insignificant coefficients and the accompanying test statistic of these zero restrictions has a p-value of .77, leading to the restricted model:

$$\nabla RS_t = \underset{(0.047)}{0.709} \nabla R20_t + \underset{(0.030)}{0.261} \nabla RS_{t-1} + \underset{(0.007)}{0.030} e_{t-1}^R + \hat{v}_{1,t}$$

$$\nabla R20_t = \underset{(0.035)}{0.304} \nabla R20_{t-1} - \underset{(0.035)}{0.126} \nabla R20_{t-2} + \hat{v}_{2,t}$$

Statistically the two models are indistinguishable as their fits are identical. There are, however, differences in their interpretations. In the second model long interest rates are strongly exogenous, as was implied by the VECM of

TABLE 15.2 Structural VECM Estimates

	$\gamma_{12,0} = 0$	$\gamma_{21,0} = 0$
$\gamma_{12,0}$	–	-0.701^a (0.049)
$\gamma_{21,0}$	-0.302^a (0.021)	–
$\gamma_{11,1}$	0.227^a (0.040)	0.236^a (0.035)
$\gamma_{12,1}$	0.270^a (0.061)	0.049 (0.056)
$\gamma_{21,1}$	-0.082^a (0.024)	-0.013 (0.026)
$\gamma_{22,1}$	0.233^a (0.036)	0.315^a (0.040)
$\gamma_{11,2}$	0.039 (0.039)	0.025 (0.035)
$\gamma_{12,2}$	-0.080 (0.062)	0.017 (0.055)
$\gamma_{21,2}$	0.008 (0.023)	0.020 (0.026)
$\gamma_{22,2}$	-0.114^a (0.036)	-0.138^a (0.040)
ψ_1	0.027^a (0.009)	0.030^a (0.008)
ψ_2	-0.012^a (0.005)	-0.004 (0.006)

VECM, Vector error correction model.
[a]Denotes significantly different from zero at 0.05 level.

Example 15.3. In the first model, by contrast, the error correction appears significantly in both equations and there is a short-run feedback from short to long rates. Which of the two models to select is thus a choice that requires further knowledge, both theoretical and institutional, about the behavior and interaction of the gilt and money markets in the United Kingdom.

CAUSALITY TESTING IN VECTOR ERROR CORRECTION MODELS

15.18 Consider a "fully partitioned" form of the marginal VECM (15.10a,b):

$$\nabla x_t = c_1 + \sum_{i=1}^{p-1} \Phi_{11,i} \nabla x_{t-i} + \sum_{i=1}^{p-1} \Phi_{12,i} \nabla z_{t-i} + \beta_1 \alpha_1' x_{t-1} + \beta_1 \alpha_2' z_{t-1} + u_{1,t}$$

$$\nabla z_t = c_2 + \sum_{i=1}^{p-1} \Phi_{21,i} \nabla x_{t-i} + \sum_{i=1}^{p-1} \Phi_{22,i} \nabla z_{t-i} + \beta_2 \alpha_1' x_{t-1} + \beta_2 \alpha_2' z_{t-1} + u_{1,t}$$

where now

$$\Phi_i = \begin{bmatrix} \Phi_{11,i} & \Phi_{12,i} \\ \Phi_{21,i} & \Phi_{22,i} \end{bmatrix} \quad \alpha' = \begin{bmatrix} \alpha_1 & \alpha_2 \end{bmatrix}'$$

The hypothesis that z does not Granger-cause x may then be formalized as

$$\mathcal{H}_0 : \Phi_{12,1} = \cdots = \Phi_{12,p-1} = 0, \quad \beta_1\alpha_2' = 0$$

The second part of $\mathcal{H}_0$, which is often referred to as "long-run noncausality," involves a nonlinear function of the α and β coefficients and this complicates testing considerably: see Toda and Phillips (1993, 1994). Basing a test on the unrestricted Π matrix, that is, $\Pi_{12} = 0$, to use an obvious notation, is invalid as the Wald test statistic will only be distributed asymptotically as χ^2 if it is known that α_2 is of rank n_2, information that is simply not available from estimating the "levels" VAR.

15.19 Because of the complexity of testing $\mathcal{H}_0$, a simpler, but necessarily less powerful and inefficient, procedure has been suggested by Toda and Yamamoto (1995) and Saikkonen and Lütkepohl (1996). Suppose we consider a VAR(p) in levels but now augment the order by one, that is, we fit a VAR($p + 1$). It turns out that the noncausality hypothesis can now be tested by a conventional Wald statistic, because the additional lag, for which $\Phi_{12,p+1} = 0$ by assumption, allows standard asymptotic inference to once again be used.[3]

If the number of variables in the VAR is small and the lag order quite large, then including an additional lag might lead to only minor inefficiencies, so that, given the ease with which tests can be constructed, this "lag augmentation" VAR (LA-VAR) approach should be seriously considered under such circumstances.

EXAMPLE 15.5 LA-VAR Causality Tests for United Kingdom Interest Rates

Since a VAR(3) has been selected for $y_t = (RS_t, R20_t)'$ and we know that RS and R20 are both $I(1)$, Granger-causality between them can be tested using the LA-VAR approach by fitting a VAR(4). The null R20 does not $\rightarrow$ RS yields a test statistic of 26.64, which is highly significant, while the test statistic for the null RS does not $\rightarrow$ R20 is 1.52, which has a p-value of just .82. There is, thus, no evidence of a feedback from RS to R20 and this is consistent with the second of the structural VECMs fitted in Example 15.4.

IMPULSE RESPONSE ASYMPTOTICS IN NONSTATIONARY VARs

15.20 As shown in §§**13.11–13.14**, the various impulse responses of the VAR are computed from the sequence of matrices

$$\Psi_i = \sum_{j=1}^{i} A_j\Psi_{i-j}, \quad \Psi_0 = I_n \quad \Psi_i = 0, \quad i < 0$$

Their computation remains exactly the same in nonstationary VARs, but if $\Pi = - \sum_{j=1}^{p} A_j$ is of reduced rank, the elements of Ψ_i will not die out as i increases, and this leads to some analytical complications.

15.21 In stationary VARs, where all the roots of the long-run matrix Π are less than one, the estimated impulse responses may be shown to be consistent and asymptotically normal and both the Ψ_i and their estimates $\hat{\Psi}_i$ tend to zero. For nonstationary VARs, where the Ψ_i do not necessarily die out as $i \rightarrow \infty$, a different limit theory holds for the impulse response estimates, as shown by the results of Phillips (1998) and Stock (1996).

These results are summarized here. When there are unit roots in the system, the long-horizon (large i) impulse responses estimated from a levels VAR by OLS are inconsistent; the limiting values of the estimated responses being random variables rather than the true impulse responses. The reason for this is that, because these true impulse responses do not die out as i increases, they carry the effects of the unit roots with them indefinitely. Since the unit roots are estimated with error (i.e., the estimated roots tend not to be exactly unity), the effects of the estimation error persist in the limit as $T \rightarrow \infty$. The limiting distribution of $\hat{\Psi}_i$ is asymmetric, so that confidence intervals for impulse responses will be asymmetric as well.

The limiting impulse responses in a CVAR, on the other hand, are estimated consistently if the cointegrating rank is either known or is itself estimated consistently, say by the tests of §§**15.10–15.11** or by using an information criterion. This is because, in a reduced-rank regression, the matrix product $\beta\alpha'$ is estimated rather than Π, so that no unit roots are estimated (either implicitly or explicitly). Nonetheless, these consistent rank order selection procedures will tend to mistakenly take roots that are close to unity as actually being unity, so that, rather than dying out, the estimated impulse responses will converge to nonzero constants, accompanied by rather wide confidence intervals.

Impulse responses for nonstationary VARs should, therefore, not be computed from an unrestricted levels VAR. Since knowing the number of unit roots in the system is necessary for obtaining accurate estimates, it is important that the cointegrating rank is selected by a consistent method that works well in practice.

EXAMPLE 15.6 Impulse Responses From the Interest Rate VECM

The VECM fitted in Example 15.3 imposes a single unit root on the long-run matrix, and the generalized impulse responses shown in Fig. 15.2 reflect this, with the impulse responses to a shock in the other variable quickly converging to nonzero constants. The levels VAR does not impose a unit root but estimates it to be 0.996. Although this is close to unity, the stationarity of the long-run matrix manifests itself in a (slow) decline of the impulse response functions toward zero, as shown in Fig. 15.3.

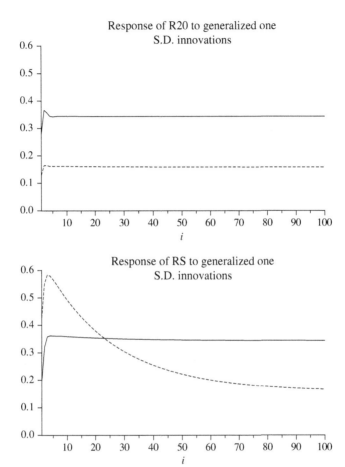

FIGURE 15.2   Generalized impulse responses from the interest rate VECM. *VECM*, Vector error correction model.

VECTOR ERROR CORRECTION MODEL-X MODELS

15.22   A straightforward extension of the CVAR/VECM model is to include a vector of $I(0)$ exogenous variables, w_t say, which may enter each equation:

$$\nabla y_t = c + dt + \sum_{i=1}^{p-1} \Phi_i \nabla y_{t-i} + \beta \alpha' y_{t-1} + \Lambda w_t + u_t \qquad (15.12)$$

Estimation and testing for cointegrating rank remain exactly as before, although critical values of tests may be affected.

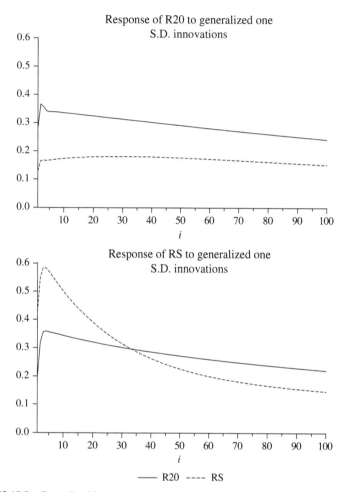

FIGURE 15.3 Generalized impulse responses from the levels VAR.

EXAMPLE 15.7 A VECM-X Model of Temperature and Total Radiative Forcing

Example 14.2 found a cointegrating relationship between the $I(1)$ variables $y_t = (\text{TEMP}_t, \text{TRF}_t)'$. It is of interest to embed this cointegrating relationship within the VECM-X model (15.12) containing the $I(0)$ exogenous vector $w_t = (\text{VOLC}_t, \text{SO}_t, \text{AMO}_t, \text{AMO}_{t-1})'$. Prior analysis suggested setting $p = 5$ and including both an intercept and a trend in the cointegrating vector. With this setup the cointegrating vector is estimated to be

$$e_t = \text{TEMP}_t - 0.115 - 0.000094t - \underset{(0.063)}{0.418} \text{TRF}_t$$

and the VECM-X may be written as

$$\begin{bmatrix} \nabla\text{TEMP}_t \\ \nabla\text{TRF}_t \end{bmatrix} = \begin{bmatrix} c_1 \\ c_2 \end{bmatrix} + \begin{bmatrix} d_1 \\ d_2 \end{bmatrix} t + \sum_{i=1}^{4} \begin{bmatrix} \phi_{11,i} & \phi_{12,i} \\ \phi_{21,i} & \phi_{22,i} \end{bmatrix} \begin{bmatrix} \nabla\text{TEMP}_{t-i} \\ \nabla\text{TRF}_{t-i} \end{bmatrix} + \begin{bmatrix} \beta_1 \\ \beta_2 \end{bmatrix} e_t + \begin{bmatrix} \Lambda_1 \\ \Lambda_2 \end{bmatrix} w_t + \begin{bmatrix} u_{1,t} \\ u_{2,t} \end{bmatrix}$$

where

$$\Lambda = \begin{bmatrix} \Lambda_1 \\ \Lambda_2 \end{bmatrix} = \begin{bmatrix} \lambda_{11} & \lambda_{12} & \lambda_{13} & \lambda_{14} \\ \lambda_{21} & \lambda_{22} & \lambda_{23} & \lambda_{24} \end{bmatrix}$$

The estimates of this model are reported in Table 15.3. From these estimates several sets of restrictions suggest themselves. The first set of restrictions, $\phi_{12,1} = \cdots = \phi_{12,4} = 0$, removes all lags of ∇TRF from the ∇TEMP equation. This has a Wald test statistic of $1.34 \sim \chi^2(4)$, which has a p-value of .86. The second set is $\phi_{21,1} = \cdots = \phi_{21,4} = 0$, which removes all lags of ∇TEMP from the ∇TRF equation. This has a Wald test statistic of $3.24 \sim \chi^2(4)$, which has a p-value of

TABLE 15.3 VECM-X Estimates

	∇TEMP Equation	∇TRF Equation
e_{t-1}	− 0.452 (0.094)	− 0.024 (0.014)
∇TEMP_{t-1}	− 0.146 (0.080)	0.018 (0.011)
∇TEMP_{t-2}	− 0.090 (0.071)	0.015 (0.011)
∇TEMP_{t-3}	− 0.101 (0.068)	0.014 (0.009)
∇TEMP_{t-4}	0.039 (0.058)	0.009 (0.009)
∇TRF_{t-1}	− 0.282 (0.511)	1.461 (0.076)
∇TRF_{t-2}	0.060 (0.894)	− 1.322 (0.013)
∇TRF_{t-3}	0.430 (0.897)	0.800 (0.133)
∇TRF_{t-4}	− 0.489 (0.515)	− 0.533 (0.076)
c	− 0.001 (0.012)	− 0.004 (0.002)
t	0.00015 (0.00017)	0.00026 (0.00002)
VOLC_t	0.072 (0.020)	− 0.003 (0.003)
SO_t	− 0.303 (0.057)	0.003 (0.008)
AMO_t	0.405 (0.048)	− 0.000 (0.007)
AMO_{t-1}	− 0.209 (0.057)	− 0.003 (0.008)
σ	0.0676	0.00100
$\mathcal{L}$	192.9	469.9
$\lvert\hat{\Omega}_5\rvert$	4.54×10^{-7}	

VECM, Vector error correction model.

.52. The third set is $\lambda_{21} = \cdots = \lambda_{24} = 0$, which removes $\boldsymbol{w}_t$ from the ∇TRF equation and has a Wald test statistic of $1.68 \sim \chi^2(4)$, which has a p-value of .79. Imposing these three sets of restrictions, with the additional restrictions $d_1 = 0$ (no trend in the ∇TEMP equation) and $\phi_{11,4} = 0$, produces:

$$
\begin{aligned}
\nabla\text{TEMP}_t = {}& \underset{(0.005)}{0.011} - \underset{(0.064)}{0.174}\,\nabla\text{TEMP}_{t-1} - \underset{(0.057)}{0.119}\,\nabla\text{TEMP}_{t-2} - \underset{(0.053)}{0.121}\,\nabla\text{TEMP}_{t-3} \\
& + \underset{(0.019)}{0.076}\,\text{VOLC}_t - \underset{(0.052)}{0.308}\,\text{SO}_t + \underset{(0.045)}{0.409}\,\text{AMO}_t - \underset{(0.053)}{0.205}\,\text{AMO}_{t-1} \\
& - \underset{(0.078)}{0.438}\,e_{t-1} + \hat{u}_{1,t}
\end{aligned}
$$

and

$$
\begin{aligned}
\nabla\text{TRF}_t = {}& \underset{(0.001)}{0.012} + \underset{(0.00002)}{0.00016}\,t + \underset{(0.071)}{1.485}\,\nabla\text{TRF}_{t-1} - \underset{(0.124)}{1.342}\,\nabla\text{TRF}_{t-2} \\
& + \underset{(0.104)}{0.811}\,\nabla\text{TRF}_{t-3} - \underset{(0.071)}{0.510}\,\nabla\text{TRF}_{t-4} - \underset{(0.007)}{0.016}\,e_{t-1} + \hat{u}_{2,t}
\end{aligned}
$$

The complete set of restrictions provides the test statistic $7.01 \sim \chi^2(14)$ with a p-value of just .93. The contemporaneous correlation between the residuals of the two equations is just 0.07, suggesting that little would be gained by considering a structural formulation.

This VECM-X model has some interesting implications. There is no short-run impact of total radiative forcing on temperature: the entire effect comes through the lagged error correcting term, so that it is the last period's deviation from the long-run equilibrium that drives temperature changes. Not surprisingly, there is no impact from the exogenous climatic variables on total radiative forcing, nor is there any short-run feedback from temperature. There is, however, a long-run feedback from temperature to total radiative forcing through the presence of the lagged error correction. The signs of the error correction term are both negative so that the system is in a stable equilibrium.

COMMON TRENDS AND CYCLES

15.23 Further implications of the presence of a linear trend in a CVAR are best analyzed by introducing the infinite-order vector polynomial $C(B)$, defined such that

$$
C(B)\Pi(B) = \nabla I_n \tag{15.13}
$$

Analogous to the decomposition of $A(B)$ in §15.1, we have

$$
\begin{aligned}
C(B) &= I_n + CB + \left(C_1^* B + C_2^* B^2 + \cdots\right)\nabla \\
&= I_n + C + \left(C_0^* + C_1^* B + C_2^* B^2 + \cdots\right)\nabla \\
&= I_n + C + C^*(B)\nabla \\
&= C(1) + C^*(B)\nabla
\end{aligned}
$$

The matrices of $C(B)$, that is, $C_0, C_1, \ldots$, are given by the recursions

$$C_i = \sum_{j=1}^{p} C_{i-j} A_j, \quad i > 0, \quad C_0 = I_n$$

so that

$$C = \sum_{i=1}^{\infty} C_i = C(1) - I_n$$

It then follows that

$$C_0^* = -C$$

and

$$C_i^* = C_{i-1}^* + C_i, \quad i > 0$$

The VAR (15.9) can then be written as

$$
\begin{aligned}
\nabla y_t &= C(B)(c + dt + u_t) \\
&= \big(C(1) + C^*(B)\nabla\big)(c + dt) + C(B)u_t \\
&= C(1)c + C^*(1)d + C(1)dt + C(B)u_t \\
&= b_0 + b_1 t + C(B)u_t
\end{aligned}
$$

where

$$b_0 = C(1)c \quad b_1 = C(1)d$$

In levels, this becomes

$$
\begin{aligned}
y_t &= y_0 + b_0 t + b_1 \tfrac{t(t+1)}{2} + C(B)\sum_{s=1}^{t} u_t \\
&= y_0 + b_0 t + b_1 \tfrac{t(t+1)}{2} + \big(C(1) + C^*\nabla\big)\sum_{s=1}^{t} u_t \\
&= y_0 + b_0 t + b_1 \tfrac{t(t+1)}{2} + C(1)s_t + C^*(B)(u_t - u_0) \\
&= y_0^* + b_0 t + b_1 \tfrac{t(t+1)}{2} + C(1)s_t + C^*(B)u_t
\end{aligned}
\tag{15.14}
$$

where

$$y_0^* = y_0 - C^*(B)u_0, \quad s_t = \sum_{s=1}^{t} u_s$$

15.24   The inclusion of a linear trend in the VAR (15.9) with $y_t \sim I(1)$ thus implies a *quadratic* trend in the levels Eq. (15.14). Furthermore, since $b_1 = C(1)d$, this quadratic trend will disappear only if $C(1) = 0$. From (15.13), $C(1)A(1) = 0$, so that $C(1) = 0$ requires that $A(1) = -\Pi \neq 0$. This will only be the case if $A(B)$ does not contain the factor $1 - B$, that is, that $y_t \sim I(0)$, which has been ruled out by assumption but would imply that Π is of full rank n.

If, however, $A(1) = 0$, so that $\Pi = 0$, is of rank zero and contains n unit roots, then there is no cointegration and $C(1)$, and hence b_1, are unconstrained. In the general case, where the rank of Π is r, it then follows that the rank of $C(1)$ is $n - r$. The rank of b_1, and hence the number of independent quadratic deterministic trends, is thus also equal to $n - r$, and will, therefore, decrease as the cointegrating rank r increases.

15.25 Without a restriction on the trend coefficient b_1, the solution (15.14) will have the property that the nature of the trend in y_t will vary with the number of cointegrating vectors. To avoid this unsatisfactory outcome, the restriction $b_1 = C(1)d = 0$ may be imposed, in which case the solution for y_t will contain only linear trends, irrespective of the value of r. The choice of r then determines the split between the number of independent linear deterministic trends, r, and the number of stochastic trends, $n - r$, in the model.

15.26 Consider then (15.14) with the restriction $b_1 = 0$ imposed and, for simplicity, initial values $y_0 = u_0 = 0$:

$$y_t = b_0 + C(1)s_t + C^*(B)u_t = C(1)(c + s_t) + C^*(B)u_t \qquad (15.15)$$

If there is cointegration, then as we have seen, $C(1)$ is of reduced rank $h = n - r$ and can be written as the product $\rho\delta'$, where both matrices are of rank h. On defining

$$\tau_t = \delta'(c + s_t) \quad c_t = C^*(B)u_t$$

(15.15) can then be expressed in the "common trends" representation of Stock and Watson (1988):

$$y_t = \rho\tau_t + c_t \qquad (15.16)$$

$$\tau_t = \tau_{t-1} + \delta'u_t$$

This representation expresses y_t as a linear combination of $h = n - r$ random walks, these being the common trends τ_t, plus some stationary "transitory" components c_t. In fact, (15.16) may be regarded as a multivariate extension of the Beveridge−Nelson decomposition (8.9) (cf. §8.4). Through a similar argument to that made about the cointegrating matrix α in §15.7, δ is not uniquely defined, so these trends are also not uniquely defined without introducing some additional identifying restrictions (see Wickens, 1996).

15.27 In the same way that common trends appear in y_t when $C(1)$ is of reduced rank, common cycles appear if $C^*(B)$ is of reduced rank, since $c_t = C^*(B)u_t$ is the cyclical component of y_t. The presence of common cycles requires that there are linear combinations of the elements of y_t that do not contain these cyclical components: that is, that there is a set of s linearly independent vectors, gathered together in the $n \times s$ matrix ϕ, such that

$$\phi' c_t = \phi' C^*(B) u_t = 0$$

in which case

$$\phi' y_t = \phi' \rho \tau_t$$

Such a matrix will exist if all the C_i^* have less than full rank and if $\phi' C_i^* = 0$ for all i, a result derived in Vahid and Engle (1993). Under these circumstances, we can write $C_i^* = G\tilde{C}_i$ for all i, where G is an $n \times (n - s)$ matrix having full column rank and $\tilde{C}_i$ may not have full rank. The cyclical component can then be written, on defining $\tilde{C}(B) = \tilde{C}_0 + \tilde{C}_1 B + \cdots$, as

$$c_t = G\tilde{C}(B) u_t = G\tilde{c}_t$$

so that the n-element cycle c_t can be written as linear combinations of an $(n - s)$-element cycle $\tilde{c}_t$, thus leading to the *common trend-common cycle* representation

$$y_t = \rho \tau_t + G\tilde{c}_t \tag{15.17}$$

The number, s, of linearly independent "cofeature" vectors making up ϕ can be at most $h = n - r$, and these will be linearly independent of the cointegrating vectors making up α. This is a consequence of the fact that $\phi' y_t$, being the vector of common trends, is $I(1)$, whereas $\alpha' y_t$, being the vector of error corrections, is $I(0)$.

15.28 An interesting special case of the representation (15.17) occurs when $r + s = n$, for in these circumstances y_t has the unique trend-cycle decomposition $y_t = y_t^\tau + y_t^c$, where

$$y_t^\tau = \Theta_1 \phi' y_t = \Theta_1 \phi' \rho \tau_t$$

contains the stochastic trends and

$$y_t^c = \Theta_2 \alpha' y_t = \Theta_2 \alpha' c_t$$

contains the cyclical components. Here

$$\begin{bmatrix} \Theta_1 & \Theta_2 \end{bmatrix} = \begin{bmatrix} \alpha' \\ \phi' \end{bmatrix}^{-1}$$

Note that y_t^c is a linear combination of the error correction $e_t = \alpha' y_t$. Since both y_t^τ and y_t^c are functions of α and ϕ, they can easily be calculated as simple linear combinations of y_t.

15.29 The $n \times s$ cofeature matrix ϕ will be identified only up to an invertible transformation, as any linear combinations of the columns of ϕ will also be a cofeature vector. The matrix can, therefore, be rotated to have an s-dimensional identity sub-matrix

$$\phi = \begin{bmatrix} I_s \\ \phi^*_{(n-s)\times s} \end{bmatrix}$$

With this specification, the s cofeature vectors can be incorporated into a VECM along with the r cointegrating vectors, with $\phi'\nabla y_t$ being considered as s "pseudo-structural form" equations for the first s elements of ∇y_t. The system is then completed by adding the unconstrained VECM equations for the remaining $n - s$ equations of ∇y_t to obtain:

$$\begin{bmatrix} I_s & \phi^{*'} \\ 0_{(n-s)\times s} & I_{n-s} \end{bmatrix} \nabla y_t = \begin{bmatrix} 0_{s \times (n(p-1)+r)} \\ \Phi_1^*, \ldots, \Phi_{p-1}^* \beta^* \end{bmatrix} \begin{bmatrix} \nabla y_{t-1} \\ \vdots \\ \nabla y_{t-p+1} \\ e_{t-1} \end{bmatrix} + u_t \quad (15.18)$$

where Φ_1^* contains the last $n - s$ rows of Φ_1, etc. The presence of s common cycles, hence, implies that $\phi'\nabla y_t$ is independent of $\nabla y_{t-1}, \ldots, \nabla y_{t-p+1}$ and e_{t-1}, and hence of all past values of y_t.

15.30 The system (15.18) can be estimated by full-information maximum likelihood or some other simultaneous equation estimation technique. A likelihood ratio statistic of the restrictions imposed by the s cofeature vectors can then be constructed, which will be asymptotically distributed as χ^2 with degrees of freedom given by the number of restrictions that have been imposed.

Ignoring intercepts, the VECM (15.6) has $n(n(p-1)+r)$ parameters, whereas the pseudo-structural model (15.18) has $sn - s^2$ parameters in the first s equations and $(n-s)(n(p-1)+r)$ parameters in the $n-s$ equations that complete the system, so imposing a total of $s^2 + sn(p-1) + sr - sn$ restrictions. Note that if $p = 1$ and $r = n - s$, the number of restrictions is zero. The system is then just-identified and no test for common cycles is needed, for the system will necessarily have r common cycles. As the lag order p increases, so the system will generally become overidentified and tests for common cycles become necessary.[4]

EXAMPLE 15.8 Is There a Common Cycle in United Kingdom Interest Rates?

In Example 15.3, a VECM with $p = 3$ and $r = 1$ was chosen to model the United Kingdom interest rate vector $y_t = (RS_t, R20_t)'$. Since $n = 2$, there can be at most a single ($s \le 1$) common cycle, in which case (15.18) would take the form:

$$\nabla RS_t = -\phi^* \nabla R20_t + u_{1,t}$$

$$\nabla R20_t = \phi_{11}^* \nabla RS_{t-1} + \phi_{12}^* \nabla RS_{t-2} + \phi_{21}^* \nabla R20_{t-1} + \phi_{22}^* \nabla R20_{t-2} + \beta^* e_{t-1} + u_{2,t}$$

A likelihood ratio test of the four restrictions imposed by the common cycle yields $\chi^2(4) = 88.5$, which is highly significant, thus rejecting a common cycle in interest rates. This is consistent with the structural model fitted in Example 15.4, in which ∇RS_{t-1} and the lagged error correction appeared significant along with $\nabla R20_t$ in the equation for ∇RS_t. A common cycle would imply that short interest rates respond immediately and without any lags to a change in long interest rates, which is clearly not the case.

ENDNOTES

1. The more general case of nonlinear and cross-vector restrictions is discussed in Pesaran and Shin (1998).
2. The concept of weak exogeneity was introduced by Engle et al. (1983). Formally, suppose that the joint distribution of $y_t = (x_t', z_t')'$, conditional on the past, is factorized as the conditional distribution of x_t given z_t times the marginal distribution of z_t. Then z_t will be weakly exogenous if two conditions hold: (1) the parameters of these conditional and marginal distributions are not subject to cross-restrictions, and (2) the parameters of interest, here α, β_1, can be uniquely determined from the conditional model alone. Under these conditions z_t may be treated "as if" it was determined outside the conditional model for x_t. Here the conditional model includes ∇z_t as an additional regressor in the marginal model (15.10b).
3. Including one additional lag will suffice if all the series are $I(1)$. In general, a VAR($p + d_{max}$) should be fitted, where d_{max} is the maximum order of integration of the series making up y_t.
4. The concept of a common feature was introduced initially by Engle and Kozicki (1993), with further generalizations given in Vahid and Engle (1997). A survey of the area is provided by Vahid (2006).

Chapter 16

Compositional and Count Time Series

Chapter Outline

CONSTRAINED TIME SERIES

16.1 In previous chapters we considered time series that generally have no restrictions placed upon them apart from when they have a natural lower bound, this often being zero. There are, however, some series, or groups of series, that are bound by further constraints. When modeling such series, a "good" model should be unable to predict values which violate the known constraints, that is, the model should be "forecast coherent." Two examples of these types of series are considered in this chapter: (1) compositional time series in which a group of series are defined as shares of a whole, so that they must be positive fractions that sum to unity; and (2) "count" time series that can only take on positive, and typically low, integer values.

MODELING COMPOSITIONAL DATA

16.2 A compositional data set is one in which the T observations on $D = d + 1$ variables, written in matrix form as

$$X = \begin{bmatrix} x_{1,1} & x_{1,2} & \cdots & x_{1,D} \\ x_{2,1} & x_{2,2} & \cdots & x_{2,D} \\ \vdots & \vdots & & \vdots \\ x_{T,1} & x_{T,2} & \cdots & x_{T,D} \end{bmatrix} = \begin{bmatrix} x_1 & x_2 & \cdots & x_D \end{bmatrix} \quad (16.1)$$

Applied Time Series Analysis. DOI: https://doi.org/10.1016/B978-0-12-813117-6.00016-8
281

where $x_i = (x_{1,i}, x_{2,i}, \ldots, x_{T,i})'$, $i = 1, 2, \ldots, D$, are such that $x_{t,i} > 0$ and $x_{t,1} + x_{t,2} + \cdots + x_{t,D} = 1$, $t = 1, 2, \ldots, T$, that is, $x_i > \mathbf{0}$ and

$$x_1 + x_2 + \cdots + x_D = \iota$$

where $\iota = \begin{bmatrix} 1 & 1 & \cdots & 1 \end{bmatrix}'$ is a $T \times 1$ unit vector. The sub-matrix

$$X^{(d)} = \begin{bmatrix} x_1 & x_2 & \cdots & x_d \end{bmatrix}$$

then lies in the *d-dimensional simplex $\mathcal{S}^d$ embedded in D-dimensional real space* with

$$x_D = \iota - \sum_{i=1}^{d} x_i \tag{16.2}$$

being the vector of 'fill-up' values and $X = \begin{bmatrix} X^{(d)} & x_D \end{bmatrix}$.[1]

16.3   There are several difficulties encountered when analyzing X within the simplex sample space, these being a consequence of the summation condition (16.2) rendering standard covariance and correlation analysis invalid. Aitchison (1982) proposed mapping $X^{(d)}$ from $\mathcal{S}^d$ to the *d*-dimensional real space $\mathcal{R}^d$ and then examining the statistical properties of the transformed data within $\mathcal{R}^d$. Several transformations have been proposed for doing this, the most popular being the *additive log-ratio* transformation which is defined as[2]

$$
\begin{aligned}
Y = \begin{bmatrix} y_1 & y_2 & \cdots & y_d \end{bmatrix} &= a_d(X^{(d)}) \\
&= \begin{bmatrix} \log\left(\dfrac{x_1}{x_D}\right) & \log\left(\dfrac{x_2}{x_D}\right) & \cdots & \log\left(\dfrac{x_d}{x_D}\right) \end{bmatrix}
\end{aligned}
\tag{16.3}
$$

The inverse transformation, known as the *additive-logistic*, is

$$X^{(d)} = a_d^{-1}(Y) = \begin{bmatrix} \dfrac{\exp(y_1)}{y} & \dfrac{\exp(y_2)}{y} & \cdots & \dfrac{\exp(y_d)}{y} \end{bmatrix}$$

$$x_D = \frac{1}{y}$$

where

$$y = 1 + \sum_{i=1}^{d} \exp(y_i)$$

16.4   If we can assume that Y is multivariate normally distributed, denoted $Y \sim N^d(\mu, \Sigma)$, where μ and Σ are the mean vector and covariance matrix, respectively, then $X^{(d)}$ will have a logistic-normal distribution, denoted as

$$X^{(d)} \sim L^d(\mu, \Sigma) = 2\pi^{-d/2} |\Sigma|^{-1/2} \left(\prod_{i=1}^{D} x_i \right)^{-1} \exp\left(-\frac{1}{2}(Y - \mu)' \Sigma^{-1}(Y - \mu) \right)$$

Although μ is the mean of Y, it is the geometric mean of $X^{(d)}$ since the inverse additive-logistic transformation $a_d^{-1}(\cdot)$ preserves the ordering of values in S^d, but does not preserve the mean and modal properties enjoyed by Y in $\mathcal{R}^d$. Thus, a difficult analysis in the "awkward" sample space S^d may be transformed using $a_d(\cdot)$ to $\mathcal{R}^d$ in which more tractable statistical analyses may be performed before using $a_d^{-1}(\cdot)$ to return to the original variables.

16.5   It is important to note that $a_d(\cdot)$ is invariant to the choice of a fill-up value so that nothing in the statistical analysis hinges on which of the "shares" or "proportions" x_i is chosen for this role. It is possible to avoid choosing a fill-up variable by using the *centered log-ratio* transformation, defined as

$$Z = c_d\left(X^{(d)}\right) = \left[\log\left(\frac{x_1}{g(X)}\right) \quad \log\left(\frac{x_2}{g(X)}\right) \quad \cdots \quad \log\left(\frac{x_D}{g(X)}\right) \right]$$

where

$$g(X) = \begin{bmatrix} \left(x_{1,1} \times x_{1,2} \times \cdots \times x_{1,D}\right)^{1/D} \\ \left(x_{2,1} \times x_{2,2} \times \cdots \times x_{2,D}\right)^{1/D} \\ \vdots \\ \left(x_{T,1} \times x_{T,2} \times \cdots \times x_{T,D}\right)^{1/D} \end{bmatrix}$$

is the vector of geometric means. Unfortunately, this has the disadvantage of introducing a non-singularity since $Z\iota = 0$.

16.6   A potential problem with the log-ratio transformation is that it cannot handle zero values, that is, if $x_{i,t} = 0$ then $y_{i,t} = \log\left(x_{i,t}/x_{D,t}\right)$ is undefined. Although zero values for proportions are ruled out in the setup of §**16.1**, they can obviously occur in actual datasets and some means of dealing with them is required. Aitchison (2003, chapter 11) offers a variety of suggestions and Mills (2007) reviews some further proposals for doing this, which essentially turn on replacing zeros with a suitably small positive value and adjusting the positive shares accordingly.

FORECASTING COMPOSITIONAL TIME SERIES

16.7   Let us now denote the tth rows of X and Y as X_t and Y_t, respectively, and let us assume that an h-step ahead forecast of Y_{t+h}, which may not yet be observed, is available. This may be denoted $Y_t(h)$ with covariance matrix $\Sigma_t(h)$. Since Y_t is multivariate normal, such forecasts may have been obtained from a wide variety of multivariate models; for example, Brunsdon and Smith (1998) consider modeling Y_t as a vector ARMA process and other regression frameworks are available in which covariates and trends may be introduced (see Mills, 2010).

A forecast for X_{t+h} is then obtained as

$$X_t(h) = a_d^{-1}(Y_t(h)) \qquad (16.4)$$

From §16.4 this forecast can be interpreted as an estimate of the geometric mean of $X_{t+h} \sim L^d(\mu, \Sigma)$. It is sometimes useful to provide forecasts for the ratios $x_{i,t+h}/x_{j,t+h}$ and these are given by

$$\left(\frac{x_i}{x_j}\right)_t (h) = \exp\left(y_{i,t}(h) - y_{j,t}(h) + \frac{1}{2}\left(\sigma_{ii,t}(h) - 2\sigma_{ij,t}(h) + \sigma_{jj,t}(h)\right)\right)$$

where $y_{i,t}(h)$ and $y_{j,t}(h)$ are the ith and jth elements of $Y_t(h)$ and the $\sigma_{ij,t}(h)$ are the appropriate elements of $\Sigma_t(h)$.

Under the normality assumption for Y_t, a $100(1 - \alpha)\%$ confidence region for X_{t+h} can be formed from:

$$\left(Y_t(h) - \log\left(\frac{X_{t+h}^{(d)}}{X_{D,t+h}}\right)\right)'\Sigma_t^{-1}(h)\left(Y_t(h) - \log\left(\frac{X_{t+h}^{(d)}}{X_{D,t+h}}\right)\right) \le \chi_\alpha^2(d) \quad (16.5)$$

where $\chi_\alpha^2(d)$ is the $100\alpha\%$ point of a $\chi^2(d)$ distribution, by mapping points from $\mathcal{R}^d$ onto the simplex $\mathcal{S}^d$. Such a region, however, is probably only informative for $D \le 3$, where graphical representations such as the ternary diagram are available.

EXAMPLE 16.1 Forecasting Obesity Trends in England

Fig. 16.1 shows the percentage of English adults (16 + years of age) that are "not overweight" [body mass index (BMI) below 25], "overweight" (BMI between 25 and 30), and "obese" (BMI over 30) annually from 1993 to 2015.[3] In 1993, 47% of adults were not overweight, but this proportion has steadily declined by approximately ten percentage points over the subsequent two decades, while the percentage of obese adults has increased by the same amount, with the percentage of those being overweight, therefore, remaining roughly constant.

Because of the leading role that obesity plays in current health debates, forecasts of future obesity levels are clearly a principal factor in helping to inform public policy in this area. The three BMI categories form a time series composition of the type (16.1) with $D = 3$ and $T = 23$. Following the original analysis of Mills (2009), $x_{1,t}$, $x_{2,t}$, and $x_{3,t}$ were therefore defined to be the proportions "not overweight," "overweight," and "obese" and the log-ratios $y_{1,t} = \log(x_{1,t}/x_{3,t})$ and $y_{2,t} = \log(x_{2,t}/x_{3,t})$ were calculated using (16.3). These are shown in Fig. 16.2.

Given the nonlinear declines of these log-ratios, they were modeled as cubic polynomials in time as

$$y_{i,t} = \beta_{0,i} + \beta_{1,i}t + \beta_{2,i}t^2 + \beta_{3,i}t^3 + u_{i,t} \quad i = 1, 2$$

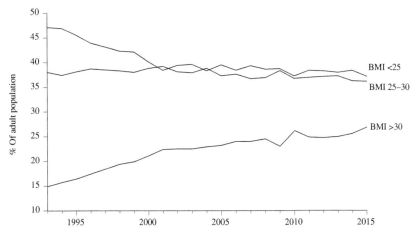

FIGURE 16.1   Percentage of English adults who are not overweight (BMI below 25), overweight (BMI between 25 and 30), and obese (BMI over 30): annually, 1993−2015. *BMI*, Body mass index.

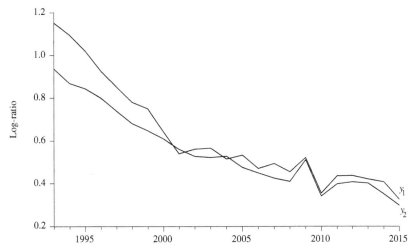

FIGURE 16.2   Log-ratios of BMI proportions, 1993−2015. *BMI*, Body mass index.

Here $u_{1,t}$ and $u_{2,t}$ are assumed to be serially uncorrelated zero-mean errors with covariance matrix

$$\Sigma = \begin{bmatrix} \sigma_1^2 & \sigma_{12} \\ \sigma_{12} & \sigma_2^2 \end{bmatrix}$$

h-step ahead forecasts of the log-ratios made at time T are, thus, given by

$$y_{i,T}(h) = \sum_{j=0}^{3} \beta_{j,i}(T+h)^j \quad i = 1, 2$$

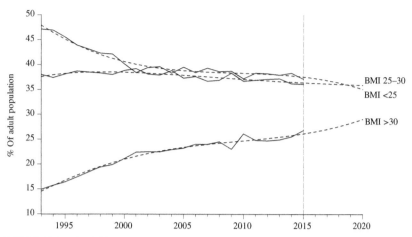

FIGURE 16.3 Fitted BMI proportions and forecasts out to 2020. *BMI,* Body mass index.

and forecasts of the proportions, $x_{i,T}(h)$, $i = 1, 2, 3$, are obtained using the inverse additive-logistic transformation (16.4).

The estimated log-ratio models are

$$y_{1,t} = \frac{1.314}{(0.039)} - \frac{0.1260}{(0.0137)}t + \frac{0.0065}{(0.0013)}t^2 - \frac{0.00012}{(0.00004)}t^3 + \hat{u}_{1,t}$$

$$R^2 = 0.977 \quad dw = 2.20$$

$$y_{2,t} = \frac{1.024}{(0.032)} - \frac{0.0754}{(0.0114)}t + \frac{0.0034}{(0.0011)}t^2 - \frac{0.00006}{(0.00003)}t^3 + \hat{u}_{2,t}$$

$$R^2 = 0.972 \quad dw = 2.45$$

with

$$\hat{\Sigma} = \begin{bmatrix} 0.001267 & 0.000772 \\ 0.000772 & 0.000884 \end{bmatrix}$$

The cubic trend specification is supported by the data, with all slope coefficients being significantly different from zero, the fits are good, and there is no indication of serial correlation in the residuals. Forecasts for 2016 to 2020 ($h = 1, \ldots, 5$) were then calculated and the fitted proportions and forecasts are shown in Fig. 16.3. In 2015, the proportions were $x_{1,2015} = 37.5$, $x_{2,2015} = 36.4$, and $x_{3,2015} = 26.1$; the forecasts for 2020 are $x_{1,2015}(5) = 35.1$, $x_{2,2015}(5) = 35.9$, and $x_{3,2015}(5) = 29.0$. Thus, the proportion of English adults "not overweight" is forecast to fall by a further 2.4 percentage points by 2020, while the proportion of "obese" adults is forecast to increase by 2.9 percentage points, with the proportion who are merely "overweight" is forecast to fall by the difference in these two numbers, that is, by 0.5 percentage points. Using (16.5) with $\chi^2_{0.05}(2) = 5.99$, 95% confidence limits for the 2020 forecasted proportions are calculated to be $23.2 < x_{1,2015}(5) < 47.5$, $22.3 < x_{2,2015}(5) < 51.7$, and $25.1 < x_{3,2015}(5) < 30.2$, so that although the forecast limits for the "not overweight" and "overweight" proportions are quite wide, those for the "obese" category are much tighter.

EXAMPLE 16.2 Modeling Expenditure Shares in the United Kingdom

We illustrate the modeling and forecasting of compositional time series using multivariate methods by analyzing the consumption (c), investment (i), government (g), and "other" (x) shares in the United Kingdom's gross final expenditure for the period 1955q1 to 2017q2 and providing forecasts of these shares out to 2020. The shares are shown in Fig. 1.11 and, after normalizing on the "other" category as the fill-up value, the additive log-ratios, $\log(c/x)$, $\log(i/x)$, and $\log(g/x)$, are shown in Fig. 16.4. Over the observation period consumption accounts for around half of final expenditure, with the remaining expenditure by 2017 being roughly accounted equally by the other three categories, although the size of these shares has fluctuated over time. The log-ratios all show consistent declines throughout the sample period and this (near) nonstationary behavior is confirmed by a fitted VAR(4) (with the trend included and order determined by information criteria), which has a largest autoregressive root of 0.98.

Consequently, we concentrate on a VAR(3) fitted to the log-ratio differences $\nabla\log(c/x)$, $\nabla\log(i/x)$ and $\nabla\log(g/x)$. At the end of the sample period, 2017q2, the expenditure shares stood at 48.9%, 12.9%, 14.7%, and 23.5% for c, i, g, and x, respectively. Using the fitted VAR, these shares were forecasted to be 48.0%, 12.6%, 14.0%, and 25.4% by the end of 2020. The increased share of "other" expenditure accompanied by the decreased shares of the other three expenditure categories clearly reflects the trends in expenditure shares seen at the end of the sample period.

Many of the coefficients in the fitted VAR(3) are insignificant, and this led, after some experimentation, to the following restricted model:

$$\nabla\log\left(\frac{c}{x}\right)_t = -\frac{0.155}{(0.040)}\nabla\log\left(\frac{c}{x}\right)_{t-3} + \hat{u}_{1,t}$$

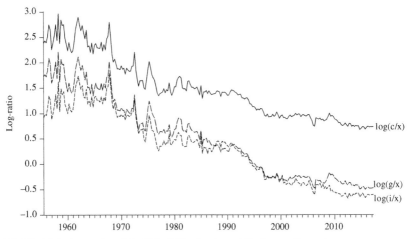

FIGURE 16.4 Log-ratios of the United Kingdom's total final expenditure shares.

$$\nabla\log\left(\frac{i}{x}\right)_t = -\frac{0.161}{(0.041)}\nabla\log\left(\frac{c}{x}\right)_{t-3} + \hat{u}_{2,t}$$

$$\nabla\log\left(\frac{g}{x}\right)_t = -\frac{0.163}{(0.065)}\nabla\log\left(\frac{c}{x}\right)_{t-2} - \frac{0.342}{(0.075)}\nabla\log\left(\frac{c}{x}\right)_{t-3}$$
$$+\frac{0.157}{(0.063)}\nabla\log\left(\frac{g}{x}\right)_{t-2} + \frac{0.183}{(0.083)}\nabla\log\left(\frac{g}{x}\right)_{t-3} + \hat{u}_{3,t}$$

The first equation shows that the growth rate of the consumption/other ratio is a pure autoregressive process, so that this ratio is exogenous. It does, however, "drive" the other two ratios with there being no evidence of any feedback between them. Modeling the log-ratios as a multivariate process, thus, produces a simple, yet rich, dynamic structure that emphasizes the interactions and driving forces existing between them.

TIME SERIES MODELS FOR COUNTS: THE IN-AR(1) BENCHMARK MODEL

16.8 Time series of small numbers of counts arise in various fields and typically consist of integer values, usually including zero, with a sample mean perhaps no higher than 10, making it inappropriate to treat the data as if it were continuous. We will focus here on the so-called *integer-valued ARMA* (IN-ARMA) models that provide an interesting class of discrete valued processes that are able to specify not only the dependence structure of the series of counts, but also enable a choice to be made between a wide class of (discrete) marginal distributions.[4]

16.9 The "benchmark" IN-AR(1) process is defined by the difference equation:

$$x_t = a \circ x_{t-1} + w_t \tag{16.6}$$

where the x_t, $t = 1, 2, \ldots$, take on values in the set of nonnegative integers, $\mathcal{N} = \{0, 1, 2, \ldots\}$. It is assumed that $0 \le a < 1$ and that w_t is a sequence of i.i.d. discrete random variables with mean $\mu_w > 0$ and variance $\sigma_w^2 > 0$: w_t is assumed to be stochastically independent of x_{t-1} for all t. The process (16.6) is stationary and the discreteness of x_t is ensured by the *binomial thinning operation*

$$a \circ x_{t-1} = \sum_{i=1}^{x_{t-1}} y_{i,t-1} \tag{16.7}$$

where the $y_{i,t-1}$ are assumed to be i.i.d. Bernoulli random variables with

$$P(y_{i,t-1} = 1) = a$$

and

$$P(y_{i,t-1} = 0) = 1 - a$$

Subsequent thinning operations are performed independently of each other with a constant probability a, so that thinning is to be regarded as a random operation with an associated probability distribution.

16.10   The unconditional moments of x_t are

$$E(x_t) = \frac{\mu_w}{(1-a)}$$

and

$$V(x_t) = \frac{(a\mu_w + \sigma_w^2)}{(1-a^2)}$$

while the conditional moments of x_t are

$$E(x_t|x_{t-1}) = ax_{t-1} + \mu_w$$

and

$$V(x_t|x_{t-1}) = a(1-a)x_{t-1} + \sigma_w^2$$

so that both are linear in x_{t-1}. The ACF of (16.6) is easily shown to be $\rho_k = a^k > 0$, $k = 1, 2, \ldots$, and is thus identical to that of a linear AR(1) process (cf. §3.10), with the qualification that only positive autocorrelation is permitted.

16.11   Of course, no distributional assumptions have been made so far. Since the Poisson (Po) distribution is a natural first choice in the analysis of counting processes, an obvious assumption to make is that $w_t \sim Po(\lambda)$ with $\lambda > 0$. From the properties of the Poisson distribution, it then follows that $\mu_w = \sigma_w^2 = \lambda$. The marginal distribution can then be shown to be $x_t \sim Po(\lambda/(1-a))$ and the resulting IN-AR(1) process with Poisson innovations may be denoted Po-IN-AR(1).

OTHER INTEGER-VALUED ARMA PROCESSES

16.12   The IN-MA(1) process is defined as

$$x_t = w_t + b \circ w_{t-1}$$

where $0 \le b < 1$ and the thinning operation is defined analogously to (16.7) as

$$b \circ w_{t-1} = \sum_{i=1}^{w_{t-1}} y_{i,t-1}$$

The autocorrelation function (ACF) of x_t is now

$$\rho_k = \begin{cases} \dfrac{b\sigma_w^2}{b(1-b)\mu_w + (1+b^2)\sigma_w^2} & \text{for} \quad k = 1 \\[2mm] 0 & \text{for} \quad k > 1 \end{cases} \qquad (16.8)$$

which is analogous to the linear MA(1) process (cf. §**3.12**). It is straightforward to show that $0 \le \rho_1 \le 0.5$ and that, if again $w_t \sim Po(\lambda)$, $x_t \sim Po(\lambda(1 + b))$ and the resulting process is Po-IN-MA(1).

16.13   A natural extension of (16.6) is to the IN-AR(2) process

$$x_t = a_1 \circ x_{t-1} + a_2 \circ x_{t-2} + w_t$$

where the thinning operations are analogous to (16.7) and, to ensure stationarity, we require that $a_1 + a_2 < 1$. The ACF of an IN-AR(2) process may be shown to be similar to that of a linear ARMA(2,1) and, indeed, a general IN-AR(p) process has an ACF similar to an ARMA($p,p - 1$).

If we assume again that $w_t \sim Po(\lambda)$, then it may be shown, on the assumption that a_1 and a_2 are independent of each other and of the past history of the process, that $x_t \sim Po\big(\lambda/(1 - a_1 - a_2)\big)$ and we have a Po-IN-AR(2) process. The ACF satisfies the second-order difference equation

$$\rho_k = a_1 \rho_{k-1} + a_2 \rho_{k-2}$$

for $k \ge 2$ with starting values $\rho_0 = 1$ and $\rho_1 = a_1$. This is different to the ACF of a linear AR(2) process (cf. §**3.18**) in that here ρ_1 depends solely on a_1 while higher order autocorrelations depend on both a_1 and a_2. If $a_2 < a_1 - a_1^2$ the ACF decays exponentially, whereas oscillatory behavior is found when $a_2 > a_1 - a_1^2$. If $a_2 = a_1 - a_1^2$ then $\rho_1 = \rho_2$. Jung and Tremayne (2003, Figs. 2 and 3) provide simulations and associated ACFs and PACFs for various Po-IN-AR(2) processes.

16.14   It is important to recognize that, under the Poisson assumption, the mean and variance of x_t are restricted to be equal. In time series of counts it is often the case that the (sample) variance is found to be greater than the (sample) mean, in which case the counts are said to be "over-dispersed." An assumption that captures such over-dispersion is that the innovations have a negative binomial (NB) distribution with parameters $n > 0$ and $0 < p < 1$, that is, $w_t \sim NB(n, p)$, for in this case:

$$E(w_t) = \frac{np}{(1 - p)} \qquad V(w_t) = \frac{np}{(1-p)^2} = \frac{E(w_t)}{(1 - p)} > E(w_t)$$

Although the resulting marginal distribution for x_t will not necessarily be NB, it will nevertheless continue to exhibit over-dispersion.

ESTIMATION OF INTEGER-VALUED ARMA MODELS

16.15   For the Po-IN-AR(1) model, the parameters a and λ must be estimated from the observed sample of counts $x_1, x_2, \ldots, x_T$. Jung et al. (2005: henceforth JRT) investigate the performance of various estimators of these parameters via a Monte Carlo simulation experiment. From their results, they recommend using a "bias-corrected" first-order sample autocorrelation to estimate a, viz., the "bias-corrected Yule-Walker" estimate (recall §**3.20**):

$$\hat{a} = \frac{1}{T-3}(Tr_1 + 1)$$

The estimate of λ is then based on the moment condition $E(x_t) = \lambda/(1-a)$:

$$\hat{\lambda} = (1-\hat{a})\bar{x}$$

By extension, the Yule-Walker estimates of a_1 and a_2 in the Po-IN-AR(2) model are given by (again see §**3.20**):

$$\hat{a}_1 = \frac{r_1(1-r_2)}{1-r_1^2} \quad \hat{a}_2 = \frac{r_2 - r_1^2}{1-r_1^2}$$

and it then follows that an estimate of λ is given by

$$\hat{\lambda}_2 = (1-\hat{a}_1 - \hat{a}_2)\bar{x}$$

Unfortunately, JRT's Monte Carlo experiments were restricted to first-order models so no bias-correction factor is available for the second-order model. JRT do, however, show that in cases of over-dispersion the bias-corrected Yule-Walker estimator still performs well and should continue to be used.

A Yule-Walker type estimate of b in the Po-IN-MA(1) model, obtained by solving (16.8) with $\mu_w = \sigma_w^2 = \lambda$, is $\hat{b} = r_1/(1-r_1)$ and, using the moment condition, this leads to $\hat{\lambda} = \bar{x}/\left(1 + \hat{b}\right)$.

16.16 Various estimators, ML-type estimators especially, have also been proposed for higher order IN-AR models, but these all require specialized routines and are, thus, not suitable for the general user.[5]

TESTING FOR SERIAL DEPENDENCE IN COUNT TIME SERIES

16.17 Before fitting a member of the IN-ARMA class of models it is important to establish the nature of the serial dependence, if any, in a time series of counts. After an extensive Monte Carlo simulation exercise, Jung and Tremayne (2003) suggest focusing attention on three tests. The first is the score test, $S^* = \sqrt{T}r_1 \sim N(0,1)$, under the null hypothesis of i.i.d. Poisson random variables, with a one-sided test being used that rejects the null for large values of the statistic. The other two tests are

$$Q_{acf}(1) = \frac{\hat{r}_2^2\left(\sum_{t=1}^T (x_t - \bar{x})^2\right)^2}{\sum_{t=3}^T (x_t - \bar{x})^2(x_{t-2} - \bar{x})^2}$$

and

$$Q_{pacf}(1) = \frac{\hat{\phi}_2^2 \left(\sum_{t=1}^{T} (x_t - \bar{x})^2 \right)^2}{\sum_{t=3}^{T} (x_t - \bar{x})^2 (x_{t-2} - \bar{x})^2}$$

where $\hat{\phi}_2$ is the second-order sample partial autocorrelation. Under the i.i.d. Poisson null hypothesis, these statistics are asymptotically distributed as $\chi^2(1)$. Note that the first-order sample autocorrelation and partial autocorrelation are, perhaps surprisingly, ignored in both statistics.

16.18 The testing strategy suggested by Jung and Tremayne (2003) is as follows. If none of the three statistics are significant then x_t may have no dependence structure, although this tentative conclusion should be tempered with the caveat that some higher order dependence, which is not readily detected by any of the tests, may be present. If both S^* and $Q_{acf}(1)$ reject but $Q_{pacf}(1)$ does not then an IN-AR(1) process may be tentatively determined, with an IN-MA(1) being indicated if the behavior of the two Q tests is interchanged. Finally, if the Q tests both reject but S^* does not, then a second-order model might be entertained.

EXAMPLE 16.3 IN-AR Models for Hurricane and Storm Counts

Fig. 1.12 shows the annual number of North Atlantic storms and hurricanes (the latter being a subset of the former) between 1851 and 2017. The annual number of storms ranges from a minimum of one (in 1914) to a maximum of 28 in 2015; that year also saw the maximum number of hurricanes, 15, while there were no hurricanes in either 1907 or 1914. The two series are clearly examples of small count time series and hence may be amenable to fitting by IN-ARMA models.

A necessary first step is to ascertain whether the series contain any serial dependencies. For the hurricane count, the first two sample autocorrelations are $r_1 = 0.118$ and $r_2 = 0.088$ and the second-order partial autocorrelation is $\hat{\phi}_2 = 0.055$. With $T = 167$ the three test statistics for serial dependence are $S^* = 1.53$, $Q_{acf}(1) = 1.45$, and $Q_{pacf}(1) = 0.56$, none of which are close to being significant. We, therefore, conclude that there is no serial dependence in annual hurricane counts which may, in turn, be regarded as an i.i.d. sequence. Since the mean number of hurricanes per year is 5.43 with a variance of 6.46 there is some indication of over-dispersion, but a standard goodness-of-fit test cannot reject the hypothesis that annual hurricane counts follow an independent Poisson process with a mean and variance of 5.4.

For the storm count we have $r_1 = 0.384$, $r_2 = 0.300$, and $\hat{\phi}_2 = 0.179$, which produce $S^* = 4.96$, $Q_{acf}(1) = 12.49$, and $Q_{pacf}(1) = 4.45$; all of which are significant at the 5% level. Since, however, $Q_{pacf}(1)$ is insignificant at the 2.5% level but $Q_{acf}(1)$ is significant, we choose to model the series as an IN-AR process. For the IN-AR(1) process the parameters are estimated to be $\hat{a} = 0.397$ and $\hat{\lambda} = 5.78$, while the IN-AR(2) process has estimates $\hat{a}_1 = 0.315$, $\hat{a}_2 = 0.179$ and $\hat{\lambda}_2 = 4.85$. Thus, storm counts clearly have a dependence structure that can be modeled as a low-order IN-AR process, although it is important to note that since $\hat{a}_1 + \hat{a}_2 = 0.494$, this process is nowhere near the nonstationary boundary so that there is no evidence of a time-changing mean. The mean number of storms is, in fact, 9.59 with variance 17.48 so here there is more evidence of over-dispersion and, hence, less chance of the process being Poisson.

Informal evidence on the adequacy of these models is provided by examining their residuals, defined, respectively, as

$$\hat{w}_{1,t} = x_t - \hat{a}x_{t-1} - \hat{\lambda}$$

and

$$\hat{w}_{2,t} = x_t - \hat{a}_1 x_{t-1} - \hat{a}_2 x_{t-2} - \hat{\lambda}_2$$

These residuals will, of course, rarely be integer values, but they can provide a rough check of model adequacy if their SACFs and PACFs are examined. For example, the first four sample autocorrelations of $\hat{w}_{1,t}$ are -0.08, 0.12, 0.11, and -0.04, while those for $\hat{w}_{2,t}$ are -0.02, -0.04, 0.01, and -0.07, thus suggesting that the second-order process leaves fewer dependencies in the data.

FORECASTING COUNTS

16.19   The approach to forecasting taken in Chapter 7, An Introduction to Forecasting with Univariate Models, is based on the conditional expectation, that is,

$$f_{T,h} = E(x_{T+h}|x_T, x_{T-1}, \ldots, x_1)$$

and is known to yield MMSE forecasts (cf. §**7.2**). The conditional expectation of the IN-AR(1) model is given in §**16.10**, so that

$$f_{T,1} = ax_T + \mu_w$$

$$f_{T,2} = af_{T,1} + \mu_w = a^2 x_T + (1 + a)\mu_w$$

and

$$f_{T,h} = a^h x_T + \left(1 + a + a^2 + \cdots + a^{h-1}\right)\mu_w \tag{16.9}$$

Since $0 \le a < 1$ the forecasts converge as $h \to \infty$ to the unconditional mean $E(x_t) = \mu_w/(1 - a)$. Despite this optimality property, forecasting based on (16.9) is beset by the problem that forecasts so obtained will be real, rather than integer, valued except in very rare cases. Of course, integer-valued forecasts may be readily obtained by, for example, the simple expedient of rounding to the nearest integer, but this rather crude solution prevents proper forecast intervals being obtained and it is not immediately obvious how forecast values should be incorporated when $h > 1$. Jung and Tremayne (2006) suggest a simple, albeit ad hoc, way of acknowledging the arbitrary nature of the rounding procedure. This is to apportion probabilities to the integers on either side of the incoherent real value in proportion to the distances from either end of that unit interval.

16.20 Such forecasting methods readily extend to the IN-AR(2) model but, not surprisingly, there have been attempts to develop a more sophisticated approach to constructing coherent forecasts. Freeland and McCabe (2004) show that the median has the optimality property of minimizing the expected absolute forecast error and suggest that the entire h-step ahead (conditional) forecast distribution should be computed. This has the following (fairly) tractable expression for the IN-AR(1) model under a Poisson innovation assumption:

$$p_h(x|x_T) = x_T! \exp\left(-\lambda\left(\frac{(1-a^h)}{(1-a)}\right)\right) C_h(x_T, x) \quad x = 0, 1, 2, \dots \quad (16.10)$$

where

$$C_h(x_T, x) = \sum_{k=0}^{m} \frac{a^{kh}(1-a^h)^{x_T-k} \lambda^{x-k}}{k!(x-k)!(|x_T-k|)!} \quad m = min(x_T, x)$$

For higher order models, numerical techniques are required to compute the forecast distribution $p_h(x|x_T)$.

EXAMPLE 16.4 Forecasting Storm Counts

Forecasts of storm counts from the IN-AR(1) model are obtained from

$$f_{2017,h} = 0.397^h x_{2017} + \left(1 + 0.397 + \cdots + 0.397^{h-1}\right) \times 5.78$$

on using $\hat{\mu}_w = (1 - \hat{a})\bar{x}$. With $x_{2017} = 17$, the forecasted number of storms for 2018 is

$$f_{2017,1} = 0.397 \times 17 + 5.78 = 12.53$$

i.e., using the ad hoc approach of Jung and Tremayne (2006) there is a 53% probability that the number of storms in 2018 will be 13 and a 47% probability that the number will be 12. To compute the forecast for 2019 we could use:

$$f_{2017,2} = 0.397^2 \times 17 + 1.397 \times 5.78 = 0.397 \times 12.53 + 5.78 = 10.75$$

Equally, we could use:

$$f_{2017,2}|(f_{2017,1} = 12) = 0.397 \times 12 + 5.78 = 10.54$$

or

$$f_{2017,2}|(f_{2017,1} = 13) = 0.397 \times 13 + 5.78 = 10.94$$

Using the former forecast there is, thus, a 25% probability of the number of storms being 10 in 2019 and a 75% probability of there being 11. Using the latter pair of forecasts there is a $0.47 \times 0.46 + 0.53 \times 0.06 = 25\%$ probability of the number of storms being 10 and $0.47 \times 0.54 + 0.53 \times 0.94 = 75\%$ probability of there being 11.

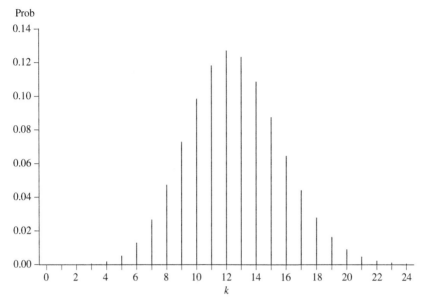

FIGURE 16.5   Forecast probability distributionof storm counts for 2018 ($h = 1$).

The drawback to this approach is that all the probability mass of the forecast distribution is concentrated on just two values, here 12 and 13 for $h = 1$ and 10 and 11 for $h = 2$. Computation of the entire forecast probability distribution using (16.10) would, therefore, seem to have an advantage in providing the complete set of probabilities although a Poisson model must be assumed. Fig. 16.5 provides the distribution for one-step ahead forecasts from the IN-AR(1) model. The probability mass is much less concentrated with there now being a 70% probability of observing a storm count in the range 11 to 16 in 2018. Freeland and McCabe (2004, Theorem 1) show that the mean and variance of the distribution at horizon h are given by

$$\overline{f}_{T,h} = a^h x_T + \lambda \frac{(1 - a^h)}{(1 - a)}$$

and

$$\sigma^2\left(f_{T,h}\right) = a^h\left(1 - a^h\right)x_T + \lambda \frac{(1 - a^h)}{(1 - a)}$$

respectively. $\overline{f}_{T,h}$ is thus given by the formula used above to produce the point forecasts for $h = 1$ and 2; the standard deviations are $\sigma\left(f_{2017,1}\right) = 3.14$ and $\sigma\left(f_{2017,2}\right) = 3.21$.

INTERMITTENT AND NONNEGATIVE TIME SERIES

16.21 When a count series contains many zeros, it is sometimes referred to as being *intermittent*, as when a stock inventory is only occasionally demanded. Traditionally, "intermittent demand forecasting" has used variants of Croston's (1972) original model in which simple exponential smoothing (cf. §§9.14–9.17) is applied to both the size of the demand and the time between demands.

The stochastic models underlying Croston's approach have been investigated by Shenstone and Hyndman (2005), who found that the implied models were inconsistent with the properties of intermittent demand data, for they must be nonstationary and defined on a continuous sample space which may contain negative values—recall from §9.15 the equivalence of simple exponential smoothing and the ARIMA(0,1,1) process. This creates difficulties when constructing forecast distributions and prediction intervals. Consequently, Shenstone and Hyndman (2005) suggest that count-type models should also be suitable for intermittent demand forecasting.

16.22 General nonnegative time series, in which the integer-value restriction is removed, have been analyzed by Bartlett and McCormick (2012, 2013), who consider ARMA models with non-Gaussian, heavy-tailed innovations, typically taken from the Pareto class of distributions. For example, they investigate the AR(1) model $x_t = \phi x_{t-1} + z_t$, where z_t is a nonnegative random variable with "regular variation" at both the right end-point of infinity and the unknown left end-point $\theta > 0$, known as the location parameter. The estimators they propose are $\hat{\phi}_{min} = \min_{1 \le t \le T}(x_t/x_{t-1})$ and $\hat{\theta}_{min} = \min_{1 \le t \le T}(x_t - \hat{\phi}_{min}x_{t-1})$, and simulation experiments show that these perform well.

EXAMPLE 16.5 A Nonnegative AR(1) Model for Storm Counts

The estimates of a nonnegative AR(1) model fitted to the storm count series were $\hat{\phi}_{min} = 0.167$ and $\hat{\theta}_{min} = 0.00004$. The estimate of the autoregressive parameter is rather smaller than that from the IN-AR(1) model fitted in Example 16.3, but the estimate of the location parameter is very close to zero, which, of course, is certainly the lower bound to storm counts but was never actually reached during the sample period (as mentioned in that example, the minimum count was one in 1914).

ENDNOTES

1. Compositional datasets clearly may contain either time series or cross-sectional observations, but obviously the focus is on the former here. Aitchison (2003) is the key textbook on the general subject of compositional data while Brunsdon and Smith (1998) is a seminal paper on compositional time series. Mills (2007) provides a concise survey of compositional data with economic applications.

2. Note that when $d = 1$, $a_1(\cdot)$ is the univariate logistic transformation $y = log(x/(1 - x))$, whose time series application is considered in Wallis (1987).

3. The BMI, defined as the ratio of weight (in kg) to height (in cm) squared, is the most popular measure of obesity used in official data of the type used here, which was provided by the Health Survey of England.

4. IN-ARMA models were initially introduced by Al-Osh and Alzaid (1987, 1988), Alzaid and Al-Osh (1990) and McKenzie (1988). Our development of these models follows that of Jung and Tremayne (2003) and Jung et al. (2005).

5. Bu et al. (2008) consider ML estimation of IN-AR(p) processes, while other efficient estimators of this model have been analyzed by Drost et al. (2008).

Chapter 17

State Space Models

Chapter Outline

FORMULATING STATE SPACE MODELS

17.1 Many time series models can be cast in *state space form* (SSF), and this enables a unified framework of analysis to be presented within which, for example, the differences and similarities of the alternative models may be assessed.

The state space model for a univariate time series x_t consists of both a *measurement equation* (alternatively known as the *signal* or *observation equation*) and a *transition equation* (alternatively *state equation*: see, e.g., Harvey, 1989, Chapters 3 and 4; Hamilton, 1994, Chapter 13; or Durbin and Koopman, 2012, for full textbook treatments). Although there are various specifications of the SSF, a popular version has the measurement equation taking the form:

$$x_t = z_t'\alpha_t + d_t + \varepsilon_t \quad t = 1, 2, \ldots, T \tag{17.1}$$

Here z_t is an $m \times 1$ vector, d_t is a scalar, and ε_t is a serially uncorrelated error with $E(\varepsilon_t) = 0$ and $V(\varepsilon_t) = h_t$. In general, the elements of the $m \times 1$ *state vector* α_t are unobservable, but are assumed to be generated by the transition equation

$$\alpha_t = T_t\alpha_{t-1} + c_t + R_t\eta_t \tag{17.2}$$

in which T_t and R_t are $m \times m$ and $m \times g$ matrices, respectively, c_t is an $m \times 1$ vector and η_t is a $g \times 1$ vector of serially uncorrelated errors with $E(\eta_t) = 0$ and $V(\eta_t) = Q_t$, a $g \times g$ covariance matrix.

Applied Time Series Analysis. DOI: https://doi.org/10.1016/B978-0-12-813117-6.00017-X
299

The specification of the state space system is completed by two further assumptions:

1. The initial state α_0 has mean vector $E(\alpha_0) = a_0$ and covariance matrix $V(\alpha_0) = P_0$; and
2. The errors ε_t and η_t are uncorrelated with each other in all time periods and uncorrelated with the initial state, that is,

$$E(\varepsilon_t \eta_s') = 0 \quad \text{for all } s, t = 1, \ldots, T$$

and

$$E(\varepsilon_t \alpha_0') = 0 \quad E(\eta_t \alpha_0') = 0 \quad \text{for all } t = 1, \ldots, T$$

17.2   The variables z_t, d_t, and h_t in the measurement equation (17.1) and T_t, c_t, R_t, and Q_t in the transition equation (17.2) are referred to generically as the *system matrices*. They are typically assumed to be nonstochastic so that, although they may change with time, they do so in a way that is predetermined. Consequently, the system is linear so that, for any t, x_t can be expressed as a linear combination of present and past ε_t's and η_t's and the initial state vector α_0.

If the system matrices do not change over time, the model is said to be *time-invariant* or *time-homogeneous*, a special case of which are stationary models.

17.3   On first sight, the state space model seems to have little connection with the range of time series models that have been introduced throughout the book. This lack of connection is illusory, however, as the following illustrations reveal:

1. The AR(2) process $x_t = \phi_0 + \phi_1 x_{t-1} + \phi_2 x_{t-2} + \eta_t$ has, on defining the state vector as

$$\alpha_t = \begin{bmatrix} x_t \\ \phi_2 x_{t-1} \end{bmatrix}$$

the SSF

$$x_t = \begin{bmatrix} 1 & 0 \end{bmatrix} \alpha_t + \phi_0$$

$$\alpha_t = \begin{bmatrix} \phi_1 & 1 \\ \phi_2 & 0 \end{bmatrix} \alpha_{t-1} + \begin{bmatrix} 1 \\ 0 \end{bmatrix} \eta_t$$

i.e., the system matrices are, with $m = 2$ and $g = 1$, so that $\eta_t = \eta_t$,

$$z_t' = R_t' = \begin{bmatrix} 1 & 0 \end{bmatrix} \quad d_t = \phi_0 \quad h_t = 0 \quad c_t' = \begin{bmatrix} 0 & 0 \end{bmatrix}$$

$$T_t = \begin{bmatrix} \phi_1 & 1 \\ \phi_2 & 0 \end{bmatrix}$$

Alternatively, we could define

$$\alpha_t^* = \begin{bmatrix} x_t \\ x_{t-1} \end{bmatrix}$$

and the SSF

$$x_t = \begin{bmatrix} 1 & 0 \end{bmatrix} \alpha_t^* + \phi_0$$

$$\alpha_t^* = \begin{bmatrix} \phi_1 & \phi_2 \\ 1 & 0 \end{bmatrix} \alpha_{t-1}^* + \begin{bmatrix} 1 \\ 0 \end{bmatrix} \eta_t$$

2. The MA(1) process $x_t = \eta_t + \theta\eta_{t-1}$ has SSF

$$x_t = \begin{bmatrix} 1 & 0 \end{bmatrix} \alpha_t$$

$$\alpha_t = \begin{bmatrix} 0 & 1 \\ 0 & 0 \end{bmatrix} \alpha_{t-1} + \begin{bmatrix} 1 \\ \theta \end{bmatrix} \eta_t$$

on defining $\alpha_t = \begin{bmatrix} x_t & \theta\eta_{t-1} \end{bmatrix}'$.

3. Consequently, the general ARMA(p,q) process, written in the form:

$$x_t = \phi_1 x_{t-1} + \cdots + \phi_m x_{t-m} + \eta_t + \theta_1\eta_{t-1} + \cdots + \theta_{m-1}\eta_{t-m+1}$$

where $m = \max(p, q + 1)$, has the SSF

$$x_t = \begin{bmatrix} 1 & \mathbf{0}_{m-1}' \end{bmatrix} \alpha_t$$

$$\alpha_t = \begin{bmatrix} \phi_1 & \vdots & & \\ \phi_2 & \vdots & & \\ \vdots & \vdots & \mathbf{I}_{m-1} & \\ \phi_{m-1} & \vdots & & \\ \cdots & \cdots & \cdots & \\ \phi_m & \vdots & \mathbf{0}_{m-1}' & \end{bmatrix} \alpha_{t-1} + \begin{bmatrix} 1 \\ \theta_1 \\ \vdots \\ \theta_{m-1} \end{bmatrix} \eta_t$$

17.4 Other models discussed in earlier chapters may also be cast in SSF form. The Muth/simple exponential smoothing model (cf. §8.1 and §9.15), when written in the notation of this chapter, viz.,

$$x_t = \alpha_t + \varepsilon_t \quad E(\varepsilon_t) = 0 \quad V(\varepsilon_t) = h$$

$$\alpha_t = \alpha_{t-1} + \eta_t \quad E(\eta_t) = 0 \quad V(\eta_t) = q = \kappa h$$

is seen to be an SSF with $m = g = 1$, $d_t = c_t = 0$ and $z_t = T_t = R_t = 1$.

Similarly, the Holt–Winters local linear trend model of §9.17 can be written as:

$$x_t = \alpha_{1,t} + \varepsilon_t$$

$$\alpha_{1,t} = \alpha_{1,t-1} + \alpha_{2,t-1} + \eta_{2,t}$$

$$\alpha_{2,t} = \alpha_{2,t-1} + \eta_{3,t}$$

and is in SSF form with $m = g = 2$, $z_t = \begin{bmatrix} 1 & 0 \end{bmatrix}$, $R_t = I_2$ and

$$T_t = \begin{bmatrix} 1 & 1 \\ 0 & 1 \end{bmatrix}$$

17.5 These illustrations make it clear that the SSF enables a wide variety of models to be specified in a coherent framework, so emphasizing their essential similarities and differences. It should be emphasized, however, that the definition of the state vector α_t for any specific model is determined by construction and, consequently, may not be able to be identified with components which have a substantive interpretation, such as a trend or a seasonal. The SSF aims to set up α_t in such a way that it contains all the relevant information on the system at time t using as few elements as possible.

17.6 As can be seen from the two SSFs given for the AR(2) process in example (1) of §**17.3**, there is not necessarily a unique SSF representation for any particular model: indeed, a unique representation is the exception rather than the rule. This can be seen easily by defining an arbitrary nonsingular $m \times m$ matrix B and considering a new state vector $\alpha_t^* = B\alpha_t$. Premultiplying the original transition equation (17.2) by B yields:

$$\alpha_t^* = T_t^* \alpha_{t-1}^* + c_t^* + R_t^* \eta_t$$

where $T_t^* = BT_t B^{-1}$, $c_t^* = Bc_t$ and $R_t^* = BR_t$. The corresponding measurement equation is then

$$x_t = z_t^{*\prime} \alpha_t^* + d_t + \varepsilon_t$$

where $z_t^{*\prime} = z_t' B^{-1}$. Thus, the two SSFs for the AR(2) process are connected by

$$B = \begin{bmatrix} 1 & 0 \\ 0 & \phi_2^{-1} \end{bmatrix}$$

17.7 The transition equation (17.2) is sometimes shifted forward one period to become

$$\alpha_{t+1} = T_t \alpha_t + c_t + R_t \eta_t \tag{17.3}$$

While in practice it makes little difference whether (17.2) or (17.3) is used in conjunction with (17.1), it does have an impact when assumption (2) of §**17.1** is relaxed to allow the errors in the measurement and transition equations to be correlated.

THE KALMAN FILTER

17.8 Once a model has been put into state space form, several important algorithms may be applied. Central to these is the *Kalman (−Bucy) filter*. The Kalman filter is a recursive procedure for computing the optimal estimate of the state vector at time t, based on the information available at that time, which consists of all the observations up to and including x_t.[1] The system matrices, together with the initial values a_0 and P_0, are assumed to be known for all t and so do not need to be included explicitly in the information set.

17.9 The derivation of the Kalman filter rests on the assumption that the errors and the initial state vector are normally distributed. It is then possible to calculate recursively the distribution of α_t, conditional on the information set at time t, for all $t = 1, \ldots, T$. These conditional distributions are themselves normal and so are completely specified by their means and covariance matrices, which are the quantities that the Kalman filter computes.[2]

  The mean of the conditional distribution of α_t is the MMSE estimator of α_t. If the normality assumption is dropped then there is no longer any guarantee that the Kalman filter will give the conditional mean of the state vector. However, it will still provide an optimal estimator in the sense that it will minimize the MSE within the class of all linear estimators.

17.10 Consider, then, the state space model of (17.1) and (17.2). Let a_{t-1} be the optimal estimator of α_{t-1} based on observations up to and including x_{t-1}, that is, $a_{t-1} = E_{t-1}(\alpha_{t-1}|x_{t-1})$, where $x_{t-1} = \{x_{t-1}, x_{t-2}, \ldots, x_1\}$, and let

$$P_{t-1} = E(\alpha_{t-1} - a_{t-1})(\alpha_{t-1} - a_{t-1})'$$

be the $m \times m$ covariance matrix of the estimation error. Given a_{t-1} and P_{t-1}, the optimal estimators of α_t and P_t are given by:

$$a_{t|t-1} = T_t a_{t-1} + c_t \tag{17.4}$$

and

$$P_{t|t-1} = T_t P_{t-1} T_t' + R_t Q_t R_t' \tag{17.5}$$

  These two recursions are known as the *prediction equations*. Once the new observation x_t becomes available, the estimator of α_t, $a_{t|t-1}$, can be updated. The *updating equations* are:

$$a_t = a_{t|t-1} + P_{t|t-1} z_t f_t^{-1} \left(x_t - z_t' a_{t|t-1} - d_t \right) \tag{17.6}$$

and

$$P_t = P_{t|t-1} - P_{t|t-1} z_t f_t^{-1} z_t' P_{t|t-1} \tag{17.7}$$

where

$$f_t = z_t' P_{t|t-1} z_t + h_t \tag{17.8}$$

Taken together, Eqs. (17.4–17.8) make up the Kalman filter. These equations may also be written as

$$a_{t+1|t} = \left(T_{t+1} - K_t z_t'\right) a_{t|t-1} + K_t x_t + c_{t+1} - K_t d_t \tag{17.9}$$

where the $m \times 1$ gain vector K_t is given by

$$K_t = T_{t+1} P_{t|t-1} z_t f_t^{-1}$$

The recursion for the error covariance matrix, known as the *Riccati equation*, is

$$P_{t+1|t} = T_{t+1} \left(P_{t|t-1} - f_t^{-1} P_{t|t-1} z_t z_t' P_{t|t-1}\right) T_{t+1}' + R_{t+1} Q_{t+1} R_{t+1}'$$

17.11 The starting values for the Kalman filter may be specified either in terms of a_0 and P_0 or $a_{1|0}$ and $P_{1|0}$. Given these initial conditions, the Kalman filter will deliver the optimal estimate of the state vector as each new observation becomes available. When all T observations have been processed, the filter yields optimal estimates of the current state vector, a_T, from (17.6), and the subsequent state vector, $a_{T+1|T}$, from (17.9). This estimate contains all the information needed to make optimal predictions of future values of both the state, $\alpha_{T+1}, \ldots$, and the observations, $x_{T+1}, \ldots$.

EXAMPLE 17.1 The Muth Model and the Kalman Filter

Consider, again, the Muth model

$$x_t = \alpha_t + \varepsilon_t \quad E(\varepsilon_t) = 0 \quad V(\varepsilon_t) = h$$

$$\alpha_t = \alpha_{t-1} + \eta_t \quad E(\eta_t) = 0 \quad V(\eta_t) = q = \kappa h$$

Since $m = 1$, the Kalman filter (17.9) becomes

$$a_{t+1|t} = (1 - k_t) a_{t|t-1} + k_t x_t$$

where the gain is

$$k_t = \frac{p_{t|t-1}}{\left(p_{t|t-1} + 1\right)}$$

and

$$p_{t+1|t} = p_{t|t-1} - \frac{p_{t|t-1}^2}{(1 + p_{t|t-1})} + \kappa$$

$$= \frac{p_{t|t-1}}{\left(p_{t|t-1} + 1\right)} + \kappa = k_t + \kappa$$

As it stands, the model does not explicitly specify any initial conditions. Setting $p_{1|0} = \varrho$, where ϱ is a positive number, would give the first set of recursions as:

$$a_{2|1} = \left(1 - \frac{\varrho}{(1 + \varrho)}\right) a_{1|0} + \frac{\varrho}{(1 + \varrho)} x_1$$

$$= \frac{1}{(1 + \varrho)} a_{1|0} + \frac{\varrho}{(1 + \varrho)} x_1$$

and

$$p_{2|1} = \varrho - \frac{\varrho^2}{(1 + \varrho)} + \kappa = \frac{\varrho}{(1 + \varrho)} + \kappa$$

However, if the random walk process for α_t started at some point in the remote past then $p_{1|0}$ should be infinity. Hence, as $\varrho \to \infty$, $a_{2|1} = x_1$ irrespective of the value of $a_{1|0}$, while $p_{2|1} = 1 + \kappa$.

The Kalman filter remains valid even if h or κ is zero. If $h = 0$ then there is no measurement error and the model is a pure random walk. If $\kappa = 0$, so that the mean is fixed at α, say, then

$$p_{t+1|t} = \frac{p_{t|t-1}}{p_{t|t-1} + 1}$$

Since now $p_{2|1} = 1$, it follows that $p_{3|2} = 1/2$, $p_{4|3} = 1/3$, and, in general, $p_{t+1|t} = 1/t$. The recursion for the estimator of the mean is, therefore:

$$a_{t+1|t} = \left(\frac{t-1}{t}\right) a_{t|t-1} + \frac{1}{t} x_t$$

The MMSE of α is, thus, the sample mean based on the first t observations and the MSE is h/t.

ML ESTIMATION AND THE PREDICTION ERROR DECOMPOSITION

17.12 The system matrices may depend on a set of unknown parameters, as with the ARMA process whose SSF was given in §**17.3**. The parameters may be denoted by an $n \times 1$ vector ψ and will be referred to as the *hyperparameters* of the SSF. These hyperparameters may be estimated by ML, the classical theory of which is based on the T observations $x_1, \ldots, x_T$ being i.i.d. This allows the joint density function of the observations to be written as:

$$\mathcal{L}(x : \psi) = \prod_{t=1}^{T} p(x_t) \tag{17.10}$$

where $x' = (x_1, \ldots, x_T)$ and $p(x_t)$ is the probability density function of x_t. Once the observations have become available, $\mathcal{L}(x : \psi)$ is reinterpreted as a likelihood function and the ML estimator is found by maximizing this function with respect to ψ.

17.13 Clearly, the principal characteristic of a time series model is that the observations are not independent so that (17.10) is not directly applicable. Instead, the definition of a conditional probability density function must be used to write the joint density as:

$$\mathcal{L}(x:\psi) = \prod_{t=1}^{T} p(x_t|x_{t-1}) \tag{17.11}$$

where $p(x_t|x_{t-1})$ denotes the distribution of x_t conditional on the information set available at time $t-1$.

If the errors and initial state vector in (17.1) are normally distributed, then the distribution of x_t, conditional on x_{t-1}, will itself be normal, with the mean and variance of this conditional distribution being given by the Kalman filter. Conditional on x_{t-1}, α_t is normally distributed with mean $a_{t|t-1}$ and covariance matrix $P_{t|t-1}$. If the measurement equation is written as:

$$x_t = z_t' a_{t|t-1} + z_t'\left(\alpha_t - a_{t|t-1}\right) + d_t + \varepsilon_t$$

then the conditional distribution of x_t is normal with mean

$$E_{t-1}(x_t) = \hat{x}_{t|t-1} = z_t' a_{t|t-1} + d_t$$

and variance f_t. The likelihood function (17.11) can then be written immediately as

$$\log\mathcal{L} = \ell = -\frac{T}{2}\log 2\pi - \frac{1}{2}\sum_{t=1}^{T} f_t - \frac{1}{2}\sum_{t=1}^{T} v_t^2/f_t \tag{17.12}$$

where $v_t = x_t - \hat{x}_{t|t-1}$ is the *prediction error*, so that (17.12) is also known as the *prediction error decomposition* form of the likelihood function.

17.14 The log-likelihood (17.12) may be computed and then maximized with respect to the unknown hyperparameters ψ, which will usually be carried out by utilizing some form of numerical optimization procedure. Suppose that $\hat{\psi}$ is the ML estimator and define the *information matrix* as $I(\psi) = P_T^{-1}$. Suppose that $I(\psi)$ converges to a positive definite matrix $I_A(\psi)$ when divided by T, that is, $I_A(\psi) = \text{plim } T^{-1}I(\psi)$. Subject to certain regularity conditions, $\sqrt{T}\left(\hat{\psi} - \psi\right)$ has a limiting multivariate normal distribution with a mean vector of zero and covariance matrix $I_A^{-1}(\psi)$: equivalently, $\hat{\psi}$ is said to be asymptotically normal with mean ψ and covariance matrix $T^{-1}I_A^{-1}(\psi)$.

PREDICTION AND SMOOTHING

17.15 Applying the Kalman filter to (17.1) and (17.2) yields a_T, the MMSE of α_T, based on all T observations. In addition, it gives:

$$a_{T+1|T} = T_{T+1}a_T + c_{T+1} \tag{17.13}$$

together with the one-step ahead prediction

$$\hat{x}_{T+1|T} = z'_{T+1}a_{T+1|T} + d_{T+1}$$

We may also consider the problem of multistep prediction, that of making predictions of future observations at times $T + 2$, $T + 3, \dots$. Extending (17.13) by substituting repeatedly into the transition equation at time $T + l$ and taking conditional expectations at time T yields

$$a_{T+l|T} = \left[\prod_{j=1}^{l} T_{T+j}\right]a_T + \sum_{j=1}^{l-1}\left[\prod_{i=j+1}^{l} T_{T+i}\right]c_{T+j} + c_{T+l}$$

The MMSE of x_{T+l} is then obtained directly from $a_{T+l|T}$ as

$$\hat{x}_{T+l} = z'_{T+l}a_{T+l|T} + d_{T+l} \tag{17.14}$$

with the accompanying MSE

$$\mathrm{MSE}\left(\hat{x}_{T+l|T}\right) = z'_{T+l}P_{T+l|T}z_{T+l} + h_{T+l} \tag{17.15}$$

The easiest way to calculate $a_{T+l|T}$ and $P_{T+l|t}$, which are required to evaluate (17.14) and (17.15), is to repeatedly apply the Kalman filter prediction equations (17.4) and (17.5) to obtain

$$a_{T+l|T} = T_{T+l}a_{T+l-1|T} + c_{T+l}$$

and

$$P_{T+l|T} = T_{T+l}P_{T+l-1|T}T'_{T+l} + R_{T+l}Q_{T+l}R'_{T+l}$$

17.16 Note that the $P_{T+l|T}$ matrices do not include errors which arise from estimating any unknown parameters in the system matrices, so that (17.15) will underestimate the true MSE because it does not incorporate the extra variation due to using $\hat{\psi}$ rather than the true ψ.

17.17 While the aim of filtering is to find the expected value of the state vector, α_t, conditional on the information available at time t, that is, $a_{t|t} = E(\alpha_t|x_t)$, the aim of *smoothing* is to take account of the information available *after* time t. This will produce the *smoothed estimator* $a_{t|T} = E(\alpha_t|x_T)$ and, since it is based on more information than the filtered estimator, it will have an MSE which cannot be greater than that of the filtered estimator.

17.18   While there are several forms of smoothing, attention is concentrated here on *fixed-interval smoothing*. This is an algorithm that consists of a set of recursions which start with the final quantities, a_T and P_T, given by the Kalman filter and work backward. These equations are:

$$a_{t|T} = a_T + P_t^*\left(a_{t+1|T} - T_{t+1}a_t\right)$$

and

$$P_{t|T} = P_t + P_t^*\left(P_{t+1|T} - P_{t+1|T}\right)P_t^{*\prime}$$

where

$$P_t^* = P_t T_{t+1}' P_{t+1|t}^{-1} \quad t = T - 1, \ldots, 1$$

with $a_{T|T} = a_T$ and $P_{T|T} = P_T$.

EXAMPLE 17.2 Prediction and Smoothing in the Muth Model

From (17.13) and (17.14) it follows immediately that

$$\hat{x}_{T+l|T} = a_T \quad l = 1, 2, \ldots$$

The set of predictions, therefore, fall on a horizontal line which passes through the final estimator of the level of the process. The accompanying MSEs, conditional on κ, are:

$$\mathrm{MSE}\left(\hat{x}_{T+l|T}\right) = \left(p_T + l\kappa + 1\right)h$$

and so increase linearly with the horizon l.

Noting that $p_t^* = p_t / \left(p_t + \kappa\right)$, it follows that

$$a_{t|T} = \left(1 - p_t^*\right)a_t + p_t^* a_{t+1|t} \quad t = T - 1, \ldots, 1$$

The smoothed estimator at time t is, thus, a simple weighted moving average of the smoothed estimator at time $t + 1$ and the filtered estimator at time t. If p_t^* is constant, then $a_{t|T}$ is similar in form to the exponentially weighted moving average of §**9.14**.

MULTIVARIATE STATE SPACE MODELS

17.19   This development of state space models has been based on modeling a univariate time series x_t. The analysis may readily be extended to modeling the $N \times 1$ vector X_t of observed series by generalizing the measurement equation (17.1) to

$$X_t = Z_t \alpha_t + d_t + \varepsilon_t$$

where Z_t is an $N \times m$ matrix, d_t is an $N \times 1$ vector, and ε_t is an $N \times 1$ vector with $E(\varepsilon_t) = 0$ and $V(\varepsilon_t) = H_t$, an $N \times N$ covariance matrix. The analysis then carries through with the necessary changes.

EXAMPLE 17.3 State Space Modeling of Global Temperatures

In Example 4.3 monthly global temperatures were fitted by an ARIMA(0,1,3) process, while in Example 9.3 the series was fitted by simple exponential smoothing. Both models can be recast as SSFs and estimated by the Kalman filter. The former model, when written in the notation of §**17.3**, has SSF

$$\nabla x_t = \begin{bmatrix} 1 & 0 & 0 & 0 \end{bmatrix} \boldsymbol{\alpha}_t \quad \boldsymbol{\alpha}_t = \begin{bmatrix} \alpha_{1,t} & \alpha_{2,t} & \alpha_{3,t} & \alpha_{4,t} \end{bmatrix}'$$

$$\begin{bmatrix} \alpha_{1,t} \\ \alpha_{2,t} \\ \alpha_{3,t} \\ \alpha_{4,t} \end{bmatrix} = \begin{bmatrix} 0 & 1 & 0 & 0 \\ 0 & 0 & 1 & 0 \\ 0 & 0 & 0 & 1 \\ 0 & 0 & 0 & 0 \end{bmatrix} \begin{bmatrix} \alpha_{1,t-1} \\ \alpha_{2,t-1} \\ \alpha_{3,t-1} \\ \alpha_{4,t-1} \end{bmatrix} + \begin{bmatrix} 1 \\ \theta_1 \\ \theta_2 \\ \theta_3 \end{bmatrix} \eta_t$$

ML estimation of the model obtains (noting the sign change) $\hat{\theta}_1 = -0.504(0.017)$, $\hat{\theta}_2 = -0.090(0.020)$, and $\hat{\theta}_3 = -0.116(0.019)$ with RMSE $= 0.1236$, which are all extremely close to those obtained previously.

Simple exponential smoothing is a special case of the Muth random walk plus noise model whose SSF was given in §**17.4**. ML estimation yields variance estimators $\hat{h} = 0.00868(0.00025)$ and $\hat{q} = 0.00318(0.00024)$, so that the signal-to-noise variance ratio is estimated to be 0.366, a little lower than the estimate of the exponential smoothing parameter (0.45). Nevertheless, the one-step ahead forecast, given by the final state, a_T, remains at 0.581(0.084).

ENDNOTES

1. The idea of sequentially updating, or recursively estimating, the parameters of a model has a history stretching back to Gauss in the 1820s, but was only rediscovered by Plackett (1950). A decade later, the engineer Rudolf Kalman published a recursive state estimation algorithm (Kalman, 1960) for stochastic dynamic systems described by discrete-time state space equations, at the core of which was a modified recursive least squares algorithm (although it was unlikely that Kalman was aware of this at the time). After something of a delay, Kalman's ideas eventually led to a huge body of research on recursive estimation across a range of different disciplines, with the algorithm becoming universally referred to as the Kalman filter. Young (2011) provides historical discussion of the links running from Gauss, through Plackett, to Kalman.

   It is generally accepted that the reasons for the delay in the uptake of Kalman's procedure by the time series community was two-fold. First, the original paper and its continuous time counterpart (Kalman and Bucy, 1961) were written for an engineering audience and so used a language, notation, and style that was alien to statisticians. Second, the original setup of the model assumed that the parameters of the underlying state space model were known exactly, so that it could only provide estimates and forecasts of the state variables of the system. This latter restriction was lifted with the development of methods for computing the likelihood function for state space models (see §§**17.12−17.14**), while the 1970s saw the Kalman filter introduced to a wider audience by casting it in more familiar terminology: see, for example, Duncan and Horn (1972).

2. A formal derivation of the Kalman filter is provided by, for example, Harvey (1989, Section 3.2).

Chapter 18

Some Concluding Remarks

18.1 My aim throughout this book has been to provide readers with a set of robust and useful techniques that they can call upon to analyze time series that occur in their own research fields. Clearly, considerations of how subject-specific theory may be incorporated into the analysis will be field-dependent but may typically influence the choice of variables to be included and provide constraints that could be imposed on the models being developed. My view would be that, in these circumstances, such constraints should be tested wherever possible, an opinion that reflects my (perhaps essentially British) "pragmatic" approach to statistical modeling in general.[1]

Related to this, my preference would always be to begin, wherever possible, with a general model and then test plausible restrictions with the aim of moving toward a simpler model that has empirical support, rather than starting with a tightly specified model whose (typically implicit) restrictions have not been subjected to statistical testing and which might, therefore, be seriously misspecified: in other words, I recommend following a *general-to-specific* modeling strategy of the type often associated with Hendry (1995).

18.2 I would also hope that readers will have gained an appreciation of the principle that the properties a time series displays will impact upon the behavior to be expected from it. To take an important current issue, the examples on modeling monthly global temperatures show that this series can be represented by an ARIMA(0,1,3) process that does not contain a significant drift term. That the series is $I(1)$ rules out the possibility that temperatures exhibit reversion to a constant mean and so invalidates any theory that posits that there is an "equilibrium setting" that temperatures inexorably return to.

However, the absence of a significant drift implies that there is also no underlying, albeit stochastic, trend, so that after three months forecasts converge on the current level of the series, so ruling out predictions of ever-increasing future temperatures. In fact, given that innovations are persistent, and that the innovation variance is relatively small when compared to the overall variability of the series (the ratio is approximately 15%), it is, thus, no surprise that there may be extended periods in which the series is generally increasing, or indeed decreasing, and also extended periods in which the

Applied Time Series Analysis. DOI: https://doi.org/10.1016/B978-0-12-813117-6.00018-1

series appears to bounce randomly around a locally constant level, all of which are features of the observed evolution of global temperatures.

The fact that temperatures are $I(1)$ also rules out the common practice of fitting deterministic trends to the entire or, more usually, segments of the series: at best these can be interpreted as descriptive exercises to which no valid statistical inference can be attached.[2]

18.3 As well as incorporating and testing relevant theory considerations, "institutional" knowledge can also be important when analyzing data and time series are no exceptions to this. One, perhaps arcane, but fondly remembered example from my own experience, relates to when I was working for the Bank of England in the early 1980s on leave from my academic position. It was here that I became interested in seasonal adjustment and signal extraction and it was also when the Bank began to monitor closely the evolution of the monetary aggregates, as monetarism and control of these aggregates was popular with the Conservative government of the time.

The "narrowest" of the selection of aggregates then available, M0, consisted primarily of the amount of notes and coin in circulation with the public, that is, cash. The Bank's statisticians, who monitored this aggregate on a weekly basis, were aware of a "spike" in the aggregate during the first two weeks of July of each year. This was known as the "wakes week" effect, referring to the practice in northern towns of the United Kingdom, primarily in Lancashire and Scotland, for all factories to shut at the same time for summer holidays. Workers and their families consequently drew out much larger amounts of cash than usual to fund their holidays, so producing the aforementioned spike in M0. The Bank statisticians, adjusted the series to remove this spike and, hence, eradicate a transitory, but predictable, uptick in the trend of the data during that month which, if left in the series, might have provoked the unwary into seeing an acceleration in the growth of this monetary aggregate.

18.4 Effects such as these, often referred to as outliers, are a recurrent feature of time series and, although mentioned briefly in Chapter 5, Unit Roots, Difference and Trend Stationarity, and Fractional Differencing, have not been afforded a chapter of their own in this book: they may, in fact, be analyzed within the transfer function setup introduced in Chapter 12, Transfer Functions and ARDL Modeling. Nevertheless, they can be important and should always be looked out for when initially exploring data.[3]

Also omitted is any discussion of *panel data*, which combines time series with cross-sectional observations. This has become a popular area of research, particularly in economics, for it enables the analysis of, typically short, time series available on a set of cross-sectional variables. Panel data warrants a textbook of its own, with Baltagi (2013) being a well-known example.

ENDNOTES

1. I use "pragmatism" here for both its vernacular meaning of indicating a "practical, matter-of-fact way of solving problems" and as a philosophical tradition that is centered on the linking of practice and theory, describing a process whereby theory is extracted from practice and then applied back to practice. Pragmatism as a philosophical movement begun in the United States during the 1870s and is most closely associated with Charles Sanders Peirce and William James (see Bacon, 2012). Although often referred to as "American pragmatism," it was heavily influenced by Charles Darwin and the earlier "British empiricists" John Locke and David Hume.

   Statistical pragmatism has been proposed by Kass (2011) as a foundation for an eclectic statistical inference that goes beyond narrow frequentist and Bayesian positions, and emphasizes the "identification of models with data," recognizing "that all forms of statistical inference make assumptions that can only be tested very crudely and can almost never be verified." A link between philosophical and statistical pragmatism has been provided by the great statistician George Box. As he memorably stated in Box (1979), "all models are wrong, but some are useful," and in Box (1984) he emphasized the importance of theory–practice interaction using many examples from the development of statistical thinking.

2. The finding of no significant drift in the ARIMA model for monthly global temperatures is, of course, at odds with anthropogenic global warming theories that radiative forcings, such as those from CO_2, which have pronounced upward trends, have a significant impact on temperatures, unless some of these forcings approximately cancel each other out. This cannot be examined within the context of modeling monthly temperatures, for forcing observations are not available at this frequency for a sufficiently lengthy period. The use of annual data, as in Example 12.2, does enable forcing effects to be isolated and there are found to be some offsets.

3. The seminal references to the identification and modeling of outliers, often referred to as *intervention analysis*, are Box and Tiao (1975); Abraham (1980); Tsay (1986b); and Chang et al. (1988); with Mills (1990, Chapter 13) providing a textbook treatment.

References

Abraham, B., 1980. Intervention analysis and multiple time series. Biometrika 67, 73−80.

Agiakloglou, C., Newbold, P., 1994. Lagrange multiplier tests for fractional difference. J. Time Series Anal. 15, 253−262.

Aitchison, J., 1982. The statistical analysis of compositional data (with discussion). J. R. Stat. Soc. Ser. B 44, 139−177.

Aitchison, J., 2003. The Statistical Analysis of Compositional Data. Blackburn Press, NJ.

Aït-Sahalia, Y., Jacod, J., 2014. High-Frequency Financial Econometrics. Princeton University Press, Princeton, NJ.

Akaike, H., 1974. A new look at the statistical model identification. IEEE Trans. Autom. Control AC-19, 716−723.

Al-Osh, M.A., Alzaid, A.A., 1987. First-order integer-valued autoregressive (INAR(1)) process. J. Time Series Anal. 8, 261−275.

Al-Osh, M.A., Alzaid, A.A., 1988. Integer-valued moving average (INMA) process. Stat. Pap. 29, 281−300.

Alzaid, A.A., Al-Osh, M.A., 1990. An integer-valued p-th order autoregressive structure (INAR (p)) process. J. Appl. Probab. 27, 314−324.

Andersen, T.G., Bollerslev, T., Diebold, F.X., 2007. Parametric and nonparametric volatility measurement. In: Aït-Sahalia, Y., Hansen, L.P. (Eds.), Handbook of Financial Econometrics. Elsevier, New York.

Andersson, M.K., Eklund, B., Lyhagen, J., 1999. A simple linear time series model with misleading nonlinear properties. Econ. Lett. 65, 281−284.

Arbia, G., 2014. A Primer for Spatial Econometrics. Palgrave Macmillan, Basingstoke.

Astill, S., Harvey, D.I., Leybourne, S.J., Taylor, A.M.R., 2015. Robust and powerful tests for nonlinear deterministic components. Oxf. Bull. Econ. Stat. 77, 780−799.

Bacon, M., 2012. Pragmatism: An Introduction. Polity Press, Cambridge.

Baillie, R.T., 1996. Long memory processes and fractional integration in econometrics. J. Econom. 73, 5−59.

Baillie, R.T., 2006. Modeling volatility. In: Mills, T.C., Patterson, K. (Eds.), Palgrave Handbook of Econometrics, Volume 1: Econometric Theory. Palgrave Macmillan, Basingstoke, pp. 737−764.

Baillie, R.T., Kapetanios, G., 2007. Testing for neglected nonlinearity in long memory models. J. Bus. Econ. Stat. 25, 447−461.

Baltagi, B.H., 2013. Econometric Analysis of Panel Data, fifth ed. Wiley, New York.

Banerjee, A., Dolado, J., Galbraith, J.W., Hendry, D.F., 1993. Co-Integration, Error-Correction, and the Econometric Analysis of Non-Stationary Data. Oxford University Press, Oxford.

Barnett, W.A., Gallant, A.R., Hinich, M.J., Jungeilges, J.A., Kaplan, D.T., Jensen, M.J., 1997. A single-blind controlled competition among tests of nonlinearity and chaos. J. Econom. 82, 157−192.

Bartlett, A., McCormick, W.P., 2012. Estimation for nonnegative first-order autoregressive processes with an unknown location parameter. Appl. Math. 3, 2133–2147.

Bartlett, A., McCormick, W.P., 2013. Estimation for non-negative time series with heavy-tail innovations. J. Time Series Anal. 34, 96–115.

Bartlett, M.S., 1946. On the theoretical specification and sampling properties of autocorrelated time series. J. R. Stat. Soc. B, Suppl. 8, 27–41.

Baxter, M., King, R.G., 1999. Measuring business cycles: approximate band-pass filters for economic time series. Rev. Econ. Stat. 81, 575–593.

Berliner, L.M., 1992. Statistics, probability and chaos. Stat. Sci. 7, 69–90.

Beveridge, S., Nelson, C.R., 1981. A new approach to decomposition of economic time series into permanent and transitory components with particular attention to measurement of the "business cycle". J. Monetary Econ. 7, 151–174.

Bhargava, A., 1986. On the theory of testing for unit roots in observed time series. Rev. Econ. Stud. 53, 369–384.

Bickel, P.J., Doksum, K.A., 1981. An analysis of transformations revisited. J. Am. Stat. Assoc. 76, 296–311.

Blanchard, O.J., 1989. A traditional interpretation of macroeconomic fluctuations. Am. Econ. Rev. 79, 1146–1164.

Blanchard, O.J., Quah, D., 1989. Dynamic effects of aggregate demand and aggregate supply fluctuations. Am. Econ. Rev. 79, 655–673.

Bollerslev, T., 1986. Generalised autoregressive conditional heteroskedasticity. J. Econom. 31, 307–327.

Bollerslev, T., 1988. On the correlation structure for the generalised autoregressive conditional heteroskedastic process. J. Time Series Anal. 9, 121–132.

Bollerslev, T., Wooldridge, J.M., 1992. Quasi maximum likelihood estimation and inference in dynamic models with time varying covariances. Econometric Rev. 11, 143–172.

Box, G.E.P., 1979. Robustness in the strategy of scientific model building. In: Laumer, R.L., Wilkinson, G.N. (Eds.), Robustness in Statistics. Academic Press, New York, pp. 201–236.

Box, G.E.P., 1984. The importance of practice in the development of statistics. Technometrics 26, 1–8.

Box, G.E.P., Cox, D.R., 1964. An analysis of transformations. J. R. Stat. Soc. B 26, 211–243.

Box, G.E.P., Jenkins, G.M., 1970. Time Series Analysis: Forecasting and Control. Holden-Day, San Francisco, CA.

Box, G.E.P., Jenkins, G.M., Reinsel, G.C., 2008. Time Series Analysis: Forecasting and Control, fourth ed. Wiley, New York.

Box, G.E.P., Tiao, G.C., 1975. Intervention analysis with application to economic and environmental problems. J. Am. Stat. Assoc. 70, 70–79.

Brännäs, K., De Gooijer, J.K., 1994. Autoregressive-asymmetric moving average model for business cycle data. J. Forecast. 13, 529–544.

Breitung, J., Hassler, U., 2002. Inference on the cointegrating rank in fractionally integrated processes. J. Econom. 110, 167–185.

Brock, W.A., 1986. Distinguishing random and deterministic systems: abridged version. J. Econ. Theory 40, 168–195.

Brock, W.A., 1988. Nonlinearity and complex dynamics in economics and finance. In: Anderson, P., Arrow, K.J., Pines, D. (Eds.), The Economy as an Evolving Complex System. Addison-Wesley, Reading, MA, pp. 77–97.

Brock, W.A., Hsieh, D.A., LeBaron, B., 1991. A Test for Nonlinear Dynamics, Chaos and Instability. MIT Press, Cambridge, MA.

Brockwell, P.J., Davis, R.A., 1991. Time Series: Theory and Methods, second ed. Springer-Verlag, New York.

Brown, R.G., 1963. Smoothing, Forecasting and Prediction of Discrete Time Series. Prentice-Hall, Englewood-Cliffs, NJ.

Brown, R.G., Meyer, R.F., 1961. The fundamental theorem of exponential smoothing. Oper. Res. 9, 673−687.

Brunsdon, T.M., Smith, T.M.F., 1998. The time series analysis of compositional data. J. Off. Stat. 14, 237−253.

Bu, R., McCabe, B., Hadri, K., 2008. Maximum likelihood estimation of higher-order integer-valued autoregressive processes. J. Time Series Anal. 29, 973−994.

Bunzel, H., Vogelsang, T.J., 2005. Powerful trend function tests that are robust to strong serial correlation with an application to the Prebish−Singer hypothesis. J. Bus. Econ. Stat. 23, 381−394.

Burbidge, J.B., Magee, L., Robb, A.L., 1988. Alternative transformations to handle extreme values of the dependent variable. J. Am. Stat. Assoc. 83, 123−127.

Busetti, F., Harvey, A.C., 2003. Further comments on stationarity tests in series with structural breaks at unknown points. J. Time Series Anal. 24, 137−140.

Chang, I., Tiao, G.C., Chen, C., 1988. Estimation of time series parameters in the presence of outliers. Technometrics 30, 193−204.

Charemza, W.W., Lifshits, M., Makarova, S., 2005. Conditional testing for unit-root bilinearity in financial time series: some theoretical and empirical results. J. Econ. Dyn. Control 29, 63−96.

Choi, I., 2015. Almost All About Unit Roots. Cambridge University Press, Cambridge.

Christiano, L.J., Fitzgerald, T.J., 2003. The band pass filter. Int. Econ. Rev. 44, 435−465.

Clements, M.P., Hendry, D.F., 1998. Forecasting Economic Time Series. Cambridge University Press, Cambridge.

Cooley, T.F., LeRoy, S.F., 1985. Atheoretical econometrics: a critique. J. Monetary Econ. 16, 283−308.

Crafts, N., Mills, T.C., 2017. Six centuries of British economic growth: a time series perspective. Eur. Rev. Econ. Hist. 21, 141−158.

Croston, J.D., 1972. Forecasting and stock control for intermittent demands. J. Oper. Res. Soc. 23, 289−303.

D'Esopo, D.A., 1961. A note on forecasting by the exponential smoothing operator. Oper. Res. 9, 686−687.

Davidson, J.E.H., Hendry, D.F., Srba, F., Yeo, S., 1978. Econometric modelling of the aggregate time-series relationship between consumers' expenditure and income in the United Kingdom. Econ. J. 88, 861−892.

De Lima, P.J.F., 1997. On the robustness of nonlinearity tests to moment condition failure. J. Econom. 76, 251−280.

Dechert, W.D., 1996. Testing time series for nonlinearities: the BDS approach. In: Barnett, W. A., Kirman, A.P., Salmon, M. (Eds.), Nonlinear Dynamics and Economics. Cambridge University Press, Cambridge, pp. 191−200.

Dickey, D.A., Fuller, W.A., 1979. Distribution of the estimators for autoregressive time series with a unit root. J. Am. Stat. Assoc. 74, 427−431.

Dickey, D.A., Fuller, W.A., 1981. Likelihood ratio statistics for autoregressive time series with a unit root. Econometrica 49, 1057−1072.

Diebold, F.X., Inoue, A., 2001. Long memory and regime switching. J. Econom. 105, 131−159.

Ding, Z., Granger, C.W.J., 1996. Modeling persistence of speculative returns: a new approach. J. Econom. 73, 185–215.

Ding, Z., Granger, C.W.J., Engle, R.F., 1993. A long memory property of stock returns and a new model. J. Empirical Finance 1, 83–106.

Dolado, J.J., Gonzalo, J., Moayoral, L., 2002. A fractional Dickey–Fuller test for unit roots. Econometrica 70, 1963–2006.

Domowitz, I., El-Gamal, M.A., 2001. A consistent nonparametric test of ergodicity for time series with applications. J. Econom. 102, 365–398.

Drost, F.C., van den Akker, R., Werker, B.J.M., 2008. Local asymptotic normality and efficient estimation for INAR(P) models. J. Time Series Anal. 29, 784–801.

Dufour, J.-M., 1982. Recursive stability analysis of linear regression relationships: an exploratory analysis. J. Econom. 19, 31–75.

Duncan, D.B., Horn, S.D., 1972. Linear dynamic recursive estimation from the viewpoint of regression analysis. J. Am. Stat. Assoc. 67, 815–821.

Durbin, J., 1960. The fitting of time-series models. Rev. Int. Stat. Inst. 28, 233–244.

Durbin, J., Koopman, S.J., 2012. Time Series Analysis by State Space Methods, second ed. Oxford University Press, Oxford.

Durbin, J., Watson, G.W., 1950. Testing for serial correlation in least squares regression: I. Biometrika 37, 409–428.

Durbin, J., Watson, G.W., 1951. Testing for serial correlation in least squares regression: II. Biometrika 38, 1–19.

Durlauf, S.N., Phillips, P.C.B., 1988. Trends versus random walks in time series analysis. Econometrica 56, 1333–1354.

Elliott, G., Rothenberg, T.J., Stock, J.H., 1996. Efficient tests for an autoregressive unit root. Econometrica 64, 813–836.

Enders, W., Lee, J., 2012. A unit root test using a Fourier series to approximate smooth breaks. Oxf. Bull. Econ. Stat. 74, 574–599.

Engle, C.R., Hamilton, J.D., 1990. Long swings in the dollar: are they in the data and do the markets know it? Am. Econ. Rev. 80, 689–713.

Engle, R.F., 1982. Autoregressive conditional heteroskedasticity with estimates of the variance of UK inflation. Econometrica 50, 987–1008.

Engle, R.F., 1983. Estimates of the variance of UK inflation based on the ARCH model. J. Money Credit Bank. 15, 286–301.

Engle, R.F., Granger, C.W.J., 1987. Co-integration and error correction: representation, estimation and testing. Econometrica 55, 251–276.

Engle, R.F., Kozicki, S., 1993. Testing for common features. J. Bus. Econ. Stat. 11, 369–380.

Engle, R.F., Lee, G.J., 1999. A permanent and transitory component model of stock return volatility. In: Engle, R.F., White, H. (Eds.), Cointegration, Causality, and Forecasting: A Festschrift in Honor of Clive W.J. Granger. Oxford University Press, Oxford, pp. 475–497.

Engle, R.F., Hendry, D.F., Richard, J.-F., 1983. Exogeneity. Econometrica 51, 277–304.

Fernández-Rodriguez, F., Sosvilla-Rivero, S., Andrada-Félix, J., 2005. Testing chaotic dynamics via Lyapunov exponents. J. Appl. Econometrics 20, 911–930.

Flaig, G., 2015. Why we should use high values for the smoothing parameter of the Hodrick–Prescott filter. Jahrbücher Nationalökonomie Statistik 235/6, 518–537.

Franses, P.H., Paap, R., 1999. Does seasonal adjustment change inference from Markov switching models? J. Macroecon. 21, 79–92.

Freeland, R.K., McCabe, B.P.M., 2004. Forecasting discrete valued low count time series. Int. J. Forecast. 20, 427–454.

Gardner Jr., E.S., 1985. Exponential smoothing: the state of the art. J. Forecast. 4, 1−28.

Gardner Jr., E.S., 2006. Exponential smoothing: the state of the art − Part II. Int. J. Forecast. 22, 637−666.

Geweke, J., 1993. Inference and forecasting for chaotic nonlinear time series. In: Chen, P., Day, R. (Eds.), Nonlinear Dynamics and Evolutionary Economics. Oxford University Press, Oxford, pp. 459−512.

Geweke, J., Porter-Hudak, S., 1983. The estimation and application of long memory time series models. J. Time Series Anal. 4, 221−238.

Ghysels, E., Granger, C.W.J., Siklos, P.L., 1996. Is seasonal adjustment a linear or nonlinear data filtering process? J. Bus. Econ. Stat. 14, 374−386.

Giles, D., 2011. Confidence Bands for the Hodrick−Prescott filter. Econometrics Beat: Dave Giles' Blog. <http://davegiles.blogspot.co.uk/2011/12/confidence-bands-for-hodrick-prescott.html>.

Glosten, L.R., Jagannathan, R., Runkle, D., 1993. Relationship between the expected value and the volatility of the nominal excess return on stocks. J. Finance 48, 1779−1801.

Gómez, V., Maravall, A., 1996. Programs TRAMO (Time Series Regression with Arima noise, Missing observations and Outliers) and SEATS (Signal Extraction in Arima Time Series). Instructions for the user. Working Paper 9628. Research Department, Banco de España.

Granger, C.W.J., 1969. Investigating causal relations by econometric models and cross-spectral methods. Econometrica 37, 424−438.

Granger, C.W.J., 1981. Some properties of time series data and their use in econometric model specification. J. Econom. 16, 121−130.

Granger, C.W.J., 1982. Acronyms in time series analysis (ATSA). J. Time Series Anal. 3, 103−107.

Granger, C.W.J., 1992. Comment. Stat. Sci. 7, 102−104.

Granger, C.W.J., Andersen, A.P., 1978. An Introduction to Bilinear Time Series Models. Vandenhoeck and Ruprecht, Gottingen.

Granger, C.W.J., Joyeux, R., 1980. An introduction to long memory time series models and fractional differencing. J. Time Series Anal. 1, 15−29.

Granger, C.W.J., Newbold, P., 1974. Spurious regressions in econometrics. J. Econom. 2, 111−120.

Granger, C.W.J., Newbold, P., 1977. The time series approach to econometric model building. In: Sims, C.A. (Ed.), New Methods in Business Cycle Research. Federal Reserve Bank of Minneapolis, Minneapolis, pp. 7−22.

Granger, C.W.J., Newbold, P., 1986. Forecasting Economic Time Series, second ed. Academic Press, San Diego.

Granger, C.W.J., Spear, S., Ding, Z., 2000. Stylized facts on the temporal and distributional properties of absolute returns: an update. In: Chan, W.-S., Li, W.K., Tong, H. (Eds.), Statistics and Finance: An Interface. Imperial College Press, London, pp. 97−120.

Granger, C.W.J., Teräsvirta, T., 1999. A simple nonlinear time series model with misleading linear properties. Econ. Lett. 62, 161−165.

Granger, C.W.J., Weiss, A.A., 1983. Time series analysis of error correcting models. In: Karlin, S., Amemiya, T., Goodman, L.A. (Eds.), Studies in Econometrics, Time Series and Multivariate Statistics. Academic Press, New York, pp. 255−278.

Graves, T., Gramacy, R.B., Watlins, N.W., Franzke, C.L.E., 2016. A brief history of long memory: Hurst, Mandelbrot and the road to ARFIMA. arXiv: 1406.6018v3.

Haggan, V., Ozaki, T., 1981. Modelling non-linear vibrations using an amplitude dependent autoregressive time series model. Biometrika 68, 189−196.

Haldrup, N., Jansson, M., 2006. Improving size and power in unit root testing. In: Mills, T.C., Patterson, K. (Eds.), Palgrave Handbook of Econometrics, Volume 1: Econometric Theory. Palgrave Macmillan, Basingstoke, pp. 252–277.

Hamilton, D.C., Watts, D.G., 1978. Interpreting partial autocorrelation functions of seasonal non-stationary time series models. Biometrika 65, 135–140.

Hamilton, J.D., 1989. A new approach to the economic analysis and the business cycle. Econometrica 57, 357–384.

Hamilton, J.D., 1990. Analysis of time series subject to changes of regime. J. Econom. 45, 39–70.

Hamilton, J.D., 1994. Time Series Analysis. Princeton University Press, Princeton, NJ.

Harrison, P.J., 1965. Short-term sales forecasting. J. R. Stat. Soc., Ser. C: Appl. Stat. 14, 102–139.

Harrison, P.J., 1967. Exponential smoothing and short-term sales forecasting. Manage. Sci. 13, 821–842.

Harvey, A.C., 1989. Forecasting Structural Time Series Models and the Kalman Filter. Cambridge University Press, Cambridge.

Harvey, A.C., Trimbur, T., 2008. Trend estimation and the Hodrick–Prescott filter. J. Jpn. Stat. Soc. 38, 41–49.

Harvey, D.I., Leybourne, S.J., Taylor, A.M.R., 2007. A simple, robust and powerful test of the trend hypothesis. J. Econom. 141, 1302–1330.

Harvey, D.I., Leybourne, S.J., Taylor, A.M.R., 2009. Simple, robust, and powerful tests of the breaking trend hypothesis. Econometric Theory 25, 995–1029.

Harvey, D.I., Leybourne, S.J., Xiao, L., 2010. Testing for nonlinear deterministic components when the order of integration is unknown. J. Time Series Anal. 31, 379–391.

Harvey, D.I., Mills, T.C., 2002. Unit roots and double smooth transitions. J. Appl. Stat. 29, 675–683.

Harvey, D.I., Mills, T.C., 2003. A note on Busetti–Harvey tests of stationarity in series with structural breaks. J. Time Series Anal. 24, 159–164.

Harvey, D.I., Mills, T.C., 2004. Tests for stationarity in series with endogenously determined structural change. Oxf. Bull. Econ. Stat. 66, 863–894.

Hathaway, D.H., 2010. The solar cycle. Living Rev. Solar Phys. 7, 1–65.

Haykin, S., 1999. Neural Networks: A Comprehensive Foundation, second ed. Prentice Hall, Upper Saddle River, NJ.

Hendry, D.F., 1977. Comments on Granger-Newbold's "Time series approach to econometric model building" and Sargent-Sims "Business cycle modelling without pretending to have too much *a priori* theory". In: Sims, C.A. (Ed.), New Methods of Business Cycle Research. Federal Reserve Bank of Minneapolis, Minneapolis, pp. 183–202.

Hendry, D.F., 1995. Dynamic Econometrics. Oxford University Press, Oxford.

Higgins, M.L., Bera, A.K., 1988. A joint test for ARCH and bilinearity in the regression model. Econometric Rev. 7, 171–181.

Higgins, M.L., Bera, A.K., 1992. A class of nonlinear ARCH models. Int. Econ. Rev. 33, 137–158.

Hilborn, R.C., 1997. Resource letter: nonlinear dynamics. Am. Phys. 65, 822–834.

Hodrick, R.J., Prescott, E.C., 1997. Postwar U.S. business cycles: an empirical investigation. J. Money Credit Bank. 19, 1–16.

Holt, C.C., 2004a. Forecasting seasonals and trends by exponentially weighted moving averages. Int. J. Forecast. 20, 5–10.

Holt, C.C., 2004b. Author's retrospective on forecasting seasonals and trends by exponentially weighted moving averages. Int. J. Forecast. 20, 11−13.

Hosking, J.R.M., 1981. Fractional differencing. Biometrika 68, 165−176.

Hosking, J.R.M., 1984. Modelling persistence in hydrological time series using fractional differencing. Water Resour. Res. 20, 1898−1908.

Hsieh, D.A., 1989. Testing for nonlinear dependence in daily foreign exchange rates. J. Bus. 62, 339−368.

Hsieh, D.A., 1991. Chaos and nonlinear dynamics: applications to financial markets. J. Finance 46, 1839−1877.

Hurrell, J.W., Kushnir, Y., Ottersen, G., Visbek, M., 2003. The North Atlantic Oscillation: Climatic Significance and Environmental Impact. American Geophysical Union, Washington, DC.

Hurst, H.E., 1951. Long term storage capacity of reservoirs. Trans. Am. Soc. Civil Eng. 116, 770−799.

Hyndman, R.J., Koehler, A.B., Ord, J.K., Grose, S., 2008. Forecasting with Exponential Smoothing: The State Space Approach. Springer-Verlag, Berlin.

Iddon, C.R., Mills, T.C., Giridharan, R., Lomas, K.J., 2015. The influence of ward design on resilience to heat waves: an exploration using distributed lag models. Energy Build. 86, 573−588.

Jarque, C.L., Bera, A.K., 1980. Efficient tests for normality, homoskedasticity and serial dependence in regression residuals. Econ. Lett. 6, 255−259.

Jenkins, G.M., 1961. General considerations in the analysis of spectra. Technometrics 3, 133−166.

Johansen, S., 1988. Statistical analysis of cointegrating vectors. J. Econ. Dyn. Control 12, 231−254.

Johansen, S., 1995. Likelihood-based Inference in Cointegrated Vector Autoregressive Models. Oxford University Press, Oxford.

Johansen, S., Juselius, K., 1994. Identification of the long-run and short-run structure: an application to the ISLM model. J. Econom. 63, 7−36.

Jones, R., 1978. Nonlinear autoregressive processes. Proc. R. Soc. London, Ser. A 360, 71−95.

Jung, R.C., Ronning, G., Tremayne, A.R., 2005. Estimation in conditional first order autoregression with discrete support. Stat. Pap. 46, 195−224.

Jung, R.C., Tremayne, A.R., 2003. Testing for serial dependence in time series models of counts. J. Time Series Anal. 24, 65−84.

Jung, R.C., Tremayne, A.R., 2006. Coherent forecasting in integer time series models. Int. J. Forecast. 22, 223−238.

Kaiser, R., Maravall, A., 2005. Combining filter design with model-based filtering (with an application to business cycle estimation). Int. J. Forecast. 21, 691−710.

Kalman, R.E., 1960. A new approach to linear filtering and prediction problems. J. Basic Eng. 82, 34−45.

Kalman, R.E., Bucy, R.S., 1961. New results in linear prediction and filtering theory. J. Basic Eng. 83, 95−108.

Kapetanios, G., Shin, Y., Snell, A., 2003. Testing for a unit root in the nonlinear STAR framework. J. Econom. 112, 359−379.

Kass, R.E., 2011. Statistical inference: the big picture. Stat. Sci. 26, 1−9.

Keenan, D.M., 1985. A Tukey nonadditivity-type test for time series nonlinearity. Biometrika 72, 39−44.

Kejriwal, M., Perron, P., 2010. A sequential procedure to determine the number of breaks in trend with an integrated or stationary noise component. J. Time Series Anal. 31, 305–328.

Kim, D., Perron, P., 2009. Unit root tests allowing for a break in the trend function at an unknown time under both the null and alternative hypotheses. J. Econom. 148, 1–13.

Koop, G., Potter, S.M., 2001. Are apparent findings of nonlinearity due to structural instability in economic time series? Econometrics J. 4, 37–55.

Koopman, S.J., Shephard, N., Doornik, J.A., 1999. Statistical algorithms for models in state space using SsfPack 2.2. Econometrics J. 2, 113–166.

Koopman, S.J., Harvey, A.C., Doornik, J.A., Shephard, N., 2009. STAMP™ 8. Timberlake Consultants Ltd, London.

Kwiatkowski, D., Phillips, P.C.B., Schmidt, P., Shin, Y., 1992. Testing the null hypothesis of stationarity against an alternative of a unit root. J. Econom. 54, 159–178.

Kyrtsou, C., Serletis, A., 2006. Univariate tests for nonlinear structure. J. Macroecon. 28, 154–168.

Lam, P.S., 1990. The Hamilton model with a general autoregressive component: estimation and comparison with other models of economic time series. J. Monetary Econ. 20, 409–432.

Lee, T.-H., White, H., Granger, C.W.J., 1993. Testing for neglected nonlinearity in time series models: a comparison of neural network methods and alternative tests. J. Econom. 56, 269–290.

Leybourne, S.J., Newbold, P., Vougas, D., 1998. Unit roots and smooth transitions. J. Time Series Anal. 19, 83–97.

Li, W.K., Mak, T.K., 1994. On the squared residual autocorrelations in nonlinear time series with conditional heteroskedasticity. J. Time Series Anal. 15, 627–636.

Lieberman, O., Phillips, P.C.B., 2008. A complete asymptotic series for the autocovariance function of a long memory process. J. Econom. 147, 99–103.

Lin, C.-F.J., Teräsvirta, T., 1994. Testing the constancy of regression parameters against continuous structural change. J. Econom. 62, 211–228.

Ljung, G.M., Box, G.E.P., 1978. On a measure of lack of fit in time series. Biometrika 65, 297–303.

Lo, A.W., 1991. Long-term memory in stock market prices. Econometrica 59, 1279–1313.

Lobarto, J.N., Nankervis, J.C., Savin, N.E., 2001. Testing for autocorrelation using a modified Box Pierce Q test. Int. Econ. Rev. 42, 187–205.

Lobarto, J.N., Nankervis, J.C., Savin, N.E., 2002. Testing for zero autocorrelation in the presence of statistical dependence. Econometric Theory 18, 730–743.

Mandelbrot, B.B., 1972. Statistical methodology for nonperiodic cycles: from the covariance to R/S analysis. Ann. Econ. Soc. Meas. 1/3, 259–290.

Mandelbrot, B.B., Wallis, J.R., 1968. Noah, Joseph and operational hydrology. Water Resour. Res. 4, 909–918.

Mandelbrot, B.B., Wallis, J.R., 1969. Some long-run properties of geophysical records. Water Resour. Res. 5, 321–340.

Maravall, A., 1983. An application of nonlinear time series forecasting. J. Bus. Econ. Stat. 3, 350–355.

Maravall, A., del Rio, A., 2007. Temporal aggregation, systematic sampling, and the Hodrick–Prescott filter. Comput. Stat. Data Anal. 52, 975–998.

McDermott, G.R., 2017. Sceptic Priors and Climate Policy. Working Paper.

McKenzie, E., 1988. Some ARMA models for dependent sequences of Poisson counts. Adv. Appl. Probab. 20, 822–835.

McLeod, A.J., Li, W.K., 1983. Diagnostic checking ARMA time series models using squared-residual correlations. J. Time Series Anal. 4, 269–273.

Mills, T.C., 1990. Time Series Techniques for Economists. Cambridge University Press, Cambridge.

Mills, T.C., 2007. Modelling compositional economic data. Indian Econ. J. 55, 99–115.

Mills, T.C., 2009. Forecasting obesity trends in England. J. R. Stat. Soc., Ser. A 172, 107–117.

Mills, T.C., 2010. Forecasting compositional time series. Qual. Quantity 44, 673–690.

Mills, T.C., 2011. The Foundations of Modern Time Series Analysis. Palgrave Macmillan, Basingstoke.

Mills, T.C., 2013a. Matrix Representation of Regression Models: A Primer. Lulu Press.

Mills, T.C., 2013b. A Very British Affair: Six Britons and the Development of Time Series Analysis. Palgrave Macmillan, Basingstoke.

Mills, T.C., 2014. Analysing Economic Data. Palgrave Macmillan, Basingstoke.

Mills, T.C., 2017a. A Statistical Biography of George Udny Yule: Loafer of the World. Cambridge Scholars Press, Newcastle.

Mills, T.C., 2017b. Stochastic modelling of rainfall patterns across the United Kingdom. Meteorol. Appl. 24, 580–595.

Mills, T.C., Markellos, R.N., 2008. The Econometric Modelling of Financial Time Series, third ed. Cambridge University Press, Cambridge.

Mills, T.C., Patterson, K.D., 2015. Modelling the trend: the historical origins of some modern methods and ideas. J. Econ. Surv. 29, 527–548.

Muth, J.F., 1960. Optimal properties of exponentially weighted forecasts. J. Am. Stat. Assoc. 55, 299–305.

Nelson, D.B., 1991. Conditional heteroskedasticity in asset returns. Econometrica 59, 347–370.

Nelson, C.R., Plosser, C.I., 1982. Trends and random walks in macroeconomic time series. J. Monetary Econ. 10, 139–162.

Newbold, P., 1988. Predictors projecting linear trend plus seasonal dummies. Statistician 37, 111–127.

Newbold, P., 1990. Precise and efficient computation of the Beveridge–Nelson decomposition of economic time series. J. Monetary Econ. 26, 453–457.

Ng, S., Perron, P., 2001. Lag length selection and the construction of unit root tests with good size and power. Econometrica 69, 1519–1554.

Park, J.Y., 1992. Canonical cointegrating regression. Econometrica 60, 119–143.

Patterson, K.D., 2010. A Primer for Unit Root Testing. Palgrave Macmillan, Basingstoke.

Patterson, K.D., 2011. Unit Root Tests in Time series, Volume 1: Key Concepts and Problems. Palgrave Macmillan, Basingstoke.

Pena, D., Rodriguez, J., 2005. Detecting nonlinearity in time series by model selection criteria. Int. J. Forecast. 21, 731–748.

Perron, P., 1988. Trends and random walks in macroeconomic time series: further evidence from a new approach. J. Econ. Dyn. Control 12, 297–332.

Perron, P., 1989. The great crash, the oil price shock, and the unit root hypothesis. Econometrica 57, 1361–1401.

Perron, P., 1990. Testing for a unit root in a time series with a changing mean. J. Bus. Econ. Stat. 8, 153–162.

Perron, P., 1997. Further evidence on breaking trend functions in macroeconomic variables. J. Econom. 80, 355–385.

Perron, P., Vogelsang, T.J., 1993. The great crash, the oil price shock and the unit root hypothesis: erratum. Econometrica 61, 248–249.

Perron, P., Yabu, T., 2009. Estimating deterministic trends with an integrated or stationary noise component. J. Econom. 151, 56−69.

Perron, P., Zhu, X., 2005. Structural breaks with deterministic and stochastic trends. J. Econom. 129, 65−119.

Pesaran, M.H., Shin, Y., 1997. Generalized impulse response analysis in linear multivariate models. Econ. Lett. 58, 17−29.

Pesaran, M.H., Shin, Y., 1998. An autoregressive distributed lag modelling approach to cointegration analysis. In: Strom, S. (Ed.), Econometrics and Economic Theory in the 20th Century: The Ragnar Frisch Centennial Symposium (Econometric Society Monograph 31). Cambridge University Press, Cambridge, pp. 371−413.

Pesaran, M.H., Shin, Y., Smith, R.J., 2001. Bounds testing approaches to the analysis of levels relationships. J. Appl. Econometrics 16, 289−326.

Phillips, P.C.B., 1986. Understanding spurious regressions in econometrics. J. Econom. 33, 311−340.

Phillips, P.C.B., 1987. Time series regression with a unit root. Econometrica 55, 227−301.

Phillips, P.C.B., 1991. Optimal inference in co-integrated systems. Econometrica 59, 282−306.

Phillips, P.C.B., 1998. Impulse response and forecast error asymptotics in nonstationary VARs. J. Econom. 83, 21−56.

Phillips, P.C.B., 2009. Long memory and long run variation. J. Econom. 151, 150−158.

Phillips, P.C.B., 2010. The Mysteries of the Trend, Cowles Foundation Discussion Paper No 1771.

Phillips, P.C.B., Ouliaris, S., 1990. Asymptotic properties of residual based tests for cointegration. Econometrica 58, 165−194.

Phillips, P.C.B., Perron, P., 1988. Testing for unit roots in time series regression. Biometrika 75, 335−346.

Pinske, H., 1988. A consistent nonparametric test for serial independence. J. Econom. 84, 205−231.

Plackett, R.L., 1950. Some theorems in least squares. Biometrika 37, 149−157.

Proietti, T., 2009a. Structural time series models for business cycle analysis. In: Mills, T.C., Patterson, K. (Eds.), Palgrave Handbook of Econometrics: Volume 2, Applied Econometrics. Macmillan Palgrave, Basingstoke, pp. 385−433.

Proietti, T., 2009b. On the model based interpretation of filters and the reliability of trend-cycle filters. Econometric Rev. 28, 186−208.

Quenouille, M.H., 1957. The Analysis of Multiple Time-Series. Griffin, London.

Ramsey, J.B., 1969. Tests for specification errors in classical linear least squares regression analysis. J. R. Stat. Soc., Ser. B 31, 350−371.

Ramsey, J.B., Rothman, P., 1996. Time irreversibility and business cycle asymmetry. J. Money Credit Bank. 28, 1−21.

Ravn, M.O., Uhlig, H., 2002. On adjusting the Hodrick−Prescott filter for the frequency of observation. Rev. Econ. Stat. 84, 371−376.

Robinson, P.M., 1977. The estimation of a non-linear moving average model. Stochastic Processes Appl. 5, 81−90.

Robinson, P.M., 1994. Time series with strong dependence. In: Sims, C.A. (Ed.), Advances in Econometrics: Sixth World Congress, Volume 1. Cambridge University Press, Cambridge, pp. 47−95.

Romano, J.L., Thombs, L.A., 1996. Inference for autocorrelations under weak assumptions. J. Am. Stat. Assoc. 89, 1303−1311.

Rothman, P., 1992. The comparative power of the TR test against simple threshold models. J. Appl. Econometrics 7, S187−S195.

Saikkonen, P., Lütkepohl, H., 1996. Infinite-order cointegrated vector autoregressive processes: estimation and inference. Econometric Theory 12, 814−844.

Sargan, J.D., 1964. Wages and prices in the United Kingdom: a study in econometric methodology. In: Hart, P.E., Mills, G., Whitaker, J.K. (Eds.), Econometric Analysis for National Economic Planning. Butterworths, London, pp. 25−63.

Schwarz, G., 1978. Estimating the dimension of a model. Ann. Stat. 6, 461−464.

Schwert, G.W., 1989. Why does stock market volatility change over time? J. Finance 44, 1115−1153.

Shenstone, L., Hyndman, R., 2005. Croston's method for intermittent demand forecasting. J. Forecast. 34, 389−402.

Shintani, M., Linton, O., 2006. Nonparametric neural network estimation of Lyapunov exponents and a direct test for chaos. J. Econom. 120, 1−33.

Sims, C.A., 1972. Money, income and causality. Am. Econ. Rev. 62, 540−552.

Sims, C.A., 1980. Macroeconomics and reality. Econometrica 48, 1−48.

Sims, C.A., 1981. An autoregressive index model for the U.S. 1948−1975. In: Kmenta, J., Ramsey, J.B. (Eds.), Large-Scale Macroeconometric Models. North Holland, Amsterdam, pp. 283−327.

Sollis, R., Leybourne, S.J., Newbold, P., 1999. Unit roots and asymmetric smooth transitions. J. Time Series Anal. 20, 671−677.

Spanos, A., 1986. Statistical Foundations of Econometric Modelling. Cambridge University Press, Cambridge.

Stock, J.H., 1996. VAR, error correction and pretest forecasts at long horizons. Oxf. Bull. Econ. Stat. 58, 685−701.

Subba Rao, T., Gabr, M., 1984. An Introduction to Bispectral Analysis and Bilinear Time Series Models. Springer-Verlag, Berlin.

Teräsvirta, T., 1994. Specification, estimation, and evaluation of smooth transition autoregressive models. J. Am. Stat. Assoc. 89, 208−218.

Teräsvirta, T., 2006. Univariate nonlinear time series models. In: Mills, T.C., Patterson, K. (Eds.), Palgrave Handbook of Econometrics, Volume 1: Theory. Palgrave Macmillan, Basingstoke, pp. 396−424.

Teräsvirta, T., 2007. Forecasting economic variables with nonlinear models. In: Elliott, G., Granger, C.W.J., Timmermann, A. (Eds.), Handbook of Economic Forecasting. North Holland, Amsterdam.

Teräsvirta, T., Lin, C.-F., Granger, C.W.J., 1993. Power of the neural network test. J. Time Series Anal. 14, 209−220.

Teräsvirta, T., Tjostheim, D., Granger, C.W.J., 2011. Modelling Nonlinear Economic Relationships. Oxford University Press, Oxford.

Toda, H.Y., Phillips, P.C.B., 1993. Vector autoregression and causality. Econometrica 61, 1367−1393.

Toda, H.Y., Phillips, P.C.B., 1994. Vector autoregression and causality: a theoretical overview and simulation study. Econometric Rev. 13, 259−285.

Toda, H.Y., Yamamoto, T., 1995. Statistical inference in vector autoregressions with possibly integrated processes. J. Econom. 66, 225−250.

Tong, H., 1990. Non-Linear Time Series: A Dynamical System Approach. Oxford University Press, Oxford.

Tong, H., Lim, K.S., 1980. Threshold autoregression, limit cycles, and cyclical data. J. R. Stat. Soc., Ser. B 42, 245–292.

Tremayne, A.R., 2006. Stationary linear univariate time series models. In: Mills, T.C., Patterson, K. (Eds.), Palgrave Handbook of Econometrics, Volume 1: Theory. Palgrave Macmillan, Basingstoke, pp. 215–251.

Tsay, R.S., 1986a. Time series model specification in the presence of outliers. J. Am. Stat. Assoc. 81, 132–141.

Tsay, R.S., 1986b. Nonlinearity tests for time series. Biometrika 73, 461–466.

Tukey, J.W., 1977. Exploratory Data Analysis. Addison-Wesley, Reading, MA.

Vahid, F., 2006. Common cycles. In: Mills, T.C., Patterson, K. (Eds.), Palgrave Handbook of Econometrics, Volume 1: Econometric Theory. Macmillan, Basingstoke, pp. 215–251.

Vahid, F., Engle, R.F., 1993. Common trends and common cycles. J. Appl. Econometrics 8, 341–360.

Vahid, F., Engle, R.F., 1997. Codependent cycles. J. Econom. 80, 199–221.

Van Dijk, D.J.C., Franses, P.H., Lucas, A., 1999. Testing for smooth transition nonlinearity in the presence of outliers. J. Bus. Econ. Stat. 17, 217–235.

Van Dijk, D.J.C., Teräsvirta, T., Franses, P.H., 2002. Smooth transition autoregressive models: a survey of recent developments. Econometric Rev. 21, 1–47.

Vogelsang, T.J., Perron, P., 1998. Additional tests for a unit root allowing the possibility of breaks in the trend function. Int. Econ. Rev. 39, 1073–1100.

Wallis, K.F., 1987. Time series analysis of bounded economic variables. J. Time Series Anal. 8, 115–123.

Wecker, W., 1981. Asymmetric time series. J. Am. Stat. Assoc. 76, 16–19.

Weiner, N., 1956. The theory of prediction. In: Breckenback, E.F. (Ed.), Modern Mathematics for Engineers. McGraw-Hill, pp. 165–190.

Weiss, A.A., 1986. ARCH and bilinear time series models: comparison and combination. J. Bus. Econ. Stat. 4, 59–70.

White, H., 2006. Approximate nonlinear forecasting methods. In: Elliott, G., Granger, C.W.J., Timmermann, A. (Eds.), Handbook of Economic Forecasting. North Holland, Amsterdam.

White, H., Granger, C.W.J., 2011. Consideration of trends in time series. J. Time Ser. Econometrics 3, 1–40.

Wickens, M., 1996. Interpreting cointegrating vectors and common stochastic trends. J. Econom. 74, 255–271.

Winters, P.R., 1960. Forecasting sales by exponentially weighted moving averages. Manage. Sci. 6, 324–342.

Wold, H., 1938. A Study in the Analysis of Stationary Time Series. Almqvist and Wiksell, Stockholm.

Yeo, I.-K., Johnson, R.A., 2000. A new family of power transformations to improve normality or symmetry. Biometrika 87, 954–959.

Young, P.C., 2011. Gauss, Kalman, and advances in recursive parameter estimation. J. Forecast. 30, 104–146.

Yule, G.U., 1926. Why do we sometimes get nonsense-correlations between time-series? A study in sampling and the nature of time series. J. R. Stat. Soc. 89, 1–63.

Yule, G.U., 1927. On a method of investigating periodicities in disturbed series, with special reference to Wolfer's sunspot numbers. Philos. Trans. R. Soc. London, Ser. A 226, 267–298.

Zakoian, J.M., 1994. Threshold heteroskedastic models. J. Econ. Dyn. Control 18, 931–955.

Zellner, A., 1962. An efficient method of estimating seemingly unrelated regressions and tests of aggregation bias. J. Am. Stat. Assoc. 57, 348–368.

Zivot, E., Andrews, D.W.K., 1992. Further evidence on the great crash, the oil price shock and the unit root hypothesis. J. Bus. Econ. Stat. 10, 251–270.

Index

Printed in the United States
By Bookmasters